# THIRD DIMENSION

# THE UNOFFICIAL AND UNAUTHORISED GUIDE TO *DOCTOR WHO* 2007

# THIRD DIMENSION

# THE UNOFFICIAL AND UNAUTHORISED GUIDE TO *DOCTOR WHO* 2007

## STEPHEN JAMES WALKER

First published in England in 2007 by
Telos Publishing Ltd
139 Whitstable Road, Canterbury, Kent, CT2 8EQ

www.telos.co.uk

This edition 2021

Telos Publishing Ltd values feedback. Please e-mail us with any comments you may
have about this book to: feedback@telos.co.uk

ISBN: 978-1-84583-176-9

*Third Dimension: The Unofficial and Unauthorised Guide to* Doctor Who *2007*
© 2007, 2021 Stephen James Walker

British Library Cataloguing in Publication Data.
A catalogue record for this book is available from the British Library.

# TABLE OF CONTENTS

| | |
|---|---|
| **Introduction** | 7 |
| **CONTEXT** | 9 |
| Chapter One: The 'Classic' Series | 11 |
| Chapter Two: The 2005 Renaissance | 16 |
| **COUNTDOWN** | 21 |
| Chapter Three: Countdown to Christmas | 23 |
| Chapter Four: It's Christmas! | 42 |
| Chapter Five: Countdown to Series Three | 50 |
| **CULMINATION** | 65 |
| Chapter Six: Series Three is Here! | 67 |
| Chapter Seven: And Meanwhile … | 69 |
| **CONTINUATION** | 81 |
| Chapter Eight: Coming Soon … | 83 |
| **CAST & CREW** | 87 |
| Chapter Nine: Main Cast | 89 |
| Chapter Ten: Principal Creative Team | 94 |
| **CREDITS** | 101 |
| Credits | 103 |
| **CRITIQUE** | 109 |
| 3.00 – Christmas Special 2006 – 'The Runaway Bride' | 111 |
| 3.01 – 'Smith and Jones' | 125 |
| 3.02 – 'The Shakespeare Code' | 140 |
| 3.03 – 'Gridlock' | 153 |
| 3.04 – 'Daleks in Manhattan' | 164 |
| 3.05 – 'Evolution of the Daleks' | 177 |
| 3.06 – 'The Lazarus Experiment' | 188 |
| 3.07 – '42' | 201 |
| 3.08 – 'Human Nature' | 213 |
| 3.09 – 'The Family of Blood' | 227 |
| 3.10 – 'Blink' | 238 |
| 3.11 – 'Utopia' | 250 |
| 3.12 – 'The Sound of Drums' | 264 |
| 3.13 – 'Last of the Time Lords' | 285 |
| Series Overview | 302 |

**COMPLEMENT**                                              305
    Appendix A: *Doctor Who Confidential*          307
    Appendix B: *Totally Doctor Who*               317
    Appendix C: *The Infinite Quest*               323
    Appendix D: Ratings and Rankings               326
    Appendix E: Original Novels                    335
    Appendix F: Original Comic Strips              339
    Appendix G: Other Original Fiction             354

About the Author                                            357

# INTRODUCTION

In 2005 – the forty-second year since it made its on-air debut, and the sixteenth year since it was last in regular production – the BBC's classic science fiction drama serial *Doctor Who* returned to TV; and, somewhat to the surprise of most media pundits, but not to its many thousands of loyal fans worldwide, proved to be a huge success all over again. In fact, this new, updated series, masterminded by acclaimed scriptwriter Russell T Davies – previously best known as the creator of *Queer As Folk* (Channel 4, 1999) – arguably brought *Doctor Who* even greater popularity than it had ever enjoyed before. It was watched by a phenomenal 7.95 million BBC One viewers on average over the course of its 13 weekly episodes (with hundreds of thousands of BBC Three viewers tuning in for repeats), absolutely trouncing the main ITV competition in the battle for ratings in its key, early-Saturday-evening slot. After suffering years of neglect, and even distain, from successive teams of senior executives at the BBC, *Doctor Who* had suddenly become their biggest hit, and it seemed they couldn't get enough of it. Even before the first series had finished transmission, they had announced the commissioning of an hour-long special for Christmas 2005; a second series and *another* Christmas special for 2006; and a *third* series for 2007 – an unprecedented demonstration of commitment in today's highly competitive broadcasting environment. As if this wasn't extraordinary enough, they even went on to commission three spin-offs: *Torchwood* (a 13-part series transmitted in 2006, and since renewed for another 13-part series scheduled to begin early in 2008); *Rose Tyler: Earth Defence* (an ultimately unproduced special); and *The Sarah Jane Adventures* (a special transmitted on New Year's Day 2007, to be followed by a full series later in the year).

The first Christmas special, 'The Christmas Invasion', proved to be a big hit on Christmas Day 2005; and the second series, which began transmission in mid-April 2006, equalled the success of the first, drawing an amazing 7.71 million viewers on average over the course of its BBC One debut transmissions, and again proving more than a match for anything that ITV could put up against it. In fact, the ITV schedulers seemed almost to give up the battle, as if they tacitly accepted that there was no way they could mount a credible challenge to *Doctor Who*'s Saturday evening ratings supremacy.

During the summer of 2006, everyone's thoughts started to turn to the second Christmas special, 'The Runaway Bride', and to the third series, due to start transmission in the spring of 2007. Could these latest episodes possibly continue the incredible run of success that *Doctor Who* had enjoyed since its return in 2005? Or would they see a cooling off of the viewers' love affair with the series? And how would they be received by the dedicated fans – who had, by and large, loved the first two series just as much as the general public had? One source of concern was the fact that Billie Piper, whose highly-acclaimed performance as Rose Tyler had been such an important factor in the success of the new *Doctor Who*, had left at the end of the second series – a move that had also necessitated the departures of popular semi-regulars Camille Coduri, who had played Rose's mother Jackie, and

Noel Clarke, her on-off boyfriend Mickey Smith. Would the relatively unknown Freema Agyeman, as successor companion Martha Jones, and the new group of semi-regulars cast as her various family members, have as great an audience appeal?

This book starts by setting the scene and establishing the context for the later chapters by looking at the lead-up to Series Three in terms of the overall history of *Doctor Who* – both the original series that ran from 1963 to 1989 and the Russell T Davies-led revival from 2005 onwards. It then notes all the main events, news stories, promotional activities and so forth that occurred in the *Doctor Who* world between the end of Series Two and the end of Series Three, pausing along the way to discuss in more detail the main developments, in what is designed to serve as a useful record of this period from the 'outside looking in' perspective of the viewing public. Following this, there are capsule biographies for all the main cast and production team members who worked on Series Three. Then comes the most substantial section of the book, which consists of a detailed guide to and analysis of all 14 episodes, including 'The Runaway Bride'. Lastly there are seven appendices, covering more peripheral matters: Series Three of *Doctor Who Confidential*; Series Two of *Totally Doctor Who*; the animated adventure 'The Infinite Quest'; the series' ratings; original *Doctor Who* novels published during the timeframe covered by this book; original *Doctor Who* comic strip stories published during the same period; and other officially-sanctioned original fiction based on the new series.

If you are reading this book, the chances are that you are already an avid follower of the good Doctor's adventures, but I hope that in the following pages you will find much to interest, inform and enlighten you, and ultimately to enhance your appreciation and enjoyment of the latest run of episodes in what is undoubtedly my favourite TV series of all time!

*Stephen James Walker*
*12 September 2007*

# CONTEXT

# CHAPTER ONE
# THE 'CLASSIC' SERIES

## SUCCESS – THE FIRST TIME AROUND

J Shaun Lyon began the opening chapter of his book *Second Flight* (Telos Publishing, 2006) with the words: 'Two years before its long-awaited return in 2005, *Doctor Who* was considered to be a relic, a television icon from an era long past.' A harsh assessment, perhaps, but one with which it is difficult to disagree. By the early 2000s, the series had been out of regular production for over a decade, and survived only through tie-in stories in other media – novels, audio CD dramas, comic strips and the like. True, it still had a loyal following of keen devotees, but these numbered in the thousands rather than the tens or hundreds of thousands. As far as the great majority of British viewers were concerned, *Doctor Who* was a part of television history, seen only in the occasional repeat on the UKTV Gold nostalgia channel. If the series was mentioned at all in the popular press, it was typically in a derogatory light, with mocking comments about wobbly sets, quarries doubling for alien planets, man-in-a-rubber-suit monsters, pepper pot aliens incapable of conquering a flight of stairs, and nerdy, anorak-clad fans. Russell T Davies, in an interview published on 17 June 2005 on the BBC News website, went so far as to say: 'You have to admit that the name of the programme had become a joke, and its reputation had become a cheap joke at that.' If one's knowledge of the original *Doctor Who* were confined to the way it was popularly perceived at the close of the 20th Century, it would be hard to understand how it could ever have become (despite the misleading statement to the contrary in *Guinness World Records 2007*) the longest running science-fiction-themed series in the world, presenting 26 seasons of episodes between 1963 and 1989. Surely it hadn't always been held in such low esteem by the general British public, had it?

The answer to that is, of course, no it hadn't. On the contrary, from virtually the outset, it had been a notable success for the BBC; and by the time of its second season, broadcast in 1964/65, it was regularly reaching the upper echelons of the weekly ratings charts, and sometimes even the top ten. This early popularity is often attributed to the introduction of the Daleks in the second story, but arguably the series would have been a winner even without the undeniable attraction of those evil machine-creatures from Skaro. Much of the first season was already in an advanced state of preparation by the time the Daleks' introductory story reached the nation's screens, and it is debatable to what extent the production team revised their plans in the light of its success; a whole year elapsed before the second Dalek story was transmitted. At any rate, close examination of the ratings and available audience research data suggests that stories such as 'Marco Polo' and 'The Aztecs', in which the Doctor and his companions ventured back into different periods of Earth's history, were actually (contrary to what has often been claimed) just as well-received by viewers as monster-fests like 'The Keys of Marinus' and 'The

Sensorites'. Certainly 'Dalekmania' – the craze that spread throughout the nation's school playgrounds in 1965, fuelled by a wealth of Dalek-related merchandise appearing on the market – was a major profile-raiser. But it was not just the Daleks that had won the hearts of Britain's TV viewers; it was *Doctor Who* itself, as a series.

In devising the character of a mysterious and eccentric alien traveller whose advanced but erratic vessel could take him and his fellow travellers literally anywhere – forwards, backwards or even sideways in time and space – the BBC's then Head of Drama Sydney Newman, and the small team of individuals who helped develop his ideas, had unwittingly come up with arguably the best and most flexible format ever created for a family adventure serial; or, come to that, for any TV drama serial. And the viewing public loved it.

This is not to say that the original *Doctor Who* – now commonly referred to as the 'classic series' to distinguish it from the modern revival (a practice that this book will also adopt) – always enjoyed the same high level of ratings success as it had attained in 1964/65. In fact, it equalled that achievement (or came close to it, at any rate) only once more, shortly after Tom Baker took over the role of the Doctor in the mid-1970s. However, the series unquestionably remained hugely popular, and a key element in the BBC's famously effective Saturday evening schedules, throughout the 1960s and 1970s. Indeed, some commentators have suggested that, at least during the 1960s, the official figures may actually have understated the true number of *Doctor Who* viewers, because the system was not well suited to measuring family audiences as opposed to adult ones (adult-orientated programmes tending, of course, to dominate the ratings charts). Certainly this author recalls that even in the late 1960s, when the official figures would suggest that the series' audience fell to a low point of around five million viewers, a good majority of his classmates at school – a fairly typical junior school of the period – continued to tune in regularly to the Doctor's adventures; and if they were watching, it is a fair bet that most of their parents were too. Did this really equate to an audience of only five million – little more than ten percent of the nation's population at that time? Whatever the answer to that question, there can be no doubt that, by the late 1970s, *Doctor Who* had firmly established itself as – to borrow a famous description coined by *Daily Sketch* journalist Gerard Garrett – 'the children's own programme which adults adore'.

How, then, could its reputation have fallen so far that, by the early 2000s, it was – in Russell T Davies's words – 'a cheap joke' to most of the British public?

## DECLINE AND FALL

The decline in the fortunes of *Doctor Who* can be traced back to the 1980s, when producer John Nathan-Turner – who occupied the post throughout that decade – took the series in a direction that was not always to its advantage.

The eras of the three 1980s Doctors – Peter Davison, Colin Baker and Sylvester McCoy – are generally considered to have been rather less successful than those of their four predecessors – William Hartnell, Patrick Troughton, Jon Pertwee and Tom Baker. This is not necessarily to the discredit of the actors concerned; they all did their best with the material they were given. But all too often that material was of questionable merit. Not only were a fair number of the stories simply poorly written – although there were notable exceptions – but the series also became overly reliant on its own mythology. Countless old foes, and even a few old friends, were brought back for return appearances, and whole plots were sometimes constructed around obscure points of *Doctor Who* lore from past eras. It has often been suggested that Nathan-Turner's aim in adopting this approach was to please the series' long-time fans – and it is, admittedly, difficult to see who else he could have been trying to please, as he must surely have realised that few members of the general viewing public would understand the numerous continuity points and back-references that permeated the scripts of this period – but if so, the irony is that it wasn't what most long-time fans wanted at all. What they really wanted was what the series had always delivered in the previous two decades: well-written, exciting, family-orientated adventure stories with a science-fiction or science-fantasy flavour. So incensed were many of the fans with Nathan-Turner's handling of the series that some of the fanzines of the time – perhaps most notably *DWB* (formerly known as *Doctor Who Bulletin* and later to become *Dreamwatch Bulletin* and ultimately the newsstand magazine *Dreamwatch*) – became filled with vitriolic criticism of the producer himself. Thus the series was gradually alienating not only the general viewing public but also many of its own fans, leaving it with few friends.

Another significant factor was that the costumes that the 1980s Doctors were given to wear in the role tended to compromise their efforts, being – certainly in Davison's and Baker's cases – more like a 'uniform' than a set of clothes; a deliberate move on Nathan-Turner's part, as he considered it useful for marketing purposes. Baker's intentionally-tasteless multicoloured costume was the worst of the lot, and had a knock-on impact on all other aspects of the series' design as well, making the whole of the sixth Doctor's era seem over-bright and garish. The 1980s companions, too, quite apart from being generally poorly conceived as characters, were all expected to wear unrealistic, uniform-like costumes that in most cases rarely changed from one story to the next. This meant that even when the scripts were of a higher calibre than usual for the period – as for instance on 'Kinda' (1982), 'Earthshock' (1982), 'The Caves of Androzani' (1984) and 'Revelation of the Daleks' (1985) – the stories still tended to be undermined by the poorly-conceived images of the lead characters, making it difficult for viewers to engage with the drama and rendering it less than fully effective.

Even in its earlier years, *Doctor Who* had sometimes been lampooned in the tabloid press as a laughable piece of nonsense in which a bizarrely-dressed alien eccentric and his dumb-but-sexy female companion battled outlandish monsters within wobbly sets and poorly-disguised quarries; but in the 1980s it was almost as if some of those involved in the making of the series actually started to be (perhaps subconsciously) influenced by this popular misconception, and thus to reflect it in their work, so that *Doctor Who* came in some respects to resemble this distorted caricature of itself. This in turn fed back into further, even more unhelpful press coverage – although Nathan-Turner appeared to take the view that any publicity was good publicity, relentlessly titilating journalists with stories about the series' latest light-entertainment guest stars and baseless hints about the possibility of him casting a woman as the next Doctor or scrapping the TARDIS's police box exterior.

Things started to look up during McCoy's time as the Doctor. His costume was a considerable improvement on his predecessor's (question-mark pullover notwithstanding); he was given a much more engaging companion in the form of

Sophie Aldred's Ace; the quality of the scripts improved markedly, with the many gratuitous continuity references that had plagued the series in the recent past being finally excised; and the standard of production became much higher all round. Whether this was due to Nathan-Turner having realised some of his past mistakes or to the positive influence brought to bear by his new script editor Andrew Cartmel is difficult to say. Perhaps it was a fortunate consequence of a number of different factors combined. The sad fact is, though, that it was all too late to reverse the damage done to the series' reputation over the previous few years, which had seen its ratings slump alarmingly – admittedly not helped by the fact that it had been scheduled opposite Britain's most popular show, *Coronation Street* (ITV, 1960- ). The writing was on the wall, and when the twenty-sixth season ended, there was no commission forthcoming from the BBC for a twenty-seventh.

## THE WILDERNESS YEARS

The period from 6 December 1989, when the last episode of the McCoy era was transmitted, to 26 March 2005, when the first of the new, Russell T Davies-overseen episodes had its debut airing, is sometimes described by fans as 'the wilderness years'; the time when *Doctor Who* was no longer an ongoing series. This is somewhat misleading, however, as it suggests that *Doctor Who* was effectively dormant throughout that period, when actually that was very far from being the case. It could even be said that *Doctor Who* did not really go on hiatus at all at the end of 1989, but simply switched to a different medium. The first ever original *Doctor Who* novel, *Timewyrm: Genesys* by John Peel, was released by Virgin Publishing less than two years later, in June 1991, and began what would prove to be a highly acclaimed and hugely influential range of books, taking the seventh Doctor and Ace on a succession of *New Adventures*. This is perhaps the greatest legacy of Cartmel's adroit realignment of the series' format during McCoy's time on TV. His more contemporary and sophisticated take on *Doctor Who* proved to be the perfect jumping-off point for the *New Adventures*, which were aimed primarily at late-teenage and adult fans and made it their mission to tell stories 'too broad and too deep for the small screen'. It is hard to imagine that any previous era of the TV series could have been so successfully spun off into a range of adult-orientated and sometimes (by *Doctor Who* standards) radical novels. Nevertheless, two years later, in July 1994, the *New Adventures* were joined by a companion range, the *Missing Adventures*, that proceeded to fit numerous exciting new stories into the gaps between the televised exploits of the first six Doctors, albeit generally told in a rather more traditional style than the *New Adventures*.

Then in 1996 came the *Doctor Who* TV Movie – an American/British co-production between Universal Television, Fox Network, BBC Television and BBC Worldwide – starring Paul McGann as the eighth Doctor. This had the status of a 'backdoor pilot' and could have spawned a whole new series had it not fallen foul of some unfortunate scheduling and internal network politics in the USA. The fact that it proved to be a one-off has sometimes been taken to mean that it was unsuccessful in the UK too, but this was emphatically not the case: its ratings were some of the best that *Doctor Who* had acheived since the mid-1970s; and although its reputation has since fallen, it should be noted that it was very well-received at the time by most who saw it, including most fans. It too would later prove very influential.

The advent of the TV Movie caused BBC Worldwide not to renew Virgin's licence to publish the *New Adventures* and *Missing Adventures*, but to bring the publication of original *Doctor Who* novels in-house to BBC Books, who essentially replicated the two ranges in their Eighth Doctor Adventures and Past Doctor Adventures, which began publication in 1997 and continued to win many plaudits, while perhaps never developing quite the same dedicated following as the Virgin ranges had.

Then, in July 1999, a company called Big Finish released the first in a new series of licensed audio CD dramas featuring the Davison, Colin Baker, McCoy and McGann incarnations of the Doctor, bringing *Doctor Who* to another new medium. This also proved to be a great success, and later spawned a number of spin-off series such as *Dalek Empire* and *Sarah Jane Smith*.

Other original *Doctor Who* fiction during this period came in the form of a range of 15 highly-regarded hardback novellas released by Telos Publishing, which aimed to present high quality writing from a mix of established *Doctor Who* authors and big names from the fantasy and horror genres.

Last but by no means least, *Doctor Who Magazine* continued to publish an acclaimed *Doctor Who* comic strip throughout this so-called wilderness period, as it had done (initially as *Doctor Who Weekly* and then as *Doctor Who Monthly*) since 1979.

Of course none of these tie-in ranges ever reached anything like the kind of mass audience that *Doctor Who* had enjoyed on TV. Even when its ratings were at their lowest, the TV series had attracted literally millions of viewers, whereas these tie-ins in other media numbered their readers and listeners in the tens of thousands at best. They were nevertheless greatly enjoyed and valued by the fans who avidly consumed them, and kept the flame of *Doctor Who* alive during its 16-year absence from regular TV production.

And, more than that, they proved to be a vital link between the classic series and the new.

# CHAPTER TWO
# THE 2005 RENAISSANCE

Around March 1962, before *Doctor Who* was even a gleam in its principal creator Sydney Newman's eye, Donald Wilson, head of the BBC's Script Department, delegated to two of his staff, Donald Bull and Alice Frick, the task of preparing a report into the suitability of literary science-fiction stories for TV adaptation.[1] Bull and Frick delivered their report to Wilson on 25 April 1962, and advised, amongst other things:

> People aren't all that mad about SF, but it is compulsive, when properly presented. Audiences – we think – are as yet not interested in the mere exploitation of ideas – the 'idea as hero' aspect of SF. They must have something to latch on to. The apparatus must be attached to the current human situation, and identification must be offered with recognisable human beings. As a rider to the above, it is significant that SF is not itself a wildly popular branch of fiction – nothing like, for example, detective and thriller fiction. It doesn't appeal much to women and largely finds its public in the technically minded younger groups. SF is a most fruitful and exciting area of exploration – but so far has not shown itself capable of supporting a large population. This points to the need to use great care and judgment in shaping SF for a mass audience. It isn't an automatic winner. No doubt future audiences will get the taste and hang of SF as exciting in itself, and an entertaining way of probing speculative ideas ... But for the present we conclude that SF TV must be rooted in the contemporary scene, and like any other kind of drama deal with human beings in a situation that evokes identification and sympathy.

It seems highly unlikely that Russell T Davies actually had this report in mind when he formulated his plans for the revival of *Doctor Who*, but clearly he must have reached essentially the same conclusions about how to present science fiction stories on TV in such a way as to appeal to a mass audience. He certainly had no illusions about the extent to which science fiction as a genre had fallen out of favour with the UK's general viewing public in the 1990s, as he told journalist Matt Wolf in an interview for the 15 October 2006 edition of *The Sunday Times*: 'There

---

[1] For a full, detailed account of the events leading up to the creation of *Doctor Who*, see *The Handbook: The Unofficial and Unauthorised Guide to the Production of Doctor Who* by David J Howe, Mark Stammers and Stephen James Walker (Telos Publishing, 2005).

was a moment when everything changed, and I can tell you exactly when it was. It was in 1990, when *Star Trek: The Next Generation* was scheduled at 6.00 pm on BBC Two. If they had run it at 8.00 pm on BBC One, science fiction would never have fallen off the radar. *The Next Generation* ran for seven years, with 26 episodes a year. It wasn't my favourite show – one of the problems was that they were members of the military – but it was a good, solid, enjoyable programme, and if it had been shown at peak time, it would have kept the sci-fi world alive.'

The way Davies responded to this public disaffection with TV science fiction was, as Bull and Frick had suggested, by ensuring that his version of *Doctor Who* was 'rooted in the contemporary scene' and offered 'identification … with recognisable human beings' in 'a situation that evokes identification and sympathy'. In short, he based the new series firmly on contemporary Earth and made ordinary shop girl Rose Tyler a pivotal character, arguably equal in importance to the Doctor himself, with her mother Jackie and on-off boyfriend Mickey also in key roles. There would be no journeys to alien planets in Series One, and although the TARDIS would visit a space station or two, these would always be within sight of the Earth. The stories would also be infused with contemporary imagery, including ersatz TV news reports (some of them presented by real-life political journalist Andrew Marr), shots of familiar London landmarks, scenes set in shopping arcades and restaurants, and so on; and even the more futuristic episodes would continue to reference familiar aspects of everyday life, for instance by presenting skewed takes on reality TV shows such as *Big Brother* and *The Weakest Link*. In other words, Davies cleverly wrapped up – and to some extent disguised – the series' science fiction aspects within a comforting package of contemporary trappings of the kind viewers were well used to seeing depicted in more conventional dramas.

This was not the first time that *Doctor Who* had been brought 'down to Earth' in a quite literal sense: Season Seven of the classic series, broadcast in 1970, had also ushered in a change of format that saw the Doctor being confined to contemporary Earth – exiled there by the Time Lords – and deprived of his ability to use the TARDIS. It was not until the following season that he was allowed to visit an alien world again – in 'Colony in Space' (1971) – and then only on a one-off mission before being sent back to Earth. Season Seven was clearly an important source of inspiration for Davies in his reconception of *Doctor Who* – this being most obviously apparent in his reuse of the Nestenes and Autons from Season Seven's opening story, 'Spearhead from Space' (1970), in his own opening episode, 'Rose' – but there were many differences in the way he treated his contemporary setting. No previous companion's family members or romantic partners had featured as regular supporting characters in the way that Jackie and Mickey would, and no previous Doctor's era had had stories grounded in such a strongly domestic context. Davies also determined that his version of *Doctor Who* should have much greater emotional depth than the classic series and tell more deeply layered stories. A small minority of long-time fans found all this rather hard to take: they wanted to see *Doctor Who* presenting the same type of overt science fiction stories as it had when they were younger, and criticised Davies's new approach as an inappropriate move toward soap-opera territory. There seems little doubt, however, that if Davies had stuck to the traditional approach they advocated, the new series would have been nothing like as big a hit as it proved to be with the general viewing public.

Davies's series was truly a *Doctor Who* for the 21st Century.

In any event, this new version of *Doctor Who* was not, as that small minority of fans clearly believed, a radical departure from what had gone before. The final classic series story, 'Survival' (1989), was based partly in present-day London, with familiar contemporary imagery and scenes set on a housing development very similar to Rose's Powell Estate; this then led on to the era of the *New Adventures*, which was the first to bring a greater emotional depth to *Doctor Who* and tell more deeply layered stories, sometimes with a domestic grounding; then came the TV Movie of 1996, which – controversially at the time – had the Doctor becoming romantically involved with and even kissing his companion, and re-imagined the TARDIS control room as a vast chamber with the console's central time rotor extending up to the ceiling in a column; then there were the Big Finish audio CD dramas, with their adoption of the *New Adventures* ethos – most obviously in the shared character of Bernice Summerfield – and clever refinement of classic series monsters with a modern sensibility. It can thus be seen that, far from being a sharp break from the past, Davies's approach to *Doctor Who* was really just the culmination of a seamless thread of development that had run from 'Survival', through the *New Adventures*, through the TV Movie, through the BBC Books, the Telos novellas and the Big Finish audio CD dramas, right up to the beginning of 'Rose'. But most influential of all were the *New Adventures*, to which Davies himself had contributed, as had other future new series writers Mark Gatiss, Paul Cornell, Matthew Jones and Gareth Roberts, and whose one-time editor Simon Winstone would go on to become one of Davies's script editors.[2] It is, I believe, fair to say that if it were not for the *New Adventures*, the new series of *Doctor Who* on TV would probably never have happened, and certainly not in the form that it took. The influence that these novels had on the series – ranging from relatively minor aspects[3] right up to an explicit adapation of one of the most popular in 'Human Nature'/'The Family of Blood' – is almost impossible to overstate.

This is not to suggest, of course, that Davies brought nothing new to *Doctor Who*. One of his biggest innovations was his recasting of the Doctor along the lines of a 'working class hero' with a Northern accent and a leather jacket, getting right away from the old-fashioned, patrician stereotype of the earlier Doctors. None of the tie-in ranges had ever taken – or, really, had the opportunity to take – such a bold new approach to the character. It is tempting to wonder what the new series would have been like if, as many fans had hoped or even expected, Paul McGann had been offered, and persuaded to accept, a chance to reprise his role as the eighth Doctor on TV (as he was already doing on audio), but with his hair cropped and wearing the same costume as was ultimately given to the ninth.[4] Such a change of

---

[2] Steven Moffat had also contributed a short story to one of Virgin Publishing's *Decalog* collections.

[3] Davies has said, for instance, that his conception of the Slitheen as a family of aliens rather than a race was inspired by the family of aliens in Paul Cornell's *Human Nature* (1995).

[4] The production team's failure to invite McGann to star in the new series was seen by some fans as being akin to the ousting of Colin Baker in 1986, in that he was arguably still the incumbent Doctor but not given the opportunity to continue in the role. There was however an important difference between the two situations, in

image would not only have been very much in line with the actor's own preferences but would also have served as a very visible indication of the way the Doctor had been affected by the Time War that had led to the destruction of his home planet and the wiping out of the rest of his race – another of Davies's major innovations for the new series. As it was, with an actor of the calibre and reputation of Christoper Eccleston cast in the lead role, the Doctor was given literally a new lease of life. But, fundamentally, the way that Davies and his main creative team saw *Doctor Who* was inescapably linked to their perspective as long-time fans of the series, as astutely observed in an article in *The Times* on Christmas Day 2005:

> This *Doctor Who* revival works so well because everyone involved is a fan, and therefore knows what other fans want from their Doctor. In many ways, it's like multi-million-pound fanfic – stories written by fans, where decades of frustration with the plot not going the way they want is vented – and so Leia and Han end up shagging frenetically, through access-panels in their snow-suits, in an ice corridor on Hoth. This sense of finally getting your hands on your idols, and making things go the way that you have always dreamt of, is why every episode of the new *Doctor Who* series has a moment that makes the Doctor fan simultaneously shivery and tearful.

Of course, not all fans are cut out to be great writers, but when you have someone who is both a fan and a great writer, it's an unbeatable combination. Such individuals understand *Doctor Who*'s strengths, and also its weaknesses, and are in an ideal postion to be able to judge what is going to work in a story and what isn't.

The end result of all this was the re-emergence of *Doctor Who* as a bigger and more mainstream success than ever before. The fact that the ninth Doctor's era lasted just one year came as a shock to many viewers. In the end, though, Davies's early 'parting of the ways' with Eccleston proved to be a blessing in disguise, as he then found in David Tennant an even better Doctor, who – now that the series was an established ratings-winner, with at least a third run of episodes guaranteed – could afford to show a little more of the eccentricity traditionally associated with the character; an eccentricity that, with perhaps understandable caution, Davies had intentionally downplayed with Eccleston's incarnation. Paired with the superb Billie Piper as Rose, Tennant quickly made the role his own, and took the series to even greater heights.

'Gareth Roberts said something interesting,' noted writer Chris Chibnall – yet another long-time fan now working on the series – in an interview in Issue 381 of *Doctor Who Magazine*, 'which is that even when Tom Baker was at his height, *Doctor Who* wasn't the huge popular cultural success that it is now. It was a great show

---

that more than eight years had passed since the TV Movie was produced, and it was understandable that the new production team would want to cast their 'own' Doctor. Whether or not McGann would have accepted an invitation to reprise the role on TV is also a moot point: he has given ambivalent and sometimes conflicting answers about this in interviews.

that everybody loved, but now it has an impact beyond the TV show. Everybody adores it, everybody loves David [Tennant], the toys are selling millions, there are two spin-off shows ...'

The measure of Davies's achievement was well summed up by journalist James Robinson in a piece in the 18 March 2007 edition of the *Observer*:

> Davies has done more than any other writer to revitalise the BBC's output, placing a witty, daring and imaginative *Doctor Who* at the heart of a revamped Saturday night schedule. It's a crucial slot, drawing in tea-time audiences that tend to stick with BBC One for the evening. The success of *Doctor Who* was a pivotal moment for an organisation stung by criticism from its governors, legislators and, yes, even viewers, that it was screening too many lifestyle shows. *Doctor Who* proved the perfect riposte, despite audience research that suggested it would not be popular. BBC executives ignored those findings and trusted their instincts; the show was a hit, and the channel has oozed confidence ever since. There are other innovative programmes too, of course. *Spooks*, to name but one, preceded it. But somehow Davies's *Doctor Who* has defined the channel, providing a creative spark that has encouraged more risk-taking and emboldened programme-makers and executives alike. How ITV, much in need of a creative catalyst despite an improved line up this year, would love its own Russell T Davies.

# COUNTDOWN

# CHAPTER THREE
# COUNTDOWN TO CHRISTMAS

As the closing credits rolled on 'Doomsday', bringing Series Two to a dramatic conclusion with the Doctor and Rose separated forever and a mouthy stranger in a wedding dress newly arrived inside the TARDIS, viewers across the UK were already starting to anticipate the continuation of the story in 'The Runaway Bride', which was expected to receive its debut transmission on Christmas Day 2006. The countdown had begun: but there were still 170 days to go! Fortunately, there would be plenty happening to maintain public interest in *Doctor Who* and keep the fans happy in the interim.[5]

Sunday 9 July 2006: T minus 169 days

A number of the national newspapers print pieces about 'Doomsday', although only the *Independent* is honest enough to admit that these were written without the journalists actually having an opportunity to view the episode in advance: 'It's the end of an era. Last night, Rose Tyler left *Doctor Who*. For weeks, since the confirmation that Billie Piper was leaving, the internet has buzzed with speculation about the manner of her departure. Granted, we'll speculate about pretty much anything on the internet, but the character of Rose has an appeal that stretches beyond fandom. In all that's been said about *Who*'s triumphant revival, one thing's clear: Everybody Loves Rose. Well, almost everybody. I should point out that, at the time of writing this, Rose's fate was still shrouded in secrecy. The crew weren't giving anything away, each new rumour contradicted the last, and when you phoned the BBC preview-tapes department they just put on a bad accent and pretended they were a kebab shop. She could be alive, she could be dead, or she could have turned into a glowing, floaty Bad Wolf demigod thing and gone off to play with the Eternals (the immortal transdimensional superbeings, not the mid-'90s girl group).' The *Daily Mail* meanwhile prints a piece about David Tennant's conspicuous lack of a suntan after a week spent on holiday in Sardinia with girlfriend Sophia Myles; apparently this is intentional on his part, as he needs to have his usual complexion when he starts work on 'The Runaway Bride'.

Monday 10 July 2006: T minus 168 days

Just two days after Series Two ends, viewers have a chance to show their support for *Doctor Who* as preliminary voting opens in the National Television Awards for

---

[5] In this and subsequent chapters, I have refrained from including details of when items of *Doctor Who*-related merchandise were released, as this is a subject that would fill a book all of its own – and is indeed covered in Telos Publishing's series of *Howe's Transcendental Toybox* titles.

2006. The series is nominated for Most Popular Drama, and David Tennant and Billie Piper for Most Popular Actor and Most Popular Actress respectively. Launched in 1995 and sponsored by the ITV network of companies, these are the most prestigious TV awards to be decided solely by public vote in the UK.

The *Daily Mail* meanwhile gives its reaction to 'Doomsday': 'Along, I imagine, with most of the population, I was distraught on Saturday night to witness the final parting of ways between Billie Piper's Rose Tyler and David Tennant's Doctor Who. In fact, I don't think I've seen anything so affecting outside the movies of Joan Crawford or Ingrid Bergman. Rose and the Doctor met on a Norwegian beach to say goodbye but she was not allowed to touch him. Remember the lump in the throat when Bergman had to say farewell, forever, to Gary Cooper in *For Whom The Bell Tolls*? Well, it was very much like that. The first half-hour or so of "Doomsday", the last episode in the present series of *Doctor Who*, hardly lived up to the rest of the finale, smothering us with tedious technical questions of parallel universes ... But it sprang into life with the war between these familiar aliens, while humans (except for a few soldiers, Rose, her parents and boyfriend Mickey) cowered in their homes ... This has been a memorable series, with the feisty Rose and the charismatic Doctor winning our affections. But having lost Christopher Eccleston as one Doctor, and now Rose, can the next series possibly rise to similar heights?'

Saturday 15 July 2006: T minus 163 days

David Tennant opens the summer fair of the Ashmount Primary School in Hornsey, London.

Sunday 16 July 2006: T minus 162 days

BBC7 – the BBC digital radio station that broadcasts comedy, drama and children's programming around the clock – begins repeating a series of *Doctor Who* audio plays, slightly re-edited from their original Big Finish CD releases, starring Paul McGann as the eighth Doctor. The run will comprise 'Shada', 'Storm Warning', 'Sword of Orion', 'The Stones of Venice', 'Invaders from Mars' and 'The Chimes of Midnight', with episodes going out on a weekly basis.

Monday 17 July 2006: T minus 161 days

The *MediaGuardian* supplement of the *Guardian* includes Russell T Davies at number 28 – down from number 14 the previous year – in its annual ranking of the 100 most influential people in British television, noting: 'With the triumphant return of *Doctor Who*, Russell T Davies single-handedly revived family TV drama. Having just finished a second series since its return last year, Davies restored BBC One's Saturday night ratings and started a trend for retro drama that will continue with *Robin Hood*, also on BBC One, and Sky One's remake of *The Prisoner*. Davies was rewarded this year with three BAFTA TV awards for *Doctor Who*, including Best Drama and the Dennis Potter award for outstanding writing. "We were told that bringing it back would be impossible, that we would never capture this generation of children," said Davies. "But we did it." Praised by critics as warm, witty and, of course, scary, *Doctor*

*Who* has also become one of the most effective satires on television, passing comment on everything from hospital superbugs to the war on Iraq. Davies has signed up for at least two more seasons of *Doctor Who*, and will oversee spin-off series *Torchwood*, starring John Barrowman as fellow time traveller Captain Jack.' BBC commissioning editor Jane Tranter also features at number 88 in the list.

The *Sun* meanwhile carries a short report on location recording for 'The Runaway Bride' taking place in Cardiff, with a picture of guest star Catherine Tate in her wedding dress costume and wearing sunglasses. There will be numerous further press and online reports about the recording over the coming week.

Tuesday 18 July 2006: T minus 160 days

Sad news for fans of the classic series as David Maloney, director of many highly regarded stories including 'The War Games' (1969), 'Genesis of the Daleks' (1975), 'The Deadly Assassin' (1976) and 'The Talons of Weng-Chiang' (1977), dies.

Monday 24 July 2006: T minus 154 days

The BBC Press Office issues press releases for BBC Three's autumn season, including the first substantial information to be made available about the *Doctor Who* spin-off *Torchwood*.

The bbc.co.uk news page meanwhile runs its own report on the location recording for 'The Runaway Bride', which has been under way since the beginning of the month. The report reads in part: 'Shoppers in sunglasses were baffled to see Christmas trees and giant snowmen on sun-baked streets in Cardiff. The seasonal time-trick of a frosty festive scene was created by the *Doctor Who* team to [record] the BBC show's Christmas special. Guest star Catherine Tate braved 30°C temperatures in full white bridal gown. When fans asked David Tennant, who plays the Doctor, how he was coping he shouted back: "It's blinking boiling." Scenes for the special, entitled "The Runaway Bride", were shot in Cardiff city centre, which will be transformed into a shopping street in London's West End for the show.'

Tuesday 25 July 2006: T minus 153 days

The *Daily Mail* runs a frank and insightful interview-cum-profile by journalist Barbara Davies on actress Anneke Wills, who played the Doctor's companion Polly in the mid-1960s. This will later inspire Wills to begin work on a two-volume autobiography.

Thursday 27 July 2006: T minus 151 days

BBC News carries a report on the official opening of the new *Doctor Who* studios at Upper Boat. It reads, in part: 'BBC Wales has opened new studios in South Wales so it can accommodate both the sci-fi show and its spin-off series, *Torchwood*, due this autumn. David Tennant, who plays the Doctor, was even on hand with his trusty sonic screwdriver to help with the opening. The television studio complex is more Pontypridd than Pinewood, situated in Upper Boat, three miles from the town that is better know as the birthplace of Tom Jones. It is the new and permanent home of the

BBC's *Doctor Who* operation, with 80 production staff and up to 400 people involved at the busiest times of the … schedule. Many of the interiors for the previous two series of *Doctor Who* were [recorded] in relatively cramped conditions at a warehouse in Newport, with some scenes shot at ITV Wales' studios in Cardiff. The new 86,000 square feet (7,400 square metres) site is more than ten times larger than BBC Wales' facilities in Cardiff, and includes workshops, video editing suites, six sound stages and a props store that is … out of this world. It is big enough to allow *Doctor Who* sets, such as that for the Time Lord's ageing and erratic spaceship, the TARDIS, to go up and stay up between production runs. Welsh Enterprise Minister, Andrew Davies, was given a whistle-stop tour of the complex during the official opening of the site.' The studios have in fact been operational for several weeks prior to this official inauguration, with recording taking place both for *Torchwood* and for 'The Runaway Bride'.

Friday 28 July 2006: T minus 150 days

Retailers Argos name remote control K-9s and remote control Daleks amongst their top ten 'hot toys' for Christmas 2006.

Tuesday 1 August 2006: T minus 146 days

The BBC's staff newspaper *Ariel* reports: 'CBBC is developing a spin-off series from *Doctor Who* based on the adventures of investigative journalist Sarah Jane, played by Elisabeth Sladen, and to be written by Russell T Davies. Sladen, who originally played the Doctor's assistant in 1973, returned for the last series where she was seen vying with young Rose Tyler for the Doctor's affections.' Although not mentioned in this short report, the working title of the new spin-off is strongly rumoured to be *Sarah Jane Investigates*.

Billie Piper is interviewed on the *Breakfast* programme, which airs on both BBC One and BBC News 24. Asked how she thinks her successor, Freema Agyeman, will get on as the new companion, she says: 'She's in good company. She's got the wonderful David Tennant. She'll handle it.'

Thursday 3 August 2006: T minus 144 days

*Doctor Who* fan and comedian Toby Hadoke premieres his play *Moths Ate My Doctor Who Scarf* at the Edinburgh Fringe Festival. It will run until 27 August.

The *Sun* newspaper reports that Zoë Lucker, one of the stars of *Footballers' Wives* (ITV One, 2002-2006), is to appear in Series Three of *Doctor Who* as the Rani, an evil Time Lady originally played by Kate O'Mara in the classic series stories 'The Mark of the Rani' (1984) and 'Time and the Rani' (1987). The story is picked up by a number of other news outlets. It is actually a false rumour spread by a fan specifically in order to spoof the tabloid press.

Sunday 6 August 2006: T minus 141 days

BBC Three begins a run of *Doctor Who* repeats starting from 'Rose'. They will air daily from this date. All bar 'The End of the World' are accompanied by their respective *Doctor Who Confidential* documentaries, mostly in their 'cutdown' rather than full versions.

## Tuesday 8 August 2006: T minus 139 days

Recording begins at Upper Boat on 'Smith and Jones', the first episode of Series Three proper, and Freema Agyeman makes her on-set debut as new companion Martha Jones.

## Wednesday 9 August 2006: T minus 138 days

David Tennant and Freema Agyeman have an early morning appointment for a rooftop photoshoot beside the TARDIS police box prop. The resulting promotional images will be widely seen in newspapers and magazines prior to the start of Series Three, showing off the Doctor's new blue suit for the first time. After the photoshoot is finished, the two actors go on to their first day's recording together for 'Smith and Jones' (the scenes that Agyeman has previously completed having not involved Tennant).

## Thursday 10 August 2006: T minus 137 days

The BBC Press Office issues a press release about Series Three, which lists some of the writers and directors who will be working on it and reads in part: 'Freema Agyeman, who will star alongside [David] Tennant in all 13 episodes in Series Three, says: "I am still pinching myself and can't wait to get started! It's been nerve-wracking but David has been brilliant in helping me to adjust on my first days on set. I am really looking forward to travelling through time and space with him over the next eight months." Russell T Davies, writer and executive producer, adds: "We were delighted and honoured by the second series' success, and we can promise new thrills, new laughs and some terrifying new aliens. The Doctor and Martha are destined to meet William Shakespeare, blood-sucking alien Plasmavores, the Judoon – a clan of galactic storm troopers – and a sinister intelligence at work in 1930s New York."'

The official *Doctor Who* website – at www.bbc.co.uk/doctorwho – also has an announcement to make: confirming rumours that have been circulating for some time, it reports that the Sci-Fi Channel has picked up Series Two for transmission in the USA, where it will debut in September. Chris Regina, Vice President of Programming for the Sci-Fi Channel, is quoted as saying: 'Our audience has clearly embraced *Doctor Who* and it has delivered a significant increase in viewers in the time period. We are looking forward to keeping the momentum going with David Tennant as the new Doctor.'

A rather less credible report appears on the news website Ananova: 'A surprise is in store ... *Doctor Who* bosses have found a way to prevent the much-loved Time Lord from dying out. By giving him a son. The revelation will be made at the end of Series Three ... The Doctor ... only has 13 lives according to lore, and is now on his tenth ... And writer Russell T Davies, who is in charge of the revamped show, decided something needed to be done in order that the programme doesn't die out. A source told the *Daily Express*: "Since there are only two regenerations left, the BBC needs a plan to make sure the show can carry on. Last year in one of the episodes it was hinted that the Doctor had a child following a doomed love affair with someone from a forgotten planet. Russell will unveil his big bombshell that he really is a dad in next year's series finale."'

## Saturday 12 August 2006: T minus 135 days

The Forbidden Planet store in London holds a well-attended signing event for the Panini-published *Doctor Who Storybook 2007*. Those autographing copies of the book include writers Steven Moffat, Mark Gatiss, Gareth Roberts, Rob Shearman, Tom MacRae and Nicholas Briggs, artists Alister Pearson and Martin Geraghty and *Doctor Who Magazine* editor Clayton Hickman.

## Sunday 13 August 2006: T minus 134 days

The *Sunday People* tabloid newspaper carries a rather alarming report: 'David Tennant has been offered millions to quit the hit BBC show [*Doctor Who*], the *People* can reveal. Beeb bosses now face a massive bidding war with ITV and Hollywood to keep their man. Tennant, 35, is paid about £500,000 to play the Time Lord in 13 episodes and a Christmas special. But he could net a fortune in films or a "golden handcuffs" deal with ITV. A show insider said: "David has yet to sign for another series of *Doctor Who*. There's a lot of talk about him going as we're all aware of deals on the table from ITV and Hollywood. A lot of film producers think he'd be great on the big screen. And ITV would love him for their dramas – and because it would mean them pinching him from the Beeb."'

## Monday 14 August 2006: T minus 133 days

Freema Agyeman gives her first TV interview for *Doctor Who* via satellite from her trailer in Cardiff to presenters Adrian Chiles and Nadia Sawalha of *The One Show*, a new early evening BBC One magazine programme of which today's is the first edition. 'We started [recording] last Tuesday,' she says, 'so it'll be a week tomorrow … It's amazing. I'm having the time of my life. Honestly, I could just sit and gush about what a good time I'm having. It's literally like I'm living a dream.' The interview is subsequently made available to view online by bbc.co.uk.

## Friday 18 August 2006: T minus 129 days

A special open-air screening of *Dr. Who and the Daleks* and *Daleks' Invasion Earth 2150 A.D.*, the two 1960s Dalek movies starring Peter Cushing as Dr Who, takes place at 8.00 pm in Walthamstow Town Square in London, hosted by the McGuffin Film Society.

## Tuesday 22 August 2006: T minus 125 days

Canadian French-language TV station Ztélé screens 'The Christmas Invasion', dubbed into French and retitled 'L'Invasion de Noel'. This is the start of a weekly run of episodes that will continue on 29 August with 'Une Nouvelle Terre' ('New Earth'), marking the Canadian debut of Series Two.

# CHAPTER THREE: COUNTDOWN TO CHRISTMAS

## Saturday 26 August 2006: T minus 121 days

Russell T Davies is named as Industry Player of the Year at the Edinburgh TV Festival 2006, as selected by a team of senior TV executives including Sky's Dawn Airey, Channel Five's Chris Shaw and ITV's Alison Sharman. He is in attendance to receive the award in person, along with producer Phil Collinson and writer Steven Moffat.

Meanwhile, at the World Science Fiction Convention in Anaheim, California, USA, Moffat is announced as winner of the coveted Hugo award for Best Dramatic Presentation (Short Form) 2006 for the Series One episodes 'The Empty Child' and 'The Doctor Dances'. Paul Cornell takes second place for 'Father's Day' and Rob Shearman takes third for 'Dalek', giving *Doctor Who* a remarkable clean sweep in its category. Julie Gardner later comments in *Doctor Who Magazine*: 'This is such an honour, and we're so delighted for Steven and [director] James Hawes. It's one of the highest accolades – if not *the* highest accolade – in science fiction, and not only to win, but to take all three top places, has just astonished us all.'

## Sunday 3 September 2006: T minus 113 days

The BBC announces the names of some new semi-regular cast members for the series. The official *Doctor Who* website reports: 'DJ and former *Top of the Pops* presenter Reggie Yates will feature as Martha Jones's brother Leo in Series Three of *Doctor Who*. Joining him to complete the Jones clan are Trevor Laird, who will play dad Clive, Adjoa Andoh as mum Francine, and Gugu Mbatha-Raw as sister Tish. Former *Casualty* actress Andoh previously appeared as cat nun Sister Jatt in the episode "New Earth". Laird is a *Who* veteran too, having played Frax in "The Trial Of A Time Lord" 20 years ago.'

## Tuesday 5 September 2006: T minus 111 days

At the TV Quick and TV Choice awards ceremony in London, *Doctor Who* wins in three categories: Best-Loved Drama, Best Actor – for David Tennant – and Best Actress – for Billie Piper. Tennant and Piper are present to collect the awards in person, and Tennant is quoted as saying: 'It was very hard to step into something that had been such a success already. It was very daunting and, because of that, this means a lot.'

## Wednesday 6 September 2006: T minus 110 days

BBC Three begins another complete rerun of Series One and Series Two episodes, with accompanying *Doctor Who Confidential* programmes, again generally in their 'cutdown' versions.

## Thursday 7 September 2006: T minus 109 days

BBC Worldwide announces that it has appointed Los Angeles, California based company Most Management LLC as its exclusive North American licensing agent for *Doctor Who*. A press release issued by the BBC Press Office quotes Julia Posen,

Sales Director of the Children's division of BBC Worldwide, as saying: 'We are excited to work with Most Management on new and unique products for one of BBC Worldwide's longest-running and most successful franchises. We want the fans in North America to have the opportunity to be a part of the *Doctor Who* phenomenon that has captivated UK and European audiences for over 40 years now.' Marc Mostman, president of Most Management, is reported as saying: 'With the success of the new *Doctor Who* series on the CBC, the market on this side of the pond has definitely grown exponentially with this evergreen franchise. We are committed to building a line of high quality licensed products for North American audiences that captures the *Doctor Who* experience.' Despite this agreement, there will actually be a dearth of North American-produced *Doctor Who* merchandise over the following year.

Friday 8 September 2006: T minus 108 days

A BBC press release announces: 'BBC Worldwide and BBC World are partnering with Amazon.com in the US to provide nearly 400 hours of content for Amazon Unbox, a new digital video download service, launched yesterday.' A number of classic series *Doctor Who* stories, all of them already released on DVD, are amongst the titles included in the deal.

Saturday 9 September 2006: T minus 107 days

The *Sun* newspaper carries a report that David Tennant has signed up to continue as the Doctor in Series Four – but that it will be his last in the lead role.

Tuesday 12 September 2006: T minus 104 days

In one of a series of storytelling-themed discussions for BBC staff at Television Centre in London, Russell T Davies is interviewed on stage by Julie Gardner. *Doctor Who* is, naturally, one of the subjects covered, and a number of clips from the series are shown, plus an exclusive preview clip from the debut episode of *Torchwood*.

Davies is also interviewed today on the *Newsround* programme, made by CBBC but transmitted first on BBC One, by presenter – and *Doctor Who* fan – Lizo Mzimba, who takes the opportunity to ask about various rumours circulating within fandom concerning 'The Runaway Bride' and Series Three, most of which Davies debunks. A transcript of a few of the questions and answers is also published on the CBBC Newsround website, part of bbc.co.uk.

Thursday 14 September 2006: T minus 102 days

The BBC Press Office issues a press release about the second *Doctor Who* spin-off, now to be entitled *The Sarah Jane Adventures*. It reads in part: 'Multi-award winning writer Russell T Davies has written a brand new series for CBBC called *The Sarah Jane Adventures*. It stars one of the Doctor's most famous companions, investigative journalist Sarah Jane Smith … Davies says: "Children's TV has a fine history of fantasy thrillers – I loved them as a kid, and they were the very first things I ever wrote. So it's brilliant to return to such a vivid and imaginative area of television." The series begins with a 60-minute special which will be broadcast in early 2007 with the series due later in the year. Set in present-day West London, the programme stars original Sarah Jane actress Elisabeth Sladen and Yasmin Paige, who plays her 13-year-old neighbour Maria. The two form an unlikely alliance to fight evil alien forces at work in Britain. Elisabeth says: "I left Sarah Jane but she never left me. I can't wait to return to Cardiff to find out what's going to happen to her next." In the special, Maria and Sarah Jane are brought together in their battle against the scheming Ms Wormwood, played by Samantha Bond. [Recording] begins next month on location in Wales, with the series going into production in spring 2007. Creative Director of CBBC, Anne Gilchrist, says: "CBBC viewers have already proved themselves to be enormous fans of *Doctor Who*. I am thrilled that they'll now have this new series as an extra-special treat."'

Also on this date, Peter Ling, writer of the classic series story 'The Mind Robber' (1968), dies at the age of 80.

### Thursday 21 September 2006: T minus 95 days

A press release issued by the BBC Press Office announces that Julie Gardner has been appointed as Head of Drama Commissioning at the BBC, although she will continue as Head of Drama for BBC Wales as well, and will retain her responsibilities as an executive producer of *Doctor Who*, *Torchwood* and *The Sarah Jane Adventures*.

### Saturday 23 September 2006: T minus 93 days

The two-day *Doctor Who* convention Regenerations begins at the Marriot Hotel in Swansea, featuring many guests connected to both classic and new series.

Writer Tom MacRae meanwhile opens the Weedon Bec Fete in Northampton and donates signed copies of his scripts for 'Rise of the Cybermen' and 'The Age of Steel' to the event's charity auction.

### Sunday 24 September 2006: T minus 92 days

A script from the classic series story 'The Time Meddler' (1965) is one of the items featured in this evening's edition of the BBC One antiques programme *The Antiques Roadshow*.

### Wednesday 27 September 2006: T minus 89 days

David Tennant is the subject in this evening's edition of the new BBC One documentary series *Who Do You Think You Are?*, in which celebrities 'trace their ancestry discovering secrets from their past'. The official *Doctor Who* website reports: 'David delves deep into his family history in a journey that takes him to the Isle of Mull and Londonderry. It's a tale of Pet Shop Boys, football and unexpected Irish roots. You'll get to meet his mum too.'

<u>Friday 29 September 2006: T minus 87 days</u>

Series Two of the new *Doctor Who* makes its US debut on the Sci-Fi Channel with a double bill of 'The Christmas Invasion' and 'New Earth'.

<u>Saturday 30 September 2006: T minus 86 days</u>

After a limited admission preview the previous evening, a new *Doctor Who: Up Close* exhibition of costumes and props from the series opens at the Spaceport Merseyside venue, scheduled to run until 4 January 2007. This complements the first such exhibition, which remains open in Cardiff.

<u>Saturday 7 October 2006: T minus 79 days</u>

The 10th Planet store, which specialises in selling *Doctor Who* merchandise, holds its second Doctor Who Day event in Barking, Essex, with guests from all eras of the series' history.

<u>Monday 9 October 2006: T minus 77 days</u>

The CBC channel in Canada screens 'New Earth' as its debut run of Series Two gets under way. Further episodes will be shown on a weekly basis, with a Christmas break after 'The Impossible Planet' on 4 December, resuming with 'The Satan Pit' on 15 January 2007. When the official ratings are released, 'New Earth' will be revealed to have pulled in an impressive 530,000 viewers. With the exception of 'Tooth and Claw', for which the figure will be rather lower at 371,000, the subsequent episodes will also attract around half a million viewers each.

<u>Monday 16 October 2006: T minus 70 days</u>

Long-running BBC One children's programme *Blue Peter* launches a competition for one lucky young viewer to win a speaking role in Series Three of *Doctor Who*. The competition is introduced by way of pre-recorded messages from David Tennant and some of the series' other cast members such as Elisabeth Sladen (Sarah Jane Smith) and Shaun Dingwall (Pete Tyler). Entrants are required to send in a one-minute-long audition recorded on videotape, performing one of three monologue scripts made available on the official *Blue Peter* website. The website also gives some guidelines for the recording and some acting tips written by *Doctor Who*'s casting director Andy Pryor. Runners-up will receive a variety of *Doctor Who*-related prizes. The closing date for entries is 10 November.

<u>Sunday 22 October 2006: T minus 64 days</u>

The *Torchwood* spin-off series makes its much-anticipated debut on BBC Three with the episode 'Everything Changes' by Russell T Davies, and becomes the highest-rated non-sports programme ever to be screened on a UK digital TV channel.

# CHAPTER THREE: COUNTDOWN TO CHRISTMAS

## Wednesday 25 October 2006: T minus 61 days

The Interalia Theatre group premiere their officially licensed *Doctor Who* play *Evil of the Daleks*, based on the 1967 TV story 'The Evil of the Daleks', at the New Theatre Royal, Portsmouth. It will have a short run, ending on Saturday 28 October, with a performance each evening plus a matinee on the Saturday.

## Saturday 28 October 2006: T minus 58 days

Author and publisher David J Howe hosts a mini-convention at the New Theatre Royal, Portsmouth, prior to the matinee performance of the *Evil of the Daleks* play.

## Tuesday 31 October 2006: T minus 55 days

At the National Television Awards ceremony in London, *Doctor Who* wins all three of the awards for which it is nominated: Most Popular Drama, Most Popular Actor and Most Popular Actress – equalling its record from the previous year. David Tennant, Billie Piper, Camille Coduri and Noel Clarke are on hand to pick up the awards. 'I think if my eight-year-old self could see me at the Royal Albert Hall winning a prize for playing the Doctor on telly,' Tennant is quoted as saying, 'he would need a stiff shot of Irn-Bru. I'm really chuffed. It's been really daunting to come into something that was such a huge success.'

## Friday 10 November 2006: T minus 45 days

BBC News reports that *Doctor Who* is one of 21 new additions to a list of 'Icons of England' voted for by the public as part of a project funded by Culture Online, part of the Department for Culture, Media and Sport.

The *Doctor Who Annual* begins a lengthy stint at the top of the Children's Best Selling Books chart published by *The Bookseller* magazine, besting the traditional bestseller *The Beano Annual* in the lucrative pre-Christmas market.

## Saturday 11 November 2006: T minus 44 days

A two-day *Doctor Who* convention called Dimensions begins in The Swallow Hotel, Stockton on Tees. TV Movie stars Paul McGann, Sylvester McCoy and Daphne Ashbrook are reunited on stage, and the event boasts many other guests from all eras of the series' history.

## Tuesday 14 November 2006: T minus 41 days

In advance of BBC One's annual *Children in Need* telethon (see below), veteran disc jockey Terry Wogan auctions on his BBC Radio 2 breakfast show some 'money can't buy' *Doctor Who* prizes, including perhaps most notably a Series Three set visit to be conducted by Russell T Davies. The auction raises £25,000 for the charity.

### Wednesday 15 November 2006: T minus 40 days

This afternoon's edition of *Blue Peter* has an item on the show's *Doctor Who* competition, which closed on 10 November. An amazing 8,057 entries have been received. Nine of the top ten finalists are announced, and an online poll is launched to allow viewers to select the tenth from a selection of ten others presented on the *Blue Peter* website. This poll will run until the end of the week. The ten finalists will then take part in an acting workshop, and the winner will be announced at a later date.

### Friday 17 November 2006: T minus 38 days

David Tennant and Freema Agyeman appear via links recorded on the TARDIS set to appeal for donations during the *Children in Need* telethon.

### Sunday 19 November 2006: T minus 36 days

The Millennium Centre in Cardiff hosts a major *Doctor Who* event. *Doctor Who – A Celebration* is a selection of Murray Gold's incidental music from the series, performed live in concert by the BBC National Orchestra of Wales and the National Chorus of Wales, conducted by Ben Foster, with occasional vocalisations by Melanie Pappenheim and clips from relevant episodes shown on a large screen above the stage. David Tennant emerges from the TARDIS police box to introduce the event, which includes a preview of the song 'Love Don't Roam', performed by Gary Williams, and a four minute clip of the 'car chase' sequence from 'The Runaway Bride'. Actors in Dalek, Cyberman, Clockwork Man and Ood costumes menace the audience at various points. David Tennant and Russell T Davies hold a short question and answer session on stage after the music. Various *Doctor Who* stars and production team members are in the audience for the event, including Freema Agyeman, Camille Coduri, Noel Clarke, Anneke Wills, Phil Collinson, Julie Gardner, Helen Raynor, Steven Moffat, Gareth Roberts and Gary Russell. Tickets sold out within about two hours when they first became available on 20 October, but the concert is broadcast live on BBC Radio Wales for those unable to attend. The whole thing is in aid of *Children in Need*. Various props and costumes from the series are auctioned online and at the event to raise further money. These include a pair of the Doctor's trainers and one of Rose's blouses. All told, these endeavours raise over £75,000 for the charity.

### Monday 20 November 2006: T minus 35 days

'The Complete Series Two' DVD box set is released by 2 Entertain. This presents 'The Christmas Invasion' and all 13 episodes of Series Two, plus extras, at a recommended retail price of £69.99; and the online retailer amazon.co.uk offers exclusive Cyber-head packaging with all copies bought over its website. The episodes themselves have already been made available earlier in the year on single-disc 'vanilla' releases, so fans generally buy the box set specifically for the extras – and many are left feeling that they have not received value for money. Some obvious and arguably essential items for inclusion on a supposedly comprehensive set such as this – the specially-filmed broadcast trailers, the 'Tardisode' teasers, the 'Attack of the Graske' digital TV game and a preview of 'The Runaway Bride' (akin to the equivalent Series One set's preview of 'The Christmas Invasion') – are omitted. In addition, of the extras that *are* included, the *Children in Need* mini episode is presented not in the transmitted version but in a rough early edit with most of the sound effects missing and a dummy music track reportedly borrowed largely from the movie *Road to Perdition* (Dreamworks/20th Century Fox, 2002); the deleted scenes section does not include a number of notable and much-discussed cuts from the transmitted episodes; the Billie Piper video diary is much shorter than the previous year's (although she may, admittedly, have shot much less material this time around, in which case this would obviously be beyond 2 Entertain's control); and the David Tennant video diary, while lengthy and well received by fans, is poorly edited, with a 15-minute out-of-sequence section tacked on the end.

Neill Gorton and his Millennium FX team meanwhile win a Royal Television Society Craft and Design Award for their work on *Doctor Who* and the BBC comedy series *Little Britain*.

## Tuesday 21 November 2006: T minus 36 days

The BBC America network in the USA screens 'Rose' as the first in a complete rerun of Series One, previously seen on the Sci-Fi Channel. The remaining episodes will be aired on a weekly basis.

A *Doctor Who* special edition of the Anne Robinson-hosted BBC One quiz show *The Weakest Link* is recorded at the famous Pinewood Studios in Iver Heath, Buckinghamshire. The guests participating are actors David Tennant, Camille Coduri, Noel Clarke, John Barrowman, Andrew Hayden-Smith, Tracy-Ann Oberman, Claire Rushbrook and Nicholas Briggs and – voiced by John Leeson and remote-controlled by Mat Irvine – K-9. Robinson's Anne-Droid double from 'Bad Wolf' is also present in the studio. Although it has been announced in advance that Freema Agyeman will be taking part, this proves to be incorrect. Recording is unexpectedly lengthy, reportedly trying the patience of some of the guests and the studio audience: it starts just after the scheduled 7.30 pm and ends not long before 11.00 pm. Camille Coduri proves victorious in the quiz.

## Friday 24 November 2006: T minus 33 days

Spanish public service station TVE Clan is the latest overseas broadcaster to pick up *Doctor Who*, beginning a run of Series One on weeknights from this date, with repeats at weekends.

## Friday 1 December 2006: T minus 24 days

The official *Doctor Who* website gets into the festive spirit by launching an advent calendar: each day in the run-up to Christmas, an additional 'window' will open to reveal a new item of content, such as an online game, an artwork or photographic image or a video or sound file, many of them relating to 'The Runaway Bride'.

# THIRD DIMENSION

## Sunday 3 December 2006: T minus 22 days

Noted *Doctor Who* author Craig Hinton dies at his London home at the young age of 42, prompting numerous tributes from friends, fans and former colleagues.

## Monday 4 December 2006: T minus 21 days

The latest issue of the TV listings magazine *TV Times* goes on sale. It reveals the recipients of its TV awards for 2006, as voted for by readers. *Doctor Who* wins the Best TV Show category and David Tennant the Best Actor category.

Big Finish launches via its website a competition for a previously-unpublished author to have a short story included in one of its licensed *Short Trips* collections of *Doctor Who* fiction during 2007. The theme for entries, which can feature any of the classic series Doctors, is 'How the Doctor changed my life'. The closing date is 31 January 2007.

## Wednesday 6 December 2006: T minus 19 days

*Doctor Who* is featured on the front cover of the BBC's *Radio Times* listings magazine in the week prior to publication of the bumper Christmas double issue. The Doctor is pictured in the foreground, holding his sonic screwdriver, with the TARDIS police box and a group of menacing robot Santas in the background, in a promotional image for 'The Runaway Bride', which is now confirmed to be scheduled for debut transmission at 7.00 pm on Christmas Day.

The BBC News website and other news outlets report that David Tennant has won a *Doctor Who Magazine* 'favourite Doctor' poll, the results of which are to be announced in the new issue due out this week. The usual winner of such polls, Tom Baker, has been knocked down to second place. 'This is a real honour, and I am totally gobsmacked,' Tennant is quoted as saying. *Doctor Who Magazine* editor Clayton Hickman meanwhile comments: 'This is an incredible result for David, and shows how quickly viewers have taken to him. The iconic image of *Doctor Who* has always been of Tom Baker in his floppy hat and long, multi-coloured scarf, but it looks like that's been replaced.'

## Thursday 7 December 2006: T minus 18 days

Pre-Christmas festivities at Peterborough Town Hall include an unlicensed amateur *Doctor Who* educational play, *A Christmas Past and Present*, in which the Doctor compares the Christmas of 1935 to that of the present day, for the benefit of an audience of children.

The BBC Press Office makes available press packs for BBC One's Winter/Spring 2007 season, including *Doctor Who*, although this contains nothing in the way of new information.

The listings magazine *TV and Satellite Week* has *Doctor Who*'s 'The Runaway Bride' as the main image on the cover of its Christmas double issue. The magazine contains a short interview with David Tennant. In response to a comment from the interviewer to the effect that a lot of viewers would like to see him stay on beyond Series Four, he says: 'That's very nice, and it's a great job, too. It's certainly not something I would walk away from lightly. But at the moment I don't know. I'll wait till I'm asked, I think.'

## Friday 8 December 2006: T minus 17 days

The BBC's *Breakfast* programme features a guest appearance by Elisabeth Sladen, discussing her return to *Doctor Who* in 'School Reunion' and her starring role in the forthcoming spin-off *The Sarah Jane Adventures*. A clip from the latter's pilot episode 'Invasion of the Bane' is shown, along with one from 'The Hand of Fear' (1976).

David Tennant is interviewed in the Christmas edition of *The Big Issue* – the street-paper published to aid the homeless – but only in the version published in Scotland.

## Saturday 9 December 2006: T minus 16 days

The Christmas double issue of *Radio Times* starts appearing on some newsagents' shelves. The listings include details of all the *Doctor Who*-related broadcasts scheduled for the festive period. All copies of the magazine also contain a free gift audio CD of the first part of the talking book version of Stephen Cole's *Doctor Who* novel *The Feast of the Drowned*; the concluding part will be given away free in the next issue, followed by Jacqueline Rayner's *The Stone Rose*, again in two parts, over the following two weeks.

Seventh Doctor actor Sylvester McCoy begins a run as one of the stars of the pantomime *Aladdin* at the Hexagon Theatre, Reading.

## Monday 11 December 2006: T minus 14 days

This afternoon's edition of *Blue Peter* on BBC One includes a behind-the-scenes report on *The Sarah Jane Adventures*: 'Invasion of the Bane', including interviews with Elisabeth Sladen, Yasmin Paige and (speaking in character as Mrs Wormwood) Samantha Bond.

## Tuesday 12 December 2006: T minus 13 days

To add further to the accolades he has received for his portrayal of the Doctor, David Tennant wins the Best TV Performance award in voting by readers of *Heat* magazine, as announced in the issue published on this date.

## Wednesday 13 December 2006: T minus 12 days

Issue 59 of the BBC's *It's Hot* magazine runs a short interview with David Tennant, in which he confesses to having been poor at maths and physics in school and says that the strangest thing about playing the Doctor is: 'Action figures. They're really, really weird. They're good likenesses, but just so unlike anything to do with real life. I collected *Star Wars* figures as a child, then suddenly someone's presenting you with one that's ... you!'

THIRD DIMENSION

## Friday 15 December 2006: T minus 10 days

Peter Fincham, the Controller of BBC One, is interviewed on the Simon Mayo show on BBC Radio 5 Live. *Doctor Who* fan Ian Robertson takes the opportunity to e-mail in a question about rumours circulating within fandom to the effect that the show may be cancelled after Series Four or Series Five. Fincham replies that there is no truth in this rumour: 'We don't necessarily plan years in advance, but *Doctor Who* is so popular, I don't see it going anywhere anytime soon.'

The *Sun* newspaper runs a short piece on Billie Piper: 'Gorgeous actress Billie Piper regrets quitting *Doctor Who* after just two series. The ex-wife of Chris Evans, who played the Doctor's sidekick Rose, admits she's "jealous" of the BBC One show's rising success. She said: "I still desperately miss Rose and everyone at *Doctor Who*. I'm jealous that I'm no longer part of it and I'm trying to keep the green-eyed monster at bay, but on the whole it felt like the right thing to do. I'd done two series, and each one takes nine months to shoot. I got so close to everybody that I thought if I didn't leave I'd be too scared to ever go, and I'd get complacent."'

## Saturday 16 December 2006: T minus 9 days

The Christmas pantomime *Jack and the Beanstalk* opens at the New Theatre, Cardiff, starring John Barrowman as Jack. The script and production make a number of subtle and not-so-subtle references to his role as Captain Jack Harkness in *Doctor Who* and *Torchwood*. Performances are due to run until 17 January 2007.

A 20-second-long trailer for 'The Runaway Bride' is broadcast just before this evening's episode of *Robin Hood* on BBC One. It is the first dedicated trailer to air for the special, although clips have been included in composite trailers advertising a number of BBC One programmes scheduled for the festive season.

## Sunday 17 December 2006: T minus 8 days

BBC One screens at 4.25 pm a repeat of the 2005 Christmas special, 'The Christmas Invasion'. This is the first BBC One repeat of a *Doctor Who* episode in over ten years.

## Monday 18 December 2006: T minus 7 days

As pre-publicity for 'The Runaway Bride' moves into top gear, a morning press launch screening of the special takes place in London. The BBC News website subsequently publishes a preview in its entertainment section, including quotes from interviews given at the event by David Tennant and guest stars Catherine Tate and Sarah Parish. It reads, in part: 'Tate … describes the role as "one of the best things I've done". "It was such a fantastic job, and so exciting," she says. "It was like making an action movie. I agreed to do it without even knowing what it was – I just said yes." "It's a fairly unconventional pairing," admits actor David Tennant … "But by the end, they've rather fallen for each other. Perhaps I'll come back and visit her some day." Tate, however, did not have to wrestle with the possibility of stepping into Billie Piper's shoes as the Doctor's new full-time assistant. "They didn't ask me," says the 38-year-old

Londoner flatly. "It's a bit of a shame, I think," says Tennant. "They could have made a great team." No *Doctor Who* episode is complete without a fiendish villain, and Parish says she jumped at the chance to play the baddie. However, that was before she realised that playing the evil Empress of the Racnoss would require extensive make-up taking four hours to apply each morning. "It was a heavy, cumbersome costume, but I loved it," she says. "It was a really interesting exercise. You really have to over-accentuate everything in order to make the prosthetics work." "Since I've started this job, Sarah has been saying 'I've got to play an alien,'" says Tennant, who previously worked with Parish on BBC One musical comedy *Blackpool* and the forthcoming ITV [sic] drama *Recovery*.[6] "All I can say is, be careful what you wish for!" Parish, however, dismisses suggestions that her arachnid villain may be too fearsome for family viewing. "It's behind-the-sofa scary, as opposed to psychiatric-ward scary," she laughs.'

Reports from the press launch also start to appear on other websites, and on radio news programmes, including on BBC Radio 1. BBC Wales's early evening *Wales Today* programme has a video report from the event, including comments from David Tennant and Sarah Parish. Tennant says: 'It's one of those shows where so much happens in post-production. All sorts of things happen to the TARDIS that have never happened before. The three of us did a scene together when we were in completely different rooms on completely different days.'

Catherine Tate appears on the Channel 4 chat show *The New Paul O'Grady Show*, where 'The Runaway Bride' is the first topic of conversation. Host O'Grady admits that he would like a cameo role in *Doctor Who*.

A new, 30-second-long trailer for 'The Runaway Bride' is now running on all the main BBC TV channels, incorporating numerous clips from the special.

Prime TV in New Zealand meanwhile screens 'Rose' as the first in a run of weekly repeats of Series One.

Tuesday 19 December 2006: T minus 6 days

The BBC's *Breakfast* programme runs its own video report on the previous day's press launch for 'The Runaway Bride', including clips and still images from the special. Comments from the report are reproduced in a further item on the BBC News website. This time, David Tennant is quoted as saying: 'The Doctor's used to his companions being rather grateful for their ride in the TARDIS. But Donna couldn't be less interested – which is an interesting new dynamic.'

*Time Out* magazine's television editor Alkarim Jivani discusses his Christmas TV highlights on the BBC Radio 4 arts programme *Front Row*. 'The Runaway Bride' is his first choice, and he explains: 'If you talk about Christmas television these days, you have to begin with *Doctor Who*. It's curious that it's rapidly establishing itself as a Christmas TV fixture for the new century in the same way that [the] Morecambe and Wise [show] was a Christmas TV fixture for the last century.'

Today's edition of the children's news magazine programme *Newsround* features interview clips with Russell T Davies, David Tennant and Catherine Tate, discussing both the Christmas special and the forthcoming Series Three. Tennant gives the show an exclusive titbit of information about the latter: 'There is a monster from *Doctor Who*'s past that nobody will be expecting to see again!' Extracts from the report are transcribed

---

[6] *Recovery* was in fact to be a BBC One drama.

on the *Newsround* website.

### Wednesday 20 December 2006: T minus 5 days

A report on the BBC News website reads: 'Hundreds of episodes of BBC programmes will be made available on a file-sharing network for the first time, the Corporation has announced. The move follows a deal between the commercial arm of the organisation, BBC Worldwide, and technology firm Azureus. The agreement means that users of Azureus's Zudeo software in the US can download titles such as *Little Britain*. Until now, most BBC programmes found on peer-to-peer file-sharing networks have been illegal copies. Beth Clearfield, vice president of programme management and digital media at BBC Worldwide, said that the agreement was part of a drive to reach the largest audience possible. "We are very excited to partner with Azureus and make our content available through this revolutionary distribution model," she said.' *Doctor Who* is one of the programmes expected to be made available to US viewers through this deal. A number of other news websites carry similar reports.

The official bbc.co.uk website for *The Sarah Jane Adventures* goes live, although for 'rights reasons' access is limited to those using UK-based internet services.

### Thursday 21 December 2006: T minus 4 days

David Tennant is heard in the role of Buttons in a performance of the pantomime *Cinderella* on DJ Christian O'Connell's breakfast show on Virgin Radio. Tennant agreed to take part in this a little earlier in the year after reacting with admirable good humour on being the victim of a prank on-air wake up call from O'Connell – who was unaware that it only a couple of hours after the actor had returned home from a night shoot on the Series Three episode 'The Shakespeare Code'.

The *Sun* newspaper runs the concluding part of an interview with Billie Piper that began the previous day. 'It was such a hard decision,' says Piper of her departure from *Doctor Who*. 'I still cry about it; I'm such a cry baby. I don't know if I'll be able to watch the next series. I'll probably have to sit behind the couch with a cushion over my eyes … I just thought it was time to do something new – not because I felt tired, the material was crap or the people were nasty – but just because I felt like doing something else. I'd spent nine months filming in Cardiff, and that's a long time to be away from your family and friends. I'm a real London girl, I absolutely love it. I found it increasingly hard to be away. I felt like if I'd stayed there any longer, I would have become a bit complacent. And, suddenly, you've been doing it for five years and you're too scared to leave.' She adds that the hardest thing was telling showrunner Russell T Davies of her decision: 'He was upset and I was upset, but he's such a wonderful man and completely supported me … Life has to move on and there are great things happening in British TV. I just hope I don't regret leaving!'

### Friday 22 December 2006: T minus 3 days

Resident TV critic Richard Arnold on the morning ITV show *GMTV* recommends 'The Runaway Bride' as one of the shows not to miss over Christmas. A clip from the special also features on the BBC's rival *Breakfast* programme, illustrating a discussion about the BBC's licence fee.

The *MediaGuardian* carries an interview with Russell T Davies, in which he again takes the opportunity to promote 'The Runaway Bride'. 'One thing that people have been saying is that it's like a *Comic Relief* sketch,' he comments, 'but it's not. It's a proper hour-long drama and Catherine Tate has a proper part. She's amazing in it; [she] and David Tennant together are a joy.'

Julie Gardner takes part in a live phone-in on the early afternoon Richard Evans show on BBC Radio Wales. She answers some wide-ranging questions put both by phone and by e-mail, and also takes a spoof call from David Tennant, pretending to be an eccentric fan from Bristol.

Journalist Charlie Brooker's late evening *Screen Wipe* show on BBC Four includes a clip from 'The Runaway Bride'

In the US, the Sci-Fi Channel has a marathon screening of Series Two episodes all day, leading up to their debut transmission of the closing two-parter 'Army of Ghosts'/'Doomsday'.

## Saturday 23 December 2006: T minus 2 days

The BBC's *Breakfast* programme features *Doctor Who* for the third time in four days, this time focusing not on 'The Runaway Bride' but on the *Doctor Who Confidential* special scheduled for transmission on BBC One at 1.00 pm on Christmas Day, which will give a behind-the-scenes account of the staging of the 19 November *Doctor Who* concert in aid of *Children in Need*. Dalek and Cyberman voice artist Nicholas Briggs and monster actor Paul Kasey are interviewed live in the BBC News 24 studio.

A day after concluding its debut run of Series Two, the Sci-Fi Channel announces via a news item on its website that it has acquired Series Three for screening in summer 2007.

## Sunday 24 December 2006: T minus 1 day

*Deep and Dreamless Sleep*, a specially-written, Christmas-themed *Doctor Who* short story by Paul Cornell, is published in *The Sunday Times*. Cornell was invited to write this by the production office after they were approached by *The Sunday Times* with the suggestion of running such a piece. 'It's the story of something strange that happens to David Tennant's Doctor when the TARDIS lands in the bedroom of a four year old boy on Christmas Eve,' Cornell is quoted as saying on the official *Doctor Who* website. 'There's fun along the way, but in the end it's quite serious and real. It's written for a family audience. It'd be nice to think it was going to be read to some children somewhere!'

# CHAPTER FOUR
# IT'S CHRISTMAS!

Christmas 2006 brought a veritable sack-load of presents for *Doctor Who* fans. Public interest in the series had never been higher, and – even leaving aside the many advance promotional spots and guest appearances by the stars and behind-the-scenes team (the main instances of which are detailed in Chapter Three) – the TV and radio schedules were packed with *Doctor Who*-related content. As Russell T Davies put it, in comments quoted in the *Guardian* on 17 December: 'It's been less than a year since David Tennant became the Doctor. It was scary this time last year: Chris Eccleston was brilliant, then he left and there was this big hole. But have you seen the BBC schedules? It's like a *Doctor Who* Christmas. I'm very pleased, obviously, but it's a bit barmy.'

The full run-down of programmes with a *Doctor Who* connection scheduled for the two weeks of the festive season in the UK was as follows (with details of the main programmes receiving their debut transmissions given below):

Saturday 23 December 2006

UKTV Gold, 8.20 am: *Doctor Who*: 'Fear Her'.
UKTV Gold + 1, 9.20 am: *Doctor Who*: 'Fear Her'.

Sunday 24 December 2006

UKTV Gold, 2.10 am: *Doctor Who*: 'Fear Her'.
UKTV Gold + 1, 3.10 am: *Doctor Who*: 'Fear Her'.
UKTV Gold, 8.20 am: *Doctor Who*: 'Army of Ghosts'.
UKTV Gold + 1, 9.20 am: *Doctor Who*: 'Army of Ghosts'.
BBC Radio Wales, 1.31 pm: *Doctor Who – Back in Time*: 'Jingle Hell – Making the Christmas Special' (debut transmission).
BBC Radio Wales, 4.30 pm: *Doctor Who: A Celebration*.
BBC 7, 6.00 pm: *Doctor Who*: 'The Chimes of Midnight' Part Three.
BBC 7, 6.30 pm: *Doctor Who*: 'The Chimes of Midnight' Part Four.
SciFi UK, 7.25 pm: *Dr. Who and the Daleks* (cinema film).
BBC Three, 9.30 pm: *Torchwood*: 'Combat' (debut transmission).

Monday 25 December 2006

BBC 7, 12.00 am: *Doctor Who*: 'The Chimes of Midnight' Part Three.
BBC 7, 12.30 am: *Doctor Who*: 'The Chimes of Midnight' Part Four.
BBC Three, 3.10 am: *Torchwood*: 'Combat'.
BBC Three, 4.00 am: *Torchwood Declassified*: 'Weevil Fight Club' (debut transmission).

UKTV Gold, 4.45 am: *Doctor Who*: 'Army of Ghosts'.
UKTV Gold + 1, 5.45 am: *Doctor Who*: 'Army of Ghosts'.
BBC One, 1.00 pm: *Doctor Who Confidential*: 'Music and Monsters' (debut transmission).
BBCi, 1.50 pm: *Doctor Who: A Celebration* (debut TV transmission) (then repeated several times).
BBC Radio 1, 4.00 pm: *Jo Whiley Meets Doctor Who* (debut transmission).
BBC One, 7.00 pm: *Doctor Who*: 'The Runaway Bride' (debut transmission).

Tuesday 26 December 2006

BBC Two Wales Digital, 7.00 pm: *On Show: Designs on Doctor Who* (debut transmission).
BBC Three, 10.30 pm: *Torchwood*: 'Combat'.

Wednesday 27 December 2006

BBC Three, 1.50 am: *Torchwood*: 'Combat'.
BBC Three, 8.00 pm: *Doctor Who*: 'The Runaway Bride'.
BBC Two, 10.00 pm: *Torchwood*: 'Combat'.

Friday 29 December 2006

BBC Three, 9.00 pm: *Torchwood*: 'Combat'.

Saturday 30 December 2006

BBC Three, 1.30 am: *Torchwood*: 'Combat'.
BBC One, 2.25 am: *Doctor Who*: 'The Runaway Bride'.
UKTV Gold, 6.35 am: *Doctor Who*: 'Frontier in Space' (compilation version).
UKTV Gold + 1, 7.35 am: *Doctor Who*: 'Frontier in Space' (compilation version).
BBC Three, 9.45 pm: *Torchwood*: 'Out of Time'.
BBC Three, 10.35 pm: *Torchwood*: 'Combat'.

Sunday 31 December 2006

BBC Three, 12.55 am: *Torchwood*: 'Out of Time'.
BBC Three, 1.45 am: *Torchwood*: 'Combat'.
UKTV Gold, 3.30 am: *Doctor Who*: 'Frontier in Space' (compilation version).
UKTV Gold + 1, 4.30 am: *Doctor Who*: 'Frontier in Space' (compilation version).
UKTV Gold, 6.15 am: *Doctor Who*: 'The Monster of Peladon' (compilation version).
UKTV Gold + 1, 7.15 am: *Doctor Who*: 'The Monster of Peladon' (compilation version).
BBC 7, 6.00 pm: *Doctor Who*: 'Blood of the Daleks – Part One' (debut transmission).

Monday 1 January 2007

BBC 7, 12.00 am: *Doctor Who*: 'Blood of the Daleks – Part One'.

UKTV Gold, 4.10 am: *Doctor Who*: 'The Monster of Peladon' (compilation version).
UKTV Gold + 1, 5.10 am: *Doctor Who*: 'The Monster of Peladon' (compilation version).
UKTV Gold, 7.45 am: *Doctor Who*: 'The Empty Child'.
UKTV Gold, 8.40 am: *Doctor Who*: 'The Doctor Dances'.
UKTV Gold + 1, 8.45 am: *Doctor Who*: 'The Empty Child'.
UKTV Gold + 1, 9.40 am: *Doctor Who*: 'The Doctor Dances'.
BBC Radio Wales, 1.05 pm: *Doctor Who: A Celebration*.
BBC One, 4.50 pm: *The Sarah Jane Adventures*: 'Invasion of the Bane' (debut transmission).
BBC Three, 9.30 pm: *Torchwood*: 'Captain Jack Harkness' (debut transmission).
BBC Three, 10.20 pm: *Torchwood*: 'End of Days' (debut transmission).

Tuesday 2 January 2007

BBC Three, 1.05 am: *Torchwood*: 'Captain Jack Harkness'.
BBC Three, 1.55 am: *Torchwood*: 'End of Days'.
BBC Three, 2.40 am: *Torchwood Declassified*: 'Blast from the Past' (debut transmission).
BBC Three, 2.50 am: *Torchwood Declassified*: 'To the End' (debut transmission).
BBC Three, 7.00 pm: *Doctor Who*: 'The Runaway Bride'.
BBC Three, 10.30 pm: *Torchwood*: 'Captain Jack Harkness'.
BBC Three, 11.20 pm: *Torchwood*: 'End of Days'.

Wednesday 3 January 2007

BBC Three, 1.35 am: *Torchwood*: 'Captain Jack Harkness'.
BBC Three, 2.25 am: *Torchwood*: 'End of Days'.
BBC Three, 7.00 pm: *Doctor Who*: 'The Christmas Invasion'.
BBC Two, 9.00 pm: *Torchwood*: 'Captain Jack Harkness'.
BBC Two, 9.50 pm: *Torchwood*: 'End of Days'.

Thursday 4 January 2007

BBC Three, 9.00 pm: *Torchwood*: 'Captain Jack Harkness'.
BBC Three, 9.50 pm: *Torchwood Declassified*: 'Blast from the Past'.

Friday 5 January 2007

BBC Three, 1.00 am: *Torchwood*: 'Captain Jack Harkness'.
BBC Three, 9.00 pm: *Torchwood*: 'End of Days'.
BBC Three, 9.50 pm: *Torchwood Declassified*: 'To the End'.

Broadcasters in the USA, Canada, Australia, New Zealand, France, Italy, South Korea, Japan and Poland also screened episodes of *Doctor Who* over this festive fortnight; and *Doctor Who Confidential*: 'Music and Monsters' and 'The Runaway Bride' could be enjoyed by overseas members of the British armed forces on their special channels, BFBS 1, BFBS 2 and BFBS Navy, initially on Christmas Day, just a short time after their BBC One transmissions.

'The Runaway Bride', as the centrepiece of BBC One's evening schedule for Christmas Day, was naturally the highest-profile of all these programmes, and it was previewed in the Christmas editions of many TV listings and other magazines. Boyd Hilton in celebrity gossip magazine *Heat*, awarding the programme a maximum five stars out of five, commented: 'Last year, Russell T Davies came up with a brilliantly dramatic yet Christmassy *Doctor Who* special. This year, he goes one better by securing the talents of TV's woman-of-the-moment Catherine Tate, playing a bride-to-be who ends up in the TARDIS rather than at the altar. Turns out she's the key to an alien plan to take over the universe, masterminded by Sarah Parish!' *All About Soap* magazine placed the special second in its list of the top five Christmas TV shows and, opening with one of Tate's comedy series catchphrases, said: 'What a liberty! The TARDIS is Rose-less for this festive episode, but David Tennant is back as the tasty time-travelling Doctor. And as a special Christmas treat, he's got a guest companion – Catherine Tate as runaway bride, Donna! While the Doctor tries his best to get Donna to her wedding before it's too late, they battle robot Father Christmases and the sinister Empress of [the] Racnoss, played by former *Cutting It* star Sarah Parish.' In *Closer* magazine, comedian Harry Hill, serving as guest TV reviewer, wrote: 'Who'd have thought *Doctor Who* would be cool again? Continuing the comic cameo trend set by Peter Kay, Catherine Tate plays a bride whose wedding is interrupted by nasty aliens. The League of Gentlemen's Mark Gatiss plays a mad scientist – is there a BBC show he hasn't been in? Personally, I'd like to see former Docs Peter Davison and Sylvester McCoy pop up.' The comment regarding Gatiss was somewhat premature: he would not be making his *Doctor Who* appearance until 'The Lazarus Experiment' in Series Three.

Most of the national newspapers previewed the special as well. The *Daily Mail* gave away some important elements of the plot when it reported (albeit not 100 percent accurately): 'A horde of alien spiders make their base under the Thames, and when the Doctor and Donna – the runaway bride in the title played by Catherine Tate – escape from the lair, water pours in, emptying the river. The scene sees the pair standing on top of the Thames Barrier, staring out across the city minus the Thames. Asked what other landmarks in the capital he wanted to target, Tennant suggested Buckingham Palace. He joked: "Let's blow that up, come on!" He added Madame Tussauds was also in the Doctor's sights. Donna, from Chiswick, becomes the first woman to turn down Doctor Who's advances at the end of the programme'. The *Sun* had some positive reaction to Tate's performance: 'Killer festive decorations, slayer Santas and a flesh-eating spider – it can only be the *Doctor Who* Christmas special. David Tennant is his usual quirky self, but "The Runaway Bride" really belongs to Catherine Tate. Her character Donna is bristling with rage at being beamed into the TARDIS while half-way up the aisle. Donna is more than a bit Lauren-esque[7] as she screeches at the Time Lord: "No stupid Martian is going to stop me getting married." Even when she gets kidnapped by a Father Christmas in a taxi, the Cockney secretary deadpans, "You *are* kidding me?"' The *Daily Mirror* noted: 'Tate has told how her

---

[7] Schoolgirl Lauren Cooper, with her 'Am I bovvered?' catchphrase, is Catherine Tate's most famous comedy character from *The Catherine Tate Show* (BBC Two, 2004-2007).

hopes of becoming Doctor Who's new sidekick were dashed when BBC bosses snubbed her, despite starring in the Christmas special. The award-winning comic appears in "The Runaway Bride" as the Time Lord's temporary assistant Donna who is mysteriously transported into the TARDIS during her wedding. But yesterday Tate claimed she was not even considered for the permanent role left vacant by Billie Piper who played Rose Tyler for two series.' The *Guardian* pronounced that the special was 'unmissable' and one of the 'best shows on the box'. The *Daily Telegraph* quoted Tennant as saying, 'It was a little bit odd going back in July – it was like going back to school and all the old team was still there except Billie, so it was very different. But I loved working with Catherine and I suppose that's what acting is about; you develop these new relationships. The show is different and just as good.' *The Times* meanwhile had an interview with Tate, in which she credited Billie Piper with getting girls interested in *Doctor Who* and noted that her own four-year-old daughter Erin loved the series and was a particular fan of the Cybermen.

The BBC's own *Radio Times* naturally also carried a photo spread and preview for 'The Runaway Bride', with Tennant quoted as saying: 'Well, the Doctor's in mourning, really. Although Rose is alive and well, she's dead to the Doctor. He can never see her again. And this is someone who not so very long ago lost his entire people. So he's coming to terms with that, and at the same time dealing with Donna, who's a bit of a handful.' Tate meanwhile described how she had become involved: 'I got a call from my agent saying Russell T Davies had been in touch, and would I be interested? I said "Yes, absolutely, whatever it is!" I thought I might be a Cyberman on the corner of the screen or something … There was lots of running for "The Runaway Bride". David would be off like a whippet and I'd be lagging behind going, "Can't you just pretend to run fast?" Then wardrobe would go, "We can see your trainers. Can you put the satin court shoes on again?" I think what they'll do in post-production is slow him down and speed me up. Get an average speed.' Sarah Parish also recalled the challenges of her role as the Empress of the Racnoss: 'From the waist down it was just me, wearing a pair of cycling shorts. From the waist up it was like a rubber suit, and from the neck up it was all prosthetics. [The head] was really heavy. A huge head sealed to my own, so you couldn't get a hand in to scratch an itch. It was on for 12 hours, so if you had an itch it was a nightmare. I'd never worked with prosthetics before, and you have to really work your face to actually see it moving.' To accompany these comments, the magazine presented a production sketch of the Empress's face and a Millennium FX model of the entire creature.

Even the BBC Radio 2 morning news bulletins on Christmas Day carried some thinly-disguised publicity for the special, in the form of a report by entertainment correspondent Colin Paterson about Tate's involvement with the production, including some brief interview quotes from the actress expressing her sympathy for the extras who had had to dress in winter clothing on location when recording was taking place on some of the hottest days of summer.

The hour-long *Doctor Who Confidential* documentary 'Music and Monsters', transmitted on BBC One six hours before 'The Runaway Bride', was devoted to presenting a behind-the-scenes insight into the staging of the *Doctor Who* concert for *Children in Need* at Cardiff's Millennium Stadium back on 19 November. The concert itself, having been given a repeat audio broadcast on BBC Wales on Christmas Eve, could now be both heard *and* seen for the first time on air (having been previously viewable only in low quality via the official *Doctor Who* website) as a 'red button' special on the BBCi digital TV service. Although scheduled to debut at 1.50 pm on Christmas Day, it actually had its first transmission that morning, at 9.15 am. The 90-minute long programme was then repeated numerous times in a loop, with occasional breaks, and would receive further transmissions on 27 and 28 December and 2 and 3 January.

BBC Radio Wales had a further treat for viewers on Christmas Eve: 'Jingle Hell – Making the Christmas Special', the latest entry in its occasional *Doctor Who – Back in Time* documentary series. As the title implied, this focused on the production of 'The Runaway Bride'.

On BBC Radio 1, Jo Whiley's three-hour-long programme beginning at 4.00 pm on Christmas Day saw the presenter accompanied by David Tennant, who in between the music chatted about his role as the Doctor and answered questions, including some sent in by listeners. The programme included pre-recorded inserts of Whiley interviewing production designer Edward Thomas on the TARDIS interior set and in the series' props store at the Cardiff studios, and visiting St Fagan's National History Museum in Cardiff for an location report on the story then still in production, 'Human Nature'/'The Family of Blood', featuring comments from Tennant, Freema Agyeman, guest actors Thomas Sangster and Jessica Stevenson (prior to her adopting her husband's surname Hynes) and producer Susie Liggat. Whiley and Tennant were also joined in the studio for part of the time by Whiley's Radio 1 colleague Reggie Yates, who spoke about his role as Leo Jones, brother of Martha, in Series Three.

The Boxing Day episode of the BBC Two Wales Digital documentary series *On Show*, not generally available in other parts of the UK, was entitled 'Designs on *Doctor Who*'. Narrated by fourth Doctor actor Tom Baker, it featured an interview with Edward Thomas discussing his design work on both *Doctor Who* and *Torchwood*.

Also on Boxing Day, *The Times* became the first of the national newspapers to run a review of 'The Runaway Bride', commenting, in part: 'Under Russell T Davies's sure guidance, the Doctor happily spent Christmas Day battling the Queen of Racnoss [sic] (Sarah Parish as a colossal, mad spider), before draining the Thames into a gigantic hole – and incorporating Catherine Tate, Slade's "Merry Xmas Everybody" and giant, web-strewn stars hanging over London on the way. Given this kind of scope, is it any wonder that, over the last two years, the *Doctor Who* Christmas special has, finally, supplanted the Christmas Day episode of *EastEnders* as the flagship of the Christmas schedules?'

The *Sun* meanwhile was looking forward to Series Three, presenting in its 27 December edition a photo spread of screen-captures from the 'Coming Soon ...' trailer at the end of 'The Runaway Bride', including one of Dalek Sec – the trailer's final image, which had been cut from the press screening on 18 December in a bid to ensure that newspaper previews focused on the special itself, rather than on the return of the Daleks the following year. That the Doctor's greatest adversaries would indeed be returning was officially confirmed in a report, also on 27 December, on the BBC News website; headed 'Doctor Battles Daleks in New York', this noted that the story would be set in Manhattan in the 1930s and quoted Davies as saying: 'This time, their plan is the most audacious Dalek scheme yet! Even the Doctor finds himself out of his depth.'

In other news, 27 January also saw John Barrowman and his partner of 16 years, architect Scott Gill, entering into a civil partnership in a ceremony conducted at St

David's Hotel, Cardiff. Davies and Barrowman's *Torchwood* co-stars were amongst the guests in attendance. 'It's been a long wait,' commented Barrowman, 'but we legitimised our relationship to each other a long time ago when we signed our mortgages together, and this is just something that forces people who don't want to recognise it that they have to.'

The 28 December edition of the *Sun* again featured *Doctor Who*, this time in a front-page story that caused consternation amongst many fans. Under the headline 'Who's Gonna Quit', the newspaper claimed: '*Doctor Who* star David Tennant is to quit the show – leaving BBC bosses looking for their eleventh Time Lord, the *Sun* can reveal. David, 35, will leave in the middle of the fourth series. The Scot is still filming the third series of the sci-fi favourite, which is set to be shown in the spring. He has told the Beeb he will return the following year – but will not do the entire nine-month shoot. David has been bombarded with film offers after appearing in the last *Harry Potter* movie. Producers are keen to get another Scot, *Trainspotting* star Robert Carlyle, 45, to step in. They are also talking to David Morrisey, who was in BBC drama *Blackpool* with Tennant, as well as in *Basic Instinct 2* … David refused to deny he was quitting when asked earlier this month, insisting he was "non-committal" about his plans. He joked: "From the moment I accepted this job, everyone said, 'When are you leaving?' A boy could get a complex!" A *Doctor Who* spokesman declined to comment.'

While the *Sun* may not have managed to persuade a spokesperson to comment, the BBC had within hours given a denial of this highly speculative story, as the Press Association reported: 'A BBC spokeswoman said that no fourth series had even been commissioned yet and negotiations with the star would not begin until it had been given the green light. "David is absolutely committed to the show and is currently [recording] the third series," said a BBC spokeswoman today. "There is no fourth series currently commissioned yet so we could not confirm his involvement in that yet. David Tennant is committed to the series. When a further series is commissioned, we will be able to confirm his involvement."'

The final significant *Doctor Who* debut transmission over the festive period was of 'Blood of the Daleks – Part One' by Steve Lyons on BBC 7 on New Year's Eve. This marked the start of the first new *Doctor Who* series specially commissioned for radio since *Doctor Who and the Ghosts of N Space* went out on BBC Radio 2 in 1996. Made by regular *Doctor Who* audio producers Big Finish, it saw Paul McGann reprising his role as the eighth Doctor, with Sheridan Smith, best known for her work on the TV comedy series *Two Pints of Lager and a Packet of Crisps* (BBC Two/BBC Choice/BBC Three, 2001- ) and *Grownups* (BBC Three, 2006- ), taking the part of his new companion, Lucie Miller.

Smith, whose audition won her the job over many other hopefuls, told *Doctor Who Magazine* Issue 374: 'Lucie's a great character to play. She's really kind of ballsy and feisty! And the relationship between her and the Doctor grows and grows throughout the episodes. The scripts are so great! Funny, dramatic and moving. Every morning, I look forward to coming into the studio and doing another one.'

Quoted in Issue 375 of *Doctor Who Magazine*, McGann said of the Doctor's part in proceedings: 'There's a more cantankerous, almost paranoid side coming out, and I've enjoyed that … We have laughs doing these, but I've always said that beside that great sense of fun in the Doctor, there's something angry in him too. You can imagine him lashing out when pushed. Actors look for tension – "Where's that tightrope I can walk?". I'm all for that.'

Producer Nicholas Briggs – known to fans of the TV series as the voice of the Daleks and the Cybermen – described in the same magazine how the series had come about: 'Since BBC 7 reran our older Paul McGann audios, our boss Jason Haigh-Ellery has been discussing doing some new ones. The previous broadcasts did well, so they've come back for more. Jason and BBC 7 then devised a season of eight 50-minute episodes, and Alan Barnes … also had a vital role, as the series' script editor.'

The subsequent episodes of the series, to be transmitted weekly, were: 'Blood of the Daleks – Part Two' by Steve Lyons, 'Horror of Glam Rock' by Paul Magrs, 'Immortal Beloved' by Jonathan Clements, 'Phobos' by Eddie Robson, 'No More Lies' by Paul Sutton, 'Human Resources – Part One' by Eddie Robson and 'Human Resources – Part Two' by Eddie Robson. The series boasted an extremely impressive guest cast list, including such household names as Timothy West, Anita Dobson, Nerys Hughes, Stephen Gately, Bernard Cribbins, Una Stubbs, Julia Mackenzie and Nigel Havers.

It seemed at times over the festive fortnight that one could scarcely open a newspaper or magazine or turn on the radio or TV without coming across some reference to *Doctor Who*. The long running BBC Radio 4 soap opera *The Archers* on Christmas Day featured a storyline in which the long-feuding brothers Ed and Will Grundy were reconciled while watching 'The Runaway Bride' together; a *Doctor Who* sketch involving the tenth Doctor inviting some of his previous incarnations to celebrate Christmas with him featured in a New Year's Eve BBC Two repeat of the previous year's *Dead Ringers* Christmas special; and in the final ever episode of the hugely popular series *The Vicar of Dibley*, transmitted on BBC One on New Year's Day, the regular character Alice Horton, played by Emma Chambers, was seen to dress as the tenth Doctor for a *Doctor Who*-themed wedding, complete with two 'home made' Daleks in attendance. In the shops, meanwhile, *Doctor Who* toys, games and novelties continued to sell by the crate-load, prompting the Scottish newspaper *Daily Record* to report: '*Doctor Who* proved the biggest hit with the kids this Christmas as merchandise from the show continued to fly off the shelves. The popularity of the BBC One show saw supplies of Daleks, Cyberman Voice Changers and Sonic Screwdrivers outstrip demand, according to the UK's biggest toy store chain. Toys R Us said stores were forced to source *Doctor Who* merchandise from across the world to keep up with demand. And in-store displays were being replenished up to five times a day in November and December.'

With not only a wealth of *Doctor Who* on offer but also the spin-offs *Torchwood* and *The Sarah Jane Adventures*[8], Christmas 2006 may well go down in the annals of broadcasting history as, to use Davies's phrase, 'a *Doctor Who* Christmas'

---

[8] *Torchwood* and *The Sarah Jane Adventures* are not covered in detail here as they are outside the remit of this book. A full guide to *Torchwood* can be found in *Inside the Hub: The Unofficial and Unauthorised Guide to Torchwood* by Stephen James Walker (Telos Publishing, 2007).

# CHAPTER FIVE
# COUNTDOWN TO SERIES THREE

After the excitement of the Christmas period, the thoughts of *Doctor Who* fans everywhere turned toward the next full series of episodes, scheduled to begin in the spring of 2007; and again they started counting the days.

Wednesday 3 January 2007: T minus 87 days

The BBC Press Office puts out a press release accompanying some new promotional pictures for Series Three. It reads, in part: 'Doctor Who's new companion Freema Agyeman takes her first trip in the TARDIS in pictures released today. Agyeman, 27, plays medical student Martha Jones opposite the Doctor (David Tennant) in the BAFTA Award-winning drama that returns to BBC One for a much anticipated third series in the spring. Guest stars already confirmed for the third series include *Shameless* star Dean Lennox Kelly – who is to play William Shakespeare – the League of Gentlemen's Mark Gatiss and comedy actress Jessica Stevenson. The most famous *Doctor Who* nemesis, the Daleks, are to also make a return in a special two-part episode. Agyeman replaces Billie Piper, who played Rose Tyler in the show, and is already familiar to *Doctor Who* fans, having appeared as Adeola in episode 12 of the second series, when she suffered a terrible fate at the hands of the Cybermen.'

The WENN Entertainment News website meanwhile carries a report that actor Jason Statham, best known for his roles in director Guy Ritchie's British gangster movies, is to take over from David Tennant in the role of the Doctor.

Friday 5 January 2007: T minus 85 days

David Tennant guests on Channel 4's comedy-variety show *The Friday Night Project*.

Wednesday 10 January 2007: T minus 80 days

The *MediaGuardian* website picks up the previous Wednesday's rumour of Jason Statham being cast as David Tennant's successor and notes: 'Apparently BBC Controller of Fiction Jane Tranter wants to "sex up" the sci-fi series once Tennant departs and thinks Statham – the former squeeze of model Kelly Brook – is the man for the job. Watch this space …'

Saturday 13 January 2007: T minus 77 days

The *Sun* reports: '*Doctor Who* fans are plotting to get a song used in the hit BBC show's Christmas special to Number One. "Love Don't Roam" – sung by The

Divine Comedy's Neil Hannon – featured in "The Runaway Bride" episode. And because the new singles chart includes downloads of old songs, fans are urging each other to download the track for 79p.' 'Love Don't Roam' will ultimately fail to chart; but Billie Piper's 1999 single 'Honey to the B', which becomes the subject of a similar campaign by BBC Radio 1 breakfast show DJ Chris Moyles a few days later, will do rather better, gaining a Number 17 place in the new chart announced on 21 January.

Monday 15 January 2007: T minus 75 days

The official *Doctor Who* website reports that, for the second year running, the series has swept the board in awards voted for by the public on the BBC Drama website, winning all five of the categories in which it is nominated: Best Drama, Best Actor, Best Actress, Favourite Moment (for Rose's exit in 'Doomsday'; the battle between the Daleks and the Cybermen in the same episode took third place in the poll) and Best Drama Website.

Tuesday 16 January 2007: T minus 74 days

'The Complete Second Series' DVD box set, released today in the USA, has the same packaging and content as the UK version, but the correct edit of the *Children in Need* special is substituted for the early edit mistakenly included on the latter.

Thursday 18 January 2007: T minus 72 days

BBC Director General Mark Thompson gives a keynote speech at The Future of Creative Content Conference, part of the Media Summit 2007 in London, in which he refers in glowing terms to *Doctor Who* and its spin-offs:

> It's incredibly important that we don't define "value" solely around productivity or cost-cutting. One of the fundamental lessons we learned from Creative Future was the value you can grow, the audiences you can build, when you think about projects not just in terms of single linear broadcast windows but across different platforms and media. It will be much harder to justify very high budgets for content that only gets a single outing on a linear channel. But that's no longer the right way to think about content commissioning. In future, major projects should extend not just across TV, the web, radio and mobile but through multiple windows across time and across different business models.
> So: Russell T Davies, Julie Gardner and BBC Wales build a brilliant sci-fi production factory to deliver *Doctor Who*. And when I say "factory" I don't just mean physical production, I mean ideas, development, brilliant scripts, design as well. A complete creative operation.
> The factory of course makes even better creative and

economic sense when you add *Torchwood* and *The Sarah Jane Adventures*. *Doctor Who* plays out across BBC and UKTV channels. The *Torchwood* website is not just commissioned on day one but is out there before the TV premiere. There's a coherent plan in place for the whole audience relationship with the content almost from the start.

Now clearly this kind of 360 degree exploitation could be creatively limiting or tawdry. Commercial priorities could distort the original commissioning intention. But it really hasn't been in this case and that's because we've had totally committed creative leaders at the centre of decision-making at every stage of the process. You'd have to talk to them directly to hear how they've found it, but my sense is that the sheer scale of the possibilities, the potential to link different titles and different platforms has been creatively inspiring and liberating.

Saturday 20 January 2007: T minus 70 days

*Doctor Who* author Stephen Cole holds a writing seminar and judges competition entries at a space-based literacy event at The Langworthy Cornerstone, a community centre in Salford, Merseyside.

Wednesday 24 January 2007: T minus 66 days

Writer Paul Cornell guests at a meeting of the British Science Fiction Association in London to talk about his work on *Doctor Who* and other projects.
The SCI FI Wire website runs an interview with David Tennant, in which he comments on Freema Agyeman taking on the role of Martha: 'Tennant said that he understands what it's like to take over for a popular *Doctor Who* cast member; he replaced former Doctor Christopher Eccleston in the second season of the show. But he let Agyeman find her own way of dealing with the pressure. "Oh, she doesn't need any advice, and I wouldn't be pompous enough to offer it," he said. "Freema hit the ground running and has inhabited Martha Jones from day one without a hint of trepidation or nervousness. I found myself quite envious of her confidence. She is going to be brilliant." But don't expect the Doctor to get over Rose so quickly. "As with any big relationship, it takes time for the scars to heal," Tennant said. "Perhaps the Doctor feels like he's dealt with it, but Martha might disagree."'

Thursday 25 January 2007: T minus 65 days

At a dinner hosted by the Toy Retailers Association, Character Options' Cyberman Voice Changer Helmet is announced as the winner of the prestigious Toy of the Year Award for 2006.
The *Daily Mirror* reports that distinguished actor Sir Derek Jacobi, best known for his starring role in *I, Claudius* (BBC One, 1976), will be guest-starring as a benevolent character called 'the Professor' in a Series Three episode.

Friday 26 January 2007: T minus 64 days

The official *Doctor Who* website carries news of a 13-part animated *Doctor Who* adventure, 'The Infinite Quest', written by Alan Barnes, directed by Gary Russell and with animation by Firestep, to be transmitted in weekly segments of about three-and-a-half minutes each as part of the second series of *Totally Doctor Who*. 'I didn't think my *Doctor Who* experience could get any more thrilling,' Freema Agyeman is quoted as saying, 'but I was absolutely blown away when they approached me about the new animation series! The prospect of becoming a cartoon character was both exciting and also a bit nerve-wracking, as it was the first time I had been asked to do voice-over work. But I needn't have worried – my first session involved being in a small recording room with [fellow cast members] David [Tennant], Anthony Head and Toby Longworth – and all of us falling about with laughter as we tried to imagine the movements of the cartoon characters and how mad it all seemed! It was such a fun experience and now I can't wait to see how it all looks!'

The *Daily Star* meanwhile reports: 'Pop babe Britney Spears is set to take on *Doctor Who* – playing a raunchy bunch of sex-mad aliens. Writer Russell T Davies is a huge fan and wants her to appear in an episode created especially for her. Blonde Brit, 25, will be cast as an entire race of lusty cloned creatures who all look identical to the twice-wed beauty. "I'd love Britney to do it – it would be so much fun," said Russell, 43. "I'm not sure if she'll come to Cardiff where the show is shot so I'm nagging the BBC to fund a Hollywood special."' This report is later denied by Davies.

Tuesday 30 January 2007: T minus 60 days

The *Sun* prints a major spoiler for Series Three, claiming that Sir Derek Jacobi's character the Professor will regenerate to become the Doctor's arch-enemy the Master in the closing episodes of Series Three, and that John Simm, star of the acclaimed BBC One drama series *Life on Mars*, is the favourite to portray the new incarnation.

Tuesday 13 February 2007: T minus 46 days

Promoting *Life on Mars* in a telephone interview on Nemone Metaxas's afternoon show on the BBC 6 Music digital radio channel, actor John Simm says in response to a question e-mailed in by a listener about rumours of his being cast as the Master: 'It's all speculation and all rumour at this point – I think it's just journalists getting a little bit over-excited.'

Wednesday 14 February 2007: T minus 45 days

Toby Hadoke performs his one-man play *Moths Ate My Doctor Who Scarf* at the Leicester Comedy Festival – the first date of a national tour running until September.

Thursday 15 February 2007: T minus 44 days

The BBC's *Radio Times* features David Tennant on its front cover – but promoting his appearance in the forthcoming BBC One drama *Recovery* rather than his role as the Doctor.

Saturday 24 February 2007: T minus 35 days

David Tennant guests on the Jonathan Ross show on BBC Radio 2. This is mainly to promote his appearance in the drama *Recovery*, but he also answers some questions about Series Three of *Doctor Who* and promises some tear-jerking storylines to come.

Billie Piper meanwhile makes her well-publicised stage debut in the play *Treats* at the Garrick Theatre in London's West End, after a day's delay due to illness, which saw an understudy taking her role the previous evening.

Monday 26 February 2007: T minus 33 days

The SCI FI Weekly website runs an interview with David Tennant. Amongst the topics covered is how the actor developed his characterisation of the Doctor: 'I've been watching *Doctor Who* since I was three years old (along with just about everyone else of my generation who grew up in Britain), so I had probably made a whole host of unconscious decisions about how I was going to do it years before it was an actual possibility. But to be honest, when it actually happened, I didn't sit down and draw up a list of quirks that I wanted to fit in to my performance. As with any other part, you take your lead from the script and what that character says and does. Once that is filtered through your own perspective and experiences, then hopefully it will be particular and unique. I was always aware of avoiding any kind of self-conscious eccentricity. The Doctor may be a 900-odd year old Time Lord from the other side of the galaxy, but he still has to be a believable character, or the whole thing collapses.'

Thursday 1 March 2007: T minus 30 days

BBC Books publish the paperback novel *Doctor Who: Made of Steel* by long-time *Doctor Who* author, and one time series script editor and writer, Terrance Dicks. Like the previous year's *I am a Dalek* by Gareth Roberts, this forms part of the 'Quick Reads' range launched by the National Literacy Trust charity on World Book Day 2006 with the stated aim to 'provide fast-paced, bite-sized books by bestselling writers for emergent readers, anyone who had lost the reading habit or simply wanted a short, fast read'. *Made of Steel* features the Cybermen and is notable for being the first officially-sanctioned story to feature new companion Martha Jones, still almost a month away from her TV debut. It also reveals for the first time that Adeola, as played by Freema Agyeman in the Series Two story 'Army of Ghosts'/'Doomsday', was Martha's cousin.

Friday 2 March 2007: T minus 29 days

The BBC Press Office issues a press release that reports: 'The BBC, BBC Worldwide and YouTube today announced the beginning of a partnership to offer Internet users across the world new and innovative ways to experience and enjoy BBC content through YouTube. This non-exclusive partnership will create branded BBC "channels" on YouTube operating under separate BBC and BBC Worldwide agreements. The partnership reflects YouTube's commitment to work with content owners to make compelling video accessible online, and the BBC's commitment to increase reach through the partnership, to bring new audiences to the proposed BBC iPlayer service, and to secure commercial revenue via BBC Worldwide, its commercial subsidiary, to supplement the licence fee.'

Amongst the initial batch of clips made available on the YouTube site from this date are short video diaries by David Tennant and Freema Agyeman recorded during the making of Series Three's debut episode 'Smith and Jones'.

Saturday 3 March 2007: T minus 28 days

Channel 4 broadcasts a programme entitled *The Fifty Greatest TV Dramas*, running down a chart compiled on the basis of a specially-commissioned poll of 200 top TV professionals. *Doctor Who* takes a disappointingly lowly twenty-sixth place, but the programme includes comments from David Tennant and the series' first producer, Verity Lambert. The winner of the poll is *The Sopranos* (HBO, 1999-2007).

John Barrowman meanwhile presents *The National Lottery: Saturday Draws* on BBC One and guests on the humorous chat chow *Al Murray's Happy Hour* on ITV1.

Monday 5 March 2007: T minus 26 days

The Digital Spy website reports: 'An "inappropriate" underwater scene was cut from an episode of *Doctor Who*, David Tennant has revealed. Actress Freema Agyeman, as loyal assistant Martha Jones, apparently stripped down to her underwear for the piece. The footage will never be seen however, thanks to producers who decided it should be cut. "There was an underwater scene in a draft of the new series but we nixed it out," explained Tennant. "It was bordering on inappropriate. You can't have shagging in the TARDIS."'

Tuesday 6 March 2007: T minus 25 days

At a sale by the Bonhams of London auction house, various costumes of five different incarnations of the Doctor – almost all of them less-than-accurate versions made for promotional or 'fancy dress' purposes rather than worn by the actors in the series itself – are amongst a large number of lots on offer. The auction has received considerable advance publicity, and been featured in an item on the ITV1 show *This Morning* on 2 March, and attracts considerable interest. A fourth Doctor costume, including striped scarf (with incorrect colours), sells for an astonishing £24,600 (about 12 times the amount expected); another fourth Doctor coat for £7,000; a second Doctor outfit for £8,000; a third Doctor ensemble, including sonic screwdriver, for £8,000; a fifth Doctor costume for £4,200; and a seventh Doctor one for £1,000. Other *Doctor Who* lots sold include Magnus Greel's cloak from 'The Talons of Weng-Chiang' (1977), which is the genuine item and fetches almost £1,600. A leather jacket supposedly worn by the ninth Doctor has been removed from the original list of items up for auction, many fans having pointed out that it looks completely different from the real one.

Friday 9 March 2007: T minus 22 days

A pair of seven-second-long teaser trailers for Series Three start to be aired by the BBC in selected breaks between programmes. These consist of split-screen images with the Doctor on the left and Martha on the right – one with the former in the foreground and the latter in the background, the other with their positions reversed – followed by the caption 'Two Worlds Will Collide'. These trailers are also made available to view on the official *Doctor Who* website.

Saturday 11 March 2007: T minus 21 days

The *Seven* magazine supplement of the *Daily Telegraph* publishes an in-depth interview with Russell T Davies. 'He has a say in everything,' reporter Richard Johnson writes, 'down to the colour of the Doctor's suit. After filming, he watches all the rushes – every single frame of them. He works across *Doctor Who*, *Torchwood* and *The Sarah Jane Adventures*, writing the key episodes. And when there's an edit, or a dub, Davies is there. It's no wonder that he hasn't had a day's holiday in three years. There's simply no time. When he had a cold, in 2006, it messed up the schedule for months.' Of the future, Johnson notes: 'A fourth series of *Doctor Who* has already been commissioned, and Davies is putting the finishing touches to scripts for Christmas 2007. His work here is – almost – done. When he does leave, it will be with happy memories, especially of the day the Doctor returned, on 26 March 2005. "That afternoon," he says, "I went into town, shopping and pottering about. There was a buzz in the air. I felt like I was eight years old again. It was like 'Mum's dragged me to town, and I've got to get home because *Doctor Who*'s going to be on.' I'll never forget that feeling. As long as I live."' This is the first suggestion in print that the 2007 Christmas special and Series Four have already been commissioned – although this has been rumoured for some time – and also gives the first hint that Davies may be considering leaving *Doctor Who* after Series Four; a prospect that generates considerable concern within fandom.

Monday 12 March 2007: T minus 19 days

The website of the genre magazine *SFX* presents a major interview with Russell T Davies, discussing many aspects of his work on *Doctor Who* and the background to Series Three. An abridged version of the interview will appear in Issue 155 of the print version of the magazine, published two days later.

Tuesday 13 March 2007: T minus 18 days

John Barrowman's latest TV appearance is on the BBC Two show *A Taste of My Life*, in which guests talk about aspects of their lives prompted by their 'personal food memories'. Also on this date, a number of online and print news outlets are reporting that a racehorse from the Hucking stables has been named 'Hucking Harkness' in honour of Barrowman's *Doctor Who* and *Torchwood* character.

Wednesday 14 March 2007: T minus 17 days

The *Sun* carries a picture of Freema Agyeman and former *EastEnders* star Tom Ellis on the Whitmore Bay location for 'Last of the Time Lords' (although the episode is not named). The brief accompanying text states that Series Three is to begin 'next month', at odds with the strongly-rumoured start date of 31 March.

David Tennant attends a performance of Billie Piper's play *Treats* in London, then goes for an after-show drink with her at the St Martin's Lane Hotel. A number of paparazzi photographs appear in the following day's newspapers.

Thursday 15 March 2007: T minus 16 days

The *Sun* again reports that John Simm has been cast as the Master in Series Three.

Friday 16 March 2007: T minus 15 days

David Tennant and Catherine Tate appear together in a sketch broadcast as part of BBC One's annual *Comic Relief* telethon for 'Red Nose Day'. Tate plays her famous mouthy schoolgirl character Lauren Cooper, while Tennant appears as a new English teacher, Mr Logan, trying to teach the class some Shakespeare. Lauren thinks that Mr Logan looks like the Doctor, and questions his capability to teach English when he is Scottish. The sketch ends with Mr Logan producing the Doctor's sonic screwdriver from his pocket and transforming Lauren into a Rose Tyler action figure.

A week after the teaser trailers first appeared, a full, 40-second-long promotional trailer for Series Three makes its on-air debut. This again makes use of a split-screen effect, and features the Doctor and Martha outside the TARDIS with the dialogue:

> **Martha:** 'I battle with my text books.'
> **Doctor:** 'I battle with monsters.'
> **Martha:** 'I try to save money.'
> **Doctor:** 'I try to save the universe.'
> **Martha:** 'I'm gonna be a doctor.'
> **Doctor:** 'I *am* the Doctor.'
> **Martha:** 'Well. Let's hope this box is big enough for the both of us!'

The two halves of the split screen then merge and a series of clips are shown, including of the Judoon from 'Smith and Jones', the Carrionites and the Globe Theatre from 'The Shakespeare Code', the New New York motorway from 'Gridlock' and Dalek Sec from 'Daleks in Manhattan'. The final shot is of Martha and the Doctor together in front of the TARDIS, with the voiceover: '*Doctor Who*: coming soon to BBC One'. Again this trailer is made available to view on the official *Doctor Who* website.The BBC Press Office also release brief details of 'Smith and Jones' as part of their advance programme information for the week beginning 31 March, although the date and time of the episode's transmission are still not confirmed here.

Saturday 17 March 2007: T minus 14 days

As pre-publicity for Series Three starts to move into overdrive, the *Sun* presents a two page interview with Freema Agyeman covering her casting as Martha and her thoughts on taking over from Billie Piper as *Doctor Who*'s female lead.

Sunday 18 March 2007: T minus 13 days

The first (and only surviving) episode of the classic series story 'The Web of Fear'

(1968) is shown on BBC Four as part of Tube Night: an evening of programming based on the theme of the London Underground system (the main setting of 'The Web of Fear').

Russell T Davies is interviewed by James Robinson in the *Observer*. As in his *Daily Telegraph* interview the previous weekend, the executive producer hints that he will not continue working on *Doctor Who* indefinitely: 'Davies will not be writing *Doctor Who* forever, of course,' notes Robinson, 'and that is a major headache for the BBC. "I'm not going to go on and on," he says, from his spacious flat overlooking Cardiff Bay, where the series is [recorded]. "I wouldn't want to do Series Seven. There are other things I want to do." As the third series begins the Saturday after next, Davies won't be packing up his typewriter until the turn of the decade, a date too far into the future to worry even the most nervy time-traveller, but one that will worry BBC executives. The show has survived the departures of both Christopher Eccleston and Billie Piper, but it couldn't outlive its re-creator.'

A 20-second version of the trailer first seen on 16 March, with truncated dialogue and a slightly different selection of clips, including one of the Face of Boe from 'Gridlock', starts to appear in BBC One programme breaks.

Tuesday 20 March 2007: T minus 11 days

On sale from today in newsagents across the UK is the BBC's *Radio Times* magazine for the week prior to the start of Series Three. In an item entitled *All New Who* in its regular *Behind the Scenes* feature, it gives readers a taste of what they are in for via some quotes from the series' stars and production team members. 'Each script that comes in just seems to be bigger than the last,' notes David Tennant. 'That's what has kept it so exciting. The scale is bigger, the locations are more extraordinary.' Freema Agyeman, meanwhile, comments: 'I've been [recording] since August and it's crazy. Every time I think I've got it under control, something else comes up – so I'm not taking anything for granted!' Producer Phil Collinson, quizzed about the series' monsters, says: 'This year there's probably a bigger selection – we've gone a bit more monster-y.'

Wednesday 21 March 2007: T minus ten days

A further 40-second-long trailer for Series Three debuts. This is very similar in style to the one first seen on 16 March, but has a different set of clips and the following dialogue:

> **Martha:** 'I need a guy who's smart.'
> **Doctor:** 'Suit and trainers works for me.'
> **Martha:** 'Who likes travelling.'
> **Doctor:** 'I've been round the block a few times.'
> **Martha:** 'Who has a big heart.'
> **Doctor:** 'Two of those, actually.'
> **Martha:** 'And someone who can make the time.'
> **Doctor:** 'Ah, now that's my speciality.'

The trailers are by this point confirming that 'Smith and Jones' will be transmitted on 31 March; and a countdown clock on the official *Doctor Who* website reveals that the scheduled start time will be 7.00 pm.

A press launch for Series Three takes place in Mayfair, London, with David Tennant, Freema Agyeman and Russell T Davies in attendance. The opening two episodes, 'Smith and Jones' and 'The Shakespeare Code', are screened for an invitation-only audience of favoured journalists and celebrity guests, including Jonathan Ross, Dawn French and Tennant's girlfriend Sophia Myles. Davies confirms during the event that Series Four of *Doctor Who* has been commissioned for some time. BBC Wales later runs a report on the launch in its evening bulletin, focusing in particular on the introduction of Martha and the series' Welsh locations.

Thursday 22 March 2007: T minus nine days

Wednesday's press launch is covered in numerous newspapers, including *The Times*, the *Sun*, the *Daily Mail* and the *Daily Mirror*; in a piece by arts correspondent David Sillito shown numerous times on the BBC's *Breakfast* programme, BBC News 24 and BBC World; on CBBC's *Newsround* programme; and on BBC Radio 1 DJ Jo Whiley's show.

John Simm is interviewed by presenter Simon Mayo on his BBC Radio 5 Live show, and confirms that he is playing a character called Mr Saxon in Series Three, but refuses to be drawn on reports that this is an alias for the Master.

It has by this point been confirmed that 'Smith and Jones' will begin at 7.00 pm on Saturday evening. This follows a period of confusion over its precise time slot, which is reported to have been caused by deliberate misinformation spread by the BBC in an attempt to wrong-foot the rival networks.

Friday 23 March 2007: T minus eight days

The official *Doctor Who* website launches a poll for the title of 'scariest new series creature'.

The *Daily Mirror* reports: 'David Tennant has agreed a £1million deal to star in the fourth series of *Doctor Who*, it was revealed last night. Despite false reports suggesting the 35-year-old would bow out halfway through next year's run, insiders have revealed he will [record] the full 13 episodes. Delighted BBC bosses are thrilled to be keeping the Scot, who has proved a smash-hit with viewers since taking over from Christopher Eccleston last year. They are overjoyed to have retained Tennant and writer Russell T Davies and have been impressed by new assistant Freema Agyeman, 27. One source said: "To be honest, David was never going anywhere. He loves to create an air of mystery about his role in *Doctor Who*, and when he might leave, so he's happy for people to speculate about his departure. But the truth is he's finished [recording] the third series and he's signed a contract to appear in the whole of the next series. That will see him [recording] throughout 2008 [sic]. It's brilliant for the show and the fans."'

The Doctor's new companion Martha Jones, still just over a week away from making her debut TV appearance, writes the first entry in a new blog she has set up on the MySpace website, www.myspace.com. This is actually a bbc.co.uk-sponsored promotional device, similar to the numerous 'fictional' websites set up the previous year in support of Series Two. The blog is really the work of *Doctor Who* tie-in fiction writer Joseph Lidster, and will continue to be updated throughout Series Three, concluding with a final entry on 3 July.

Saturday 24 March 2007: T minus seven days

David Tennant is a guest this morning on BBC Radio 1's morning show, presented by Fearne Cotton and Series Three semi-regular Reggie Yates.

In today's edition of the *Daily Telegraph*, journalist Sam Leith offers a thoughtful and admiring opinion on the revived *Doctor Who*, identifying 'its underlying deep melancholy' as a defining characteristic: 'Mr Davies has taken a rickety old 1970s science-fiction series, and – by applying a little psychological seriousness to the premise; by asking what it would mean to be able to travel through time, and to live more or less forever – turned it into an extraordinary study of loss. Its deep theme is loneliness. Loneliness goes through the series like the lettering through a stick of rock. The Doctor is described at one point as a "lonely god". He has something close to the perspective of a god: he can munch, if he so chooses, his breakfast bagel shortly after the Big Bang and have supper the same day in the Restaurant at the End of the Universe. But he does not have the power of a god: he can't go back and change the course of events. So everybody he cares about or ever will care about is always already dead; every companion he picks up will, sooner or later, be gone. I've mentioned before, in connection with this, T S Eliot's notion that if "all time is eternally present, all time is unredeemable". Eliot was interested (inter alia) in the theology of this; Russell T Davies in the psychology.'

Tuesday 27 March 2007: T minus four days

The BBC's national and local radio stations begin airing a trailer for 'Smith and Jones'. This is accompanied by a section from pop artist Robbie Williams' recording of the song 'Have You Met Miss Jones?' and incorporates some dialogue from the episode. It runs:

> **Announcer:** 'The Doctor's back on BBC One, and he's got a new companion.'
> **Martha:** 'You never even told me who you are.'
> **Doctor:** 'I'm the Doctor. I'm a Time Lord.'
> **Martha:** 'Right. Not pompous at all, then.'
> **Announcer:** 'When their two worlds collide, anything can happen.'
> **Doctor:** 'Ready?'
> **Martha:** 'No … Landing's a bit bumpy!'
> **Doctor:** 'Welcome aboard, Miss Jones!'
> **Announcer:** 'Brand new *Doctor Who*, starts Saturday night at 7.00 on BBC One.'

Freema Agyeman makes two guest appearances on BBC One today: the first on the *Breakfast* programme, and the second on the long-running children's magazine programme *Blue Peter*. On *Breakfast*, clips from 'Smith and Jones' are shown and the actress is interviewed. She explains how she first learnt that she had got the part of Martha on 16 February 2006 when her agent phoned while she was in a car with her brother and sister; the call was taken by her sister, who asked her to stop the car and phone back, and on doing so, she was given the good news. *Blue Peter* first sees presenter Konnie Huq paying a surprise visit to a young fan of the series in his school hall and features several clips from 'Smith and Jones', as well as one of Agyeman's previous role as Adeola in 'Army of Ghosts'. Arriving in the *Blue Peter* studio in the TARDIS – after a number of humorous 'diversions' – Agyeman tells of how she came to be cast as Martha, of watching *Doctor Who* as a child when Sylvester McCoy was the Doctor and Bonnie Langford his companion, and of advice she received from predecessors Billie Piper and Elisabeth Sladen to play the part in her own way. She also responds to some of the more than 2,000 questions sent in by viewers via the *Blue Peter* website, covering amongst other things Martha's character – which she describes as 'headstrong, academic and tolerant' – the differences between her and Rose and the pride she feels on being the Doctor's first Black companion on TV.

Russell T Davies guests on Channel 4's *Richard & Judy* chat show.

The new *Radio Times* goes on sale today, with a choice of two *Doctor Who* covers: one with Martha in the foreground and the Doctor in the background, and the other vice versa, echoing the style of the specially-shot TV trailers for Series Three. The new series is extensively previewed within the magazine.

## Wednesday 28 March 2007: T minus three days

Freema Agyeman is interviewed in today's edition of the *Sun*, and reveals that she is a science fiction fan. 'I even went to a couple of *Star Trek* fan conventions,' she is quoted as saying. '*The Next Generation* was my favourite show and I loved Patrick Stewart as Captain Jean-Luc Picard. I grew up with *Doctor Who* when it starred Sylvester McCoy, but I was more interested in *Star Trek* at the time. Now I can't wait to go to a *Doctor Who* convention as a member of the cast … The fans have been really, really encouraging. I've had some great letters saying that they'll miss Rose but they're looking forward to meeting Martha. It warms my heart to know that the fans are backing me.'

The *Radio Times* website reports: 'Recently we ran a survey on *Radio Times* asking you who you thought was the coolest person on TV. Over 4,000 of you took part, and your votes easily put David Tennant as *Doctor Who* at the top of the list. That ranking places him higher than Jack Bauer and the Fonz, and miles above Russell Brand.'

At the John Nicholson Auction Rooms in Haslemere, Surrey, David Tennant's script for 'The Satan Pit' is auctioned in aid of the Parent-Teacher Association of a primary school that Tennant supports because it is attended by his godson, the son of actress Arabella Weir. The script is signed by Tennant, Billie Piper and Russell T Davies. The event is covered by the ITV1 show *Dickinson's Real Deal*. Tennant originally planned to attend the auction in person, but has had to pull out due to other commitments.

*Blue Peter* features *Doctor Who* for the second day running as presenter Zoë Salmon tells viewers how to make a chocolate Dalek cake.

## Thursday 29 March 2007: T minus two days

A 90-second-long Series Three trailer, with many previously-unseen clips, is made available to view on the 'red button' BBCi digital TV service. It is captioned: 'When Two Worlds Collide – The Adventure Begins'.

Hot on the heels of Russell T Davies's appearance two days earlier, John Barrowman guests on the *Richard & Judy* show on Channel 4.

David Tennant meanwhile guests on *The Graham Norton Show* on BBC Two.

## Friday 30 March 2007: T minus one day

The 90-second-long Series Three trailer that debuted the previous day on BBCi is now made available to view via the official *Doctor Who* website.

*The Times* today devotes substantial coverage to the start of Series Three. Journalist and confessed *Doctor Who* fan Caitlin Moran reports on a visit to the series' Cardiff studios and interviews David Tennant: '"This is a terrible anecdote, so I must tell it," he says, settling into a chair with a coffee. "Last year Billie [Piper] and I kept getting invited to guest at award ceremonies but we could never go – we were either [recording] in Cardiff or we would be presenting Best Wig or something, and what's the point of that? But when the BRIT Awards rolled around, we let it be known through our 'people' that we'd love to present a BRIT for Best Drunkard or something. But, pleasingly for the laws of hubris, they said 'No, we'll be fine, thank you'. They turned down the Doctor and Rose! Famous across the universe!" Tennant does a self-deprecating boggle.

Talking to him is a mildly surreal experience. On the one hand, it's the Doctor! You're talking to the Doctor! On the other hand, he is as obsessive and passionate about the show as any fan ... Every detail ... thrills him, even the clothes. Indeed, perhaps the most surprising moment is when he explains how the image of his Doctor was, unguessably, based on [an outfit worn by celebrity chef] Jamie Oliver. "I'd always wanted a long coat, because you've kind of got to. You've got to swish. Then Billie was on [ITV1 chat show *Parkinson*] the same week as Jamie Oliver, who was looking rather cool in a funky suit with trainers. And I rang Russell T Davies and said, 'Are you watching this? Could we do this for the Doctor?' They had wanted me to wear a stompy pair of posh boots, but the trainers were the one thing I did go to the wall on."'

John Barrowman visits the Hucking racehorse stables to see the Hucking Harkness colt named after his character. Later, he makes his latest TV guest appearance on *The Charlotte Church Show* on Channel 4.

The BBC News website runs an interview with Freema Agyeman in its Entertainment section: 'She grins as she says the infamous sonic screwdriver is "not just a blue torch – it's magic," then cringes with embarrassment as she recalls how she nearly broke it. "We were rehearsing and David threw the sonic screwdriver to me and it landed on the floor," she says. "We were both looking at each other like, 'You did it,' but it turned out it was me. Luckily it was a rehearsal prop and not the real thing. The BBC would probably have charged me for a replacement! But David's always breaking things off the TARDIS by mistake," she adds.'

Agyeman also guests on DJ Simon Mayo's afternoon show on BBC Radio 5 Live.

As she did three days before transmission of 'The Runaway Bride' back in December, Julie Gardner answers listeners' questions on the Richard Evans phone-in programme on BBC Radio Wales. Again she has a surprise caller: this time, David Tennant's father, who talks to her about his son's lifelong passion for *Doctor Who*.

The *Doctor Who* special edition of the popular quiz show *The Weakest Link*, recorded back on 21 November 2006, finally gets its debut transmission on BBC One at 8.30 this evening (apart from in Scotland).

Classic series writer Dave Martin, who with Bob Baker created the popular K-9, dies of lung cancer at the age of 72.

# CULMINATION

# CHAPTER SIX
# SERIES THREE IS HERE!

Advance publicity for *Doctor Who*'s latest run was organised not by the BBC itself, as had been the case for the previous two series, but by the independent PR company Taylor Herring, who had first been given this outsourced responsibility for 'The Runaway Bride'. The Taylor Herring employee assigned to the task was Lesley Land – perhaps somewhat ironically, given that her uncle, Michael Grade, had been notoriously hostile toward *Doctor Who* when he was Controller of BBC One in the 1980s – and the resulting campaign, with the slogan 'When Two Worlds Collide', focused on the contasting lives of the Doctor and his new companion Martha Jones, suggesting the potential for sexual tension between the two, reminiscent of that between Steed and Mrs Peel in the cult classic *The Avengers* (ITV, 1961-1969). This angle was strongly foregrounded in the specially-shot TV trailers for 'Smith and Jones' and in promotional material provided to the press, as well as in content on the official *Doctor Who* website, which was updated as the series' debut date approached and then on a weekly basis throughout its 13-week run.

Given that David Tennant was returning for his second full year as the Doctor, and that the behind-the-scenes team was also essentially unchanged, the arrival of Freema Agyeman as Martha was certainly the most immediately noticeable innovation for Series Three. Quoted in the 17 March 2007 edition of the *Sun*, Agyeman recalled her delight on learning, back in February 2006, that she had won the role as Billie Piper's successor: 'I was too over the moon to cry – I was absolutely elated. Look up elated in the dictionary and you will see my face. I hadn't allowed myself to entertain the thought that I would get it. But all of a sudden it was all bombarding me, a million miles an hour. My mum and dad were just so shocked. They know *Doctor Who* for what it was in the old days: iconic – huge.'

Agyeman's casting as Martha had been announced, and extensively reported in the press, in July 2006, just prior to the end of transmission of Series Two, so viewers had had a long time to anticipate the arrival of the new companion.[9] In an interview for genre magazine *SFX*, posted in an expanded version on its website on 12 March 2006, Russell T Davies commented on what Agyeman and her character would bring to the show: 'It's simply the new energy of having someone new. There's a whole different slant to the [Doctor and companion] relationship in having unrequited love – which is ... not laboured, it's there as little moments. It's a chance to explore the whole mythology from scratch, which is always good ... And she gives a lot of Freema, that's the greatest strength, as Billie brought an awful lot of Billie to Rose. Y'know, we're so lucky with these women, because in

---

[9] For full details of the casting announcement, see Shaun Lyon's *Second Flight: The Unofficial and Unauthorised Guide to Doctor Who 2006* (Telos Publishing, 2006).

nine months [of recording, Freema] never had a bad day, never had an off day, which you're entitled to with nine months [of recording] ... Martha's got a career, and there's a sense that the Doctor's interrupted her life. With Rose you felt like the Doctor made her life. With Martha it's more like she was interrupted. There's a family, and the family's got all sorts of ongoing situations in it as well. And the Doctor interrupts ... and of course she loves him and goes with him, but she has got that to go back to.'

As the promotional effort for the series continued, the morning of Saturday 31 March 2006 saw Davies guesting on Jonathan Ross's BBC Radio 2 show. He spoke of his lifelong love of *Doctor Who*, of the pleasures of working in Wales, and of his favourite stories from the classic series. Looking ahead, he confirmed that there would be another Christmas special in 2007 and that he had already planned out the stories of Series Four, which was tentatively scheduled for transmission in the spring of 2008. Primarily, however, he took the opportunity to publicise that evening's BBC One debut transmission of 'Smith and Jones'. Later in the day, he also appeared on the BBC Radio 4 programme *Loose Ends*, again promoting the new series. David Tennant meanwhile guested on *Radio 1 with Fearne and Reggie*, the morning show presented by Fearne Cotton and Reggie Yates, and BBC Radio Wales in its 1.00 pm slot presented a new edition in its occasional *Doctor Who – Back in Time* documentary series.

Dozens of lucky fans in Wales were given a chance to see 'Smith and Jones' a few hours ahead of everyone else, as free tickets were made available via a phone line on a first-come-first-served basis for a number of big-screen previews scheduled for 10.30 am on the day of transmission. The five venues were: Cardiff Bay Odeon, Swansea Odeon, Wrexham Odeon, Aberystwyth Arts Centre and Pwllheli Neuadd Dwyfor. Other tickets for these events were given away to BBC Radio Wales and BBC Radio Cymru listeners as competition prizes. Initial reactions from these preview screenings were extremely positive, and viewers elsewhere in the UK didn't have long to wait before they too could enjoy the episode. After nine months in production, and several more in pre-production before that, Series Three of *Doctor Who* finally reached Britain's TV screens at 6.59 that evening as the series' familiar title sequence and theme music heralded the start of a new run of thrilling adventures for the Doctor and his latest companion.

# CHAPTER SEVEN
# AND MEANWHILE …

While Series Three was in transmission, there were still plenty of other things going on in the *Doctor Who* world; the most notable of these are recorded in the following diary.

Saturday 31 March 2007

On the day when Series Three begins on TV, a new *Doctor Who: Up Close* exhibition – claimed to be the largest ever staged – opens at Manchester's Museum of Science and Industry, due to run until 5 November. It joins the *Up Close* exhibition in Cardiff (the Merseyside one having by this point closed) and the *Doctor Who Museum* in Blackpool.

The *Sun* runs a lengthy, and well illustrated, centrespread interview with the series' leading monster actor, Paul Kasey, who comments: 'I've had the pleasure of deleting a lot of people in often gruesome ways. Often I will delete an actor and they'll tell me it was a great honour to be killed by a Cyberman. It's the only way to go! I haven't managed to exterminate the Doctor so far, but I won't give up trying!'

The 'Invasion of the Bane' introductory special of *The Sarah Jane Adventures* is repeated on CBBC three hours prior to 'Smith and Jones' making its BBC One debut.

Monday 2 April 2007

The BBC's Open Centre in Leicester invites members of the public to come in and meet a Dalek and a Cyberman; the event lasts until Thursday of this week.

Saturday 7 April 2007

A further *Doctor Who: Up Close* exhibition opens, at Land's End in Cornwall.

Sunday 8 April 2007

The *Doctor Who* special edition of *The Weakest Link* is transmitted by BBC One Scotland – its first airing north of the border.

Wednesday 11 April 2007

In the latest issue of the genre magazine *SFX*, which goes on sale today, *Doctor Who* picks up six awards in the annual readers' poll: Best TV Series, Best TV Episode (for 'The Girl in the Fireplace'), Best TV Actor (David Tennant), Best TV Actress (Billie Piper), Sexiest Man (John Barrowman) and *SFX* Hall of Fame (Russell T Davies).

## Thursday 19 April 2007

The official *Doctor Who* website announces that the Daleks have won the online poll launched on 23 March to determine the series's scariest monsters. More than 21,000 people voted in the poll. Actor Nicholas Briggs comments: 'I've been fortunate enough to provide the voices for a wide variety of *Doctor Who* villains over the years, but the Daleks seem to have stood the test of time as the scariest and most iconic space terrors that the Doctor has ever encountered.'

## Sunday 22 April 2007

The Sunday tabloid *News of the World* carries the first report that Australian actress and pop star Kylie Minogue is being lined up to appear in the 2007 *Doctor Who* Christmas special: 'A BBC insider said: "Kylie jumped at the chance to be in the show and is really looking forward to acting again. She is flattered to be asked to be in such a classic TV show. The *Doctor Who* team are delighted they've got someone as sexy and high profile as Kylie to ensure they win the annual ratings battle with ITV."' Both Minogue and her friend and regular stylist Will Baker are known to be *Doctor Who* fans; Minogue's stage shows have regularly featured *Doctor Who*-inspired designs, and recently presented a group of dancers wearing Cyberwoman costumes like that seen in *Torchwood*.

## Friday 27 April 2007

In the BBC staff magazine *Ariel*, Russell T Davies dismisses reports from the previous weekend that Kylie Minogue is being lined up to guest star in the 2007 Christmas special. He is quoted as saying, 'Don't be stupid. I haven't even written the script yet, and a woman like that is booked up two years in advance.'

## Saturday 28 April 2007

*Doctor Who* and *Torchwood* are big winners at the Welsh BAFTA Awards ceremony this evening, as detailed in a report on the BBC News website: 'The *Doctor Who* show has cleaned up at the BAFTA Cymru Awards for the second year running, managing to win in eight of 13 nominations. Actor David Tennant, who plays the Time Lord, won Best Actor, with lead writer Russell T Davies Best Screenwriter. *Doctor Who* spin-off *Torchwood* won four gongs including Best Drama Series and Best Actress for Eve Myles. Both programmes are made by BBC Wales. Controller Menna Richards said she was "very proud indeed". *Doctor Who*'s success was even better than last year, when it won five awards. Its accolades this year included: Best Lighting Director – Not Camera; Best Editor; Best Original Music Soundtrack; Best Make-Up; Best Costume; and Best Director: Drama. Sci-fi thriller *Torchwood* also picked up Best Director of Photography: Drama, and Best Design. The programme's success rounded off a night which saw BBC Wales pick up 24 BAFTA Cymru Awards – more than any other broadcaster – at the Cardiff International Arena on Saturday.'

## Monday 30 April 2007

The BBC News website carries another report of interest to *Doctor Who* fans: 'BBC shows such as *Doctor Who* and *EastEnders* are to be made available on-demand after the BBC's iPlayer service was given the green light. The service – which will launch later this year – allows viewers to watch programmes online for seven days after their first TV broadcast. Episodes can also be downloaded and stored for up to 30 days. The BBC Trust gave the iPlayer the go-ahead after consultations with members of the public.'

## Wednesday 2 May 2007

Today's edition of the *Sun* reports: 'A string of bets on an unknown bald actor becoming the next Doctor Who has left bookies in a spin. Enthusiastic punters have staked cash on 5ft 7in Julian Walsh taking over the TARDIS in the BBC sci-fi hit. One even asked for a £2,500 bet – amid rising speculation that current Doctor David Tennant, 35, will stop playing the Time Lord after the third series. Gamblers piled in after bookies began taking bets on who will become the eleventh Doctor. And many backed Mancunian Julian, 37 – even though he is best known as a child star from '80s show *Jossy's Giants* and his current claim to fame is an ad for Warburton's bread. Darren Haines of bookies Paddy Power said last night: "Julian might not look the part as he's a bit squat and bald. But he's the one people have been trying to back in the last 48 hours. At first he was not even on our books, but we've had to slash his odds to 12/1. We fear punters might know something we don't. We're not convinced they're right, but we have to sit up and take note." A spokesman for Julian said last night: "He is bemused by all of this. Nobody has approached us yet."'

## Friday 4 May 2007

The BBC Two business programme *Working Lunch* features an item on Neill Gorton's Millennium FX company, focusing on its prosthetics work for *Doctor Who*. Gorton is interviewed by former footballer Graeme Le Saux. The item is subsequently made available to view via the 'watch again' feature on bbc.co.uk's *Working Lunch* homepage.

## Saturday 5 May 2007

David Tennant is the first guest on a new series of the ITV1 chat show *Parkinson*, the interview having been recorded two days earlier. The programme starts 15 minutes earlier than originally scheduled, causing many disappointed fans to miss the segment featuring Tennant.

## Sunday 6 May 2007

A one-day *Doctor Who* event, Who in the Cavern 2, takes place in Liverpool.

Saturday 12 May 2007

A number of press reports today revive the rumour that Kylie Minogue is to appear in this year's *Doctor Who* Christmas special. These have apparently been prompted by an interview with the star in *InStyle* magazine, in which she is quoted as confirming that she has accepted a role, although not as a villain.

The SyFy Portal website today carries a report on a supposed *Doctor Who* movie project: 'Were you a big fan of Paul McGann and his trip to San Francisco in the TARDIS back in 1996? Well, now that interest has once again been reignited in the *Doctor Who* franchise thanks to the popular BBC series starring David Tennant and Freema Agyeman, there is word … that [the] BBC is planning to do a new *Doctor Who* movie featuring not Tennant as the tenth Doctor, or even Christopher Eccleston as the ninth Doctor. Empire Online is reporting that [the] BBC and director Geoffrey Sax want to continue the story of McGann's eighth Doctor in a way to separate it from the popular television franchise. "Because of the demand for eighth Doctor stories on film, due to the popular Big Finish audios and BBC 7 radio audios made specifically for those productions, a film is finally in negotiations," Empire reported, courtesy of <u>Crave Online</u>. "There are still many things to finalise, such as if Paul McGann is interested in portraying the Doctor on film again. The TARDIS interior from the 1996 TV movie [was] auctioned off back in 1999, but they plan on recreating the same interior from the TV movie, which is a popular design." If such a film is made, it will be without popular bad guys like the Daleks, Cybermen or even the Master, who was featured in the first film. Instead, it will focus on a new alien species, and instead of traveling to the United States, would instead be on Earth for just a few minutes before heading to three different alien worlds.' This report is generally dismissed by fans as the result of a hoax.

Tuesday 15 May 2007

In its latest *Doctor Who*-related report, the *Sun* claims: 'Film legend Woody Allen is being lined up for a starring role – in the Christmas special of *Doctor Who*. Show bosses have made an astonishing approach to the geeky Oscar-winning American director and actor. An insider on the BBC One sci-fi hit said: "Producers are going all out for big names. Kylie confirmed last week, now Woody Allen's in the frame. They want him to play Albert Einstein. They chose Einstein because they want historical figures in the special. Einstein's also linked with *Doctor Who* themes, like time travel."' This is believed by some fans to be a garbled report based on the fact that David Tennant is due to appear in the role of Eddington in a BBC film project *Einstein and Eddington*, and that his co-star in that production, Rebecca Hall, has been cast in Allen's latest movie, as noted in a rather confused 11 May *Daily Mail* story headed, 'Woody Allen's new film is a mixture of Gollum and Dr Who'.

Thursday 17 May 2007

Actress Michelle Collins guests on the BBC's *Breakfast* to promote her forthcoming appearance in the Series Three episode'42', two preview clips from which are shown.

# CHAPTER SEVEN: AND MEANWHILE …

Friday 18 May 2007

John Barrowman guests on the *Friday Night with Jonathan Ross* chat show on BBC One to promote his forthcoming return to *Doctor Who*. A preview clip from 'Utopia' is show, of Captain Jack grabbing onto the TARDIS exterior as the ship takes off from Cardiff and travels through the time vortex.

Monday 21 May 2007

The official *Doctor Who* website reports: 'We've teamed up with BBC Blast[10] to find the next generation of game designers. Together we've launched a competition that will give the winner the chance to design and create a *Doctor Who* game that will take pride of place on the *Doctor Who* and Blast websites. Using *Doctor Who* as an inspiration, your goal is to design the most exciting and addictive game possible. The winner will have their *Doctor Who* game brought to life, with runners-up receiving Blast and *Doctor Who* goodie bags.' The competition is restricted to teenagers.

Tuesday 22 May 2007

From today until Saturday 26 May, an exhibit called *A Garden in Time*, created by Cardiff Council Landscape Officer Mo Dorken, features as part of the Royal Horticultural Society's annual Chelsea Flower Show. With a full-size TARDIS police box as its centrepiece, complete with light and sound effects, one half of the exhibit depicts a typical 1960s urban garden, and the other half a modern garden with a focus on sustainability and recycling of waste, the intention being to highlight how things have changed in the gardening world over the four decades since *Doctor Who* began. Her Majesty the Queen expresses interest in the exhibit when she visits the Show, and Dorken explains its concept to her.

Friday 25 May 2007

A week after John Barrowman's appearance on the same show, Freema Agyeman guests on *Friday Night with Jonathan Ross*.

Saturday 26 May 2007

The *Sun* prints one of its more sensationalist *Doctor Who* reports: 'Doctor Who actress Freema Agyeman has been axed from the next series, the *Sun* can reveal. Pretty Freema, 27, only joined the BBC One sci-fi hit as the Time Lord's new companion Martha Jones at the beginning of the current Series Three. We told how the struggling actress scooped the role after Billie Piper quit. But show chiefs think her performance is not as strong as in her earlier episodes. And they are planning a storyline where the Doctor, played by David Tennant, will lose her and travel through the universe searching for her. The decision to dump Freema comes as a bolt from the blue after her performance for the first couple of episodes was

---

[10] Blast is the games section of bbc.co.uk.

praised. A source said: "Freema is very talented but we don't think she is just right on *Doctor Who*. None of this is being done with any malice. Freema's a lovely girl." Freema has previously admitted that she had a tough job to fill Billie [Piper]'s boots. Billie, who played Rose Tyler, left at the end of the second series. Christopher Eccleston stunned the BBC by quitting as the Time Lord after the first series of the revamped drama in 2005. Meanwhile current star Tennant is still believed to be making just part of Series Four, which starts filming in Wales this summer. A spokeswoman for the show refused to comment.'

The BBC issues an official statement in response to this: 'It is absolute rubbish that Freema Agyeman has been axed or sacked from *Doctor Who*. However we do not comment on future storylines.'

Thursday 31 May 2007

A flurry of reports appear concerning the future of *Doctor Who*, and of Russell T Davies's involvement in it. The *Sun* has picked up on unsubstantiated fan rumours that Davies and David Tennant have both decided to leave at the end of Series Four, and that the BBC, not wanting to continue it without them, will then put *Doctor Who* on long-term hiatus, as happened at the end of the 1980s: 'Hit show *Doctor Who* will be exterminated next year – after the fourth series. Boss Russell T Davies has decided to axe the BBC One sci-fi drama and concentrate on other projects. He and senior staff have hatched a plot to hand in a group resignation in summer 2008. A source said: "The heavy workload – nine months of 16-hour days every year – has started to take its toll. It was decided the best thing for the show was to go out at the top next year." Davies was behind the relaunch of *Doctor Who* in 2005 – 16 years after it was originally axed.' A report on the *MediaGuardian* website, however, quotes a 'senior BBC Wales drama source' as responding to this by commenting, 'Russell has always said that he wouldn't be with the show forever and he has made no secret that the hours are quite exhausting ... But there isn't any way it would be axed even if he left. He loves the show and he does feel that maybe it would benefit from some new blood'. The report goes on to state: 'If Mr Davies does leave *Doctor Who*, the BBC will want to keep such a popular show going by bringing in a new executive producer to take over his creative responsibilities.'

Friday 1 June 2007

The United Press International agency runs a report following on from the previous day's speculation about *Doctor Who*'s post-Series Four future. It notes: 'Speculation was high that writer Russell T Davies, who revived *Doctor Who* in 2005, was scrapping the show to concentrate on other projects. Davies and other senior staff working on the series were said to be thinking about handing in their resignations, news reports indicated. "We are a long way away from even thinking about Series Five when the current series hasn't ended and we have yet to start [recording] Series Four. But the BBC has a long-term commitment to *Doctor Who*," the programme's creators said in a statement.'

CHAPTER SEVEN: AND MEANWHILE ...

Tuesday 5 June 2007

At an evening ceremony in London, Freema Agyeman takes the Best Newcomer title in the *Glamour* magazine's Women of the Year Awards 2007. Asked about how she was affected by the *Sun*'s recent story about her having been 'axed' from *Doctor Who*, she is quoted as responding: 'I'm not axed. I haven't been sacked ... For about five minutes ... you do think, "Oh no," but then you know you're not going to have 100 percent of people all the time. It's just life. What is important is that the fans are enjoying it, and I just decided to focus on that and it didn't bother me any more.' Agyeman has in fact been given special dispensation by the *Doctor Who* production team to rebut the *Sun*'s story, although she is still not permitted to discuss the extent of her involvement in Series Four.

Saturday 9 June 2007

Australian cable broadcaster UK-TV begins a weekend-long marathon of *Doctor Who* screenings for the Queen's Birthday national holiday, with Series One scheduled for today and Series Two for tomorrow. Also to be shown are the 15-minute 'cutdown' versions of *Doctor Who Confidential*, making their Australian broadcast debut.

BBC Radio Wales broadcasts 'Top Tennant', the first in a new run of three weekly 1.00 pm programmes in its occasional *Doctor Who – Back in Time* documentary series. The publicity blurb promises: 'Julian Carey meets David Tennant and gets the lowdown on life as the tenth Doctor.'

Sunday 10 June 2007

At the forty-seventh Monte Carlo Television Festival, which begins today and runs until Thursday, *Doctor Who* is represented by Freema Agyeman but fails to win any awards. Fifth Doctor actor Peter Davison, however, receives a Golden Nymph for Outstanding Comedy Actor for his role in the series *Fear, Stress and Anger* (BBC Two, 2007).

Monday 11 June 2006

A 20-second-long trailer for 'Utopia' starts airing between selected programme breaks on BBC One.

Tuesday 12 June 2006

The edition of *Radio Times* that goes on sale today launches a special offer for readers to obtain a 124 cm by 45 cm, double-sided, panoramic *Doctor Who* poster, one side of which depicts an array of Series Three monsters and the other side of which shows the Doctor, Martha and Jack inside the TARDIS control room. In order to obtain the poster, readers have to collect two tokens – one in this week's edition, one in next week's (although, in the event, the special version of the latter produced for Virgin Media customers will omit the second token, causing much annoyance to fans in that group) and send in a cheque for £2.99.

A special edition of the BBC's *Blue Peter* wholly devoted to *Doctor Who* and entitled *Who Peter* is broadcast at 4.35 pm today, just ahead of the regular Wednesday edition of the programme. Its main focus is the competition, launched on 16 October 2006, for one young viewer to take an acting role in *Doctor Who*. The winner is revealed to be nine-year-old John Bell, who is given the news in a phone call from Russell T Davies, and who is subsequently shown recording his role as Creet in 'Utopia'. The two runners-up, Jonathan Wharton and Lizzie Watkins, have been given non-speaking roles in the same episode. Also on the programme, John Barrowman assists presenter Gethin Jones in making a TARDIS interior model out of household items.

Saturday 16 June 2007

The second in BBC Radio Wales's latest run of *Doctor Who – Back in Time* documentaries is entitled 'Made in Wales'. The publicity blurb reads: 'Julian Carey discovers the benefits and knock-on effects of having the *Doctor Who* series made in Wales and explores the *Who* HQ in downtown Pontypridd.'

Monday 18 June 2007

CBC in Canada airs 'Smith and Jones' at 8.00 pm as the first in a complete debut run of Series Three, with episodes going out weekly on Monday evenings. 'The Runaway Bride' then gets its first screening, out of order, at midnight tonight. (Both episodes go out half an hour later in the Newfoundland region than elsewhere.)

Starting today, two 12-second-long trailers for 'The Sound of Drums' air in selected programme breaks on BBC One. The first consists of testimonials for Harold Saxon from celebrities Sharon Osbourne, McFly and Ann Widdecombe, with a 'VOTE SAXON – the man you can trust!' caption scrolling across the screen from right to left and a blue Archangel logo revolving in the top right-hand corner of the screen, to the accompaniment of an insistent drum beat. (These celebrity clips differ slightly from the ones that will eventually be seen in the episode itself; Widdecombe's in particular shows her on her own, whereas in the version in the episode, she is standing beside Saxon.) The trailer ends with a graphic of a black cross being marked in a 'Vote Saxon' box, as on an election form, in the bottom right-hand corner of a red screen giving the day, time and channel of transmission. The second is a more standard trailer showing brief shots of Saxon, Jack, Martha and the Doctor, and Saxon saying, 'What this country really needs, right now, is a Doctor', then giving a broad smile. An announcer's voice then states that the episode will be airing at 7.15 pm on Saturday on BBC One, as the graphic of the black cross being marked in a 'Vote Saxon' box appears, as on the first trailer. There is also a radio trailer for the episode. In addition, the main BBC TV channels have begun running a trailer for a complete omnibus screening of 'The Infinite Quest' – the animated adventure being shown in segments as part of *Totally Doctor Who* – that is now scheduled for the morning of 30 June.

CHAPTER SEVEN: AND MEANWHILE ...

<u>Tuesday 19 June 2007</u>

The winner of Big Finish's short story writing competition, launched on 4 December , is announced today on the official *Doctor Who* website: it is Michael Coen, whose entry, *What I Did On My Holidays*, is the one that has most impressed the judges, led by editor Simon Guerrier, out of the more than 1,000 received. It will be published in the forthcoming *Short Trips* anthology *Defining Patterns*; and the judges have been so impressed by the 24 runners-up that it has been decided that they will be collected together into a special anthology of their own, entitled *How the Doctor Changed My Life*.

The subject of today's '60 Second Interview' in *Metro*, the newspaper distributed free to commuters in many UK cities, is Freema Agyeman. Asked how the small role of Adeola in 'Army of Ghosts' led on to the co-starring role of Martha, she explains: 'After I did the first show, my agent called and said they wanted me to audition for a role in *Torchwood*. When I arrived, I found out it was actually for the role of the new companion. I was thrilled, because I'd had such a good time before. I guess when you're enjoying something, it shows. I never forget the advice – do your best no matter how small the part is, because you never know what it might lead to. It's definitely what I did with the first part, because it was quite small but I attacked it.'

<u>Saturday 23 June 2007</u>

The last of the current run of BBC Radio Wales's *Doctor Who – Back in Time* programmes is 'Interrogation': 'In March,' reads the publicity blurb, 'BBC Radio Wales opened up its e-mail address to thousands of *Doctor Who* fans, challenging them to ask the cast and crew any question they liked about the show – these are the results. Featuring David Tennant, Freema Ageyman, Russell T Davies ... and a Dalek.' A video clip of Tennant's interview for this programme has been available to view on the official *Doctor Who* website since 10 April.

<u>Sunday 24 June 2007</u>

A new, 30-second-long trailer for 'Last of the Time Lords' starts airing in programme breaks on the main BBC TV channels. It opens with the words 'The Master Has Returned', then features a succession of clips from the episode and concludes with an image of the Doctor and Martha beside the TARDIS as seen in the original pre-series trailers, all to the accompaniment of an insistent drumbeat.

<u>Tuesday 26 June 2007</u>

The new edition of *Radio Times*, for the week of the Series Three finale, matches that for the week of its debut, coming with a choice of two *Doctor Who* covers. One features David Tennant as the Doctor, the other John Simm as the Master. When placed side by side, the two make up a single composite image, which is also made available to buy separately as a high-quality, limited-edition print from the Science and Society Picture Library.

Freema Agyeman guests on the *Richard & Judy* show on Channel 4.

Freema Agyeman is a guest on Christian O'Connell's breakfast show on Virgin Radio UK, taking calls from listeners – including David Tennant, who spoofs her by pretending to be a fan called 'Derek', repeatedly mispronouncing her name as 'Frida' and criticising the performance of 'David Eccleston' as the Doctor, at which point Agyeman guesses his true identity.

Thursday 28 June 2007

'The Runaway Bride' receives its Australian debut transmission on ABC.
   The BBC News website reports: 'Strong overseas sales of shows such as *Doctor Who* and *Planet Earth* helped the BBC's commercial arm, BBC Worldwide, to increase its profits by 24% last year. The division reported record pre-tax profits including exceptional items of £111.1 m, up from £89.4 m a year earlier.' *Torchwood* is also mentioned in the report as one of the 'notable success stories'.

Friday 29 June 2007

John Barrowman guests on ITV1's breakfast programme *GMTV*, speaking live from his trailer during a break from recording on Series Two of *Torchwood*. He displays some sketches of Captain Jack as the character is to be depicted when added to the 'comic maker' feature on the official *Doctor Who* website. A clip from 'Last of the Time Lords' is shown.
   Tom Ellis, who plays Thomas Milligan in 'Last of the Time Lords', appears on ITV1's *This Morning* show to promote the episode. A clip is shown.
   Freema Agyeman guests on the *Steve Wright in the Afternoon* show on BBC Radio 2.
   The *Daily Mirror* meanwhile has some exclusive news on Series Four, from apparently well-informed sources: 'Doctor Who is to get a brand new companion, we can reveal. The Time Lord, played by dishy David Tennant, has been rather mean to poor old Martha of late. And by the start of the fourth series next year, she's had enough. A show insider reveals: "Martha will still be in *Doctor Who*, but her relationship with the Doctor will have changed. The truth is that she loves him but he doesn't feel the same way. She is going to have to share him, because he'll be getting a different sidekick. And this is a major addition to the cast." Bosses are remaining tight-lipped over whether the new companion is male or female. But the new arrival prompts Martha, played by Freema Agyeman, to take a bit of a back seat. She is expected to flit in and out of the show, also popping up in spin-off series *Torchwood*. Freema will definitely not be appearing in the Christmas special, which starts [recording] next week – Kylie Minogue will be helping out the Doctor instead. The end of the next series will also see us bidding a fond farewell to writer Russell T Davies, who is hanging up his cyber pen to work on other projects. And David Tennant has admitted to having decided when he's off (er, it's then, too). These departures don't mean *Doctor Who* will be exterminated – the Beeb's drama supremo Jane Tranter has big things planned for the hit sci-fi series. She insists: "One thing is certain, *Doctor Who* will be around on BBC One for years to come."'
   *Doctor Who* is ranked 22 out of 30 in a list of the 'Top Cult Shows Ever' in the US

listings magazine *TV Guide. Star Trek* takes first place in the list.

The UKTV Drama website launches a 'favourite Doctor' poll, with a closing date of 13 July. The results are to be revealed during a *Doctor Who* weekend on the channel on 14 and 15 July. David Tennant will ultimately prove to be the winner.

Saturday 30 June 2007

Following Thursday's airing of 'The Runaway Bride', ABC in Australia shows 'Smith and Jones' as the first in its regular weekly run of Series Three.

# CONTINUATION

# CHAPTER EIGHT
# COMING SOON ...

The flurry of advance promotional activities and press hype for *Doctor Who*'s Series Three finale culminated on 30 June 2007, the day of its BBC One debut transmission, with most of the national newspapers running previews of the episode and John Barrowman and Freema Agyman making personal appearances at the Gay Pride event in London's Trafalgar Square, although plans for the episode itself to be shown on a giant screen there had to be called off, to the disgruntlement of many of those present, when the police and Westminster Council imposed an 8.00 pm curfew on the event in response to recent terrorist threats.

'Last of the Time Lords' finally aired at 7.05 pm that evening, bringing the latest run of Britain's favourite family drama series to a highly dramatic conclusion as the Doctor's arch-enemy the Master was apparently killed and Martha Jones walked out of the TARDIS to resume the life that was interrupted when she first came on board in 'Smith and Jones'. The series' fans barely had time to draw breath, however, before the BBC followed this up with three major cast-related *Doctor Who* announcements, on three successive days. The first of these came on Monday 2 July with a press release about Agyeman's future as Martha. This read in part:

> The production team has now confirmed that the character is set to make a triumphant return in the fourth series. Freema, who gained rave notices for her portrayal of Martha Jones, is also set to join the cast of *Torchwood*, where she will continue to play the character in three new episodes before returning to *Doctor Who* in the middle of the fourth series. *Doctor Who* executive producer and head writer Russell T Davies said: 'Series Three has gained outstanding reviews and Freema has been a huge part of that success, gaining rave notices for her portrayal of Martha. Now we are taking the character of Martha into brand new territory with a starring role in *Torchwood*.' Freema said: 'I can't wait to start [recording] on *Torchwood* and the new series of *Doctor Who*. It's a huge new challenge for me and I'm delighted Russell has decided to expand the character of Martha Jones.' The announcement leaves a vacant space in the TARDIS, and a new companion for the Doctor, who will join the new series for the entire 13-week run, will be announced shortly.

The following day, Tuesday 3 July, the focus was on the forthcoming Christmas special, 'Voyage of the Damned', which was about to enter production in Cardiff. Finally substantiating a long-standing casting rumour, which had been previously denied by the BBC, the press office reported:

> The BBC has confirmed that Kylie Minogue will be joining the *Doctor Who* cast in a major lead role in an hour-long Christmas special to be broadcast in December 2007 on BBC One. Kylie will be joining David Tennant for the episode, 'Voyage Of The Damned', which starts [recording] in July in Cardiff. The production team has also confirmed that the storyline will follow on directly from the ending of Series Three where viewers witnessed the *Titanic* crash through the TARDIS walls ... The episode has been written by *Doctor Who*'s executive producer and head writer Russell T Davies. He says: 'We are delighted and excited to announce that Kylie Minogue will be joining the Doctor. *Doctor Who* Christmas specials are always a joy and we feel very confident that this will be the most ambitious and best Christmas episode yet.' Kylie says: 'It is an incredible thrill to be joining David and the entire *Doctor Who* production for this year's Christmas special. *Doctor Who* enjoys a unique history and it is going to be very exciting to be a part of that.' Full details are currently under wraps with more information to be announced shortly.

A publicity photograph of David Tennant and Kylie Minogue together in Cardiff was also released to the press.

On Wednesday 4 July, the trio of announcements was completed with one that no-one outside production circles had seen coming. Headed 'Doctor Who Series Four: Catherine Tate Confirmed as New Companion', the press release read:

> Hot on the heels of the critically-acclaimed Series Three finale of *Doctor Who*, the BBC has announced that Catherine Tate is set to return to the TARDIS for the complete 13-week run of the new BBC One series. Award-winning comedian Catherine Tate has been confirmed as the Doctor's new companion, returning to her role as Donna who featured in last year's Christmas special 'The Runaway Bride' ... Tate was asked if she would like to become the Doctor's new companion at the press screening of 'The Runaway Bride'. She replied: 'I would love to, but no-one has asked!' ... *Doctor Who*'s executive producer and head writer Russell T Davies said: 'Catherine was an absolute star in "The Runaway Bride" and we are delighted that one of Britain's greatest talents has agreed to join us for the fourth series. Viewers can expect more ambitious storylines and a whole host of guest stars in 2008.' Catherine Tate said: 'I am delighted to be returning to *Doctor Who*. I had a blast last Christmas and look forward to travelling again through time and space with that nice man

from Gallifrey.' The fourth series of *Doctor Who* goes into production this July and will hit UK screens in Spring 2008.

These announcements were quickly picked up by online news outlets and in press reports not only in the UK but also – particularly in the light of Minogue's status as an international pop star – in numerous other countries around the world. The *Doctor Who* fan community was also naturally buzzing with excitement and debate. It seemed that, for many, Christmas 2007 could not come soon enough ...

# CAST & CREW

# CHAPTER NINE
# MAIN CAST

## DAVID TENNANT (THE DOCTOR)

David Tennant was born David John McDonald in Bathgate, West Lothian, on 18 April 1971 and grew up in Ralston, Renfrewshire, where his father was a Church of Scotland minister. His later stage name, adopted in order to avoid confusion with another actor called David McDonald, was inspired by that of pop star Neil Tennant of the Pet Shop Boys. He became a fan of *Doctor Who* at a young age and, partly inspired by that, made it his ambition to become an actor. He joined a Saturday youth theatre while still attending Paisley Grammar School and went on to train at the Royal Scottish Academy of Music and Drama, to which the youth theatre was affiliated. In his twenties he joined a radical Scottish theatre company called 7:84, making his professional debut in their production of *The Resistable Rise of Arturo Ui*. He broke into TV with small parts in *Strathblair* (BBC One, 1992) and a 1993 episode of *Rab C Nesbitt* (BBC Two, 1988-1999) and then won his first lead role – as a manic-depressive radio station manager – in a drama called *Takin' Over The Asylum* (BBC Two, 1994). After moving from Scotland to London, where he rented rooms from actress Arabella Weir of *The Fast Show* (BBC, 1994-2000), he gained more theatre work, including in numerous Royal Shakespeare Company productions. He also made his feature film debut in *Jude* (Universal Pictures/PolyGram Filmed Entertainment, 1996), in which he shared a scene with its star Christopher Eccleston, later to play the ninth Doctor. Further film roles followed, including in Stephen Fry's *Bright Young Things* (Film Four, 2003) and *Harry Potter and the Goblet of Fire* (Warner Brothers, 2005). It was for his TV work that he became best known, however, taking parts of increasing prominence in programmes such as: *The Mrs Bradley Mysteries* (BBC One, 1999), in which he appeared opposite fifth Doctor actor Peter Davison; *Randall and Hopkirk (Deceased)* (BBC One, 2000-2001); a first season episode of *Foyle's War* (ITV, 2002- ); and *He Knew He Was Right* (BBC One, 2004). His rise to star status came with major roles in two acclaimed series in quick succession: as DI Carlyle in *Blackpool* (BBC One, 2004) and, even more memorably, as the title character in Russell T Davies's *Casanova* (BBC Three, 2005), which gained him his first picture on the front cover of the *Radio Times*. *Casanova* effectively served as Tennant's 'audition' for the part of the tenth Doctor, for which he was the only actor seriously considered when Eccleston departed. He accepted the role after a brief hesitation, and quickly became a household name following his full debut in 'The Christmas Invasion' on Christmas Day 2005. This was not in fact his first connection with *Doctor Who*: he had previously played voice parts in a number of Big Finish's audio CD dramas – 'Colditz' (2001); 'Sympathy for the Devil' (2003); 'Exile' (2003) (one of the *Doctor Who Unbound* range); the spin-off series *Dalek Empire III* (2004); 'Medicinal Purposes' (2004); and 'The Wasting' (2005), an episode of the *UNIT* spin-off – and also in an episode of the webcast story 'Scream of the Shalka' (2003). His portrayal of the tenth Doctor was, however, the first time he had been associated with the series in the general public's eyes, and it saw him becoming Britain's most popular TV actor, winning numerous awards and other accolades.[11] He has still found time to take on a number of other roles during breaks in production on *Doctor Who*, including in the TV plays *Recovery* (BBC One, 2007) and *Learners* (BBC One, 2007), and has made numerous guest appearances on talk shows and the like. On 9 July 2007, the *MediaGuardian* supplement of the *Guardian* newspaper ranked him the twenty-fourth most influential person in the UK's media.

## FREEMA AGYEMAN (MARTHA JONES)

Freema Agyeman was born in 1979 to an Iranian mother, Azar, and a Ghanaian father, Osei. She is one of three children, with an older sister, Leila, and a younger brother, Domenic. Her parents divorced when she was young, and she lived with her mother and siblings in a flat on the Woodberry Down housing estate in Finsbury Park, North London. She was educated at Our Lady's Convent in Stamford Hill and the Anna Scher Theatre School in Islington. Although as a child she had had ambitions to be a doctor and a marine biologist and had enjoyed science, she eventually chose English, Fine Art and Theatre Studies as her A Level subjects. She later studied at Middlesex University, graduating in 2000 with a BA (Honours) in Performing Arts and Drama, and also at Radford University in Virginia, USA. She had plans to work with children if her acting career stalled, but in fact she soon won a regular role as Lola Wise in the revived soap opera *Crossroads* (Carlton, 2001-2003), and this led on to further TV work, including in a 2004 episode of *Casualty* (BBC One, 1986- ), a 2005 episode of *Mile High* (Sky One, 2003-2005), a 2005 episode of *Silent Witness* (BBC One, 1996- ) and three episodes between 2004 and 2006 as a semi-regular in *The Bill* (ITV, 1983- ). She also played the femme fatale Nana in the independent film production *Rulers and Dealers* (RDL Productions, 2006). Having auditioned unsuccessfully for the part of Sally in 'The Christmas Invasion', she made her *Doctor Who* debut as Adeola Oshodi in 'Army of Ghosts' and immediately impressed the production team with her performance and personality. She was earning a living working shifts at a Blockbuster video rental store when, shortly afterwards, she was invited to audition for what she was initially told was a regular role in the spin-off series *Torchwood*. She eventually learned what part she was really being considered for – that of the companion in *Doctor Who* – when she was called back for a further, top-secret audition opposite David Tennant in producer Phil Collinson's Cardiff flat. She won the role, and went on to appear as medical student Martha Jones in every episode of Series Three. Although Martha then parted company with the Doctor, she is due to feature in three episodes of Series Two of *Torchwood* – allowing Agyeman to contribute to the spin-off after all – and in five episodes of Series Four of *Doctor Who*.

---

[11] See earlier chapters of this book for further details.

## JOHN BARROWMAN (CAPTAIN JACK HARKNESS)

John Barrowman was born on 11 March 1967 in Glasgow, Scotland. He grew up in his native city until, when he was aged eight, his family emigrated to live in the USA, in the Illinois town of Aurora, just south of Chicago. He had always been keen on performing – both acting and singing – and pursued this interest during his education at Joliet West High School, Illinois, where he appeared in a number of student productions between 1983 and 1985. An early job was as a musical entertainer in a Nashville, Tennessee theme park called Opryland. He returned to the UK in 1989, initially to study Shakespeare at a London university, and his theatrical career really took off when he won a role opposite Elaine Paige in *Anything Goes* in London's West End. He also started gaining TV work during the 1990s, including as a regular presenter on the BBC children's series *Live and Kicking* (1993). Roles in the American series *Central Park West* (1996) and *Titans* (2000) followed, and more theatre work, including in a couple of productions on New York's Broadway. His starring roles in the theatre have come mainly in musicals, such as *Chicago, Sunset Boulevard, Miss Saigon, Evita, Beauty and the Beast* and *Phantom of the Opera*, although he has also had a number of non-singing parts, including in productions of *Rope* and *A Few Good Men* (2005). On the big screen he has appeared in *De-Lovely* (2004), a biography of composer Cole Porter, and in Mel Brooks's *The Producers* (2005). He has sung on a number of original-cast soundtrack recordings of musicals, and has also released three solo CDs: *Aspects of Lloyd Webber* (1998), *Reflections from Broadway* (2000) and *John Barrowman Swings Cole Porter* (2004). When, in 2004, his agent was approached by casting director Andy Prior about the possibility of him playing Captain Jack, he was eager to take the role, having long been a fan of *Doctor Who*. He was, in fact, the first regular to be cast in the revived series. So popular did he prove as Captain Jack that he was soon offered the opportunity to star in his own spin-off series, *Torchwood*. He appeared in pantomime – *Cinderella* at the New Wimbledon Theatre – over the 2005/2006 Christmas holiday season, and early in 2006 could again be seen on TV, in the variety shows *The Magic of Musicals* for the BBC and *Dancing on Ice* for ITV. He also had a stint as presenter of the ITV morning talk show *This Morning*, standing in for regular host Phillip Schofield. Later in 2006, he was one of the judges on the BBC show *How Do You Solve a Problem Like Maria?*, about the search for a newcomer to star in a West End revival of the musical *The Sound of Music*. Since then, he has appeared as a guest on almost every talk show and celebrity quiz programme on TV, cementing his position as one of the most high-profile and popular stars in the British entertainment industry. Following his return as Captain Jack in Series Three of *Doctor Who*, he is to continue in the role throughout Series Two of *Torchwood*.

## JOHN SIMM (THE MASTER)

John Ronald Simm was born on 10 July 1970 in Leeds, West Yorkshire, and raised in the small town of Nelson in Lancashire. He initially followed in the footsteps of his musician father Ronald, learning to play the guitar and accompanying him on stage for performances at working men's clubs and the like under the name Us2. This led on to him becoming the guitarist in the band Magic Alex during the 1990s and singing backing vocals on an album by Ian McCulloch, former leader of Echo and the Bunnymen, with whom Magic Alex had toured as a support act. In the meantime, he had been studying acting, first at Blackpool Drama College for three years from the age of 16, and then at the Drama Centre in London. While still performing as a musician, he started to take acting jobs as well, winning his first TV role in a 1992 episode of *Rumpole of the Bailey* (ITV, 1975-1992). Further notable TV parts came in a 1995 episode of *Cracker* (ITV, 1993-1996, 2006), in two series of *The Lakes* (BBC One, 1997-1999) and in a 2000 episode of *Clocking Off* (BBC One, 2000-2003). He also found work in feature films, with roles in *Boston Kickout* (CNC, 1995), *Diana & Me* (BVI/Village Roadshow Pictures, 1999), *Understanding Jane* (Scala Productions, 1998), *Human Traffic* (Metrodome/Miramax, 1999), *Wonderland* (Universal Pictures, 1999), *Miranda* (First Look/ Pathé/Film Four, 2002) and *24 Hour Party People* (United Artists, 2002), the latter of which saw him playing Bernard Sumner of the group New Order and led on to him performing a song live on stage with them at a concert in Finsbury Park, London, the same year – by which point he had otherwise effectively given up working as a musician to concentrate fully on acting. With his reputation steadily growing, he returned to TV with parts in productions including *Crime and Punishment* (BBC Two, 2002), *State of Play* (BBC One, 2003), *The Canterbury Tales* (BBC One, 2004) and *Sex Traffic* (Channel 4, 2004), before taking on the starring role for which he is now best known, as policeman DI Sam Tyler in *Life on Mars* (BBC One, 2006-2007). After completing work on the second season of *Life on Mars* and portraying artist Vincent Van Gogh in the biographical drama *The Yellow House* (Channel 4, 2007), Simm took up temporary residence in Cardiff to play the Master in 'Utopia'/'The Sound of Drums'/'Last of the Time Lords'. Subsequently he went on to take the title role in the play *Elling* for a week's run at London's Bush Theatre, and began work – alongside his wife, actress Kate Magowan – on a crime film entitled *Tuesday* (in production, scheduled for 2008).

## ADJOA ANDOH (FRANCINE JONES)

Adjoa Andoh was born in 1969. An early interest in rock music led her to dye her hair turquoise blue at one point in her youth, and she also played cello in a jazz trio for a while in hotels around Bristol, where she studied for a law degree for two years at Bristol Polytechnic before dropping out to concentrate on acting. She has worked extensively in the theatre since the mid-1980s and also has a lengthy list of TV credits to her name in a wide variety of roles dating back to 1990. In addition, she is an accomplished voice artist, having done many audiobook readings, perhaps most notably for the popular series of Alexander McCall Smith novels that began with *The No. 1 Ladies' Detective Agency*. She first appeared in *Doctor Who* under heavy prosthetic make-up as Sister Jatt, one of the cat-like Sisters of Plenitude, in 'New Earth', and then won the semi-regular role of Martha's mother Francine. She has one other *Doctor Who* connection: she took a role in the audio CD drama 'Year of the Pig' (Big Finish, 2006). She lives in South London with her husband Howard, whom she married in 2001 after some years together, and her three daughters, Jesse, Lily and Daisy.

## TREVOR LAIRD (CLIVE JONES)

Born in the Islington area of London in 1957, Trevor H Laird attended the Anna Scher Stage School (where Freema Agyeman would also later study) from around the age of 15. His big break came in 1976 when he won a part in Stephen Frears' award-winning *Playhouse* drama *Play Things* (BBC Two). He has worked regularly in TV and film ever since, generally in supporting character roles. One of these roles was as the guard captain Frax in the 'Mindwarp' segment of the classic series *Doctor Who* story 'The Trial of a Time Lord' (1986). He is perhaps best known, though, for having played the mod character Beefy in the cult film *Quadrophenia* (The Who Films, 1979). In 1998 he took up residence in the Harlesden area of London with his partner Kerry, with whom he subsequently had a daughter named Theo. In addition to his ongoing work as an actor, he has taught drama at a local adult education college.

## GUGU MBATHA-RAW (TISH JONES)

Gugu Mbatha-Raw was educated at the Henry Box School in Oxfordshire and later trained at the Guildhall School of Speech and Drama and the Royal Academy of Dramatic Art (RADA), graduating in 2004 at the end of a three year course. She is a skilled dancer, singer and saxophonist as well as an actor. After taking a number of theatre roles, she gained her first TV experience in a 2005 episode of *Holby City* (BBC One, 1999- ). Other TV parts then came in productions such as *Vital Signs* (ITV, 2006- ), two 2006 episodes of *Bad Girls* (ITV, 1999-2006) and perhaps most notable as the semi-regular character Jenny in eight 2006 episodes of *Spooks* (BBC One, 2002- ) (US title: *MI-5*). She made her feature film debut in a supporting role in the disturbing thriller *Straightheads* (Verve Pictures, 2007).

## REGGIE YATES (LEO JONES)

Reginald 'Reggie' Yates was born on 31 May 1983 in the Archway area of London. He made his TV debut as a child actor in a 1993 episode of *Between the Lines* (BBC One, 1992-1994) but got his big break in 2002 playing the regular character Carl Fenton in *Grange Hill* (BBC One, 1978- ). He is as well-known now for his presenting work as for his acting, having fronted numerous shows for CBBC and BBC One, perhaps most memorably *Top of the Pops* alongside Fearne Cotton, with whom he now co-hosts a regular show on BBC Radio 1. In 2005, he appeared in the BBC's celebrity singing contest *Comic Relief Does Fame Academy*, finishing fourth.

# CHAPTER TEN
# PRINCIPAL CREATIVE TEAM

RUSSELL T DAVIES (SHOWRUNNER, EXECUTIVE PRODUCER, LEAD WRITER)

Russell T Davies was born in Swansea, South Wales, in 1963. (He in fact has no middle name: he started using 'T' as an initial in the 1980s in order to distinguish himself from an actor, journalist and broadcaster also named Russell Davies.) He was educated at Olchfa School, a huge comprehensive, and had an early involvement with the West Glamorgan Youth Theatre in Swansea. He then studied English Literature at Oxford University, graduating in 1984. His TV career began with posts as a floor manager and production assistant at the BBC, where in the late 1980s he also trained as a director and gained a presenting credit on *Play School* (1987). He produced the children's series *Why Don't You ...?* for BBC Manchester from 1988 to 1992, during which time he also started to work as a writer, gaining credits on *The Flashing Blade* (1989), *Breakfast Serials* (1990) and *Chucklevision* (1991). His writing career moved up a gear when he was responsible for the acclaimed BBC children's serials *Dark Season* (1991) – which he also novelised for BBC Books – and *Century Falls* (1993). In 1992, he moved from the BBC to Granada, where he produced and wrote for the popular children's drama *Children's Ward* (1992-1996). He also started to gain writing credits for family and adult programmes, including *Cluedo* (1993), *Families* (1993), *The House of Windsor* (1994) and *Revelations* (1994). He worked briefly as a storyliner and writer on the hugely popular *Coronation Street* (1996) and contributed to Channel 4's *Springhill* (1996). It was at this time that he had his first professional association with *Doctor Who* – having been a long-time fan of the series – when he wrote the *New Adventures* novel *Damaged Goods* (1996) for Virgin Publishing. The following year, he was commissioned to contribute to the ITV period drama *The Grand* (1997), and ended up scripting the whole series after a number of other writers dropped out. He subsequently left Granada and joined a company called Red Productions, where he had a major success as creator, writer and producer of *Queer as Folk* (1999-2000), a ground-breaking two-season drama series for Channel 4 about a group of gay men in Manchester, which also spawned a US remake. Since then, his career has gone from strength to strength, with writer and executive producer credits on *Bob and Rose* (2001) and *Mine All Mine* (2004) for ITV and *The Second Coming* (2003), *Casanova* (2005) and of course *Doctor Who* (2005- ), *Torchwood* (2006- ) and *The Sarah Jane Adventures* (2007- ) for the BBC. He is now frequently cited as one of the most influential and powerful people in the British TV industry.

JULIE GARDNER (EXECUTIVE PRODUCER)

Julie Gardner was born in South Wales, near Neath, in 1969. Having gained a degree in English at London University, she began her working life as a teacher of English to secondary school pupils in Wales. In her mid-twenties, however, she decided that this was not the career for her, and she successfully applied for a job at the BBC, as the producer's secretary on the series *Our Friends in the North* (1996). She quickly ascended the ladder of promotion to script reader in the Serial Drama Department, then to script editor and then to producer, working on shows including *Silent Witness* (1996), *Sunburn* (1999) and *The Mrs Bradley Mysteries* (2000). In 2000, she left the BBC and took up a post as development producer at London Weekend Television. There she was responsible for dramas including a controversial modern-day retelling of Shakespeare's *Othello* (2001) and *Me and Mrs Jones* (2002). She was working on further ideas at LWT when, in 2003, she was head-hunted to become Head of Drama at BBC Wales. The new *Doctor Who* series gave her one of her first executive producer credits, and she has since gone on to fulfil a similar role on *Torchwood* and *The Sarah Jane Adventures*. Other projects she has overseen at BBC Wales include *Casanova* (2005), *Girl in the Café* (2005) and *Life on Mars* (2006-2007). On 21 September 2006 it was announced that she had been promoted to the post of the BBC's Head of Drama Commissioning, and would have special responsibility for implementing a cohesive independent drama strategy across the UK. She would however remain as Head of Drama, BBC Wales, for the foreseeable future, and would continue as executive producer of *Doctor Who*, *Torchwood* and *The Sarah Jane Adventures*.

## PHIL COLLINSON (EXECUTIVE PRODUCER, PRODUCER)

Phil Collinson started his career as an actor. The major role of Alexander in *Queer as Folk* (Channel 4, 1999-2000) was originally written specially for him by his long-time friend Russell T Davies, but ultimately went to another actor, Antony Cotton, on the strength of a superb audition. Collinson ultimately decided to concentrate on working behind the scenes in TV, having already had stints as a script editor and a writer on series such as *Springhill* (Sky One, 1996-1997) and *Emmerdale* (ITV, 1972- ). He gained his first job as a producer on *Peak Practice* (ITV, 1993-2002), then went on to fulfil the same role on a number of series for the BBC, including *Linda Green* (BBC One, 2001-2002) and the first seasons of *Born and Bred* (BBC One, 2002-2005) and *Sea of Souls* (BBC One, 2004-2007). A long-time *Doctor Who* fan, he jumped at the opportunity to become its producer when work began on the revived series in 2004. He continued in that capacity throughout the first three series, save for a short period of time when Susie Liggat deputised for him while he took a holiday, which saw him being accorded an executive producer credit instead. He also serves as series producer on *The Sarah Jane Adventures*. The *Daily Star* reported on 24 June 2007 that Collinson would be shortly moving on to become producer of the hugely popular soap opera *Coronation Street* (ITV, 1960- ), but this has not been confirmed at the time of writing.

## SUSIE LIGGAT (PRODUCER)

Susie Liggat's TV credits have come mainly as a first assistant director, including on series such as *Teachers* (Channel 4, 2001-2004) and *Casanova* (BBC Three, 2005). In 2006 she produced both *The Sarah Jane Adventures*: 'Invasion of the Bane' and, as holiday relief for Phil Collinson, one recording block on *Doctor Who*, comprising the episodes 'Human Nature' and 'The Family of Blood'. She is also serving as producer on two episodes of Series Four.

THIRD DIMENSION

## HELEN RAYNOR (SCRIPT EDITOR, WRITER)

After graduating from Cambridge University in the mid-1990s, Helen Raynor began her career in the theatre, as an assistant director and director for a number of companies, including the Bush Theatre, the Royal Shakespeare Company and the Royal Opera House. She then joined the BBC, where she became script editor of BBC One's daytime serial *Doctors* (2002-2004). This led on to a post as one of the two script editors on the new *Doctor Who* (2005- ). She has also gained credits as a writer for the theatre (*Waterloo Exit Two*, Young Vic, 2003), for radio (*Running Away With the Hairdresser*, BBC Radio 4, 2005) and for TV (*Cake*, BBC One, 2006). She contributed the episode 'Ghost Machine' to Series One of *Torchwood*, which then led on to her commission to write 'Daleks in Manhattan'/'Evolution of the Daleks' for *Doctor Who*.

## GARETH ROBERTS (WRITER)

Gareth Roberts was born in 1968. He studied drama at college and worked as a clerk at the Court of Appeal while also pursuing an interest in writing. In the 1990s he authored seven acclaimed *Doctor Who* novels, plus novelisations of two episodes of *Cracker* (ITV, 1993-1996), for Virgin Publishing. He also wrote for *Doctor Who Magazine* and for Big Finish's tie-in audio CD drama range before coming to work on the new series via the digital mini-adventure 'Attack of the Graske' and the 'Tardisode' teasers for Series Two. He has written the new series novels *Only Human* (BBC Books, 2005) and *I Am A Dalek* (BBC Books, 2006) and numerous *Doctor Who* short stories. He is also the lead writer on *The Sarah Jane Adventures*. His other TV credits include: storylines for *Springhill* (Sky One, 1996-1997); episodes of *Emmerdale* (ITV, 1972- ) in 1998; episodes of *Brookside* (Channel 4, 1982-2003) over a four year period from 1999; and co-written episodes of *Randall and Hopkirk (Deceased)* (BBC One, 2000-2001) and *Swiss Toni* (BBC Three, 2004-2004).

## STEPHEN GREENHORN (WRITER)

Stephen Greenhorn was born on 5 September 1964 in West Lothian, Scotland. He has written extensively for the stage – including the hit play *Passing Places* (2000) and the musical *Sunshine on Leith* (2007) based on the songs of the Proclaimers – as well as for TV. His earliest TV writing credits came on two episodes of *The Bill* (ITV, 1983- ) in 1996 and 1998 respectively, and on two episodes of *Where the Heart Is* (ITV1, 1996-2006) in 1998. He went on to script the series *Glasgow Kiss* (BBC One, 2000) and the docudrama *Derailed* (BBC One, 2005) and to create and write for the Scottish soap opera *River City* (BBC One Scotland, 2002- ). More recent credits include an acclaimed adaptation of Jean Rhys's novel *Wide Sargasso Sea* (BBC Four, 2007), which led on to his commission to contribute 'The Lazarus Experiment' to *Doctor Who*.

## CHRIS CHIBNALL (WRITER)

Chris Chibnall was raised in Lancashire and began his TV career as a football archivist and occasional floor manager for Sky Sports. He then took a succession of

96

administrative jobs with different theatre companies including, between 1996 and 1999, the experimental group Complicite. He subsequently became a full-time writer, initially for the theatre, with credits including *Gaffer!* – a single-actor piece about homophobia in football, first staged in 1999 – and *Kiss Me Like You Mean It* – which premiered at the Soho Theatre in 2001 and has also been staged in a number of European venues, including Paris under the title *Un Baiser, Un Vrai*. On the strength of his play scripts, he was invited by the BBC to develop a period drama series for them. This became *Born and Bred* (2002-2005), which he not only created but also contributed to as consultant producer and lead writer throughout its four seasons. His other TV writing credits include episodes of *All About George* (2005) and *Life on Mars* (2006). He is lead writer on *Torchwood*, and contributed four episodes of his own to its first series.

## PAUL CORNELL (WRITER)

Paul Cornell was born on 18 July 1967. He first became known as a writer within *Doctor Who* fandom in the 1980s and went on to become one of the most acclaimed contributors to the series' tie-in novel and audio CD drama ranges. He later scripted the animated webcast story 'Scream of the Shalka' (2003). For the novel *Love and War* (Virgin Publishing, 1992), he created the Doctor's companion Bernice Summerfield, who has since featured in her own spin-off ranges, to which Cornell has also contributed. His debut TV credit came when he won a BBC young writers' competition with his script for *Kingdom Come* (BBC Two, 1990). This led on to him writing some episodes of *Children's Ward* (ITV1, 1988-1998) and creating and writing his own children's series, *Wavelength* (ITV1, 1997). He was one of the principal writers on *Springhill* (Sky One, 1996-1997), had a short stint working on *Coronation Street* (ITV, 1960- ) and scripted an episode of *Love in the 21st Century* (Channel 4, 1999). During the early 2000s he has written mainly for the BBC, contributing episodes to *Doctors* (BBC One, 2000- ), *Casualty* (BBC One, 1986- ), *Born and Bred* (BBC One, 2002-2005), *Holby City* (BBC One, 1999- ), *Robin Hood* (BBC One, 2006- ) and, of course, *Doctor Who*. He is the author of two non-*Doctor Who* novels, *Something More* (Gollancz, 2001) and *British Summertime* (Gollancz, 2002), and has scripted a number of comic book stories, most notably his own six-issue mini-series *Wisdom* (Marvel Comics, 2007).

## STEVEN MOFFAT (WRITER)

Steven Moffat was born in 1961 in Paisley, Scotland. He had gained a degree in English and begun working as a teacher when a chance encounter between his father and a TV producer led to him being commissioned to write the children's series *Press Gang* (ITV, 1989-1993), which quickly acquired cult status. He went on to create and write the sitcom *Joking Apart* (BBC Two, 1993-1995), which was inspired by the breakdown of his first marriage and won the Bronze Rose of Montreux award, and the less-well-received *Chalk* (BBC One, 1997). His biggest success to date came with the sitcom *Coupling* (BBC Two/BBC Three, 2000-2004), which was also the subject of a short-lived American remake (NBC, 2003). More recently, he wrote the acclaimed drama *Jekyll* (BBC One, 2007) as a modern take on Robert Louis Stevenson's *Strange Case of Dr Jekyll and Mr Hyde* (Longmans, Green &

Co, 1886). He scripted the spoof *Doctor Who* story 'The Curse of Fatal Death' for BBC One's *Comic Relief* telethon in 1999 and has contributed a number of short stories to various *Doctor Who* collections. He has the distinction of being the only writer other than Russell T Davies to have scripted episodes for each of the first three series of the new *Doctor Who.*

## CHARLES PALMER (DIRECTOR)

Charles Palmer is the son of well-known British actor Geoffrey Palmer (who has made a number of *Doctor Who* appearances). He made his directorial debut on the short film *The Magic of Vincent* (2001). Other credits include episodes of *Linda Green* (BBC One, 2001-2002), *Night and Day* (ITV1, 2001-3), *Marple* (ITV1, 2004- ), *Life Begins* (ITV1, 2004-2006), *The Ghost Squad* (Channel 4, 2005- ) and *Vital Signs* (ITV1, 2006- ).

## RICHARD CLARK (DIRECTOR)

Richard Clark's other directorial credits include: *Metroland: The Card Game* (ITV1, 1995); *My Dead Buddy* (Channel 4, 1997), which won the 1997 Lloyds Bank/Channel 4 Film Challenge; *Hungry* (Channel 4, 1999), *Shockers: Dance* (Channel 4, 1999), *Waitress* (Channel 4, 2001), *Whistleblower* (ITV1, 2007) and *Life on Mars* (BBC One, 2006-2007).

## JAMES STRONG (DIRECTOR)

James Strong's first TV credits were as a documentary maker, on *Critical Mass* (Carlton, 1998), *World in Action* (ITV, 1998/99), *My FC* (Channel 5, 2000) and *Crimewatch UK* (BBC1, 2000). He then moved into directing comedy and drama programmes, including *Otis Lee Crenshaw* (Channel 4, 2000), *Jack Dee's Happy Hour* (BBC One, 2001), *Doctors* (BBC1, 2000-2001), *Nothing but the Truth* (ITV1, 2001), *Blood on her Hands* (ITV1, 2002), *Mile High* (Sky One, 2002), *Holby City* (BBC One, 2002-2004), *Casualty* (BBC One, 2004), *The Good Citizen* (BBC One, 2004), *Rocket Man* (BBC One, 2005) and *Doctor Who*: 'The Impossible Planet'/'The Satan Pit' (BBC One, 2005). He both wrote and directed the comedy short film *Sold* (2002) and the TV dramas *Lady Jane* (ITV1, 2003) and *Billie Jo* (ITV1, 2004).

## GRAEME HARPER (DIRECTOR)
Graeme Harper was born on 11 March 1945. He started his working life as a child actor, appearing in TV adaptations of *The Pickwick Papers* (Associated Redifussion, 1956) and *The Silver Sword* (BBC, 1957), amongst other productions, before becoming a floor assistant at the BBC in 1965. It was in the latter capacity that he first worked on *Doctor Who*, on stories including 'The Power of the Daleks' (1966). He was promoted to assistant floor manager in 1969, being assigned to *Doctor Who* again on 'Colony in Space' (1971), 'Planet of the Daleks' (1973) and 'Planet of the Spiders' (1974). His next promotion, in 1975, was to production assistant, in which capacity he worked on 'The Seeds of Doom' (1976) and 'Warriors' Gate' (1981). He then successfully completed the BBC's directors' course. The fifth Doctor's swansong 'The Caves of Androzani' (1984) was the first job he got as a freelance

director, after handling some of the final episodes of the hospital drama *Angels* (BBC One, 1975-1983) in-house at the BBC. He went on to direct one further classic series story, 'Revelation of the Daleks' (1984), and would also have handled the third story of Season 23 had the series not then been put on temporary hiatus by Michael Grade, Controller of BBC One at that time. He subsequently became one of Britain's most sought-after TV directors, building up an impressive list of credits on shows such as: *The District Nurse* (BBC One, 1984-1987); *Star Cops* (BBC Two, 1987); *Boon* (ITV, 1986-1992); *The House of Elliot* (BBC One, 1991-1994); numerous episodes of *Casualty* (BBC One, 1986- ); *The Royal* (ITV, 2003- ); some 2003 and 2005 episodes of *Byker Grove* (BBC One, 1989-2006); and three episodes of *Robin Hood* (BBC One, 2006- ). He came close to working on *Doctor Who* again both in 1989, when he was approached to direct 'Battlefield' (an assignment he was prevented from taking on as he was already committed to *Boon*), and in 1993, when he was scheduled to helm the planned, but ultimately unmade, thirtieth anniversary story 'The Dark Dimension'. He finally returned to direct the episodes 'Rise of the Cybermen', 'The Age of Steel', 'Army of Ghosts' and 'Doomsday' for Series Two, and '42' and 'Utopia' for Series Three. He has since worked on episodes for Series One of *The Sarah Jane Adventures* and will be returning to *Doctor Who* again on Series Four.

## HETTIE MACDONALD (DIRECTOR)

Hettie Macdonald has worked mainly in the theatre. She studied English at Bristol University, then in 1985 joined the Royal Court Theatre under a scheme for trainee directors. Her career really took off when in 1986, at the age of 24, she became the youngest woman ever to direct a play in London's West End, taking over a production of *The Normal Heart* at the Albery Theatre. In 1991 she became associate director at the Wosley Theatre, Ipswich, her credits including *A View From the Bridge* and *Who's Afraid of Virginia Woolf?*. Early in 1995 she directed Carol Braverman's play <u>*The Yiddish Trojan Women*</u> for the Soho Theatre Company. Having also directed a production of Jonathan Harvey's play *Beautiful Thing* at the Bush Theatre in 1993, she was then asked by World Productions to helm their film adaptation of it. Although originally intended for TV, this was eventually given a theatrical release in 1995, winning considerable acclaim for its realistic portrayal of a gay teen romance. Aside from *Doctor Who*, Macdonald's other TV credits include two 1997 episodes of *Casualty* (BBC One, 1986- ), three episodes of *Servants* (BBC One, 2003), a 2005 instalment of *Agatha Christie's Poirot* (ITV, 1989- ) and the play *Banglatown Banquet* (BBC Two, 2006).

## COLIN TEAGUE (DIRECTOR)

Colin Teague's directorial credits include the feature films *Northwest One* (1999), *Shooters* (2002), *Spivs* (2004) and *The Last Drop* (2005), all of which apart from *Shooters* he also co-wrote, and episodes of *London's Burning* (ITV1, 2002) and *Holby City* (BBC One, 2003-2006). He directed the episodes 'Ghost Machine' and 'Greeks Bearing Gifts' for the first series of *Torchwood* and the 'Invasion of the Bane' special for *The Sarah Jane Adventures*, making him the only director to date to have worked on both of the spin-offs as well as on *Doctor Who* itself.

## EDWARD THOMAS (PRODUCTION DESIGNER)

Edward Thomas took a foundation course in art and design after leaving school, and then studied at the Wimbledon School of Art, from which he graduated with a BA (Hons) degree in 3-D Design, specialising in theatre. He began his career as a designer on a wide variety of commercials and a number of theatrical productions, including *Turandot* for the Royal Opera Company at Wembley Arena, *Under Milk Wood* for the Dylan Thomas Theatre Company and Shakespeare's *Twelfth Night* and *Cymbeline* for the Ludlow Festival. This was followed by work on numerous feature films, including over a dozen South African productions in the early 1990s and *The Mystery of Edwin Drood* (1993), *Resurrection Man* (1998), *Darkness Falls* (1999) and *The Meeksville Ghost* (2001). He also gained credits on a wide range of TV shows including, for BBC Wales, *Jones*, *The Coal Project* and, of course, *Doctor Who* (2005- ) and *Torchwood* (2006- ). He has sometimes been credited as Edward Alan Thomas or simply as Ed Thomas, and is represented by the Creative Media Management agency.

# CREDITS

# DOCTOR WHO
# THE RUNAWAY BRIDE and
# SERIES THREE (2007)

CREDITS[12]

Producer: Phil Collinson (3.00, 3.01, 3.02, 3.03, 3.04, 3.05, 3.06, 3.07, 3.10, 3.11, 3.12, 3.13), Susie Liggat (3.08, 3.09)

MAIN CAST

David Tennant (The Doctor) and (Smith) (3.08)[13]
Catherine Tate (Donna Noble) (3.00)
Freema Agyeman (Martha Jones) (3.01-3.13)
Adjoa Andoh (Francine Jones) (3.01, 3.06, 3.07, 3.12, 3.13)
Gugu Mbatha-Raw (Tish Jones) (3.01, 3.06, 3.12, 3.13)
Reggie Yates (Leo Jones) (3.01, 3.06, 3.12, 3.13[14])
Trevor Laird (Clive Jones) (3.01, 3.12, 3.13)
John Barrowman (Captain Jack Harkness) (3.11, 3.12, 3.13)
John Simm (The Master) (3.11[15], 3.12, 3.13)

PRODUCTION TEAM

1st Assistant Director: Peter Bennett (3.00, 3.04, 3.05, 3.12, 3.13), Gareth Williams (3.01, 3.02, 3.07, 3.10, 3.11), Dan Mumford (3.03, 3.06), Richard Harris (3.08, 3.09)
2nd Assistant Director: Steffan Morris (3.00, 3.01, 3.02, 3.04, 3.05, 3.07, 3.08, 3.09, 3.11, 3.12, 3.13), Jennie Fava (3.03, 3.06), Anna Evans (3.10)
3rd Assistant Director: Sarah Davies (all except 3.10), Paul Bennett (3.10)
Location Manager: Patrick Schweitzer (3.00), Gareth Skelding (3.00, 3.01, 3.02, 3.04, 3.05, 3.07, 3.10, 3.11), Lowri Thomas (3.03, 3.06, 3.08, 3.09), Antonia Grant (3.12, 3.13)
Location Scout: Bronwen Evans (3.08, 3.09)
Unit Manager: Rhys Griffiths (3.00, 3.01, 3.02, 3.03, 3.06, 3.07, 3.11, 3.12, 3.13), Huw

---

[12] Where an episode number (or more than one) appears in brackets after a person's name in the listing, this means that they were credited only on the episode (or episodes) indicated. Otherwise, the person concerned was credited on all 14 episodes. Some production roles were credited only on certain episodes.
[13] For 'Human Nature', David Tennant was credited as 'The Doctor/Smith' on screen and as 'John Smith' in *Radio Times*.
[14] Has no dialogue in 3.13, and is seen only in the background of one shot.
[15] Not credited in *Radio Times* for 3.11, to preserve the surprise of the Master's return.

Jones (3.04, 3.05, 3.08, 3.09), Geraint Havard Jones (3.10)
Production Co-ordinator: Jess van Niekerk
Production Secretary: Kevin Myers
Production Assistant: Debi Griffiths
Production Runner: Victoria Wheel (3.00), Siân Eve Goldsmith (3.01, 3.02, 3.03, 3.05, 3.08, 3.09, 3.11)
Driver: Wayne Humphreys (3.00, 3.04, 3.05, 3.08, 3.09, 3.11, 3.13), Malcolm Kearney (3.00, 3.04, 3.05, 3.08, 3.09, 3.11, 3.13)
Floor Runner: Barry Phillips (3.00, 3.02, 3.04, 3.06), Heddi Joy Taylor (3.01, 3.03, 3.05, 3.07, 3.08, 3.09, 3.11, 3.12, 3.13), Lowri Denman (3.03, 3.04, 3.05, 3.06, 3.07, 3.08, 3.09, 3.13), Glen Coxon (3.10), Tom Evans (3.10)
Contracts Assistant: Bethan Britton (3.00, 3.01, 3.03, 3.05, 3.07, 3.09, 3.11, 3.13), Kath Blackman (3.02, 3.04, 3.06, 3.08, 3.10, 3.12)
Continuity: Non Eleri Hughes (all except 3.10), Llinos Wyn Jones (3.10)
Script Editor: Simon Winstone (3.00, 3.01, 3.02, 3.03, 3.06, 3.07, 3.11, 3.12, 3.13), Lindsey Alford (3.04, 3.05, 3.08, 3.09), Helen Raynor (3.10)[16]
Camera Operator: Julian Barber (3.01, 3.02), Roger Pearce (3.04, 3.05, 3.07, 3.11)
Focus Puller: Steve Rees (all except 3.10), Ant Hugill (3.10)
2nd Camera Operator[17]: Siân Elin Palfrey (3.00), Steven Hall (3.01, 3.02, 3.08, 3.09), Erik Wilson (3.12, 3.13)
2nd Unit Focus Puller[18]: Jamie Southcott (3.08, 3.09, 3.12, 3.13)
Polecam Operator: Andy Leonard (3.06)
Grip: John Robinson (all except 3.10), Clive Baldwin (3.10)
Camera Assistant: Penny Shipton (3.06), Tom Hartley (3.08, 3.09, 3.12, 3.13), Stephen Andrews (3.10)
Boom Operator: Jon Thomas (3.00, 3.03, 3.04, 3.05, 3.06, 3.12, 3.13), Jeff Welch (3.01, 3.02, 3.07, 3.08, 3.09, 3.10, 3.11), Bryn Thomas (3.04, 3.05, 3.06, 3.08, 3.09, 3.13), Jillian Speed (3.10)
Gaffer: Mark Hutchings (all except 3.10), Peter Chester (3.10)
Best Boy: Peter Chester (3.00, 3.01, 3.02, 3.03, 3.04, 3.05, 3.06, 3.07, 3.11, 3.12, 3.13), Steve Slocombe (3.08, 3.09), Chris Davies (3.10)
Electrician: Clive Johnson (3.04, 3.05, 3.08, 3.09, 3.11), Ben Griffiths (3.04, 3.05, 3.08, 3.09, 3.11), Steve Slocombe (3.05, 3.11)
Stunt Co-ordinator: David Forman (3.00), Tom Lucy (3.01, 3.02, 3.03, 3.04, 3.05, 3.06, 3.12, 3.13), Crispin Layfield (3.01, 3.02, 3.03, 3.10, 3.13), Abbi Collins (3.07, 3.11), Glenn Marks (3.08, 3.09, 3.10)
Stunt Performer: George Cottle (3.00, 3.01), Tina Amskell (3.00), Richard Hammett (3.00), Gary Hoptrough (3.00), Rob Hunt (3.00), Nina Armstrong (3.00), Will Willoughby (3.01, 3.05), Dean Forster (3.01), Maxine Whittaker (3.02), Andy Smart (3.05), Guy List (3.05), Charles Jarman (3.06), Gordon Seed (3.12), Dani Biernat (3.12), Curtis Rivers (3.12)
Wires: Bob Schofield (3.02), Kevin Welch (3.07)
Choreographer: Ailsa Berk[19] (3.01, 3.04, 3.05, 3.08, 3.09)

[16] Gary Russell also worked as a script editor, uncredited, during Series Three.
[17] Credit given as '2nd Unit Camera Operator' on 3.08 and 3.09.
[18] Credit given as '2nd Focus Puller' on 3.12 and 3.13.
[19] First name misspelt 'Alisa' on 3.04.

CREDITS

Chief Supervising Art Director: Stephen Nicholas
Art Department Production Manager: Jonathan Marquand Allison
Art Department Co-ordinator: Matthew North (3.00, 3.01, 3.02, 3.03, 3.04, 3.05, 3.06, 3.07, 3.08, 3.09, 3.10, 3.11)
Chief Props Master: Adrian Anscombe
Supervising Art Director: Arwel Wyn Jones
Associate Designer: James North
Set Decorator: Tristan Peatfield (3.00, 3.12, 3.13), David Morison (3.01, 3.02, 3.08, 3.09), Malin Lindholm (3.03, 3.06), Julian Luxton (3.04, 3.05, 3.07, 3.11), Keith Dunne (3.10)
Standby Art Director: Lee Gammon (3.00, 3.04, 3.05, 3.07, 3.11), Tim Dickel (3.01, 3.02, 3.08, 3.09), Leonie Rintler (3.03, 3.06), Dafydd Shurmer (3.10), Lisa McDiarmid (3.12, 3.13)
Design Assistant: Peter McKinstry (3.00, 3.02, 3.04, 3.06, 3.07, 3.08, 3.09, 3.10, 3.11, 3.12, 3.13), Ben Austin (3.00, 3.02, 3.06), Ian Bunting (3.01, 3.03, 3.05, 3.07, 3.09, 3.10, 3.11, 3.12, 3.13), Al Roberts (3.01, 3.03, 3.05, 3.07, 3.09, 3.10, 3.11, 3.12, 3.13), Rob Dicks (3.04, 3.08, 3.09, 3.10)
Cyfle Trainee: Anna Coote (3.01), Jon Grundon (3.02), Christian Ibell (3.03), Kate Meyrick (3.04), Katherine Lewis (3.05), Naseem Sayed (3.06), Christina Tom (3.08, 3.09), Sarah Payne (3.10)
Storyboard Artist: Shaun Williams (3.00, 3.01, 3.03, 3.05, 3.07, 3.09, 3.11, 3.13)
Standby Props: Phill Shellard (all except 3.10), Clive Clarke (3.00, 3.01, 3.02), Nick Murray (3.03, 3.04, 3.05, 3.06, 3.07, 3.08, 3.09, 3.11, 3.12, 3.13), Gareth Thomas (3.10), Rhys Jones (3.10)
Standby Carpenter: Paul Jones (all except 3.10), Will Pope (3.10)
Standby Painter: Louise Bohling (3.00), Ellen Woods (3.01, 3.02, 3.03, 3.04, 3.05, 3.06, 3.07, 3.08, 3.09, 3.11, 3.12, 3.13), Julia Challis (3.10)
Standby Rigger: Bryan Griffiths (all except 3.10), Keith Freeman (3.10)
Property Master: Paul Aitken (3.00, 3.03, 3.06, 3.08, 3.09, 3.12, 3.13), Phil Lyons (3.01, 3.02, 3.04, 3.05, 3.07, 3.11), Dewi Thomas (3.10)
Props Buyer: Joelle Rumbelow (3.00), Catherine Samuel (3.01, 3.02, 3.08, 3.09, 3.12, 3.13), Bloanid Maddrell (3.03, 3.06), Ben Morris (3.04, 3.05, 3.07, 3.11), Sue Jackson-Potter (3.10)
Props Chargehand: Gareth Jeanne (3.01, 3.03, 3.05, 3.07, 3.09, 3.11, 3.12, 3.13), Martin Broadbent (3.10)
Props Storeman: Stuart Wooddisse (3.01), Martin Griffiths (3.03, 3.05, 3.09, 3.10)
Forward Dresser: Amy Chandler (3.01, 3.03, 3.05, 3.09), Austin Curtis (3.10)
Practical Electrician: Albert James (3.01, 3.03, 3.05, 3.07, 3.09, 3.11, 3.13)
Props Maker: Barry Jones (3.00), Penny Howarth (3.02, 3.04, 3.06, 3.08, 3.09, 3.10, 3.12), Mark Cordory (3.02, 3.04, 3.06, 3.08, 3.09, 3.10), Nick Robatto (3.02, 3.04, 3.06, 3.08, 3.09, 3.10, 3.12)
Senior Props Maker[20]: Barry Jones (3.01, 3.02, 3.04, 3.06, 3.08, 3.09, 3.10, 3.12, 3.13)
Construction Manager: Matthew Hywel-Davies
Construction Chargehand: Allen Jones (3.02, 3.04, 3.06, 3.08, 3.09, 3.10, 3.12), Scott Fisher (3.08, 3.09, 3.10, 3.12)
Graphics: BBC Wales Graphics
Assistant Costume Designer: Rose Goodhart (3.00), Marnie Ormiston (3.01, 3.02, 3.03,

---

[20] Credited as 'Chief Props Maker' on 3.06, 3.10, 3.12 and 3.13.

3.04, 3.05, 3.06, 3.07, 3.08, 3.09, 3.11, 3.12, 3.13)

Costume Supervisor: Lindsay Bonaccorsi (all except 3.10), Charlotte Mitchell (3.10)

Costume Assistant: Sheenah O'Marah (all except 3.10), Kirsty Wilkinson (all except 3.10), Bobby Peach (3.10), Sara Morgan (3.10)

Make-Up Artists: Pam Mullins (all except 3.10), Steve Smith (all except 3.10), John Munro (all except 3.10), Alison Sing (3.10)

Casting Associate: Andy Brierley, Kirsty Robertson (3.07, 3.08, 3.09, 3.10, 3.11, 3.12, 3.13)

Assistant Editor: Ceres Doyle (3.00, 3.01, 3.02, 3.03), Tim Hodges (3.03, 3.04, 3.05, 3.06, 3.07, 3.08, 3.09, 3.10, 3.11, 3.12, 3.13), Matthew Mullins (3.08, 3.09, 3.10, 3.11)

Post Production Supervisor: Samantha Hall, Chris Blatchford

Post Production Co-ordinator: Marie Brown

Special Effects Co-ordinator: Ben Ashmore (all except 3.07)

Special Effects Supervisor: Paul Kelly (3.00, 3.01, 3.02, 3.03, 3.04, 3.05, 3.06, 3.08, 3.09, 3.10, 3.11), Danny Hargreaves (3.12, 3.13)

Special FX Technician: Danny Hargreaves (3.05, 3.06, 3.08, 3.09, 3.10), Henry Brook (3.05, 3.06, 3.08, 3.09, 3.10), Dan Bentley (3.10, 3.11, 3.12, 3.13), Richard Magrin (3.10, 3.11, 3.12, 3.13)

Prosthetics Designer: Neill Gorton (all except 3.07)

Prosthetics Supervisor: Rob Mayor (all except 3.07)

On Set Prosthetics Supervisor: Pete Hawkins (3.05, 3.11), Lotta Hogvist (3.08, 3.09), Matt O'Toole (3.10)

Prosthetics Technician: Matt O'Toole (3.05), Helen Rowe (3.06), Alex Wathey (3.06), Lisa Crawley (3.08, 3.09), Anthony Parker (3.09, 3.11, 3.12, 3.13), Claire Folkard (3.10), Gustav Hoegen (3.12, 3.13[21])

VFX Editor: Ceres Doyle (3.04, 3.05, 3.06, 3.07, 3.08, 3.09, 3.10, 3.11, 3.12, 3.13)

On-Line Editor: Matthew Clarke (3.00, 3.01, 3.02, 3.03, 3.04, 3.05, 3.06, 3.07), Mark Bright (3.08, 3.09, 3.11, 3.12, 3.13), Simon C Holden (3.10)

Colourist: Mick Vincent

3D Artist: Paul Burton (3.00, 3.03, 3.11, 3.12), Nick Webber (3.00, 3.02, 3.03, 3.07, 3.11, 3.13), Matthew McKinney (3.00, 3.01, 3.03, 3.05, 3.12), Mark Wallman (3.00, 3.01, 3.05, 3.11, 3.13), Andy Guest (3.00, 3.02, 3.07, 3.13), Chris Tucker (3.00, 3.02), Nicolas Hernandez (3.00, 3.06, 3.07, 3.11, 3.12, 3.13), Jean-Claude Deguara (3.00, 3.03, 3.06, 3.07, 3.11, 3.12, 3.13), Bruce Mogroune (3.01, 3.02, 3.03, 3.07, 3.12), Will Pryor (3.01, 3.05, 3.07, 3.12, 3.13), Neil Roche (3.03, 3.06, 3.13), Jeff North (3.03, 3.06, 3.12), Serena Cacciata (3.03, 3.05, 3.07, 3.12), Adam Burnett (3.04, 3.13), Jean Yves Audouard (3.04, 3.06, 3.13)

2D Artist: Sara Bennett (3.00, 3.01, 3.02, 3.03, 3.04, 3.06, 3.07, 3.11, 3.12, 3.13), Russell Horth (3.00, 3.01, 3.02, 3.04, 3.05, 3.07, 3.11, 3.12), Melissa Butler-Adams (3.00, 3.01, 3.02, 3.05, 3.06, 3.13), Bryan Bartlett (3.00, 3.01, 3.02, 3.04, 3.05, 3.06, 3.07, 3.11, 3.12), Astrid Busser-Cassas (3.00), Adam Rowland (3.00, 3.02, 3.03, 3.04, 3.06, 3.07, 3.11, 3.12), Simon C Holden (3.00, 3.01, 3.05, 3.13), Greg Spencer (3.00, 3.04, 3.05, 3.06, 3.11, 3.13), Joseph Courtis (3.00, 3.01, 3.02, 3.04, 3.07, 3.11, 3.13), Tim Barter (3.01, 3.03, 3.04, 3.06, 3.07, 3.11, 3.12), Adrianna Logo[22] (3.05, 3.12)

VFX Co-ordinator: Jenna Powell (3.00, 3.01, 3.02, 3.03, 3.04, 3.05, 3.06, 3.07, 3.11, 3.12,

[21] Also worked on 3.01, uncredited.
[22] First name spelt 'Ariana' on 3.12 and 3.13.

3.13), Rebecca Johnson (3.00, 3.01, 3.02, 3.03, 3.04, 3.05, 3.06, 3.07, 3.11, 3.12, 3.13)
VFX Production Assistant: Marianne Paton (3.08, 3.09, 3.10, 3.12, 3.13)
Digital Matte Painter: Simon Wicker (3.01, 3.02, 3.03, 3.04, 3.05, 3.06, 3.12, 3.13), Charlie Bennett (3.01, 3.04, 3.05, 3.06, 3.13), Alex Fort (3.02, 3.04, 3.05, 3.11)
On Set VFX Supervisor: Barney Curnow (3.00, 3.01, 3.02, 3.03, 3.04, 3.05, 3.06, 3.07, 3.11, 3.12, 3.13)
Model Unit: Lucas FX (3.00)
Dubbing Mixer: Tim Ricketts
Supervising Sound Editor: Paul McFadden
Sound Editor: Doug Sinclair (3.01, 3.02, 3.03, 3.04, 3.05, 3.06, 3.07, 3.08, 3.09, 3.10, 3.11, 3.12, 3.13)
Sound FX Editor: Paul Jefferies
Foley Editor: Kelly-Marie Angell (3.04, 3.05, 3.06, 3.08, 3.09, 3.10, 3.11)
Finance Manager: Chris Rogers
Vocals: Neil Hannon (3.00)

With thanks to the BBC National Orchestra of Wales

Original Theme Music: Ron Grainer
Casting Director: Andy Pryor CDG
Production Executive: Julie Scott
Senior Production Accountant: Endaf Emyr Williams (3.08, 3.09, 3.12, 3.13)
Production Accountant: Endaf Emyr Williams (3.00, 3.01, 3.02, 3.03, 3.04, 3.05, 3.06, 3.07, 3.10), Oliver Ager (3.08, 3.09, 3.11, 3.12, 3.13)
Sound Recordist: Julian Howarth (3.00, 3.01, 3.02, 3.03, 3.06, 3.08, 3.09, 3.12, 3.13), Ron Bailey (3.04, 3.05, 3.07, 3.11), Ray Parker (3.10)
Costume Designer: Louise Page (all except 3.10), Ray Holman (3.10)
Make-Up Designer: Barbara Southcott (all except 3.10), Emma Bailey (3.10)
Music: Murray Gold
Visual Effects: The Mill
Visual FX Producer: Will Cohen, Marie Jones
Visual FX Supervisor: Dave Houghton
Special Effects: Any Effects
Prosthetics: Millennium FX (all except 3.07)
Editor: John Richards (3.00, 3.03, 3.06), Matthew Tabern (3.01, 3.02, 3.08, 3.09), Mike Jones (3.04, 3.05), Will Oswald (3.07, 3.11), Jamie McCoan (3.10), Mike Hopkins (3.12, 3.13)
Production Designer: Edward Thomas
Director of Photography: Rory Taylor (3.00, 3.03, 3.06, 3.08, 3.09, 3.12, 3.13), Ernie Vincze BSC (3.01, 3.02, 3.04, 3.05, 3.07, 3.10, 3.11)
Production Manager: Tracie Simpson (3.00, 3.03, 3.06, 3.08, 3.09, 3.12, 3.13), Patrick Schweitzer (3.01, 3.02, 3.04, 3.05, 3.07, 3.11), Debbi Slater (3.10)

Executive Producer: Russell T Davies, Julie Gardner, Phil Collinson (3.08, 3.09)

BBC Wales in association with the Canadian Broadcasting Corporation

# CRITIQUE

The durations quoted in the episode guide below are for the complete versions of the episodes on the BBC's master tapes. The durations on transmission were generally a few seconds shorter, as each episode tended to be cut into slightly by the preceding and/or following continuity caption and announcement.

Readers who have yet to see the episodes may wish to bear in mind that this guide is a comprehensive one that contains many plot 'spoilers'.

# 3.00 – CHRISTMAS SPECIAL 2006 THE RUNAWAY BRIDE

Writer: Russell T Davies
Director: Euros Lyn

DEBUT TRANSMISSION DETAILS

BBC One
Date: 25 December 2006. Scheduled time: 7.00 pm. Actual time: 7.00 pm.

BBC Three
Date: 27 December 2006. Scheduled time: 8.00 pm. Actual time: 8.00 pm.

Duration: 60′ 19″

ADDITIONAL CREDITED CAST[23]

Sarah Parish (Empress), Don Gilet (Lance Bennett), Howard Attfield (Geoff Noble), Jacqueline King (Sylvia Noble), Trevor Georges (Vicar), Glen Wilson (Taxi Driver), Krystal Archer (Nerys), Rhodri Meilir (Rhodri), Zafirah Boateng (Little Girl), Paul Kasey (Robot Santa).

PLOT

It is Christmas Eve, and Donna Noble is on the point of marrying her fiancé Lance when she suddenly vanishes from the church and reappears inside the TARDIS, where the Doctor is still trying to come to terms with the loss of his companion Rose. It transpires that Donna's body has been infused with huon energy – a remnant of which also exists in the heart of the TARDIS, explaining why she was drawn to the ship. It is Lance who has poisoned her with the huon particles, acting under the direction of the Empress of the Racnoss, the last survivor of an ancient and destructive race, who has promised to show him the wonders of the universe. The spider-like Empress wants to use Donna as a 'key' to reawaken her children, who are in hibernation in a spaceship at the Earth's core. Ultimately it is Lance who fulfils this purpose, when the Empress has him force-fed with huon particles and dropped into a shaft that has been cut down to the spaceship. The Doctor offers to relocate the Racnoss to another, uninhabited world, but when the Empress refuses, he destroys her children by draining water from the Thames into the shaft. Army tanks then open fire on the Empress's spaceship, destroying it. The Doctor invites

---

[23] David Tennant, Catherine Tate and Sarah Parish were the only cast members credited in *Radio Times*.

Donna to join him on his travels, but she declines, and he departs in the TARDIS.

## QUOTE, UNQUOTE

- **Doctor:** 'Oh, but that's what you do, the human race: make sense out chaos, marking it out with weddings and Christmas and calendars. This whole process is beautiful, but only if it's being observed.'
- **Doctor:** 'You've seen it out there. It's beautiful.'
  **Donna:** 'And it's terrible. That place was flooding and burning, and they were dying, and you stood there like ... I don't know ... a stranger. And then you made it snow. I mean, you scare me to death.'
- **Donna:** 'Am I ever going to see you again?'
  **Doctor:** 'If I'm lucky.'

## CONTINUITY POINTS

- This episode is set in London on Christmas Eve, a year after 'The Christmas Invasion'. As evidence from Series One and Two indicates that the events of 'The Christmas Invasion' take place around Christmas 2006, this dates 'The Runaway Bride' to 24 December 2007. It is possible that the very last scene is set the following day, as Donna implies that her parents are about to have Christmas dinner.
- The (fictional) church is St Mary's in Chiswick, West London.
- On the wall outside the room where the wedding reception takes place there is a sign with an arrow pointing to 'Manchester Suite'; presumably another room in the same building. This was also the name of the hall where the alien delegates were seen to gather on Platform One around the year Five Billion AD in 'The End of the World'.
- When the Doctor uses his sonic screwdriver on a mobile phone to try to gain information about Donna's employers, H C Clements, a number of web pages flash up briefly on the phone's screen. These include a page from the UNIT website (www.unit.org.uk); a revised version of a page from the Torchwood House website (www.visittorchwood.co.uk); a page from the Leamington Spa Lifeboat Museum website (www.leamingtonspalifeboatmuseum.co.uk); a page from the Deffry Vale High School website (www.deffryvaleschool.org.uk/archive.shtml); the CheapServe webpage (www.cheapserve.co.uk); and a revised version of a page from the Project Guinevere website, mentioning the British Rocket Group (www.guinevere.org.uk/index2.html). Aside from CheapServe, which was created for general use in TV and film productions, these are all fictional *Doctor Who*-related websites that were set up to promote Series Two.
- The Doctor says that huon energy has not existed since 'the Dark Times', save for a remnant at the heart of the TARDIS. The Time Lords got rid of huon particles because they 'unravelled the atomic structure' and were deadly. The Empress of the Racnoss, however, has been manufacturing them anew, via a process involving the use of water from the Thames, and has conspired to have Donna dosed with them, in liquid form, over a period of six months; the particles are inert, and need something living to catalyse inside; a process

aided by the fact that, with the stress and excitement of her wedding day, Donna's body has become a chemical 'pressure cooker'.

- The Racnoss existed in the Dark Times; they were omnivores who devoured whole planets. The Doctor says that the Empress should not exist: 'Way back in history, the fledgling empires went to war against the Racnoss; they were wiped out.' The Empress responds that she survived. Later, when the Doctor's mentions his home planet Gallifrey – the first time the name has been used since *Doctor Who* returned in 2005 – the Empress hisses, 'They murdered the Racnoss'; this suggests that the Time Lords themselves were heavily involved in the war in question.
- The Doctor uses the surfboard-like tribophysical waveform macro-kinetic extrapolator device taken from the Slitheen in 'Boom Town', and seen also in 'The Parting of the Ways', to shift the TARDIS to a nearby location after it is pulled to the Empress's lair by the huon particles force-fed to Lance. It has now been incorporated into the TARDIS controls, and consequently a coral-like growth has spread over part of it.
- The Doctor takes Donna back 4.6 billion years to the creation of the Earth and the other planets of the solar system, commenting: 'We're going further back than I've ever been before.' It is unclear, though, whether he means further back in time, or just further back into the Earth's history. The latter would appear most likely, as the TARDIS is seen to journey far back in time in a number of classic series stories, and even approaches Event One – apparently the creation of the universe itself – in 'Castrovalva' (1982).
- The Earth was formed around a star-shaped Racnoss spaceship bearing the Empress's children, who have remained in hibernation ever since, awaiting revival with a key of huon particles.
- The Doctor states that his pockets are bigger inside than out.
- As suggested in a number of classic series stories, the TARDIS has a protective force field that can protect the occupants when the doors are opened while it is hovering in space (as opposed to travelling through the time vortex). This is demonstrated first when Donna opens the doors shortly after her initial arrival in the TARDIS, and later when the Doctor takes her back in time to the creation of the Earth.
- The TARDIS can fly like a conventional spaceship; at the end of the episode, it takes off by rising vertically up into the air, as seen – or at least implied – only once before in the series, in 'Fury from the Deep' in 1968.

## TORCHWOOD REFERENCES

- Donna tells the Doctor that she works as a temporary secretary at H C Clements, a security company – the sole proprietor of which, he quickly discovers, is Torchwood. Infiltrating the company's headquarters, the Doctor, Donna and Lance gain access to a secret underground base bedecked with the Torchwood logo. 'H C Clements was bought up 23 years ago by the Torchwood Institute,' says the Doctor. 'Torchwood was destroyed, but H C Clements stayed in business. I think someone else came in and took over the operation.' The secret base, it transpires, extends below the Thames Flood Barrier – 'Torchwood snuck in and built this place underneath,' explains the

Doctor – and has at its heart a borehole leading down to the centre of the Earth – 'Very Torchwood.'

## SAXON REFERENCES

- The mysterious Mr Saxon received his first mention in a newspaper headline seen briefly in Series Two's 'Love & Monsters'. What few viewers realised at the time was that this foreshadowed a story arc that would be developed via a series of further references in Series Three, akin to the Bad Wolf arc in Series One and the Torchwood arc in Series Two. 'The Runaway Bride' affords the first of these further references as a tank commander is told: 'Order from Mr Saxon: fire at will.'

## PRODUCTION NOTES

- 'The Runaway Bride' was a story originally intended for inclusion in Series Two, but was moved by Russell T Davies after he learnt that a Christmas Special had been commissioned for 2006. Its place in the Series Two schedule was taken by 'Tooth and Claw'.
- Although presented as a one-off special on transmission, this episode was made as Block 1 of production on Series Three for planning purposes.
- The series' title sequence was slightly revised for this episode, not only with the inclusion of Catherine Tate's name in place of Billie Piper's but also with some re-editing and the substitution of a different version of the logo, essentially the same as the one previously used on the series' tie-in merchandise. The latter changes would be retained for Series Three.
- The sequence of Donna's arrival in the TARDIS was not material reused from the end of the Series Two finale 'Doomsday' but a reshot version so as to ensure that it matched up with the subsequent scenes, particularly in lighting terms.
- Mendelssohn's 'Wedding March' is the music played on the church organ during the opening wedding scene. (As pointed out by incidental music composer Murray Gold during recording, this is arguably an error, as it is a piece traditionally played not at the beginning of a wedding ceremony but at the end, as the newlywed couple walk back down the aisle.)
- The two music tracks heard at the wedding reception are Slade's classic single 'Merry Xmas Everybody' from 1973 (also used in the previous year's 'The Christmas Invasion') and the specially-written-and-recorded 'Love Don't Roam' by Murray Gold, with vocals by Neil Hannon of the band The Divine Comedy. 'Love Don't Roam' appears to have been inspired by Al Wilson's 1968 soul single 'The Snake', to which it bears a strong similarity.
- Recording for 'The Runaway Bride' took place mainly in Cardiff at the height of summer, making it difficult at times to convey the impression that it was really late December. The hot weather conditions caused discomfort for Catherine Tate in Donna's heavy wedding dress and for the actors playing the robot Santas in their thick clothing, in particular during the St Mary Street location scene where the Doctor creates his diversion with the cash dispenser, which was shot in blazing sunshine on 24 July 2006. The church scenes were

recorded at the Church of St John the Baptist in the city centre a little earlier, on 13 and 14 July. The scenes in the Torchwood underground base were recorded at Cardiff's Millennium Stadium on 19 July. The shots of the crowd reacting to the Empress's spaceship hovering in the sky and firing destructive rays down upon them were recorded in Wharton Street and St Mary Street on the night of 25 July, with a London bus and taxi used to help create the illusion that this was actually taking place in London, along with military vehicles. A real tank was used in St Mary Street; it caused some damage to the road surface, which BBC Wales later paid to have repaired. The closing scene of the Doctor bidding farewell to Donna outside her house was shot in Princes Avenue in the Roath area of Cardiff on 26 July. Finally, the scenes of Sarah Parish as the Empress were recorded at the Impounding Station, Newport Docks, on 2 August.

- The 'car chase' sequence, supposedly set on the M4 motorway heading out of London, was recorded partly on the Chiswick Flyover in London but primarily on a road in Cardiff, with the real road signs (which bore directions in Welsh as well as English) covered up or kept out of shot. Director Euros Lyn drew part of his inspiration for this recording from a sequence of a chase through the streets of Moscow in the movie *The Bourne Supremacy* (Universal Pictures, 2004).

- The bank notes spewed out by the cash dispenser were not genuine but specially designed for the episode: the £10 ones bore a portrait of David Tennant and the words 'I promise to pay the bearer on demand the sum of ten satsumas' and 'No second chances – I'm that sort of man' (references back to the dialogue of 'The Christmas Invasion'), while the £20 ones carried the likeness of producer Phil Collinson and the legend 'There's no point being grown up if you can't be a little childish sometimes' (a slight misquote of a phrase used by the fourth Doctor in his debut story 'Robot' (1974/1975)).

- The studio scenes for this story were the first *Doctor Who* material to be recorded at the series' new permanent base at Upper Boat.

- When repeated on 30 December 2006, this became the first *Doctor Who* story ever to be broadcast with in-vision British Sign Language interpretation for the deaf.

- The Empress of the Racnoss was constructed primarily of fibreglass, with foam latex for the soft joints. It was mounted on one end of a pole-arm rig – essentially a large steel 'see-saw' – with a counterbalance of steel weights on the other end, which meant that it could be easily moved up and down by a single operator pushing it by hand. At the 'head' of the creature, actress Sarah Parish knelt with her legs in a capsule created from a cast of her lower body, which provided maximum comfort and security. The actress then wore a prosthetic body suit on her upper torso and matching prosthetic make-up on her face and head, and had to operate the two front legs with her own arms. It took four hours for the prosthetic make-up to be applied. Parish had long wanted to make a guest appearance in *Doctor Who*, specifically as an alien, and found the experience 'amazing'.

- According to director Euros Lyn, one of his tonal guidelines for 'The Runaway Bride' was to make 'a more real version of *Four Weddings and a Funeral*', with the 'opulence and richness' of a Christmas celebration but 'without some of the fakery'.

## UNFOUNDED PRE-TRANSMISSION RUMOURS

- 'The Runaway Bride' would be transmitted in three half-hour segments on different days, possibly divided into the past/present/future format of Charles Dickens' *A Christmas Carol*.[24]
- Former companions Sarah Jane Smith and K-9 would make a cameo appearance.
- The Doctor would save Donna when she tried to commit suicide by throwing herself off the roof of a building, possibly presaging a story akin to that of the classic movie *It's a Wonderful Life* (RKO Radio Pictures, 1946).
- The action would be concurrent with that of the previous Christmas Special, 'The Christmas Invasion', explaining the presence of the robot Santas and allowing for a cameo appearance by Billie Piper as Rose.
- The bride would grow to giant proportions, and possibly explode if the Doctor was unable to get her back to the church on time.

## OOPS!

- Although only briefly visible on screen, prop advertising posters used during the St Mary Street location recording of the scene where the Doctor uses a cash dispenser and Donna hails a cab give the date as Christmas 2006, whereas (as discussed in 'Continuity' above) the action must actually take place at Christmas 2007. (Could these have been items left over or reused from the previous year?)
- Cardiff Castle can be glimpsed in the background of some of the supposedly London-set shots involving the tank.

## PRESS REACTION

- 'Catherine Tate [wore a] drab rag of a wedding dress in *Doctor Who*. But given that this ... was a Christmas special, and therefore an episode in which a certain levity and deftness of touch wouldn't – and indeed in the case of David Tennant's sweetly boyish Doctor didn't – go amiss, perhaps the award-winning comic actress (lest we forget) giving us an utterly charmless, strident and humourless performance meant that she got the frock she deserved. What a huge, messy disappointment it was, full of Tate shouting and Tennant looking like he really, really missed Billie Piper, and all of it drowned in hideously overwrought music. And what on earth – or even outer space – was the point in disguising the beauteous Sarah Parish as a giant red spiderthing? If you ask me, there was mix-up in both the casting and costume departments, and Tate and Parish were wearing each other's parts.' Kathryn Flett, *The Observer*, 31 December 2006.

---

[24] *A Christmas Carol* had previously inspired the format of the classic series story 'The Trial of a Time Lord'.

- 'There were no concessions to those who'd overdone it with the champagne and brandy sauce on Christmas Day, as "The Runaway Bride" erupted in a giddying cocktail of action, thrills and quick-fire wit. This was an important episode for the series – the first without any of the original cast since *Doctor Who*'s reinvention in 2005 – and it served as a reminder that the format is the star. Billie Piper's passing was acknowledged with some sweet moments, but the emphasis was on moving forward, and Donna couldn't have made a more different companion. Catherine Tate's brash performance was certainly pitched at those who have seen her BBC Two sketch show – we were almost anticipating the catchphrases – but she fitted the spirit of this romp, though fortunately the rush to get Donna to the church on time was resolved early in the episode.' David Richardson, *Starburst* Issue 346, February 2007.
- '*Doctor Who* has never really done anything like "The Runaway Bride" before. There's a bit of *The 39 Steps* in there and a heavy dumping of screwball comedy too. Then, when the Doctor attempts to rescue Donna from a robot Santa, it suddenly becomes a Hollywood action movie, only on the M4. Never in two years of peacock *Doctor Who* or in 26 years of pawn shop *Who* have we seen anything as jaw-slackening as this sequence. .... When Sarah Parish's Empress of the Racnoss eventually turns up, it becomes as big and visual as *Who*'s ever [been]. She's a masterpiece of prosthetics and visual effects: slightly naff but a the same time brilliant. Catherine Tate's a curious celebrity in that she wins awards and has hit TV shows, and yet a sizeable amount of the public not only can't warm to her, but actively dislike her. Her gnarly, sarky Donna won't win over those people, but it's she who really makes "The Runaway Bride", and in the touching final scene, your mind races through the possibilities of having Donna go on more adventures with the Doctor.' Steve O'Brien, *SFX* Issue 153, February 2007.

## FAN COMMENT

- 'Russell T Davies pulls off exactly the same trick he did in last year's "The Christmas Invasion", opening with a delirious first act designed to allow the family to settle down, wake up and pay attention. Plot is minimal – instead there is screwball ditziness, the return of the robot Santas, the continuation of a hopefully annual tradition of playing Slade's "Merry Xmas Everybody", and a crowd-pleasing chase-by-TARDIS to capture the attention (and provide a focal point for the pre-broadcast media to latch onto without ruining the plot). It's instantly clear why Russell wanted to cast Catherine Tate as Donna Noble. She launches herself into the role with the same broadness that characterises her sketch show, but at least here's a character who is more than just a catchphrase – although the way Tate delivers Russell's one-liners suggests she's trying to add one or two to her repertoire and, in the sublimely quotable "Santa's a robot!", she might actually have done so. But she's also a fine companion, if only a temporary one (and kudos to RTD for the wit of actually making Donna a temp).' Simon Kinnear, Shockeye Online website, December 2006.
- 'This story just isn't quite as compelling as last year's, and even the threat of the Racnoss, while certainly as global as that of the Sycorax invasion, lacks the same sense of impending doom. A huge rock-like ship hovering over UK

landmarks somehow packs a lot more punch than a flashlight shining up from a shaft with dialogue telling us that yes, trust us, there are lots of spiders coming up from there soon. And when the Doctor defeats the imminent spider attack, he does so by flushing a lot of water down the drain …which is where some of my enthusiasm went as well.' Arnold T Blumberg, A Panel With No Borders blog, 9 April 2007.

- 'My biggest worry was always Catherine Tate – her programme is the sort of sub-*Little Britain* schlock that pollutes British comedy at the moment. It's all endlessly repeated catchphrases and gross-out "humour". What happened to the Pythons, hmm? Intelligent, witty and 100 times funnier than a man dressed as a WI member being sick on a vicar. Of course, I needn't have worried, because the comedienne wasn't writing and, as a character, Donna really grew on me over the course of the episode. She's a brash, selfish type; but whose heart didn't bleed when Lance said he'd prefer being the Empress's escort to spending a night with Donna? Ouch! That's just mean. She also fulfilled the wishes of many a blogger and kept the Doctor in check – delivering a quick slap when he started getting smug and flippant.' Felicity, Behind the Sofa website, 11 January 2007.

- 'For an episode that ostensibly tries to reunite a discontented bride with her jilted groom, it's rather fitting that "The Runaway Bride" fulfils the remit of the wedding day tradition itself. Something old. Something new. Something borrowed. And something blue. In fact, at times I thought I was tuning in to last year's Christmas special, so redolent with some of the iconography of *la* Tennant's seasonal debut of 12 months ago was this year's episode. Zoom down from space into the opening action? Check. Robot Santas causing havoc for the Doctor's "companion"? Double check. Christmas trees that go homicidal at the most inopportune times? Triple check with a psychotic fairy on top. And that's without even mentioning the fact that Doctor Ten once again gets to show his real steel when given the opportunity to show mercy for an invading menace. All we wanted was to get a few shots of iconic London landmarks and the picture would have been completed. Oh, what do you mean we did …?' Sean Alexander, Behind the Sofa website, 25 December 2006.

- 'It was a complete rehash of the previous year's Christmas special, hitting the same narrative beats to the same pace and to the same resolution, but with less originality and genuine flair. Last year's special was stylish and self-assured, whereas 2006's Christmas episode was neurotic and narratively timid. *Doctor Who*, like all good science fiction, works best when it is layered – you can enjoy it on many levels. "The Runaway Bride" was monothematic and mono-toned, a madcap childish mishmash of loud, brash, confusing CGI strung together by tenuous plotting with the odd attempt to inject a sense of poignancy about a character who left in the previous series, and who would be a total mystery to any potential new viewer.' Peter Crispin, *Celestial Toyroom* Issue 346, January 2007.

## ANALYSIS

After only two years, the *Doctor Who* Christmas special seems to have acquired the status of a cherished national institution for British viewers, in much the same way as the Morcambe and Wise Christmas shows did back in the 1970s. This is quite amazing, and proof positive of the incredible impact made by the Russell T Davies-led 21st Century incarnation of the series.

Coincidentally, both Christmas specials to date have also marked pivotal points in the series' development: 'The Christmas Invasion' fulfilled the crucial role of introducing David Tennant in his first full story as the tenth Doctor, and 'The Runaway Bride' had the huge challenge of proving that the series could continue successfully even in the absence of the superb Billie Piper as Rose Tyler.

In a typically astute move, Davies decided against using 'The Runaway Bride' as the vehicle for introducing a new regular character – although he did briefly consider retaining the eponymous bride as Rose's successor – and thus avoided the problem of having to try to establish a new companion here when she would not be seen again until the start of Series Three some three months later. Instead he chose to make the Christmas special a kind of stand-alone transitional adventure with a one-off guest star in the lead female role – again recalling the Morcambe and Wise tradition of featuring big-name guest stars in their Christmas shows, often in very different types of roles from those for which they were best known. There are certainly few bigger names in British TV at the moment than Catherine Tate, and on paper it must have seemed a great coup to secure this cult favourite – albeit not universally popular – comedienne in the relatively straight role of Donna Noble, the eponymous bride. Certainly it garnered a huge amount of publicity and interest. Sadly, however, it turned out to be a highly regrettable piece of casting in dramatic terms.

I am by no means one of those people who dislike everything that Tate does; I think she is great in her own BBC Two sketch show, and has created some truly inspired comic characters. It is also fair to say that she has a good track record in straight dramatic roles, although this is not the type of work for which she is generally noted. Sadly, however, she is pretty awful in 'The Runaway Bride', giving an unappealing, one-note performance that sees her delivering most of her lines in a raucous shout. What Davies seems to have been aiming for in the relationship between the Doctor and Donna is something akin to the 'romantic sparring' typically seen in the screwball caper films that enjoyed their heyday in the 1930s and 1940s, featuring memorable pairings such as those of Clark Gable and Claudette Colbert in *It Happened One Night* (Columbia Pictures, 1934), William Powell and Carole Lombard in *My Man Godfrey* (Universal Pictures, 1936) and Cary Grant and Katharine Hepburn in *Bringing Up Baby* (RKO Radio Pictures, 1938) and *Holiday* (Columbia Pictures, 1938) – and indeed, coming more up to date, Richard Gere and Julia Roberts in *Runaway Bride* (Paramount Pictures, 1999), the film from which this episode's title appears to have been drawn. In order for such a relationship to work, though, the viewer needs to sense that beneath the ostensible antagonism between the male and female leads there lies a smouldering attraction, or at least that there is a palpable chemistry between the two. This is not something that can really be manufactured, and unfortunately there seems to be no chemistry at all between Tennant and Tate.

The problem lies not only in Tate's grating, unsubtle performance, however, but also in the conception of Donna. There is nothing remotely engaging or attractive about her as a person, and – surprisingly, given that she is obviously intended to be an audience identification character – Davies's script goes out of its way to highlight just how stupid she is: the Doctor is astonished to discover that she has somehow failed to notice the recent alien incursions by Daleks, Cybermen and the like; and Lance, her treacherous fiancé, says, 'God, she's thick. Months I've had to put up with her. Months. A woman who can't even point to Germany on a map … I was stuck with a woman who thinks the height of excitement is a new flavour Pringle. Oh, I had to sit there and listen to all that yap, yap, yap: "Ooh, Brad and Angelina." "Is Posh pregnant?" "X-Factor." "Atkins diet." "Feng shui." "Split ends." "Text me, text me, text me." Dear God, the never ending fountain of fat, stupid trivia.'

The episode opens in exactly the same way as 'Rose' – with a shot zooming down to Earth from space and focusing in on the London setting where the viewer first encounters the title character[25] – and ends in much the same way too – with a scene of chaos and destruction in a secret underground base beneath a familiar London landmark (a similarity even jokingly alluded to in the dialogue[26]), during the course of which the Doctor's new-found friend swings across to him on a cable (more successfully in one case than in the other). Is Davies seeking here to draw some sort of parallel between Rose and Donna? Or perhaps, alternatively, inviting the viewer to compare and contrast their respective qualities? Or is he simply, and more prosaically, reprising a successful formula with a new twist? If the aim is to suggest that Donna could, in her own way, make just as good a companion as Rose, this is very wide of the mark. It is actually difficult to see why the Doctor would want to associate with Donna at all, apart perhaps from out of a sense of moral obligation arising from the fact that she has got caught up in one of his adventures – although, even then, it is through no fault of his. When, at the end of the story, he astonishingly invites her to accompany him on his travels – using, significantly, almost exactly the same words as when, in his previous incarnation, he first asked Rose to join him; just as Donna then, in asking if she will ever see him again, echoes Rose's words at the end of 'Doomsday' – the viewer is fervently willing her to decline; which one suspects is exactly the opposite of the reaction Davies was aiming for.

The Doctor's companions should always have something special about them – as he himself puts it in 'The Long Game' and the digital-only adventure 'Attack of the Graske', 'I only take the best' – and, although she does seem to have her eyes opened to some extent by what she goes through here, Donna at no point displays the qualities of intelligence, courage, curiosity and resourcefulness that would qualify her for such a role. She is, quite simply, not companion material, and the attempt to imply that she and the Doctor develop some sort of bond during the course of the story, and that their eventual parting is replete with highly-charged

---

[25] The same shot was also used to open 'The Christmas Invasion' and 'Army of Ghosts'.

[26] Other stories in which a secret base is revealed to exist beneath or within a prominent London landmark include not only 'Rose' (the London Eye) but also 'The Christmas Invasion' (the Tower of London), 'The Age of Steel' (Battersea Power Station), 'Army of Ghosts' (Canary Wharf) – and, going back to 1966, 'The War Machines' (the Post Office Tower). The Torchwood Hub is similarly sited beneath a prominent Cardiff landmark (the water tower in the Roald Dahl Plass) in *Torchwood*.

emotion, falls flat – particularly as it evokes memories of the genuinely heart-rending departure of Rose at the end of Series Two, and very much pales by comparison with that. The Doctor's appeal to Donna to accompany him in the TARDIS actually smacks of desperation on his part, as if he is so incredibly lonely in the wake of losing Rose – something emphasised by repeated references to her throughout the episode, including visual references such as her blouse in the TARDIS control room and shots of the exterior of the (fictional) Henrik's department store where she used to work, and even two brief flashbacks to 'New Earth' – that he is willing to take on almost anyone as his new companion, regardless of their suitability; which is really rather demeaning to the character. The whole thing comes across as an unsuccessful attempt to emulate the excellent build-up of the relationship between the eighth Doctor and Grace Holloway, with similar screwball comedy aspects, in the 1996 TV Movie, which likewise ended with the Doctor being turned down by his potential new companion; in that case to the viewer's genuine disappointment, not least because Grace was a much more appealing and better-acted character than Donna.

With this major flaw at its very heart, 'The Runaway Bride' was never going to be amongst my favourite new series episodes, but unfortunately it has other shortcomings too. For one thing, it reaches its peak of excitement after only about 12 minutes, in the thrilling and wonderfully-executed 'car chase' sequence where the Doctor rescues Donna from the robot Santa's taxicab by pursuing it down the Chiswick flyover in the TARDIS; after this breathtaking incident, which is really the highlight of the episode and unlike anything ever seen in *Doctor Who* before (not something that is easy to achieve after some 43 years), everything that follows comes as something of an anticlimax. One of the main reasons for this is that the Empress of the Racnoss, when she is finally revealed, is not a particularly good monster. The decision to build the creature as a full-size rig in the studio, rather than realise it as a CGI effect, was apparently taken more for artistic reasons than on cost grounds, to ensure that it looked as 'real' as possible. While one can understand and sympathise with that aim, and the end product is an undeniably ambitious and impressive piece of construction work, it regrettably means that the Empress remains disappointingly static: one would expect to see a spider-like creature scuttling around its lair, not staying rooted to the spot. Even actress Sarah Parish is quite restricted in her movements, being effectively encased in a disconcertingly phallic protuberance as the head of the creature – which, coupled with its deep red coloration, actually makes it look like a strange sort of spider-lobster hybrid – and compensates for this by turning in an extraordinary, albeit entertaining, performance of scenery-chewing intensity. As a character, the Empress is also given a somewhat unoriginal backstory: her status as the previously-unsuspected sole survivor of a war against the Time Lords, now trying to unleash a new generation of her kind on the universe, is exactly the same as that of the Dalek Emperor in 'The Parting of the Ways', and also recalls that of the Nestenes in the aftermath of the Time War – yet another reference back to the end of 'Rose'.

The idea of the Doctor ending the threat of the Racnoss by flushing the spiders back down what amounts to a gigantic plughole is a good joke, but again the sequence falls short of achieving its full potential, because the budget apparently wouldn't run to showing any of the Empress's children physically emerging from the hole, or even extending a hairy leg or two through the opening, and the viewer has to be content with being told about them, rather than actually seeing them. (It would, admittedly, have taken them quite a long time to have got all the way to the top from the centre of the Earth, so perhaps it is more realistic this way.) Davies's tendency occasionally to over-egg certain of his plot elements – as previously witnessed for instance in 'New Earth' in his decision to have the cloned test subjects unbelievably infected with every disease under the sun rather than just certain specific viruses – is seen again here in the suggestion that the laser-cut shaft extends right down to the very core of the Earth, and that it completely drains the Thames of water when opened up to it. These ideas are superficially amusing but, if given even a second's thought, raise all sorts of problematic issues, such as the wider impact of the Doctor's actions in terms of damage to the environment, not to mention in terms of death or injury to the occupants of any vessels that happened to be on the river at the time.[27] The classic series story 'Inferno' (1970) dealt far more sensibly and fittingly with the awe-inspiring idea of a borehole being drilled down to the centre of the Earth; and even the oft-derided 'The Underwater Menace' (1967) gave rather more consideration to the potentially disastrous effects of a large body of cold water being drained into the planet's superheated core (although in that case, admittedly, the body in question was a whole ocean rather than just a river).

Perhaps I am being a bit too po-faced about all this, given that the main aim of 'The Runaway Bride' was obviously to deliver an hour's worth of undemanding, colourful entertainment for a Christmas Day audience settling comfortably into their sofas after maybe watching the Queen's Speech and consuming copious quantities of turkey and figgy pudding. That said, though, there is precious little Christmas spirit in evidence in the way the Doctor mercilessly despatches the Empress's children, to her obvious and considerable distress. This is a very grim sequence and clearly recalls the original idea from 'The Christmas Invasion' of the tenth Doctor being a 'no second chances' sort of man; although, since this was not really followed up on at all in any of the Series Two episodes, and was arguably even contradicted when the Doctor gave Cassandra what amounted to a second chance at the end of 'New Earth'[28], perhaps it is a character trait that is destined to surface only in Christmas specials!

In fact, despite Davies having spoken in a number of interviews of being determined to ensure that his Christmas specials remain suitably 'Christmassy', this is much less true of 'The Runaway Bride' than it was of 'The Christmas Invasion'. The Christmas elements this time are really confined to just a few bits of superficial imagery – principally, the Santa disguises adopted by the Empress's robot drones, the death-dealing Christmas tree, the star-shaped Webstar spaceship hovering over London and the artificial snowstorm at the end – all of which could have been quite easily changed to something non-Christmassy without any impact

---

[27] Some fans have speculated that the North Sea, as well as the Thames itself, would be completely drained into the shaft, but this is not the case as, although the Thames is a tidal river, it is above sea level.

[28] This was a point that was originally addressed in Davies's script for 'New Earth', but the sequence in question was deleted due to problems encountered shooting in bad weather conditions on location.

whatsoever on the plot, had the episode been transmitted at a different time of year. All these elements bar the star-shaped spaceship are also directly repeated from 'The Christmas Invasion' – albeit that the robot Santas have been slightly redesigned this time around, that the Christmas tree utilises a new killing method involving exploding baubles and that the artificial snowstorm has a different cause – which seems rather unimaginative and gives the impression that Davies is already running out of inventive ways of presenting Christmas-themed *Doctor Who* episodes. ('The Christmas Invasion' had its own spaceship hovering over London, too, although in that case it resembled simply a lump of rock rather than a star.) To find a *genuinely* Christmassy piece of *Doctor Who* writing in December 2006, one really needed to read Paul Cornell's excellent short story *Deep and Dreamless Sleep* published in the Christmas Eve edition of *The Sunday Times* – further evidence of the series' new-found national institution status – which concerns itself with the true meaning of Christmas, not just the surface trappings.

Even composer Murray Gold rather underperforms on this occasion, turning in one of his least impressive scores for the series, the worst parts probably being the irritating and wholly inappropriate muzak-type accompaniment to Donna's initial scenes inside the TARDIS and the ill-fitting quote from George Gershwin when the Doctor emerges from the Torchwood base and finds himself atop a Thames Barrier pier.

On the positive side, 'The Runaway Bride' sees David Tennant in extremely impressive form. The tendency he showed at some points during Series Two toward over-the-top goofing – usually, it has to be said, in the weaker episodes, most notably the terrible 'Fear Her', where he was perhaps trying a little too hard to compensate for the script's shortcomings – seems to be very much a thing of the past now. Here he turns in a winning performance of great energy and enthusiasm, skilfully counterpointing his Doctor's now-familiar geeky eccentricity – just a little reminiscent at times of the trademark camp persona of the wonderful Kenneth Williams – with moments of steely intensity. It is clear that, one year in, he has well and truly got to grips with the role – something that bodes very well indeed for Series Three. Could he be the best Doctor ever? While it is perhaps a little too early to be making that judgment, I certainly no longer find myself thinking, as I did during much of Series One, 'This is absolutely brilliant, but it would have been even better if they had got Paul McGann to continue in the lead role.'

Donna's fiancé Lance – the only supporting character of any substance, further evidencing just how closely the action focuses on the central Doctor-and-Donna pairing – is well portrayed by Don Gilet. Particularly amusing is the scene where he creeps up behind the Empress with an axe, as if to attack her, only to burst out laughing and reveal that – as has already been guessed by the Doctor, and probably by most viewers as well by this point, but not by the slow-witted Donna – he is actually in league with the creature. The theme of the qualities required of someone to make them suited to become the Doctor's companion interestingly resurfaces here, albeit obliquely, when Lance's reason for helping the Empress – that she has promised him the chance to go out into space, get away from the triviality of life on Earth and see 'the big picture' – turns out to be a kind of dark mirror of Rose's reason for embarking on her travels in the TARDIS back at the beginning of Series One.

Other plus points include some excellent design work and effects – including a couple of superb CGI shots of the Doctor, and later Donna too, on the aforementioned Thames Barrier pier – and the occasional nice moment of quirky humour, such as when the Doctor creates a diversion by using his sonic screwdriver to cause bank notes to fountain out of a cash dispenser, and when he, Donna and Lance trundle their way through the Torchwood base on Segways. It is actually rather a pity that the originally-intended running joke of them using various different, and generally inappropriate, forms of transport throughout the story – including a bus[29] and Donna's tiny pink 'smart car' or (in a reshoot done because Julie Gardner disliked the original version) green Volkswagen when travelling from the wedding reception to the H C Clements building – was cut during editing, as it would have provided some welcome added moments of light relief in between the more highly dramatic sequences.

All the statistical evidence, along with press and fan reviews, would seem to suggest that 'The Runaway Bride' was well received by the great majority of the viewing audience. For me, though, despite having a number of enjoyable aspects, it stands as one of the most disappointing episodes since the series returned in 2005.

There are some *Doctor Who* stories that grow in reputation and stature with the passage of time, and some that diminish, and I feel that 'The Runaway Bride' is destined to fall into the latter category.

---

[29] The deleted bus scene featured actress Bella Emberg briefly reprising her role as Mrs Croot from 'Love & Monsters'.

# 3.01 – SMITH AND JONES

Writer: Russell T Davies
Director: Charles Palmer

## DEBUT TRANSMISSION DETAILS

BBC One
Date: 31 March 2007. Scheduled time: 7.00 pm. Actual time: 6.59 pm.

BBC Three
Date: 1 April 2007. Scheduled time: 8.00 pm. Actual time: 8.01 pm.

Duration: 44' 31"

## ADDITIONAL CREDITED CAST[30]

Anne Reid (Florence Finnegan), Roy Marsden (Mr Stoker), Kimmi Richards (Annalise), Ben Righton (Morgenstern[31]), Vineeta Rishi (Julia Swales), Paul Kasey (Judoon Captain), Nicholas Briggs (Judoon Voices)[32],[33]

## PLOT

An ordinary working day for trainee doctor Martha Jones is thrown into turmoil when London's Royal Hope Hospital is transported to the Moon by a force of Judoon – rhino-like space police – seeking to bring to justice a fugitive Plasmavore who has murdered a young princess on a far-distant world. The vampiric Plasmavore has used its shape-changing ability to assume the guise of an elderly patient named Florence Finnegan, and is being protected by two humanoid but non-sentient Slabs. She threatens to use a readjusted MRI scanner to kill every living thing in the hospital, and incidentally also on the side of the Earth facing the Moon; but, aided by Martha, the Doctor, who has also been posing as a patient, ensures that she is apprehended by the Judoon, who execute her and then depart, returning the hospital to Earth. Martha accepts the Doctor's invitation to join him for a trip in the TARDIS.

---

[30] Two of the uncredited actors playing the Judoon were Ken Hosking and Ruari Mears.
[31] First name given in dialogue as 'Oliver'.
[32] Not credited in *Radio Times*.
[33] Leo's partner Shonara was played uncredited by Channon Jacobs.

## QUOTE, UNQUOTE

- **Martha:** 'We're on the Moon! We're on the bloody Moon!'
- **Judoon Captain:** 'Bo! Sco! Fo! Do! No! Kro! Blo! Co! Sho! Ro!'
- **Doctor:** 'Oh, look down there, you've got a little shop. I like a little shop.'
- **Martha:** 'Oh my god, you can travel in time! But hold on, if you could see me this morning, why didn't you tell me not to go into work?'
- **Doctor:** 'Crossing into established events is strictly forbidden; except for cheap tricks.'

## CONTINUITY POINTS

- The action of this episode unfolds over the course of a single day. It is uncertain when it is set, although it must take place sometime after the Series Two finale 'Army of Ghosts'/'Doomsday', because the events of that two-parter are referred to; and they are dated no earlier than autumn 2007. The relevant entry in Martha's (fictional but BBC-originated) blog on the MySpace website (www.myspace.com/marthajonesuk) is dated 31 March 2007, but this cannot possibly be when the action actually takes place, unless something has happened to disrupt Earth history quite radically in the interim.[34] The Big Ben clock tower appears now to have been completely repaired following the damage it sustained in the spring of 2006 in 'Aliens of London', in consequence of which it is seen still to have scaffolding around it in December 2006 in 'The Christmas Invasion'. The Thames is also flowing again, having been drained in December 2007 in 'The Runaway Bride'. There is nothing in 'Smith and Jones' to indicate whether or not the events of the latter story have occurred yet from Martha's perspective, but she refers to them in another entry in her MySpace blog. A notice seen on the back of a hospital door in one shot refers to 'Sizing for new uniforms' taking place during the weeks 'Mon 22 Sep - Fri 26 Sep' and 'Mon 29 Sep - Friday 3 Oct', but it is possible that this has been there for some time and is out of date. A 'Vote Saxon' poster on the wall of the alley in the scene where Martha enters the TARDIS suggests (and this is confirmed by later episodes) that a General Election has been called but has not yet been held. Similar posters are seen in the *Torchwood* episode 'Captain Jack Harkness', the most probable dating for which is January 2008. In one scene in 'Love & Monsters', an edition of the *Daily Telegraph* newspaper is seen with headlines including 'Saxon leads polls with 64 percent', 'Election Countdown: Four more months of government paralysis' and 'Fourth minister resigns: so who's running the country?'. As this scene probably takes place in late summer or early autumn 2007, shortly before the events of 'Army of Ghosts'/'Doomsday', the most probable dating for the General Election is late

---

[34] Later entries in Martha's blog appear to have been written in the TARDIS and then somehow transmitted through time and space to the MySpace website, appearing on a succession of dates in 2007 regardless of when they were actually written. The first two entries, however, clearly date from before Martha joins the Doctor on his travels.

2007 or very early 2008. Taking all these things into account, it seems most likely that 'Smith and Jones' is set in late December 2007 (post Christmas) or early January 2008, with only the dating of Martha's original MySpace blog entries being inconsistent with this.

- The Doctor uses his usual 'John Smith' alias. He has had himself admitted to the hospital supposedly suffering from severe abdominal pains.

- Martha says that her first meeting with the Doctor, when he came up to her and took off his tie (as part of what is later revealed to be a 'trick' to demonstrate that he can travel in time), took place in 'Chancellor Street'. This is a fictional location, as there is no such road in the area where the Royal Hope Hospital is supposedly situated.

- When Martha, examining the Doctor in the hospital, asks him, 'Have you got a brother?', he replies 'No, not any more. Just me.' This is the first suggestion in the series that the Doctor may have had a brother – who would presumably have been killed in the Time War between the Time Lords and the Daleks – although it is possible that he may not mean it literally. Irving Braxiatel, a Time Lord character who features in the original book and audio CD drama series, was suggested to be the Doctor's brother in the New Adventures novel *Tears of the Oracle* (1999), written by his creator Justin Richards and edited by 'Smith and Jones' script editor Simon Winstone. The possibility that the Doctor's arch-enemy the Master might be his brother has also long been the subject of fan speculation.

- Adeola Oshodi, who died at Canary Wharf, aka Torchwood Tower, during the events of 'Army of Ghosts', was Martha's cousin, hence their similarity in appearance.

- It appears that some members of the public now accept the reality of recent alien incursions and attacks such as those seen in 'Aliens of London'/'World War Three', 'The Christmas Invasion' and 'Army of Ghosts'/'Doomsday', but that others continue to believe that these were fakes or hallucinations, possibly brought on by drug poisoning.

- The Doctor states that he has met Benjamin Franklin (1706-1790), one of the founding fathers of the USA and inventor of the lightning rod ('My mate Ben. That was a day and a half. I got rope burns off that kite, and then I got soaked. And then I got electrocuted!'), and famous suffragette Emmeline Pankhurst (1858-1928), who he says stole his laser spanner ('Cheeky woman').

- Under Galactic Law, the Judoon have no jurisdiction over the Earth. They transport the hospital to the Moon using an '$H_2O$ Scoop'.

- The Doctor is exposed to an ultra-powerful burst of Röntgen radiation (aka X-rays) when he destroys one of the Slabs, but it has no harmful effects on him – he says 'We used to play with Röntgen bricks in the nursery' – and he is able to shake it out of him via his left shoe. (It has however been established in earlier stories, including the first Dalek serial in 1963/64, that other forms of radiation can be harmful to the Doctor and his fellow Time Lords.)

- The Doctor mentions the TARDIS's helmic regulator – first referred to in 'The Ark in Space' (1975) – gravitic anomaliser – which featured in 'The Horns of Nimon' (1979/80) – and handbrake – which debuted in the *Doctor Who* TV Movie (1996).

- The Plasmavore says, just before she dies: 'Enjoy your victory, Judoon, because you're gonna burn with me; burn in hell!' Martha asks, 'What did she mean, "burn with me"?' This question is left unanswered, but foreshadows '42', in which the phrase 'Burn with me' will take on particular significance.

## SAXON REFERENCES

- Martha's colleague Morgenstern says during a radio interview: 'I looked out at the surface of the Moon. I saw the Earth suspended in space. And it all just proves Mr Saxon right: we're not alone in the universe; there's life out there; wild and extraordinary life'. There are also some 'Vote Saxon' posters on the wall of the alley where the Doctor picks up Martha at the end of the story.

## PRODUCTION NOTES

- 'Smith and Jones' was made with 'The Shakespeare Code' in Block 2 of production on Series Three.
- This episode is only the second since the new *Doctor Who* began to have no pre-credits teaser sequence. (The first was 'Rose'.)
- The music track heard over the episode's opening scene is 'Sunshine' by Arrested Development from their 2006 album *Since the Last Time*.
- Having liked the interaction between the Doctor and Madame de Pompadour in Series Two's 'Girl in the Fireplace', Russell T Davies briefly considered giving the new companion a period background – either the Victorian era or possibly the years immediately prior to the First World War. This idea was not well received by BBC drama head Jane Tranter when he ran it past her. In the end, he decided to make Martha another contemporary character like Rose, in order to provide a stronger point of audience identification. He viewed this as being akin to the transition from Jo Grant to Sarah Jane Smith in the classic series.
- The scene where the Doctor first meets Martha and removes his tie and the scene where Martha walks along talking on her mobile phone at the beginning of the episode were shot consecutively on the corner of Quay Street and St Mary Street in Cardiff on 10 August 2006. The hospital interiors and exteriors were recorded on various dates during August and September in a number of different locations, including Singleton Hospital, Swansea, a mock-up hospital ward used for training purposes in the Care Science building at Glamorgan University and a deserted glass factory on Trident Park industrial estate in Cardiff (the latter of which had been used as a location before on the series, notable for 'The Impossible Planet'/'The Satan Pit'). The foyer scene was shot over two nights in a library foyer on the Swansea University campus, with a fake 'little shop' constructed by the crew. The small hospital kitchen was not a location but a set constructed in the Upper Boat studio kitchen, with a fake wall and cupboards fitted with pistons for the scene where the building is shaken about as it is transported to the Moon. The scene of the argument beween Martha's family in the street after Leo's party was shot on 2 October outside the Market Tavern in Pontypridd.
- Freema Agyeman had not had any other acting work between completing her

scenes as Adeola in 'Army of Ghosts' and making her debut as Martha. She was pleased that her first day on set for 'Smith and Jones' involved her simply rushing about the hospital corridors, with no dialogue to deliver and no scenes opposite David Tennant, as this allowed her to ease herself in gradually.

- In an interview for Issue 156 of the genre magazine *SFX*, publishing in May 2007, Freema Agyeman commented on the differences between Rose and Martha: 'With Rose, you got the sense that she was searching for a life, and the Doctor helped her find who she was. With Martha you get more of a sense that he's interrupted a life that she's set up. She's got her own flat, she's training to be a doctor and she's got this huge family unit that she's a rock for ... Because she's slightly older than Rose, she doesn't idolise [the Doctor] in quite the way that Rose did; she challenges him a little more. Rose was unique in that she loved the Doctor and he loved her back. With Martha it's pretty much a one-way street. Her affections are ... unrequited!'

- The hospital consultant's name, 'Mr B Stoker' (the initial revealed on a sign on his office door, although this is barely visible on screen), recalls that of Bram Stoker, author of the seminal vampire novel *Dracula*, but was actually taken from that of a hospital consultant character in the series *Children's Ward* (ITV, 1992-1996), which Russell T Davies had produced and written for.

- There were eight Judoon costumes made for the episode; the impression of large numbers of the creatures was created by the use of multiple images of them. Only one rhino head was made, for the Captain, hence the other Judoon kept their helmets on.

- Unlike his previous vocal characterisations for the series (most notably the Dalek and Cyberman voices), the Judoon voices were created by Nicholas Briggs without any electronic aid.

- When Martha asks if the Slabs come from 'the planet Zovirax', this is a reference to a TV commercial, familiar to UK viewers, for a brand of cold-sore treatment. The commercial features a woman who, because she is suffering from a cold sore, conceals her features behind a dark-visored motorcycle helmet.

- For the scene where Martha performs CPR on the Doctor, Freema Agyeman was given brief on-set instruction by someone medically qualified (although the technique she uses is reportedly somewhat out of date and not in line with current hospital practice).

- The scenes in the X-Ray room were directed, uncredited, by James Strong, as recording had overrun and principal director Charles Palmer was required to be elsewhere working on scenes for 'The Shakespeare Code'.

- When first edited together, the episode was found to under-run, so Russell T Davies wrote some short additional scenes, which were shot later and then added in. These included the scene of Martha in her flat toward the end of the episode, this set having been constructed for use in 'The Lazarus Experiment'.

- Russell T Davies's script for this episode was made available for download from the BBC's Writers' Room blog (www.bbc.co.uk/blogs/writersroom) from 19 April 2007.

## UNFOUNDED PRE-TRANSMISSION RUMOURS

- Classsic series monsters the Ice Warriors would appear in this episode.
- The Judoon would be revealed as a cloned sub-group of the classic series monsters the Sontarans.

## OOPS!

- Members of the production crew are occasionally visible in reflections in the Slabs' helmets.
- Martha's reflection in the hospital window, when she first realises that the building has been transported to the Moon, is a static image, even though she is moving.
- In 'Aliens of London', the (fictional) Albion Hospital was said to be the nearest one to where the 'space pig' was recovered from the Thames, but here the (equally fictional) Royal Hope Hospital is located on the same site as the (real-life) St Thomas's Hospital, just on the opposite side of the Thames from the Houses of Parliament, which must mean that it is nearer. (Possibly the Royal Hope Hospital is newly-opened?)

## PRESS REACTION

- 'It's a baptism of laser fire for Freema Agyeman, who acquits herself honourably in her new role and adroitly communicates the spontaneity and excitement so essential to Russell T Davies's rip-roaring new adventures of the tenth Time Lord.' Mike Bradley, *The Observer*, 31 March 2007.
- '"That's aliens, aliens, real proper aliens!" Pulling off a line like that without sounding like an asteroid-sized chump takes some chutzpah, but mega-hyped new *Doctor Who* sidekick Martha Jones – welcome on board Freema Agyeman – pulled it off with aplomb, turning in a debut that had even this hardened Whovian whispering "Rose who?" It looks like trainee-medic-turned-interplanetary-adventurer Martha will be giving the good Doctor a run for his money over the coming weeks, and the good news is they've got the big snog out of the way, even if the randy Time Lord tried to shrug it off as a "genetic transfer". Agyeman and David Tennant have the kind of chemistry you can only buy on Planet Phwoar.' Keith Watson, *Metro*, 2 April 2007.
- 'Here is some good news ... followed by even better news. The good news is that *Doctor Who* is back and – yes! – it's as exhilarating as ever. Russell T Davies's script is exciting and imaginative and very funny. The monsters are as scary as scary can be without sending kids into psychological meltdown. The special effects are sensational, and David Tennant's Doctor is so wacky and endearing that his performance is getting perilously close to definitive. But here's the even better news. The Doctor's new companion (Freema Agyeman) takes over the role from Billie Piper and immediately makes it her own, imbuing it with strength and fun and warmth. It is such a good episode that I almost forgot to mention that the wonderful Anne Reid plays an evil old crone who does disgusting things with a straw. Lucky children. Lucky parents.' David Chater, *The Times*, 31 March 2007.

- 'As with last year's series opener, "New Earth" – also written by Russell T Davies and also set in a hospital – the science-fiction element of the story doesn't stand up to close scrutiny. An MRI scanner, capable of being tweaked to kill everything within 250,000 miles? On an NHS budget? (Seriously though, it could kill everything on Earth – even from the Moon – but Anne Reid plans to escape by hiding behind a screen?) Also in common with last year's episode, though, the sci-fi is secondary to character development – in particular, how a new Doctor-companion team works together. And there are loads of great character moments for both. We get to see that Martha is analytical, methodical, but caring – pausing to give Roy Marsden's dead consultant what little dignity she can. And Agyeman proves that she's up to the job, thus far at least. She's certainly more than capable of acting the straight man to David Tennant's Doctor – on top form here, serious and intense when needed, but superbly comedic when allowed.' Scott Matthewman, *The Stage* website, 31 March 2007.
- 'Billie Piper is a long-forgotten memory of blonde hair and bushy black eyebrows. But is her replacement, Freema Agyeman, much cop? If wooden, bland, unoriginal is your thing, then she's fantastic. Let's hope she settles in as the series progresses. When *Doctor Who* burst back on our screens two years ago shinier than one of Alan Sugar's Bentleys, it was exciting and fresh. Billie took time to warm into her role as sidekick Rose Tyler but, before long, she carried the show while the Doctors changed. Writer Russell T Davies injected a sense of fun and excitement back into the cult series with impressive special effects and a modern glossy shiny sheen. But as we embark on a third series, minus the brilliant Billie, that gloss has vanished. What was once new and exciting is now boring and repetitive. It feels a struggle to have to engage with a new sidekick for the Doctor. The constant changing of actors leaves a continuity problem larger than Simon Cowell's ego. A problem that could have been overcome if this series offered something new to distract. But if the opener is anything to go by, then we're in for the same tricks over again.' Jon Wise, *People*, 1 April 2007.
- 'Agyeman is simply a pleasure to watch, with Martha's excitement at her journey putting a smile on our faces. She's also smart and confident enough to hold her own with Tennant in both the serious and lighter scenes, with their moments of banter well delivered. Our introduction to Martha's family wasn't particularly absorbing, but that's easily forgivable. At this stage of the series the foundations are being laid for later events. Swiping aside the characterisation, the actual alien-related plot is slightly underwhelming and not overly consumed with the sense of menace and danger that pervades the finest *Doctor Who* episodes. The Plasmavore threat to the Earth never has much gravity (like the rain in the episode), despite Anne Reid's fun performance. Still, you can imagine children around the country running around with straws in the playground, which is probably a tad healthier than imaginary machine guns ... As for David Tennant, he feels so natural in the role. He is the Doctor. His physical comedy skills are particularly foregrounded by the radiation ejection scene, which echoes a similar moment beating out a samba in the "New Earth" episode last year. He's not just a clown though, as packaged within this one-liner emitting figure is still a Time Lord who has

anger, fear and loneliness. Overall, this episode succeeded in its aim of endearing the character of Martha Jones to us, so that by the end of the episode we're delighted to have her on board for the trip of a lifetime. Job done lads.' Ben Rawson-Jones, Digital Spy website, 31 March 2007.

- 'There are strange things going on at the hospital where Martha is a medical student. The Doctor is a patient there, for a start. Next the Stig from *Top Gear* turns up and starts causing trouble (and then another one – two Stigs! I knew it wasn't just one person). It starts to rain upwards outside. Then, before you know it, the whole hospital has been teleported to the moon. And the Doctor and Martha are having a romantic earthlit moment on the balcony. Then he's snogging her! Bloody hell, he's so totally over Rose. Okay, so it's not actually a snog snog – it's part of the Doctor's plans to trick the Judoon, the scary space-rhino aliens that are running all over the place. But it certainly looks like a snog snog. That's it then, the chemistry in place, in episode one. It's almost too quick. But Agyeman is great. If I do have one criticism, it's that she's too much like her predecessor – in the way she speaks, her mannerisms, the way she flirts with the Doctor. I hope as the series goes on, she'll develop more of her own identity. But it'll do for now. Bloody hell, I'm so over Rose too. Billie who, frankly.' Sam Wallaston, *Guardian*, 2 May 2007.

- 'As Martha, Freema Agyeman hit the ground running, which was fortunate since there was much running to be done, mostly down NHS corridors. The London hospital in which she worked had been sucked up and relocated on the Moon, a primary care reorganisation too far, you'll agree. The Moon was being used as some kind of Guantanamo Bay for the Judoon, intergalactic policemen with the faces of rhinos (pigs would have been too obvious). The Judoon were firm but fair. Hit them over the head and they would vaporise you, but for a wrongful arrest you got a compensation form to complete. With the Doctor and Martha's help, they got their man in the end, or rather an alien woman, Mrs Florence Finnegan, wanted for murdering an irritating princess in another galaxy. It was all accomplished with great energy and at a frantically entertaining pace. It looks wonderful. I think, though, that Davies knows he is entering a zone of diminishing returns by setting so many stories in present-day Britain: both of the last two episodes have contained references to the unlikely amount of alien activity there has been. The humour also worries me. I liked the compensation gag but the Doctor shaking the radiation out of his trousers was as stupid as the bicycle pump he needs to get the TARDIS going.' Andrew Billen, *The Times*, 2 April 2007.

FAN COMMENT
- 'Davies has written Martha's character really, really well. She's sassy, clever and calm. The fact that she kept her head when the building that she's in magically appeared on the Moon was fantastic. Granted Britain has been through a few changes recently with spaceships crashing into Big Ben and Cybermen taking over, but I'd still freak out if I ended up on the Moon in a big bubble! The explanation of her cousin being in Canary Wharf answered my question of "How are they going to get over the fact she died in the last series as a different character?" beautifully. The sadness in Ten's eyes as he said that he was in Canary Wharf at the time had me thinking of Rose, but only for a

second. The Judoon ships averted my attention. They were seriously … cool ships! And the Nu-rock boots. Excellent! Gothic monsters. And the drinking-blood-through-a-straw lady? Awesome!' Melissa, Emerge website, 31 March 2007.

- 'Oh wow. Forget your soaps. Forget your reality TV shows. Forget your night time quiz shows. Forget your police dramas. Give me a fleet of Judoon spaceships touching down on the Moon any time. In that moment – and in the subsequent sequence of the Judoon entering the hospital – I found my jaw dropping, my gob smacking, and my flabber gasting. Quite frankly, the effects in this opening episode of the new series were nothing short of awesome. If the Mill don't win some awards for their work on this episode … it'll be because they've bettered themselves in later episodes. This was stunning stuff.' David Brider, LiveJournal blog, 2 April 2007.

- '"Smith and Jones" was a superb opener. A crowd pleaser on every level, Davies's script shone with witty one liners and action, a really cool monster, and of course the introduction of a new companion. In some respects, I found the opening of "Smith and Jones" reminiscent of the start of "Rose", with the new girl – here, Martha Jones, medical student – and her family/affairs being introduced in a snappy shorthand style which is very attractive. This also introduces Martha as very much a 2000s girl, reliant on her mobile phone to stay in touch, and talking with everyone simultaneously while juggling her job and family relationships effortlessly. She's also quite a fox, easy on the eye and very natural on-screen.' David J Howe, Howe's Who website, 4 April 2007.

- 'The "camp fest" that is Russell T Davies's Doctor Who is back on screen, and I began to wonder if Graham Norton mightn't have been a more appropriate choice for his conception of the Doctor. David Tennant's Doctor is all levitas, even in what should be grave situations. Mind you, faced with the like of the Judoon, rhino-headed humanoids, you might well make a joke of it yourself. What's scary about a rhino? Surely something truly alien could have been imagined. A hospital sucked up to the Moon? Somehow this kind of thing convinced in "The Three Doctors": in "Smith and Jones" it seemed ridiculous. I truly believe that it happened only because RTD thought of the phrase "Judoon on the Moon" and thought it hilarious. "But it will appeal to children," some will say. Yes, but when the children have grown up, they may have grown out of Doctor Who and be looking back at that "childish nonsense", whereas those of us who grew up with the "classic series" still love the stories because there's depth in them, as well as sincere acting.' Paul Pritchard, Celestial Toyroom Issue 347[35], May 2007.

- 'Part of the enjoyment of this episode was … a quiet sense of relief at being free of Rose's extended family and her "journey". I liked quite a bit of that journey over the last two years, and I understand why RTD needed to use Rose as some kind of touchstone for a new audience. But the show has its audience now, and it felt genuinely liberating to have a new companion (not saddled with a boyfriend?) with a family that already show signs of being less dominating than the last lot. The other liberating thing was being in space – it

---

[35] Although numbered Issue 347 on the cover, this is actually Issue 348, as the Doctor Who Appreciation Society mistakenly published two issues numbered 346.

took me a while to realise it, but I had a big smile on my face for a lot of the episode because big spaceships were landing on something other than the Earth and aliens were marching across a lunar landscape. Perhaps I'm not that sophisticated a viewer after all.' John Williams, Behind the Sofa website, 6 April 2007.

## ANALYSIS

The main focus of this episode is obviously the introduction of Martha Jones as the Doctor's new companion; in fact, it is rather a surprise that it wasn't called simply 'Martha'. Having said that, 'Smith and Jones' is an excellent title, and does highlight the fact that what we see here is not just the debut of a new companion but also the inception of a new Doctor-and-companion relationship.

It seems that, perhaps picking up on the advice that Donna gave him at the end of 'The Runaway Bride', the Doctor is actively on the lookout for a successor to Rose, albeit – as he is quick to point out – not a replacement. He effectively auditions Martha for this role during the course of the story, noting each time she makes an intelligent comment or a shrewd deduction. The first example of this comes when, shortly after the hospital is transported to the Moon, she dismisses her colleague Julia's concern that opening the window will allow all the air to escape, pointing out that the seals aren't airtight and that there must therefore be something preventing this from happening. 'Very good point,' the Doctor observes. 'Brilliant, in fact.' He then invites Martha to join him out on the balcony, but the tearful Julia has clearly failed to make the grade: 'Not her,' he says. 'She'd hold us up.'

Admittedly, not even Martha thinks to express surprise that the hospital still has Earth-type gravity (presumably courtesy of the Judoon, who would doubtless have found it difficult to catalogue everyone if they were bouncing around semi-weightless) and an electricity supply (perhaps more easily explained if one recalls that hospitals have their own generators, which automatically kick in if the mains current is interrupted); but writer Russell T Davies's reason for focusing on the question of the air supply becomes apparent a little later on, when the fact that it is limited, and that the hospital's occupants are finding it harder and harder to breathe, becomes a source of increasing tension – making their plight a race against time – and is also used to good symbolic effect when Martha ultimately revives the Doctor by performing mouth-to-mouth resuscitation on him, giving virtually her last breath to save him and thereby confirming her suitability for companion status. (It actually seems rather curious that a conventional CPR technique, designed for humans, works on a Time Lord; but then Martha does remember that he has two hearts – as she discovered when she examined him earlier on – and tries to make allowances for it by switching the compressions from one side of his chest to the other, so perhaps that is why!)

Billie Piper's Rose – in many ways the definitive *Doctor Who* companion – was always going to be a very hard act to follow, but Agyeman gives an excellent performance in her debut as Martha (after her creditable but brief appearance as Adeola – now revealed to have been Martha's cousin – in 'Army of Ghosts' at the end of Series Two) and shows every sign of having the energy, charisma and sheer likeability needed to make her a worthy successor. In terms of characterisation,

Davies does a superb job of establishing Martha as a young woman who is in some ways similar to Rose – in that she is intelligent, brave, inquisitive and resourceful and, more superficially, has a similar London accent – but in others very different. She is a little older than Rose; is better educated; has a more challenging and rewarding job; is more independent, with her own (rented) flat and no boyfriend; and comes from a larger, more middle-class family of a different ethnic origin. Just as Rose's mother Jackie and boyfriend Mickey were introduced in a fairly low-key way in 'Rose', giving little indication of the prominent parts they were to play in later episodes, so Martha's family have only an incidental role in proceedings in 'Smith and Jones'. They are sketched in by Davies in fairly broad, humorous strokes – the smartly-dressed, no-nonsense mother Francine, who takes an executive briefcase to work; the estranged father Clive, showing obvious signs of going through a mid-life crisis with his sports car and trashy blonde girlfriend Annalise; the cute, friendly younger sister Tish; and the handsome 21-year-old brother Leo with, as seen in the background of a couple of shots, his partner Shonara and baby Keisha (neither of whom are actually named on screen) – but this helps to ensure that they are quickly established, and that they stick in the viewer's mind; an important consideration, given that none of them will be seen again until five episodes later.

Davies's script cleverly points up the significance that Martha is going to have in the Doctor's life by drawing a number of subtle parallels between her introduction and Rose's. The prime example comes when, as the Slabs stride menacingly toward them, the Doctor takes Martha's hand and says 'Run!', obviously recalling the action from his first meeting with Rose in the basement of Henrik's in 'Rose', as also mentioned in the *Children in Need* special of 2006 and seen in flashback at the start of 'Army of Ghosts'. Where this works a little less well, however, is in the scene toward the end of the episode where the Doctor entices Martha to take a trip in the TARDIS by telling her 'I can travel in time as well.' When, in his previous incarnation, he said something very similar – 'Did I mention, it also travels in time' – to convince Rose to join him on his travels, it came across as a simple, spontaneous invitation to adventure. The fact that he says essentially the same thing here, though, makes it seem more like a corny chat-up line, and one is uncomfortably reminded of Martha's father trying to impress his trophy girlfriend with his sports car.

There is something almost a little creepy about the way the Doctor lures Martha into the TARDIS in this alley scene – did no-one ever warn her about accepting lifts from strangers? – but fortunately things improve rapidly when the action moves inside the ship, to the accompaniment of the wonderfully haunting new theme composed for Martha by Murray Gold. The Doctor's silent mimicking of Martha when she notes, predictably, 'It's bigger on the inside' – a piece of business suggested by David Tennant himself during recording – is very funny; although, to her credit, Martha has also made, a few moments earlier, the striking observation that the TARDIS is a spaceship made of wood – something that none of the Doctor's previous companions has ever thought to comment upon. One can easily see how, from Martha's point of view, the Doctor might appear to be sending her mixed signals here. He has given every impression that he is flirting with her – as she points out, he did kiss her, and he has now gone to some lengths to track her down and invite her out on a 'date' – but when she responds to his advances, making it clear that she finds him attractive in his 'tight suit', he coyly back-pedals, pointing out that the kiss was just a genetic transfer and telling her to 'Stop it'. (Again Tennant seems almost to be channelling Kenneth Williams in his performance here, although he just holds back from using the latter's 'Stop messin' about' catchphrase.) Kisses do appear to hold a special significance in Davies's view of the universe: the Doctor saved Rose's life, and sacrificed his own ninth incarnation, by drawing the time vortex out of her with a kiss in 'The Parting of the Ways'; there were a number of instances of life-force being transmitted via a kiss in the first series of *Torchwood*; and now the Doctor has performed a genetic transfer on Martha through a kiss, and Martha, in a kind of reciprocation, has resuscitated him using the 'kiss of life' technique. Was it really necessary for the Doctor to kiss Martha, full on the lips, in order to effect a temporary transfer of Time Lord genetic material to her? In scientific terms, probably not; in symbolic terms, definitely so. Martha's defensive response to being rebuffed – 'For the record, I'm not remotely interested; I only go for humans' – isn't really fooling anyone.

This again shows Davies astutely establishing a relationship between the Doctor and Martha that is in some ways similar to that between the Doctor and Rose but in others very different. Whereas with Rose there was clearly a strong mutual attraction – and even, ultimately, love – with Martha the feelings seem to be – so far, at least – one-sided. To have had the Doctor falling for another young woman so soon after losing Rose would have been almost unthinkably crass, so arguably Davies had little option but to come up with something different this time around, but he has really made a virtue out of necessity here, crafting a new Doctor-and-companion dynamic that seems fresh and full of potential. It is, in fact, not far removed from the type of relationship the writer had originally envisaged for the Doctor and Rose: in his initial treatment document for the new *Doctor Who*, prepared in the autumn of 2003, he stated that they would love each other platonically and be 'soulmates', and that the Doctor would not select his companions on the basis of whether or not he fancied them; it was only later, at the scriptwriting stage, that he developed their attachment into the highly intense one that it ultimately became.

The relationship between the Doctor and Martha is thus rather more 'traditional' in *Doctor Who* terms; and while the classic series never featured a companion character who had overt romantic feelings for the Doctor that he either failed to reciprocate or even register, there are precedents for this – as for so many other aspects of Davies's *Doctor Who* – in the original novels. Perhaps the most notable of these is Sam Jones, who is the eighth Doctor's first companion in the BBC novels series, and whose feelings for him really come to the fore when, in Michael Collier's *Longest Day* (1998), she performs CPR on him, and finds herself kissing him passionately. The fact that Martha has the same surname as Sam is probably just a coincidence in view of Davies's well-known predilection for giving his characters Welsh names, and certainly in other respects they are very different character types, but the scene where the former first enters the TARDIS in 'Smith and Jones' does bear a number of striking similarities to that where the latter does so in Terrance Dicks's novel *The Eight Doctors* (1997), even down to the handshake between them and the 'just one trip' idea.

The exchange of dialogue at the very end of 'Smith and Jones', where the Doctor says 'Welcome aboard Miss Jones,' and Martha responds 'It's my pleasure,

Mr Smith,' as the TARDIS buffets them about in flight, apart from being a homage of sorts to the fifth Doctor's greeting to his new companion Peri at the close of 'Planet of Fire' (1984), somewhat recalls the mock formality, playfulness and unrequited sexual tension of the relationship between John Steed (Patrick Macnee) and Emma Peel (Diana Rigg) – or 'Steed' and 'Mrs Peel', as they customarily addressed each other – in the most-fondly-remembered era of the classic fantasy espionage series *The Avengers* (ABC, 1961-1969) (another brainchild of *Doctor Who's* principal creator Sydney Newman), suggesting an interesting avenue for possible future development.

The only slightly questionable aspect of this excellent final scene is that the Doctor actually refers to Rose directly and by name. After 'The Runaway Bride', which seemed to have been designed at least in part as a transitional adventure to allow the Doctor, and the audience at home, to get over Rose's departure, it might have been possible, and indeed preferable, to have avoided any further specific mentions of this kind, leaving the Doctor's enduring sadness at the loss of his former companion to be conveyed rather more subtly, perhaps simply through nuances in Tennant's performance. It actually seems rather unfair to Agyeman, when she is trying hard to establish herself as the series' new female lead, that the dialogue insists on reminding the viewer so forcefully of her brilliant predecessor; something that will indeed continue throughout Series Three.

Quite apart from introducing a very promising new companion, 'Smith and Jones' has a lot of other things going for it. David Tennant is again on superb form, and it is good to see him getting a new suit to wear, in a nice shade of blue, which thankfully avoids him being stuck in what amounts to a 'uniform' (albeit a very good one), as a couple of the earlier Doctors were. His hair seems to have gone a bit mad here, too, his exaggerated quiff occasionally giving him something of a Stan Laurel look. The fact that the Doctor is already posing as a hospital patient when the story begins means that he is thrown straight into the action without any tiresome preliminaries, and this works well in helping to get things off to a flying start. This approach of having the Doctor already ensconced in a key position at the start of a story is again one that was pioneered in some of the *New Adventures* novels in the 1990s; and it was also adopted to good effect in the Series Two episode 'School Reunion', which opened with the Doctor standing in as a science teacher at Deffry Vale High School.

Also introduced in 'Smith and Jones' is an excellent new race of aliens in the form of the Judoon, superbly voiced by the estimable Nicholas Briggs. Although obviously reminiscent of classic series monsters the Sontarans in their design, with their domed helmets matching the shape of their heads, and also to some extent of the Cybermen in the way they march along in formation, the idea of them being interplanetary 'police for hire' who are bound to follow certain rules is quite original in *Doctor Who* terms. It provides a good motivation for them temporarily removing the hospital to the neutral territory of the Moon – an idea possibly inspired by the transportation of a church to the Moon in Paul Cornell's acclaimed *New Adventures* novel *Timewyrm: Revelation* (1991) – as well as a pretext for some amusing incidents such as when they act as prosecutor, judge and executioner to a patient who hits one of them over the head with a vase ('Justice is swift,' as the Judoon Captain says) and when they give Martha compensation after at first wrongly thinking that she may be a non-human. Probably their closest *Doctor Who* antecedents in this respect are the Megara, from what is said to be one of Davies's favourite classic series stories, 'The Stones of Blood' (1978); these justice machines were also obliged to abide by set laws, and were likewise seeking an alien criminal who had assumed human female form in a tale involving blood-sucking monsters.

As characters, the Judoon are also somewhat reminiscent both of the Vogons, a race of hidebound bureaucrats from *The Hitchhiker's Guide to the Galaxy* by one-time *Doctor Who* script editor and writer Douglas Adams, and of the inflexible, black-helmeted law-enforcers of the *Judge Dredd* comics series from *2000 AD*. Their 'space rhino' appearance is again suggestive of a comic book influence, and recalls the 'space cows' seen in Gareth Roberts' 'The Lunar Strangers' story in *Doctor Who Magazine*, as well as the 'space turtle' Chelonians featured in some of the same author's *Doctor Who* novels and short stories.

In terms of their on-screen realisation, the Judoon are impressive, imposing creations, and the prosthetic head of the Captain is a truly superb piece of work by designer Neill Gorton, featuring possibly the most convincing animatronic movement seen in the series to date. In fact, all aspects of the episode's design work are well up to par, giving the production a polished, high-budget look.

Just to prove, though, that the series doesn't need expensive special effects to present an effective alien, 'Smith and Jones' also gives us a deadly, blood-sucking Plasmavore disguised in human form as the elderly Florence Finnegan, played by veteran actress Anne Reid in her second *Doctor Who* appearance (something of a role-reversal from her first, as a nurse whose blood is sucked by the vampire-like Haemovores in 'The Curse of Fenric' (1989)). Reid gives a superbly creepy performance here, making Florence a far more effective villain than the murderous old ladies of 'Paradise Towers' (1987), probably her nearest forerunners in the series (although the Sontarans' perennial enemies the Rutans were also shapeshifters, suggesting that 'Smith and Jones' could have been presented as a Sontarans versus Rutans story without too much rejigging). It was an inspired notion on Davies's part to have her use a bendy straw to perform her exsanguinations; something that can be easily mimicked by kids in playgrounds across the country without even having to fork out for a toy replica. It is quirky, imaginative ideas such as this – another good example being the Judoon identifying the catalogued patients with a cross in marker pen on the back of the hand (although presumably this means the Doctor could have avoided them without the need for a genetic transfer if he had just happened to have a marker pen in his bigger-inside-than-out pockets!) – that help to make modern *Doctor Who* so much fun; and they are one of the hallmarks of Davies's writing for the series.

There is even a third set of new creatures introduced here in the shape of the Slabs (although 'creatures' is probably not quite the right word in this instance, as they are 'basic slave drones' supposedly made of solid leather), and these are realised almost outrageously cheaply, as two men wearing what appear to be motorbike leathers and standard black-visored helmets – almost the proverbial 'man in a rubber suit' creations – but, incredibly, they actually work, and serve as a very menacing presence as they stalk around the hospital.

Another of Davies's hallmarks as a writer is his superb, sparkling dialogue, and 'Smith and Jones' provides many further examples of this; it is an episode packed with great lines and memorable exchanges, some particularly quotable gems being Florence's 'Look, I've even brought a straw,' the Doctor's 'Judoon platoon upon the

Moon', and Martha's father Clive's 'I'm putting my foot down! This is me, putting my foot down!'. Where Davies sometimes falls down a little is in his plotting, but even that is very sound here, the only slip coming when, in another example of his tendency to over-egg things a little (as discussed in the 'Analysis' section on 'The Runaway Bride'), he has Florence reconfiguring an MRI scanner in such a way that it threatens to wipe out all life on the side of the Earth facing the Moon; an unfortunate elaboration not only because it is scientifically impossible – in a way that the idea of a hospital being transported to the Moon really isn't, because in that case one can rely on the catch-all explanation that it involves the use of some highly advanced alien technology, the capabilities of which have to be taken as read in a series like *Doctor Who* – but also because it is unnecessary in the context of the story, the danger to the 1,000-odd patients and staff in the hospital being quite sufficient to sustain the drama without the need for this extra, over-the-top layer.

This, though, is a rare lapse in an otherwise outstanding script. Davies has consistently proved himself a master craftsman when it comes to writing introductory episodes – as seen with the superb 'Rose', the tenth Doctor's excellent debut adventure 'The Christmas Invasion' and *Torchwood*'s brilliant opening instalment 'Everything Changes' – and 'Smith and Jones', presenting Martha to the viewing public, is no exception. Far superior to the muddled Series Two opener 'New Earth', and possibly better even than 'Rose' itself, it is actually one of his strongest ever *Doctor Who* scripts. On the production front, the thing that really comes across loud and clear here is a huge sense of confidence on the part of all concerned, as they embark on making a third run of episodes in what has already firmly established itself as a ratings-dominating, award-winning and much-loved series. It is a confidence that is not misplaced: amusing, thrilling, bright, fresh and optimistic, 'Smith and Jones' is an example of 21st Century *Doctor Who* at the very top of its game.

# 3.02 – THE SHAKESPEARE CODE

Writer: Gareth Roberts
Director: Charles Palmer

DEBUT TRANSMISSION DETAILS

BBC One
Date: 7 April 2007. Scheduled time: 7.00 pm. Actual time: 6.59 pm.

BBC Three
Date: 8 April 2007. Scheduled time: 8.00 pm. Actual time: 8.01 pm.

Duration: 45' 38"

ADDITIONAL CREDITED CAST

Dean Lennox Kelly (Shakespeare), Christina Cole (Lilith), Sam Marks (Wiggins), Amanda Lawrence (Doomfinger), Linda Clark (Bloodtide), Jalaal Hartley (Dick[36]), David Westhead (Kempe[37]), Andrée Bernard (Dolly Bailey), Chris Larkin (Lynley), Stephen Marcus (Jailer), Matt King (Peter Streete)[38], Robert Demeger (Preacher)[39], Angela Pleasence (Queen Elizabeth)[40].

PLOT

The Doctor takes Martha to London, 1599, to see a performance at the Globe Theatre. Three witch-like Carrionites are attempting to influence Shakespeare to write into his latest play, *Love's Labour's Won*, some lines of dialogue that will free the others of their kind from their ancient banishment. At the Doctor's urging, Shakespeare ad-libs some new words that trap the Carrionites within their crystal globe, which the Doctor determines to consign to an attic in the TARDIS.

QUOTE, UNQUOTE

- **Martha:** 'What if I kill my grandfather?'
  **Doctor:** 'Are you planning to?'
  **Martha:** 'No.'
  **Doctor:** 'Well then …'

---

[36] Richard Burbage, a member of Shakespeare's company.
[37] William Kempe, another member of Shakespeare's company.
[38] Not credited in *Radio Times*.
[39] Not credited in *Radio Times*.
[40] Not credited in *Radio Times*.

- **Shakespeare:** 'The Doctor may never kiss you. Why not entertain a man who will?'

## CONTINUITY POINTS

- When Lynley, the Master of the Revels, dies by drowning on dry land, the Doctor says, 'I've never seen a death like it.' This is technically true, although he did once see, after the event, the body of a man who had been killed in a similar way in 'The Mind of Evil' (1971).
- Martha asks the Doctor if witchcraft is real, and he replies, 'Of course it isn't … Looks like witchcraft, but it isn't. Can't be … There's such a thing as psychic energy, but a human can't channel it like that, not without a generator the size of Taunton.'
- The Doctor identifies the 'witches' as Carrionites after recalling the '14 stars of the Rexel planetary configuration,' echoed in the 14-sided shape of the Globe as designed under their influence by craftsman Peter Streete. He later says that they 'disappeared, way back at the dawn of the universe,' and that they now want to create a 'new empire, on Earth; a world of bones and blood and witchcraft'.
- The Doctor refers to the seventh book in the *Harry Potter* series, and assumes that Martha will not have read it. Given the likelihood that Martha comes from 2008, as indicated in 'Smith and Jones', this suggests that, in the *Doctor Who* universe, the book in question, *Harry Potter and the Deathly Hallows*, may have not have been published until 2008 (or later), whereas in our universe it came out on 21 July 2007. Either that, or the Doctor has simply made a mistake with his dates, although Martha's reaction to his comment gives no indication that this is the case.
- The Carrionites are said to have been banished into 'deep darkness' by the Eternals, a race introduced in the classic *Doctor Who* story 'Enlightenment' (1983) and also mentioned in 'Army of Ghosts'.
- Queen Elizabeth I describes the Doctor as her 'sworn enemy', although he has no idea what she means.
- In a contribution to the book *Doctor Who: Creatures and Demons*, published in May 2007, writer Gareth Roberts expands on the Carrionites' background with additional details not revealed in the transmitted story: 'The 14 Stars of the Rexel Planetary Configuration have been a mystery since the dawn of understanding in the universe. Legend has it that [they] are a prison door, sealed billions of years in the past, keeping the Carrionites in Deep Darkness. The Carrionites, legendarily, ate their own husbands and children. They are said to have developed a malevolent science of their own – using shapes, words, numbers and names to effect their attacks on hundreds of their neighbouring planets back at the dawn of time. They used the grief and suffering of others to enhance this science – which to us is indistinguishable from magic.'

## PRODUCTION NOTES

- 'The Shakespeare Code' was made with 'Smith and Jones' in Block 2 of production on Series Three.
- This episode had the working title 'Love's Labour's Won'.
- Consideration was given to a number of other possible settings for the story, including Shakepeare's home town of Stratford-upon-Avon, before London was settled upon. It was felt that an urban setting would give the story a higher-budget look and be, as writer Gareth Roberts later put it in an interview, 'more audacious and fun'. Other possibilities mooted at an early stage included having the action take place at a time when Shakespeare was still a child, or alternatively an old man approaching death; it was eventually decided that it would be preferable to show the playwright in, or at least approaching, his prime. Ideas dropped from the script as it developed through its various drafts included featuring Shakespeare's daughter Susanna in the unconvincing guise of a boy, and having Martha audition for Shakespeare's company in the manner of a contestant on ITV1 talent contest *The X Factor* (2004- ).
- The character Wiggins was named after long-time *Doctor Who* fan and commentator Dr Martin Wiggins, who is renowned as a leading academic authority on Shakespeare.
- Freedonia, the place that the Doctor tells Shakespeare that Martha comes from, is a fictional country from the Marx Brothers classic comedy film *Duck Soup* (Paramount Pictures, 1933). It may also refer to the forename of actress Freema Agyeman.
- The scene where the Doctor confronts Lilith in the 'crooked house' in All Hallows Street was originally to have had them engaging in a sword fight. This, unusually, was planned to be done on film rather than video, at the request of director Charles Palmer. After two days of rehearsals for it, however, it was ultimately judged not to work, and was dropped just before it was shot. The stand-off thus became a more understated one, with Lilith attempting to seduce the Doctor and he telling her that that sort of magic would not work on him.
- The dialogue that the Carrionites induce Shakespeare to add to his play includes words and phrases drawn by writer Gareth Roberts from a number of different sources, including earlier *Doctor Who* stories ('Dravidian', used in 'The Brain of Morbius' (1975)), '70s science-fiction series *The Tomorrow People* ('Rexel 4', used in 'The Blue and the Green' (1974)), the film *The Monster Club* (Amicus Productions, 1980) ('Shadmock', the name of a monster in the film, based on a collection of short stories by R Chetwyn-Hayes) and (inadvertently on Roberts' part) *Blake's 7* ('co-radiating crystal', used in 'Power' (1981)).
- Location recording took place in Coventry – at Ford's Hospital in Greyfriars Lane (used for a number of settings, including the witches' house) – in Warwick – at Lord Leycester's Hospital, a home for retired servicemen, in the High Street (for the street where the TARDIS materialises) – and at the reconstruction of the Globe Theatre in London, all at the end of August 2006. About a week before the recording at the Globe was due to take place, contractual problems arose that almost ruled it out, and the production team

had to consider relocating the relevant scenes to another setting, possibly a country house; but the problems were then resolved. Recording at this location took place over three nights, starting on 31 August, with work beginning immediately after each evening's public performance ended and continuing round to 9.00 the following morning. Part of the theatre was subsequently recreated in the Upper Boat studios for recording of additional scenes in early September 2006, where the impression of a full audience was achieved by having a block of around 50 extras, all in appropriate period dress, moved into a succession of different positions around the stage, with the resultant shots then being put together in post-production to form a composite image. The interiors of Bethlem Hospital were shot in cellars beneath Newport Market on 7 September 2006.

- Quoted in the *Radio Times* of 7-13 April 2007, actor Dean Lennox said of his portrayal of Shakespeare; 'One thing I thought was: "What do I do with my body?" I'm a modern person! ... I just went slightly camp, slightly Johnny Depp in *Pirates of the Caribbean*[41], a bit of Liam Gallagher, a bit of Kev from *Shameless*[42], a bit of me, a bit of eyeliner – there you go! For a whole load of kids, their vision of Shakespeare is gonna be me, prancing about. I could inspire a generation of Shakespeare lovers. Or not. But that's going to be great ... Imagine me being in a shop and a little kid comes up and goes, "Excuse me, Mr Shakespeare!"'
- In April 2007, the costume worn by the Carrionite Bloodtide in this episode was placed on display at the Globe Theatre as part of its Shakepeare's Globe Exhibition.

OOPS!

- The architecture of the Bethlem Hospital exterior, as seen in an establishing shot, is anachronistic, being about a century too modern.
- The fillings in actress Christina Cole's teeth are clearly visible when Lilith cackles.

PRESS REACTION

- 'With much hey-nonny-no-ing, *Doctor Who* pitched up in Elizabethan times and a Shakespearean witchcraft romp that, for all its tricksy wordplay, felt suspiciously like marking time. Casting Kev from *Shameless* (Dean Lennox Kelly) as the Bard was a cute piece of TV in-jokery but by the fifth time he'd quipped "I might use that one" after the Doctor had quoted his quotes back at him, things had got a little too clever-clever for their own good. The Doctor needs scarier foes than a trio of hags in bad wigs to keep him on his toes.' Keith Watson, *Metro*, 10 April 2007.

---

[41] A trilogy of films released by Walt Disney Pictures and Buena Vista Pictures in 2003, 2006, 2007 respectively, in which Depp plays a flamboyant pirate character, loosly based on Keith Richards of the Rolling Stones.
[42] An ongoing Channel 4 comedy series, launched in 2004, in which Kelly plays the role of Kev.

- 'The theme of the power of words has been dealt with before in *Doctor Who*. In 2005's "The Long Game", for example, humanity was being subdued by journalists working under the control of a malevolent proprietor. "The right word, in the right broadcast, repeated often enough," says that episode, "can destabilise an economy, invent an enemy, change a vote ..." That's a theme worth repeating, and the power of theatre if anything makes the point both more firmly and more effectively here, two years on.' Scott Matthewman, *The Stage* website, 8 April 2007.

- 'This is a work of fiction ... incorporating characters who were real people ... It includes a play within a play, containing fictional dialogue attributed to a real author ... Now pay attention, that was the easy bit. On encountering this missing adventure, Martha suggests capturing it on MiniDisc, so that even with the folio lost, future fans of Shakespeare can enjoy it. A bit like the soundtracks to "The Power of the Daleks" and "The Macra Terror" in the BBC Radio Collection, really, which are of course parts of *Doctor Who*, in which Martha herself is a fictional character. And then the Doctor, played by David Tennant, talks about *Harry Potter* – in which Tennant himself has apppeared. The Doctor even eulogises the *Harry Potter* author J K Rowling, who was herself invited to write for *Doctor Who*. Fictional Martha even tells real Shakespeare a joke about himself told by real comedian Peter Kay, who appeared in *Doctor Who* playing the fictional Abzorbaloff last year. I'm not sure what to call this. There must be a term, somewhere between "metatextual conjuring" and "smartarse in-jokes", but it kept me tickled for hours.' Dave Owen, *Doctor Who Magazine* Issue 383, May 2007.

- 'The most expensive episode of *Doctor Who* yet, but it's not all about the spectacle. This is a full-blooded historical romp, shot through with wit, colour and such smart ideas as the Carrionites building reality out of words while humanity uses numbers. Dean Lennox Kelly brings a Gallagher swagger to Shakespeare while Christina Cole is edibly evil as Lilith, but it's the chemistry between Tennant and Agyeman that makes this intoxicating. And it's a story unafraid to draw on the archetypal power of old-school cackling hag witches ...' Nick Setchfield, *SFX* Issue 157, June 2007.

FAN COMMENT

- 'Guest star Dean Lennox Kelly plays Shakespeare as the swaggering, cocky rock star of the 16th Century, all high kicks on stage and weariness of the attentions of his fans. It's an interesting, tongue-in-cheek portrayal that might cause purists the odd palpitation, but it makes the character far more palatable to a modern audience than the rather stuffy, patrician image generally associated with Shakespeare. The sparks fly when Shakespeare becomes entranced by Martha (another cracking performance by Freema Agyeman, easily cementing her position as a more than worthy replacement for Billie Piper's iconic Rose), and David Tennant is clearly in his element here, coolly confronting the Carrionite leader Lilith ... and ultimately encouraging Shakespeare to resolve the whole situation in his own very special way. The Carrionites themselves are creations that veer wildly from the pantomime (their cackling, crooked-nose witch-forms) to the creepy (the swooping, ethereal CGI creatures at the climax). But they're an enemy not to be trifled with and one or two scenes are genuinely quite unsettling – the (off-camera) destruction of Lilith's would-be suitor and, especially, a surprisingly-graphic "dry-land drowning" complete with spluttering and liberal doses of choking water-regurgitation. It's hard not to smile at the scene where Lilith escapes her first confrontation with the Doctor by means of a broomstick. Well, some clichés are just too delicious to resist ...' Paul Mount, SciFind website, 10 April 2007.

- 'Shakespeare was a great writer ... It doesn't take a high-school English literature teacher ramming the commentary down your throat to see that [he] had an uncanny ability to write about the human condition. (Unless you believe the Earl of Oxford wrote [the plays] instead.) Nonetheless, there's nothing to attribute great, spontaneous, blinding genius in the man. Certainly not the type that would be immune to psychic paper or be able, in 1599, to grasp and work out that Martha is from the future and the Doctor is an alien. The constant adulation of Shakespeare detracts from the story and yet, at the same time, it is *critical* to the story because it is his genius with words that is the catalyst of the plot. I find that strikes an unpleasant balance. The notion [that] Shakespeare's writing accidentally opened the void and let [in] the first three Carrionites is ludicrous, and if the point is that it is his genius alone that can release the rest, why then does Lilith have to write the actual words that accomplish the task? How, with no real concept of what he's done, can Shakespeare start to close the void, and how is it possible that Martha can fling a bit of J K Rowling in at the end to finish the job?' Eugene Glover, Lone Locust website, 12 April 2007.

- 'Greetings, mortal. Fear me, for I am a dark being from the dawn of time. I was born in the chaos when blood and magic still ruled the universe. I can travel through language itself. I am everywhere and nowhere. Yes, I look like a witch. A stereotypical, cackling, broomstick-riding witch. So what? Clearly it's just how people in the 16th Century personify my awe-inspiring fear as witchcraft. One of us is hot though. Sometimes. I see this awkwardness concerning my ridiculous appearance is undermining my threat. In that case, let me reveal to you my name; for as we all know, there is much magical power in names. Are you ready? *Carrionites!* What? I do *not* sound like some crazy cross between a vulture and a termite. I'm ancient and terrible! Oh, fine. My name sounds lame. I could really do with some long "ah" sound somewhere, and perhaps a "k" or a "z". While we're talking about words, I should mention that I'm connected to your puny universe through the words and language of William Shakespeare. Yes, mortal, I come to you through the now-traditional "celebrity historical" *Doctor Who* story for Series Three. Yes, these puny bipeds still fear writing a story set in the past without dumping monsters in it.' Tom Charman, AtypicalReview website, 26 April 2007.

- 'I loved the idea that the actors and indeed the audience were used to finding chunks of Shakespeare difficult to follow, and so accepted the incomprehensible instructions [in the code] as par for the course. There are whole generations of schoolchildren who could sympathise with that. I was more impressed by the wordplay than by the story, though, and the older witches reminded me of Statler and Waldorf [from *The Muppet Show* (ITV,

1976-1981)] sitting in their box seat jeering at the performance. But in the scheme of things that hardly seemed a big deal – the whole thing looked great, Lilith the young witch was heart stopping in more ways than one, and David Tennant uttered nary a shriek nor a titter but got on with the job in his new toned-down style. I'm also keen on the fact that the Doctor isn't giving Martha the goo-goo eyes despite her best efforts to encourage him, and even Shakespeare (an astute man) told her "The Doctor [may] never kiss you." I wasn't averse to the Doctor/Rose love interest, but it would have been a mistake to do the same thing again, and this new dynamic has given the series a lift. The Doctor and Martha seem more light-hearted than the Doctor and Rose – just having fun rather than *Just 17*.' John Williams, Behind the Sofa website, 7 April 2007.

ANALYSIS

In the classic *Doctor Who* series, historical stories fell into two main categories. First there were the 'pure historicals', which saw the Doctor and his companions encountering fictionalised versions of real-life historical figures such as Marco Polo, Robespierre, Emperor Nero and Richard the Lionheart but had no other science-fiction aspects apart from the TARDIS. These began with 'Marco Polo' in 1964 and ended with 'The Highlanders' in 1967.[43] Then there were the 'pseudo-historicals', which conversely featured no such real-life figures but involved the Doctor and his companions dealing with alien incursions in period settings. The first of these was 'The Time Meddler' in 1965 and the last was 'The Curse of Fenric' in 1989. Only on a couple of occasions was there a story that crossed the boundary between these two types by juxtaposing real-life historical figures with aliens and other science-fiction elements: 'The Mark of the Rani' and 'Timelash', both in 1984. ('Time and the Rani' in 1987 also featured a couple of historical 'geniuses', but only as non-speaking extras.) Russell T Davies, however, has made this type of story, which he terms the 'celebrity historical', a staple ingredient of his revival of the series, in the form of 'The Unquiet Dead' (involving Charles Dickens) in Series One, 'Tooth and Claw' (featuring Queen Victoria) and 'The Girl in the Fireplace' (with Madame de Pompadour and King Louis XV) in Series Two and now 'The Shakespeare Code' in Series Three, with at least one more planned for Series Four. This approach has the considerable virtue of acquainting viewers with the episode's chosen historical subject, in whom they might previously have taken little or no interest, while at the same time entertaining them with the kind of fantastical adventure story they have come to expect from the series. In fact, without getting too pompous about it, this actually harks back to the original, partly educational remit of *Doctor Who*, as laid down by its principal creator Sydney Newman, and again illustrates how Davies has cannily updated the series for a modern audience but at the same time kept it very true to its roots.

Certainly it seems likely that most younger viewers, and no doubt many adult

[43] 'Black Orchid' (1982) is also sometimes placed in this category, in that it has a period setting and no science-fiction elements (apart from the four regular characters and the TARDIS), although in this case the plot involves no real-life historical figures.

ones too, will have had their preconceptions of Shakespeare confounded by this episode. Often thought of as rather dry and inaccessible by those with little knowledge of them, or simply as something one is obliged to study at school, the Bard's plays are presented here as possessing literally magical qualities. The power of words is, indeed, the key theme around which the story revolves: as the Doctor puts it, 'The theatre's magic, isn't it? ... Stand on this stage, say the right words with the right emphasis at the right time, oh, you can make men weep, or cry with joy; change them. You can change people's minds just with words in this place. And if you exaggerate that ...' It is precisely this power that forms the basis of the Carrionites' supposed witchcraft. 'It's just a different sort of science,' the Doctor tells Martha and Shakespeare. 'You lot, you chose mathematics – given the right string of numbers, the right equation, you can split the atom. The Carrionites use words instead.' The Doctor eventually discovers that the three Carrionite survivors, whom Shakespeare has unwittingly freed from their ancient banishment with 'new, glittering' words written in a grief-stricken state following the death of his son, are now planning to restore the rest of their kind, having influenced the Globe's architect to design it in the form of a 14-sided energy converter and got the playwright to include the requisite words in the closing dialogue of his latest work, *Love's Labour's Won*.

The closest *Doctor Who* precedent for this is probably provided by the fourth Doctor's swansong 'Logopolis' (1981), in which the Logopolitans' technique of performing their block transfer computations by speaking the arcane codes aloud is essentially akin to that of wizards casting spells – possibly the last thing one would have expected from that story's writer, arch-rationalist Christopher H Bidmead. It is really rather a pity that the Carrionites' spells in 'The Shakespeare Code' are not described, in passing, as block transfer computations – numbers and words both being combinations of sounds, and thus essentially the same thing, when spoken aloud, as apparently acknowledged in the fact that the code actually includes a sequence of numbers, presumably representing planetary coordinates – but the principle is nevertheless the same. *Doctor Who* is a series that has always drawn heavily yet astutely on a wide range of literary sources, and it seems appropriate that 'The Shakespeare Code' should be a story in which the danger is averted through an explicitly linguistic solution, rather than, as is so often the case (one of the few other exceptions being 'The Mind Robber' (1968)), a scientific or pseudo-scientific one.

It is not only his plays but also Shakespeare himself who is presented in a lively, exciting light in this story, at odds with the traditional public perception of him as a stuffy, serious person. This perception has been challenged before in productions such as the BBC Four drama *A Waste of Shame* (2005), starring Rupert Graves, and even more so the multi-award-winning romantic comedy movie *Shakespeare in Love* (Bedford Falls/Miramax/Universal, 1998), with Joseph Fiennes in the lead role. 'The Shakespeare Code', while obviously being influenced to a degree by *Shakespeare in Love*, goes one step further by depicting Shakespeare as a kind of 16th Century equivalent of a charismatic Northern rock star, like Liam Gallagher of Oasis or Richard Ashcroft of the Verve. Dean Lennox Kelly – best known for his role as Kev in the Channel 4 comedy-drama *Shameless* (2004-2007) – is an excellent choice of actor to play the character in this mould, and he rises to the occasion with a bravura performance that sees a dashing Bard taking to the stage with a flamboyant kick, baiting his audience in the manner of a stand-up comedian ('Oh, that's a wig!') and later flirting outrageously with Martha and even, briefly, the Doctor. ('Fifty-seven academics just punched the air,' says the Doctor, in reference to the long-standing debate amongst experts regarding Shakespeare's sexuality – making this arguably one of the few occasions in its history when *Doctor Who* has 'broken the fourth wall' and directly acknowledged the viewing audience.) As relatively little is actually known about what Shakespeare was really like as a person, this interpretation certainly seems as valid as any.

More generally, Gareth Roberts' script sticks pretty faithfully to established historical fact. Shakespeare and his company, the Lord Chamberlain's Men, really did co-own and perform at the newly-opened Globe Theatre on the south bank of the Thames in Southwark in the autumn of 1599, the year in which the story is set; Shakespeare did indeed have 'a wife in the country', as mentioned in the dialogue, and a son named Hamnet who died of the plague at the age of 11 in 1596; and, sometime prior to 1609, he wrote a series of 26 sonnets to a mysterious 'Dark Lady' of unknown identity, implied here to have been inspired by his memories of Martha. Bethlem Hospital, known colloquially as Bedlam, was by all accounts very much the kind of horrific institution depicted in the rather disturbing sequence where the Doctor, Martha and Shakespeare pay a visit to the unhinged Peter Streete (albeit that his real-life counterpart was not killed by a Carrionite in 1599, as seen here, but went on to build the Fortune Theatre the following year). What's more, there really does appear to have been a now-lost play of Shakespeare's called *Love's Labour's Won*, a sequel to *Love's Labour's Lost*; and although one of the very few pieces of evidence for this indicates that it must have been written and first performed no later than 1598, Roberts can be forgiven this small piece of dramatic licence, without which the story wouldn't really work (or, at least, not without it being relocated to a different theatre – perhaps the Curtain Theatre in Shoreditch, where the Lord Chamberlain's Men are believed to have staged their plays between 1597 and 1599).

After years of writing acclaimed *Doctor Who* novels, audio CD dramas, short stories and comic strips, plus the digital-only adventure 'Attack of the Graske', the 'Tardisode' online teasers for Series Two and (with Davies) the 'Invasion of the Bane' pilot for *The Sarah Jane Adventures*, not to mention much unrelated TV work, Roberts at last gets his chance here to contribute to the series proper, and his script shows every sign of him relishing the task. The whole thing has a wonderful energy and exuberance to it, and is so incident-packed that it actually seems amazing that it is all contained within just a single 45-minute episode; there is enough going on here to sustain a feature film. The pacing and structure are excellent and the dialogue rich, clever and witty – not to mention very bold, in that it actually attributes some newly-written lines to Shakespeare (albeit that one of these, 'The eye should have contentment where it rests,' is actually borrowed from the classic *Doctor Who* historical story 'The Crusade' (1965); a neat in-joke for the fans to spot).

On the downside, the initially amusing running gag of Shakespeare gaining inspiration for some of his most famous lines from things that he, the Doctor and Martha say during the course of the action is perhaps a little overused by the end, and essentially repeats the idea of Dickens being prompted to write his *A Christmas Carol* by things he witnesses in 'The Unquiet Dead' (which likewise has a scene featuring a spectral entity flying around a theatre), and indeed that of H G Wells basing his stories on things he sees in 'Timelash' (1984). The lionising of the Bard is also taken a touch too far at times: the Doctor's description of him as 'the most human human there's ever been' is definitely excessive, even allowing for the fact that he is carried away with enthusiasm at the time. A sense of *déjà vu* arises, too, from the explanation that the three Carrionites are the last survivors of a race from the dawn of time now trying to unleash their kind anew upon the universe, which is very similar to the backstory of the Empress of the Racnoss in 'The Runaway Bride' and, again, the Dalek Emperor in 'The Parting of the Ways' and the Nestene Consciousness in 'Rose', not to mention the ancient threats posed by the Beast in 'The Satan Pit'/'The Impossible Planet' and Abaddon in *Torchwood*'s 'End of Days'. These are only minor quibbles, though: overall, Roberts' long-awaited debut story for the series is a brilliant piece of work, and it is very good to know that it will not be his last.

Part of the inspiration for the plot appears to have been drawn from Justin Richards' *New Adventures* novel *Theatre of War* (1994), which involves a dream machine on the planet Menaxus containing 'living scenes' from a number of plays, including *Hamlet* by Shakespeare and the (fictional) legendary lost work *The Good Soldier* by Stanoff Osterling; the machine causes the action from the plays to affect the real world, and the Doctor ultimately triumphs by rewriting the end of *The Good Soldier* and delivering an improvised speech about time and decay that causes its marauding killer robots to rust away to nothing before they can attack the audience. This has clear parallels in 'The Shakespeare Code' in the idea of the end of the lost play being rewritten by the Carrionites to revive the others of their kind, and of Shakespeare (with a little help from Martha) ad-libbing some new dialogue to foil this plan. The Globe also features as a setting in one of the *Missing Adventures*, Stephen Marley's *Managra* (1995), in which its destruction by fire in 1613 is attributed to arson by one of Shakespeare's rivals; this novel likewise involves the idea of living theatre transforming reality, in a process referred to as 'mimesis'. Roberts' own *Missing Adventures* novel *The Plotters* (1996) has the first Doctor's companions Ian and Barbara attempting to attend a performance at the Globe in 1604, although they are prevented from getting there when they run into a crowd watching a bear-baiting.

Shakespeare himself has featured in *Doctor Who* on a number of previous occasions. In the TV story 'The Chase' (1965) he is seen briefly, via the screen of a Time-Space Visualiser device, in an encounter with Queen Elizabeth I and the philosopher, statesman and essayist Francis Bacon (claimed by some to have been the true author of the Bard's works), during which he appears to gain inspiration for both *The Merry Wives of Windsor* and *Hamlet*. Given that both these plays are believed to have been written around 1602, or possibly a little earlier, the fact that Shakespeare looks quite a bit older and more careworn here than in 'The Shakespeare Code' (although the Queen looks not too dissimilar) is difficult to account for within the fiction of the series; possibly his experience with the Carrionites aged him, or he failed to heed the Doctor's warning that rubbing his head might make him bald! The fourth Doctor also makes two mentions of having met Shakespeare, the first of these coming in 'Planet of Evil' (1975) and the second in 'City of Death' (1979), when he claims to have transcribed some of *Hamlet* himself because the Bard had sprained his wrist writing sonnets; and in 'The Mark of the Rani', the sixth Doctor also refers to having met him. Other, non-TV appearances by Shakespeare have come in Andy Lane's 1609-set *Missing Adventures* novel *The Empire of Glass* (1995); as a young boy in Justin Richards' audio play 'Time of the Daleks' (2002) and Ian Potter's follow-up short story *Apocrypha Bipedium* (2003); in Nev Fountain's audio play 'The Kingmaker' (2006), according to which an encounter with the fifth Doctor in 1597 ultimately leads to him being left in 1485, while King Richard III is transported forward in time from 1485 to take his place in 1597; and in Roberts' own *Doctor Who Magazine* comic strip *A Groatsworth of Wit* (2006), which can almost be seen as a 'trial run' for 'The Shakespeare Code', in that it features similar-looking (albeit in this case male) monsters, is set partly in the Globe, has (a straight, and balding) Shakespeare flirting with the Doctor's companion (Rose) and even uses some very similar dialogue, although it is set some seven years earlier (and its use of the Globe is thus anachronistic). This is obviously one of those instances where the details of different stories conflict to such a degree that it is very difficult if not impossible to reconcile them, and Roberts and the production team made a conscious decision not to acknowledge even the previous TV series references to Shakespeare: an early draft of the script did have the Doctor telling the Bard 'See you earlier' (a line also used in 'City of Death') – reflecting the fact that, while for Shakespeare this was their first meeting, for the Doctor it was not – but this was subsequently omitted on the basis that it would be mystifying for casual viewers and confusing even for fans.

The budding relationship between the Doctor and Martha is nicely developed in their second episode together, as he treats her to the 'one trip' he has promised and she gets used to the idea of having travelled back in time. The scene where they first arrive in the street beside the Thames in 1599 is particularly good, with the Doctor pointing out parallels between life in Elizabethan times and in Martha's era and amusingly making light of her concerns about how the future would be changed if she were to step on a butterfly or kill her grandfather – well-worn clichés of other time travel fiction. It is good, too, to see the mock formality of them addressing each other as 'Mr Smith' and 'Miss Jones' being carried over from the end of 'Smith and Jones'. Also very effective is the scene where they retire to their room in the inn and the Doctor remains completely oblivious of the significance to Martha of the idea of them sharing a bed, upsetting her by tactlessly talking about how Rose would know the right thing to say if she were there. This neatly emphasises the point that Martha's romantic interest in the Doctor is unlikely to be reciprocated, and reinforces the impression that this Doctor-and-companion relationship is going to be more akin to those seen in the classic series than to that between the Doctor and Rose.

In production terms, 'The Shakespeare Code' is an absolute *tour de force*, and another tribute to the abilities of director Charles Palmer after his excellent *Doctor Who* debut on 'Smith and Jones'. The location work, probably the most ambitious yet attempted in the new series, is superb, the scenes shot at the modern reconstruction of the Globe being a particular highlight, and the studio sets are equally good – it is actually difficult to tell sometimes whether a given setting is studio or location. The excellent CGI establishing shots of London and the area around the Globe (one of which is completely different, and very much improved, from the version seen in the series trailer at the end of 'The Runaway Bride') are the icing on the cake; indeed, the Mill have really excelled themselves with their work on this episode, as all the CGI effects are outstanding, and the flying Carrionites that whirl around the theatre at the climax are an excellent and original new monster design.

The only less than fully successful aspect of the production is the prosthetic make-up created for the three Carrionites, which looks obviously fake at times and is too close to the clichéd hook-nosed hag image of the wicked witch of popular perception, as seen on many a Halloween mask and in many a pantomime (a connotation that unfortunately seems to have been picked up by Amanda Lawrence and Linda Clark in their over-the-top performances as the cackling Doomfinger and Bloodtide, although thankfully not by the superb Christina Cole in the more prominent role of their daughter Lilith); it would have been better had a more subtle approach been taken here, with the actresses' features less heavily augmented by special make-up or even left free of such make-up altogether. Lilith is certainly at her best and most menacing as a character when she appears in her human guise; as, fortunately, she does for much of her time on screen. Then again, the obvious implication here is that the Carrionites are the source of inspiration for Shakespeare's three Weird Sisters in *Macbeth*, believed to have been written around 1605, which presented them in very much the stereotypical hag mould (well established even by the 16th Century), so arguably they needed to be depicted in that way in 'The Shakespeare Code' as well.

Surprisingly, given that they feature so prominently in myth and folklore, this is the first time that witches have been used as the basis for a race of *Doctor Who* monsters – on TV, at least[44] – although the classic series had a few human practitioners of witchcraft, including the 'white witch' Miss Hawthorne in 'The Dæmons' (1971) and a couple of occult covens, perhaps most notably the one in the *K-9 and Company* spin-off. The time was certainly ripe for this development, with popular interest in all things magical having been raised to an all-time high by J K Rowling's extraordinarily successful *Harry Potter* novels and their film adaptations. As Davies himself has observed, having one of the witches revealed right up-front in the pre-titles teaser is a shrewd move on Roberts' part, as it virtually guarantees children's engagement with the story, even if they are predisposed to think of Shakespeare as rather dull subject matter. *Harry Potter* is a very rare example of a cultural phenomenon that has matched *Doctor Who*'s incredible achievement of appealing to children and adults alike, making it another true family entertainment, and it is fitting that both it and Rowling herself are explicitly referenced in Roberts' dialogue, with Martha's appropriation of the familiar spell 'Expelliarmus' being instrumental in capping the defeat of the Carrionites. If nothing else, it proves that the production team took no offence when Rowling declined an invitation to write for *Doctor Who* a couple of years earlier! Whether or not children will have understood the Doctor's reference to the movie *Back to the Future* (Amblin Entertainment, 1985) is rather more open to question; but many of their parents will no doubt have appreciated it.

---

[44] In *TV Comic*, a 1968 comic strip story entitled 'The Witches' featured real, broomstick-riding witches from throughout the universe attending a gathering on the planet Vargo. This was followed up in the 1968 *TV Comic Holiday Special* with 'Return of the Witches'.

There has been a certain amount of debate within fandom regarding the possibility that the somewhat hackneyed depiction of the Carrionites as evil old crones – in contrast to the generally positive portrayal of witches in series such as *Buffy the Vampire Slayer* (The WB, 1997-2001, UPN, 2001-2003) and *Charmed* (The WB, 1998-2006) – might be considered insulting or offensive to real-life witches, and a retrograde step. It seems clear, though, that in likening the Carrionites to witches, the Doctor and Martha are referring simply to the folklore archetypes, rather than to practitioners of the Wiccan religion, so perhaps this is a case of – to borrow a phrase of the Doctor's, albeit used in a slightly different context – 'political correctness gone mad'. That said, the stereotypical image of witches is arguably grounded in misogynistic ideas about women's sexuality and power, and Roberts certainly does nothing to subvert those in his script (or in his contribution to the *Doctor Who: Creatures and Demons* book, in which he suggests that the Carriorites 'ate their own husbands and children'), so perhaps a trick has indeed been missed here.

Whatever shortcomings there may be in the depiction of the witch-form Carrionites, this is again no more than a minor niggle when viewed in perspective. Overall, 'The Shakespeare Code' is probably the series' most lavish and accomplished episode to date. As well-made as Series One and Series Two were, it seems fair to say that a production of such comprehensive and sustained high quality would not have been achievable even that short while ago; which just goes to show how all concerned have grown in experience and expertise, as well as how certain techniques such as CGI have been refined and become more affordable as time has gone by.

The finishing touch is provided by the excellent closing scene in which Elizabeth I (a cameo role for the distinguished Angela Pleasence) arrives at the Globe and denounces a bemused Doctor as her sworn enemy – obviously referring to events that, from his point of view, have yet to occur – causing him and Martha to flee back to the TARDIS, which departs with an arrow fired by one of the Queen's bowmen lodged in the door. Not only does this serve as a nice homage to the series' previous foray into the Elizabethan era, 'Silver Nemesis' (1989), which likewise features a scene in which an arrow is fired into the TARDIS door – and also, incidentally, has the Doctor telling his companion 'Just act like you own the place', as he does at the beginning of 'The Shakespeare Code' – but it also lays the foundation for a potential future 'celebrity historical' featuring Elizabeth I. If that were to be anywhere near as good as 'The Shakespeare Code', then it would be well worth the wait.

# 3.03 – GRIDLOCK

Writer: Russell T Davies
Director: Richard Clark

## DEBUT TRANSMISSION DETAILS

BBC One
Date: 14 April 2007. Scheduled time: 7.40 pm. Actual time: 7.40 pm.

BBC Three
Date: 15 April 2007. Scheduled time: 8.00 pm. Actual time: 8.01 pm.

Duration: 45' 03"

## ADDITIONAL CREDITED CAST

Ardal O'Hanlon (Brannigan[45]), Anna Hope (Novice Hame), Travis Oliver (Milo), Lenora Crichlow (Cheen), Jennifer Hennessy (Valerie), Bridget Turner (Alice), Georgine Anderson (May), Simon Pearsall (Whitey), Daisy Lewis (Javit), Nicholas Boulton (Businessman), Erika Macleod (Sally Calypso), Judy Norman (Ma), Graham Padden (Pa), Lucy Davenport (Pale Woman), Tom Edden (Pharmacist # 1)[46], Natasha Williams (Pharmacist # 2)[47], Gayle Telfer Stevens (Pharmacist # 3)[48], Struan Rodger (The Face of Boe)[49].

Macra created by Ian Stuart Black

## PLOT

The Doctor brings Martha to the city of New New York on New Earth in the year 5,000,000,053. They arrive in the grimy, enclosed undercity, where Martha is kidnapped and taken by her captors, Milo and Cheen, to their flying car – one of countless similar vehicles moving slowly around a gridlocked motorway. The Doctor, intent on rescuing Martha, makes his way gradually towards her, jumping from car to car, meeting *en route* a number of diverse individuals, including cat person Brannigan, his wife Valerie and their litter of kittens. Those cars with three adult occupants are entitled to descend to the 'fast lane' – which is why Martha was kidnapped – but there are rumours that something terrible lies in wait down

---

[45] Full name given in dialogue as Thomas Kincaid Brannigan.
[46] Not credited in *Radio Times*.
[47] Not credited in *Radio Times*.
[48] Not credited in *Radio Times*.
[49] Not credited in *Radio Times*.

there … These rumours prove well-founded: lurking below is a nest of fearsome, crab-like Macra. The Doctor is waylaid by Novice Hame, one of the cat-nuns he met on his last visit to New Earth, who is now a reformed character. She teleports him to the Senate building in the city proper, where he is reunited with the Face of Boe. He learns that the Face of Boe, assisted by Novice Hame, trapped the population in the undercity to save them from a virus that wiped out the rest of the city's inhabitants before expiring itself. The Doctor manages to restore the power, opening the undercity and releasing the cars from the motorway. The Face of Boe, life force now exhausted, finally dies, but not before imparting a last great secret to the Doctor: 'You are not alone.'

## QUOTE, UNQUOTE

- **Martha:** 'When you say "last time", was that you and Rose?'
  **Doctor:** 'Erm, yeah. Yeah, it was, yeah.'
  **Martha:** 'You're taking me to the same planets that you took her?'
  **Doctor:** 'What's wrong with that?'
  **Martha:** 'Nothing. Ever heard the word "rebound"?'
- **Valerie:** 'He's completely insane!'
  **Brannigan:** 'That, and a bit magnificent!'
- **Face of Boe:** 'Everything has its time. You know that, old friend, better than most.'
  **Novice Hame:** 'The legend says more …'
  **Doctor:** 'Don't. There's no need for that.'
  **Novice Hame:** 'It says that the Face of Boe will speak his final secret to a traveller.'
  **Doctor:** 'Yeah, but not yet. Who needs secrets, eh?'

## CONTINUITY POINTS

- The episode is set 30 years after 'New Earth'.
- The Doctor describes his home planet Gallifrey to Martha: 'The sky's a burnt orange, with a Citadel enclosed in a mighty glass dome, shining under the twin suns. Beyond that, the mountains go on forever, slopes of deep red grass, capped with snow.' Later he elaborates: 'Oh, you should've seen it, that old planet. The second sun would rise in the south, and the mountains would shine. The leaves on the trees were silver, and when they caught the light every morning it looked like a forest on fire. When the autumn came, the breeze would blow through the branches …' These desciptions echo the one given by his granddaughter Susan in 'The Sensorites' (1964): 'Oh, it's ages since we've seen our planet. It's quite like Earth, but at night the sky is a burnt orange, and the leaves on the trees are bright silver.'
- The action of 'Gridlock' appears to carry straight on from that of 'The Shakespeare Code', as on arrival in New New York the Doctor pulls from the TARDIS door the arrow that Queen Elizabeth I's bowman shot into it at the end of the previous episode.
- The booths in the Pharmacy Town alley bear a white-crescent-on-green-background logo that is the reverse of the green-crescent-on-white-

background one seen on the side of the hospital in 'New Earth'. Some boxes and bins in the alley bear a green crescent logo, as do the mood patches sold by the vendors.

- The Doctor plays with one of Valerie's kittens and appears to have overcome the aversion to cats that he expressed in 'Fear Her', which was brought on by his previous encounter with the cat-nuns in 'New Earth'. (In his earlier incarnations, notably the sixth and – in the tie-in novels – the seventh and eighth, he was seen to be something of a cat lover.)
- The cars have 'antigravs' that lift them from the ground, and engines run on self-replicating fuel that then propel them along. When the engines are switched off, the antigravs continue to work.
- The Doctor says that he was given his coat by American rock singer Janis Joplin (1943-1970). This begs the question how it comes to have pockets bigger inside than out, as he claimed in 'The Runaway Bride'. (Perhaps he adapted it using Time Lord technology after he acquired it from Joplin?)
- In an article written by Russell T Davies for the *Doctor Who Annual 2006* (Panini, 2005), a description is given of hieroglyphics related to the last great Time War carved on a mountainside on the distant planet Crafe Tec Heydra: under an image of a lone survivor walking away, the message 'You are not alone' has been been scratched. This clearly foreshadows the Face of Boe's message for the Doctor in 'Gridlock'.

## BAD WOLF REFERENCES

- In the car belonging to the two Asian girls, there is a poster bearing kanji writing that is a rough translation of 'Bad Wolf' in both Japanese and Chinese.

## PRODUCTION NOTES

- 'Gridlock' was made with 'The Lazarus Experiment' in Block 3 of production on Series Three.
- This episode had a later-than-usual start time for its debut BBC One transmission owing to live coverage that afternoon of a football match: the FA Cup semi-final between Manchester United and Watford. Had the match gone to extra time, the episode – and its accompanying *Doctor Who Confidential* documentary on BBC Three – would have been held over to be transmitted the following week instead (despite a trailer for it having been shown during the match's half-time interval). In the event, however, Manchester United won 4-1.
- One of Russell T Davies's aims in writing this story was to have action taking place within a CGI environment, as opposed to the usual approach of keeping sets and CGI effects as essentially separate elements. He did an initial sketch of the motorway, which was then developed by members of the Art Department into a series of concept drawings and storyboards. These were discussed with director Richard Clark and other members of the team over a period of some six weeks, and gradually refined. Issues that had to be addressed included how close to each other the cars should be – given that in a real traffic jam they are often bumper-to-bumper, which if translated into three dimensions would result simply in a wall of cars – and how to create the impression of lanes of

traffic creeping forward when, due to the jam, the cars would all be essentially stationery.

- Story ideas dropped during the scripting process included having people still living in the overcity; a sea at the base of the undercity with the Macra swimming in it; small, red, baby Macra devouring the occupants of cars on the lowest level of the motorway, leaving only skeletons; and the full-sized Macra giving chase to the Doctor by crawling up the undercity walls.
- The costumes and make-up of the couple, Ma and Pa, whose car is attacked in the pre-opening titles teaser sequence were designed to make them resemble the two people pictured in the famous 1930 painting 'American Gothic' by Grant Wood (1891-1942). This was because writer Russell T Davies considered it to be a quintessential image of American pioneers.
- The information screen that the Doctor consults on arriving in the undercity shows a view of flying cars approaching New New York: CGI work reused from 'New Earth'.
- Two sessions of location recording were carried out in Cardiff for this story: the Senate building material was shot in the Temple of Peace (previously used as a location on 'The End of the World') on 18 and 19 September 2006 and the Pharmacy Town alley scenes were taped at the Maltings on East Tyndall Street on 28 and 29 September 2006, with additional shots recorded at the Ely Papermill on the latter date.
- The car rig was a solid metal framework construction with exterior panels clamped onto it; the construction of these exterior panels was contracted out to an external company, Icon. There were certain removable elements, such as the windscreen, to facilitate getting the required camera shots. The car interior was built in-house at Upper Boat and took about 45 minutes to redress each time it had to be changed to represent a different vehicle. The windows were made dirty so that little could be seen through them from inside; the impression of the exhaust-fume fog and other cars outside was created with some dry ice mist and two red lights moved around on a pole. The rear panel of another car was also built for use in certain shots. All the cars had to look identical externally as it would have been prohibitively expensive to have used numerous different designs, particularly in the extensive CGI work.
- Brannigan's appearance was based on that of Ratz, a disembodied CGI cat's head that was (alongside, amongst others, John Barrowman) a 'virtual presenter' of BBC One's *Live & Kicking*, a Saturday morning children's magazine show, in the mid-1990s.
- In an entry that he contributed to the book *Doctor Who: Monsters and Villains* (BBC Books, 2005), Russell T Davies wrote, 'Legend has it that if the Face of Boe should die one day, then the sky will crack asunder'. This idea was subsequently referenced in 'New Earth'. The sky does indeed 'crack asunder' in 'Gridlock' when the Doctor opens the roof of the undercity and allows the cars to escape from the motorway, but Davies has since admitted that this was unintentional – or perhaps subconscious – on his part, as he had forgotten about the supposed legend at the time when he wrote the script.
- Bridget Turner, who played Alice in this story, is married to classic series *Doctor Who* director Frank Cox.

- The two hymns heard in the episode are 'The Old Rugged Cross', composed in 1912 by George Bennard, and 'Abide with Me', with lyrics written by Henry Francis Lyte in 1943 and music composed by William H Monk in 1861. At one point during the production, 'Abide with Me' was dropped in favour of a new, wordless choral piece composed by Murray Gold, but Russell T Davies felt that this made it seem as if the Doctor and Martha could suddenly hear the incidental music, owing to the similarity of the orchestration, so the traditional hymn was reinstated.
- Russell T Davies made a small addition to the Face of Boe's scripted lines before the dialogue was added to the episode in ADR (additional dialogue recording) to have him refer to the Doctor as an 'old friend'. This was specifically in order to foreshadow a revelation to be made about the Face of Boe's origins at the end of 'Last of the Time Lords'.

## OOPS!

- The BBC One Wales debut transmission of this episode was briefly interrupted by the beginning of a trailer for the series *Belonging* (starring *Torchwood*'s Eve Myles) mistakenly cut away to by the presentation department at the start of the closing scene with the Doctor and Martha in the alley by the TARDIS. Other BBC One regions were unaffected.

## PRESS REACTION

- '"Gridlock" takes contemporary issues such as mass congestion, pollution and designer drugs and stretches them to their logical conclusion to create some engaging science fiction. Since returning to our screens, *Doctor Who* has succeeded at doing this on several occasions, such as the Guantanamo Bay analogies in "Dalek" and the constant craving for upgraded technology in the Cybermen episodes. On the subject of old enemies, what a nice touch to have the Macra back for a bit of an encore, although the poor crabs have devolved, as the Doctor observed. Huge credit goes to Russell T Davies' writing skills and notable performances from Ardal O'Hanlon ... and Lenora Crichlow ... for generating enough emotional pathos for their characters' predicaments without any sense of contrivance or schmaltz. When required, the visual effects are also astounding and cleverly not over-used. That final fleeting glimpse of the orange New Earth skyline (harking back to the Doctor's Gallifreyan memories) lives on in our minds ... Our emotions are also heightened by a rather touching ensemble scene when the daily hymn is broadcast to the masses in their cars. Eerily reminiscent of the singing portion of Paul Thomas Anderson's opus *Magnolia*, the scene was a creative risk but managed to blend in perfectly and bring a tear to more eyes than those of Martha.' Ben Rawson-Jones, Digital Spy website, 14 April 2007.
- '*Who* delivers a quirky sci-fi realm as near to the vision of *Blade Runner* as possible on a BBC budget – great! Once you start questioning [the] plot it begins to fall apart, though. Could the undercity really be unaware of the end of civilisation? Why would anyone choose this life: surely living in a slum's better than years stuck in a traffic jam? But the script's so replete with

audacious notions that you can forgive all that. Brimming with oddball ideas and visual treats, "Gridlock" may not stand up to rigorous analysis, but God it's fun!' Ian Berriman, *SFX* Issue 157, June 2007.

- 'Davies's script's a rich satire, full of broadly drawn characters and one-liners to bring a smile to Saturday night audiences. The idea of a society locked into a congested motorway is a bold observation of car-obsessed times, though for the first half hour this sense of inertia is reflected in the narrative, which takes a long time to move into high gear. And when it does, the story is revealed to be so full of holes it falls apart.' David Richardson, *Starburst* Issue 350, June 2007.

- 'After superficial similarities between the reborn *Doctor Who* and the old series' last bow, "Survival", "Gridlock" now evokes other serials from that time, none more so than "Paradise Towers", another extrapolation on civil engineering gone horribly wrong, how ordinary people are forced to adapt to survive in it, and how they soon become unrecognisable to outsiders. By placing New New York so unimaginably far in the future, writer Russell T Davies takes viewers beyond any reasonable hope of second-guessing what is normal. Cat-men and mousey women can interbreed? Fair enough! Flying cars in the year Five Billion have old-fashioned needle gauges? Well, why not? For us, the drama is more about exploring this world than sharing the travails of its inhabitants.' Dave Owen, *Doctor Who Magazine* Issue 383, 27 June 2007.

## FAN COMMENT

- 'I found that episode strange and confusing. I had no idea where it was going, what sort of story it was supposed to be, or how it was meant to turn out. After the first half-hour, I *still* had no idea where it was going, what sort of story it was supposed to be, or how it was meant to turn out. Its structure was utterly unlike old-fashioned *Doctor Who*, utterly unlike newfangled *Doctor Who*, and utterly unlike anything else on television. (The best summary I can come up with, for a comedy-drama about people trapped in little boxes in the middle of a hostile CGI world, is "Harold Pinter Gets Giant Crabs"... or possibly "Harold Pinter Re-Writes *Attack of the Clones*", which is even more interesting.) In short: I thought it was ... fantastic. I like *anything* I can't see coming a mile off, and this was so bizarre that even *I* found it surprising. God help the little children-stroke-fanboys, since it may have been a bit non-monstery for their tastes, as with "Love & Monsters" last year. But speaking as a grown-up, the sheer, relentless unpredictability of "Gridlock" made it even more exciting than the preceding football match that determined whether or not it was actually broadcast.' Lawrence Miles, The Beasthouse website, 14 April 2007.

- '"Gridlock" has become my favourite episode of the new series since its resurrection in 2005, and while it's becoming increasingly difficult to marry this bold new series with the classic series, I'd probably go as far as to say this one would be right up there with the very best episodes ever made. Visually it's astounding; the Mill are right at the top of their game here, providing FX work rivalling the best Hollywood studios, from the gridlock itself, New Earth and, for drooling long-term fans, the return of the Macra, crab-monsters first seen in a long-lost 1967 Patrick Troughton four-parter. This is the way to reintroduce old elements to the series without baffling a new audience. So far this year the Doctor has encountered both the Judoon and the Carrionites – and it's quite clear he's met them both before in adventures we've not seen. So here, when the Doctor gazes down through the fug and proclaims "Macra!" it doesn't matter a jot to new viewers who'll just assume that these are creatures he's familiar with, but the old guard can feel a swell of excitement knowing that Davies has cleverly used his plot to slide in an old enemy that is never going to make the cover of *Radio Times* but serves as a nice reminder that, at the end of the day, this is still the same old series it ever was.' Paul Mount, SciFind website, 18 April 2007.

- 'I had hardly any preconceptions of "Gridlock" yet still it managed to confound me. It confounded my expectations of *Doctor Who* as a television programme. It confounded my expectations of television as a medium. It was, to be frank, a weird and bemusing 45 minutes. It was impossible to predict, impossible to second guess. It left me feeling like I'd seen TV for the first time and was running to catch up with the rules of a medium I'd never encountered before. And I bloody loved it. It was undoubtedly the finest episode of *Doctor Who* since the revival began. It was a continuation, an expansion and a fulfilment of everything good about the old series. It had concept and character, emotion and intelligence, romance and sentimentality, colour and coherence ... and all these things were balanced with daring and precision. It was satirical, polemical, allegorical, figurative, discursive, metaphorical ... yet it was never pompous or preachy or boring ... In a world in which 99% of all TV is 99% predictable 99% of the time, "Gridlock" seems like an impertinent rejoinder to everything else on the screen, as though the *Doctor Who* production team are blowing contemptuous raspberries at the people who churn out all the beige wallpaper that constitutes most modern telly.' Jack Graham, Shabogan Graffiti website, 18 April 2007.

## ANALYSIS

Having initially offered Martha just one trip in the TARDIS, the Doctor now makes that two, simply because – as he later admits – he wants to show off. In doing so, he courts disaster, and almost ends up losing her.

'New Earth' was one of the weaker entries in Series Two, so the prospect of a return visit to New New York was not an immediately appealing one. 'Gridlock', though, quickly confounds expectations by having the TARDIS arrive not in the gleaming, futuristic city seen in the distance in that earlier episode, but in the dank, grimy undercity, and specifically in Pharmacy Town, where street vendors peddle mood-altering drugs. This is a great setting, obviously influenced by the noirish visuals of Ridley Scott's movie masterpiece *Blade Runner* (Warner Brothers, 1982), and the story gets off to a dramatic and unsettling start as the Doctor almost immediately becomes separated from Martha when she is dragged off at gunpoint by two desperate strangers – later revealed to be the unusually sympathetic kidnappers Milo (nicely played by Travis Oliver) and Cheen (equally well portrayed by Lenora Crichlow, best known for her role as Sugar in the Channel 4 series *Sugar Rush* (2005-2006)). The Doctor's determination to track down and rescue his new companion then becomes the driving force of the narrative, and leads him swiftly on to the story's main setting: the motorway where serried ranks of outwardly identical flying cars, looking somewhat akin to old Commer or Volkswagen camper vans, crawl along in a perpetual traffic jam.

Russell T Davies has spoken on a number of occasions of liking to write stories in which the action moves in a vertical plane rather than a horizontal one, because this is unusual and exciting and, again, confounds expectations. This is why his stories often feature towers or other multi-level buildings that the characters pass up and down as events unfold. It is an approach exemplified by the lift shaft scenes in 'New Earth' but given perhaps its ultimate expression here in 'Gridlock'. The idea of the Doctor making his way down through the 'lanes' of the motorway by jumping from car to car, entering each through a panel in the roof and exiting through one in the floor, is absolutely inspired, and gives the whole thing a unique dynamic. Whereas the standard format for a story is to have a more or less fixed group of characters who move between a succession of different and varied settings, here the pattern is reversed, as the Doctor drops in on a succession of different characters who remain in more or less fixed and identical settings. Having said that, the attention to detail in the dressing of the various car interiors – all of which were realised on the same basic rig – is phenomenal; and this, along with the idiosyncratic costume and make-up designs, helps to ensure that each of their respective occupants sticks in the mind as a distinctive individual, even if seen only briefly as the Doctor passes through (or, in a couple of cases, speaks to them over a video link).

In the finest traditions of *Doctor Who*, Davies's scripts themselves tend to work on more than one level, with a deeper subtext discernible within what is ostensibly a lighthearted fantasy adventure story; and often that subtext relates to some issue of serious contemporary concern. 'Gridlock' is no exception to the rule, and here the issue in question is that of urban traffic overload and the associated problems of pollution and damage to the environment. The story's biggest surprise is undoubtedly the return of the crab-like Macra, whose one and only previous appearance in the series came 40 years earlier in 'The Macra Terror' (1967), but they actually fit in extremely well here, as their defining characteristic – at least in the eyes of their creator, the late Ian Stuart Black – is that they thrive on a gaseous atmosphere that to humans is poisonous: which makes the exhaust-fume-choked undercity a perfect environment for them to inhabit.

Certainly anyone who has regularly experienced the traffic jams of major cities such as London and Los Angeles will sympathise with the plight of those who find themselves stuck on New New York's ultra-congested motorway. In fact, if the script has a weakness, it is the implausibility of the idea that large numbers of people might willingly face the prospect of spending literally years of their lives on the road, confined to the cramped interior of a car (save perhaps for the occasional stop at a lay-by), in the vague hope of finding a better life when they eventually reach the exit. Surely, however terrible their situation was to start with, it could never have been so bad as to have justified them taking this drastic step? The ultimate revelation that the Face of Boe has sealed them all in the undercity to save them from being exposed to a deadly virus obviously explains why they have been unable to enter the city proper, but not why so many have chosen to join the motorway. One way around this might have been to give the Macra a bigger role in the story, and have it turn out that a Macra Controller had taken over, released the virus and set up the motorway as a trap to provide a regular supply of human meat for the creatures' feeding ground below the fast lane. The Face of Boe and Novice Hame could then have been seen to have been acting clandestinely behind the scenes to try to rid the city of the Macra's influence; which would also have provided a more satisfactory explanation as to why they could not simply release the undercity dwellers once the virus died out. This would have required little extra screen time – if necessary, it could have been done simply through dialogue substituted for the backstory given in the transmitted episode – and would have had the added advantage of avoiding having to 'dumb down' the Macra (although the idea that they have 'devolved' is admittedly intriguing, turning on its head the usual principle of evolution through survival of the fittest).

In a way, though, the plot is incidental here. The heart of this story is the optimistic premise of a population who have managed to bond together as a society, through electronic communication with those on their 'friends list', despite being physically separated from one another in their own individual cars. This could be seen as a metaphor for the way that online communities spring up amongst internet users connecting via their own individual computers (on an information 'superhighway' that often moves more slowly than one would like); and while it might not be true to say that the members of such communities always 'sing from the same hymn sheet', the undercity dwellers of New New York certainly do, quite literally, as becomes apparent when, at an appointed time, they join in a communal rendition of the evangelical gospel hymn 'The Old Rugged Cross'. There have been many extraordinary and surprising scenes in *Doctor Who*'s 43-year history, but arguably none more so than this; in fact, nothing even remotely like it has ever been presented before, either in this or in any other telefantasy series. It is not only completely unexpected but also very moving, as Martha clearly finds within the story; although the other side of the coin is that this ritual daily 'contemplation' serves to engender a sense of apathy amongst the car dwellers, so that none of them ever seems to question their situation or do anything to try to break out of it. One cannot help but wonder whether this unique community will endure once everyone returns to the overcity at the end of the episode or whether it will soon dissipate and be lost for good – there is an old saying, coined by Robert Louis Stevenson in 1881, 'It is better to travel hopefully than to arrive' – but some cause for optimism presents itself when, on returning to Pharmacy Town, the Doctor and Martha hear the city's inhabitants start up a new round of communal singing, this time of the hymn 'Abide with Me'. It is perhaps a little surprising that Davies, as an avowed atheist, should have his far-future descendents of humanity singing Christian hymns, but there is no denying the dramatic power of these moments.

A major influence on the episode, as acknowledged by Davies himself, is the *2000 AD* comic, which began publication in 1977 and went on to acquire a cult following. The endless motorway scenario recalls aspects of the *2000 AD* story 'Terror Tube'; the bowler-hatted Businessman character is directly inspired by Max Normal from the comic's famous *Judge Dredd* series; newsreader Sally Calypso is a homage to Swifty Frisco from the acclaimed *The Ballad of Halo Jones* series; and, more generally, the whole ethos of the undercity recalls that of *Judge Dredd*'s Mega-City One, a huge city-state covering much of what in our world is the East Coast of the USA. Partly for this reason, the episode also bears some similarities to the *2000 AD*-influenced classic series *Doctor Who* story 'The Happiness Patrol' (1988), which likewise is set in a noirish city, features a bowler-hatted, business-suited character and sees the Doctor setting things to rights in the space of a single night. The mood-altering drugs of Pharmacy Town, while again alluding to an issue of contemporary concern, also recall a *2000 AD* idea, although more direct inspirations in this case were the treatment of a similar concept in Gareth Roberts' ninth Doctor novel *Only Human* (2005) and Davies's own use of nicotine patches to help him give up smoking.

Another comic strip source for 'Gridlock' may well have been the story *End of the Line*, first published in Marvel's *Doctor Who Monthly* Issues 54 and 55 in 1981 and reprinted in Panini's *Dragon's Claw* collected edition in 2004, which is set in a grim future city and features a train system that is locked on automatic and going endlessly round and round, while waste pollution from the city filters down to the lower levels and makes its inhabitants ill. Davies's naming of New New York's virus-spreading drug as Bliss may have been a nod to Margaret Attwood's dystopian novel *Oryx and Crake* (McClelland and Stewart, 2003), in which a lethal drug called BlyssPluss becomes airborne and brings about the downfall of human civilisation, or possibly even to Grant Naylor's book *Red Dwarf* (1989), based on the popular TV series, which also mentions a drug called Bliss. The bringing back of one of the 'lesser' classic series monsters for a highly unexpected return appearance is an idea first exploited in the *Doctor Who* tie-in ranges, for instance with the use of the Krotons[50] in the novel *Alien Bodies* (1997) by Lawrence Miles and of the Nimon[51] in the audio play *Seasons of Fear* (2002) by Paul Cornell and Caroline Symcox.

As the last part of a loose Year Five Billion trilogy, following on from 'The End of the World' in Series One and 'New Earth' in Series Two, 'Gridlock' also sees the revelation of the Face of Boe's much-anticipated four-word 'final message' on the point of death, in what is another strangely moving scene. The 'traveller' for whom the message is intended turns out to be Doctor – as it was always obvious it would – and the four words are: 'You are not alone.' What exactly this means will become apparent only in subsequent episodes, but for the time being it clearly astounds and puzzles the Doctor. This leads on to the excellent closing scene in the Pharmacy Town alley, where the Doctor comes clean to Martha and admits that – contrary to what he suggested when they first arrived in New New York – his planet is no more, having been destroyed in the last great Time War between the Time Lords and the Daleks, and that – despite, he maintains, what the Face of Boe said – he is the last of his kind. This neatly reminds the viewer of the Doctor's status as 'the last of the Time Lords', helping to set the stage for the concluding episodes of Series Three, and also serves to take the development of his relationship with Martha to the next level.

Richard Clark acquits himself very well indeed on his debut assignment as a *Doctor Who* director; and, as is now becoming the norm, the production values on the episode are very high. The CGI work is surely the most ambitious and impressive yet seen on the series, and while it never totally convinces that the motorway is a real location – it still has that slightly artificial look that seems

---

[50] From 'The Krotons' (1968/69).
[51] From 'The Horns of Nimon' (1979/80).

almost characteristic of the effect – it certainly conveys the required impression well enough. The Macra also look great – a lot more fearsome than their forebears of 1967! – and the shot where they are first revealed, just a moment before the Doctor actually says their name, is guaranteed to bring a grin of delight and amazement to the faces of those classic series fans who remember them from their debut appearance. The return of the Face of Boe and Novice Hame is equally welcome, albeit far less unexpected, and Anna Hope again gives a good performance in the latter role, beneath the excellent cat fur prosthetic – the slightly greyer tint of which neatly conveys the ageing of the character since last seen in 'New Earth'. It is good, too, to encounter a male cat this time around in the shape of Thomas Kincaid Brannigan, whose make-up is also very well realised and convincing, and who is superbly portrayed by Ardal O'Hanlan (best known for his role as Dougal in the Channel 4 comedy series *Father Ted* (1995-1998)); although exactly how Brannigan and his human partner Valerie – also well played by Jennifer Hennessy – managed to produce their kittens is a question over which it is probably best that a discreet veil be drawn!

One might have been forgiven for thinking that, after some 43 years of *Doctor Who*, every possibility for presenting different types of story within its format had been exhausted. 'Gridlock' proves that not to be the case. This really is quite unlike anything seen previously in the series; which is a huge tribute to the distinctiveness, ingenuity and sheer audaciousness of Russell T Davies's writing.

With three outstanding stories in a row, Series Three has got off to a very strong start.

# 3.04 – DALEKS IN MANHATTAN

Writer: Helen Raynor
Director: James Strong

## DEBUT TRANSMISSION DETAILS

BBC One
Date: 21 April 2007. Scheduled time: 6.35 pm. Actual time: 6.36 pm.

BBC Three
Date: 22 April 2007. Scheduled time: 8.00 pm. Actual time: 8.00 pm.

Duration: 46' 57"

## ADDITIONAL CREDITED CAST

Miranda Raison (Tallulah), Ryan Carnes (Laszlo), Hugh Quarshie (Solomon), Andrew Garfield (Frank), Eric Loren (Mr Diagoras), Flik Swan (Myrna), Alexis Caley (Lois), Earl Perkins (Man # 1), Peter Brooke (Man # 2), Ian Porter (Foreman), Joe Montana (Worker # 1), Stewart Alexander (Worker # 2), Mel Taylor (Dock Worker), Barnaby Edwards, Nicholas Pegg, Anthony Spargo, David Hankinson (Dalek Operators), Nicholas Briggs (Dalek Voices), Paul Kasey (Hero Pig).

Daleks created by Terry Nation.

## PLOT

The Doctor and Martha arrive in New York in 1930, the era of the Depression, and investigate the mystery of people disappearing from the Hooverville camp set up in Central Park by the city's destitute. With the aid of the Hooverville residents' leader, Solomon, and a music hall showgirl, Tallulah, whose boyfriend Laszlo has also disappeared, the two time travellers discover that the missing people are being abducted through the sewers and taken to an underground base. There the four Daleks of the Cult of Skaro are converting the less intelligent of the abductees into part-human, part-pig slaves and using the more intelligent in an unspecified experiment. The Daleks have secretly taken control of the construction of the Empire State Building and, through their human intermediary Mr Diagoras, are harrying the labourers to carry out extra work on the building's mast by that night. But this is not the only use they have for Diagoras: as their 'final experiment' is initiated, Dalek Sec draws the man into its casing and melds with him to produce the first of a new breed of human-Dalek hybrid …

## QUOTE, UNQUOTE

- **Foreman:** 'These new bosses, what's their names?'
  **Diagoras:** 'I think you can say they're from outta town.'
  **Foreman:** 'Italians?'
  **Diagoras:** 'Bit further than that.'
  **Foreman:** 'How much further?'
  **Diagoras:** 'Beyond your imagination.'
- **Tallulah:** 'It's the Depression, sweetie. Your heart might break, but the show goes on. 'Cause if it stops, you starve.'
- **Dalek Caan:** 'We are the only four Daleks in existence, so the species must evolve. A life outside the shell. The children of Skaro must walk again.'

## CONTINUITY POINTS

- Martha finds a newspaper dated 1 November 1930. This suggests that the TARDIS arrives on that date, or possibly a day or two later if the newspaper is an old one. Martha says that this is 'nearly 80 years ago', consistent with her hailing from a couple of years before 2010. The action in the opening teaser, when Laszlo is attacked by the Pig-Slave in the theatre, takes place two weeks earlier, according to Tallulah.
- The green blob that the Doctor finds in the sewers slightly resembles a Rutan as seen in 'Horror of Fang Rock' (1977) but he later finds that it has 'Fundamental DNA type 467–989', from which he deduces that its planet of origin is Skaro.
- Dalek Caan says that its planet was destroyed in a great war. This could be a reference to the events of 'Remembrance of the Daleks' (1988), in which the Doctor believed that he had destroyed the Daleks' home world, Skaro. If so, it would suggest that these events are viewed as part of the Time War. In the original novels series, however, John Peel's 'War of the Daleks' (BBC Books, 1997) indicates that it was actually a different planet that was destroyed at the end of 'Remembrance of the Daleks'.
- When Dalek Sec's casing opens and Mr Diagoras is sucked inside, it is revealed that the skirt section of the casing is empty, save for the Dalek creature's tentacles (which appear larger than usual) extending down from above. This is at odds with many speculative 'Anatomy of a Dalek'-type features that have appeared in annuals, drawing books, comics and the like over the years, which have tended to show the casing packed with advanced equipment, but is in fact consistent with what has been previously established in the TV series. In the first Dalek story (1963/64), the Doctor's companion Ian is able to climb inside a Dalek casing and operate it himself, once the Dalek creature has been removed, and in 'Planet of the Daleks' (1973), the Thal woman Rebec does the same thing. It would be impossible for them to do this if there were lots of equipment inside the casing. This suggests that the technology that gives the Dalek its motive power etc must be contained within the dome section and built around the sides and into the base of the casing itself.
- A document on the Torchwood Institute System Interface website refers to an infestation of Weevils (monsters featured in the *Doctor Who* spin-off *Torchwood*)

occurring in New York in the 1930s and being attributed to reptiles or similar specimens escaped from the zoo. Could this perhaps have been a misreporting of sightings of the Daleks' Pig-Slaves ...?

## PRODUCTION NOTES

- 'Daleks in Manhattan' was made with 'Evolution of the Daleks' in Block 4 of production on Series Three. The two episodes constitute a two-part story.
- Helen Raynor came up with the idea of using the Empire State Building as a setting at an early stage of the writing process. This contributed to her decision to have the Doctor and Martha arrive in 1930, the year of the Building's construction. Her curiosity was piqued by the fact that it was the tallest building in the world and, with the mooring mast at its apex, effectively also the tallest lightning conductor. The 1930 setting led her to think of the film *Frankenstein*, released by Universal Pictures the following year, in which the monster played by Boris Karloff is animated by lightning, and she determined to make her story a 'family-show take on 1930s horror films'. Russell T Davies suggested featuring a theatre and showgirls, and this led Raynor to think also of *King Kong*, the RKO Radio Pictures film released in 1933 that famously includes scenes of the titular giant ape climbing up the Empire State Building, and *Phantom of the Opera*, the Gaston Laroux novel, of which Lon Chaney's film version had been released by Universal Pictures in 1925. Another story element prompted by the 1930 setting was the economic Depression that gripped America at that time. As Raynor noted in an interview for Issue 349 of *Starburst*, published in May 2007: 'We wanted to look at how the social fabric was crumbling, which gives you a very good way of getting together a mix of characters. The ideas of society having to regroup and being driven by the need to survive fed very nicely into the idea of a Dalek story.' Realising that it would not be possible to have many exterior scenes, as it would be too difficult and expensive to recreate the look of the New York streets of 1930, Raynor set most of the action indoors. The idea of the Pig-Slaves being underground was inspired in part by the urban myth of alligators living in the New York sewers.
- Helen Raynor's initial outline for the story involved scenes of the Daleks lurking underwater in the New York docks, with only their dome lights visible from above, moving about beneath the surface. The intention was that these scenes would be shot at Cardiff docks. This idea was ultimately dropped. Also abandoned was an early notion to feature a group of gangster characters; it was felt that this would be out of keeping with the tone of the story. Another idea dropped during scripting, partly because it was felt to be too gruesome, was that Tallulah would stumble upon a cage containing hideously deformed survivors of the Daleks' earlier, failed genetic experiments. Also dropped, because it was considered too downbeat, was the original idea that Laszlo would die at the end of the story.
- It was director James Strong's suggestion to take a small unit to New York, at the same time as the *Doctor Who Confidential* team were planning to fly writer Helen Raynor over there for an interview, to capture plate shots for use in the story's CGI work. The unit set off for New York on 11 October 2006 and returned four days later. It was also Strong's suggestion that the TARDIS

should materialise beside the Statue of Liberty; as originally scripted, it would have arrived on the roof of a building overlooking Broadway. The Majestic Theatre in Manhattan was used for the exterior shot of the (fictional) Lorenzi Theatre in the story.

- Studio recording for this two-part story took place at Upper Boat over a week, beginning on 23 October 2006.
- The Dalek laboratory scenes were shot from 1 to 7 November 2006 at a disused glass factory on Cardiff's Trident Park industrial estate, previously used as a location on a number of other stories, including 'The Impossible Planet'/'The Satan Pit' and 'Smith and Jones'. The wall beside which the TARDIS materialises was on a primary school playing field opposite Penarth Leisure Centre, where recording took place on 9 November; the New York-recorded shots of the Statue of Liberty above were added in post-production. Central Park's Hooverville was recreated in Bute Park on the estate of Cardiff University, where scenes were shot over one day and four nights (the last of them hampered by heavy rain), starting on 10 November; the New York buildings in the background were again added in post-production. The theatre interiors were shot at the Parc and Dare Theatre, Treorchy, starting on 15 November, and at Headlands School – previously used as a location on 'The Unquiet Dead' and 'Tooth and Claw' – on 20, 21 and 22 November.
- In the scene where the Doctor and Martha arrive at the base of the Statue of Liberty, Murray Gold's incidental music quotes from George Gershwin's 'Rhapsody in Blue', composed in 1924 and often associated with New York, perhaps most notably in Woody Allen's movie *Manhattan* (United Artists, 1979). Other songs featured in the music include 'Happy Days are Here Again', written in 1929 by Milton Ager (music) and Jack Yellen (lyrics), and 'Puttin' on the Ritz', an Irving Berlin composition, also from 1929.
- Tallulah was inspired by the similarly-named character portrayed by Jodie Foster in the film *Bugsy Malone* (Fox-Rank/Paramount Pictures, 1976). The song originally intended to be used for her musical number was Cole Porter's *Anything Goes*, but when it was discovered that this had not been composed until 1934, four years after the story's setting, a specially-written piece by Murray Gold was substituted.
- Because of its longer-than-usual running time (despite a number of edits having been made in post-production to reduce this), 'Daleks in Manhattan' was allocated a 50-minute slot in the BBC One schedule for its debut transmission, rather than the usual 45-minute slot.

## UNFOUNDED PRE-TRANSMISSION RUMOURS

- This story would feature redesigned 'art deco' Daleks with a chrome finish to their casings.
- This story would see an appearance by the father or grandfather of Morton Dill, the character (played by Peter Purves) encountered by the Daleks at the top of the Empire State Building in the classic series story 'The Chase' (1965).

## OOPS!

- The gloves that Mr Diagoras is seen putting on when he is taken to meet Dalek Sec, before he gets sucked inside the casing, have mysteriously disappeared by the time the Dalek Sec Hybrid emerges. (This was because it was initially thought that the prosthetics being created for the hybrid creature by Millennium FX would not include hands, hence it would need to be gloved, but it later transpired that hand appliances had been made after all, and it was decided to go ahead and use them.)
- There are various continuity errors where the different Daleks, identifiable by the individual name plates on their casings and differently-pitched voices, are used interchangeably during recording.
- The Empire State Building is not as close either to the Statue of Liberty or to Central Park as is suggested here.
- The Statue of Liberty's torch, and the arm holding it, looked different in 1930; the versions seen here are replacements fitted in the mid-1980s.

## PRESS REACTION

- 'In previous [Dalek] outings for the new series, the iconic villains have been used as the big "ta da!" moment, a way of showing how clever *Doctor Who* can be at that climactic cliffhanger moment. Here, they are just *there*, already in New York, and our first sight of them is barely ten minutes in as one arrives in a lift … Being used in this manner recalls the early days of the classic series, where Dalek stories were ten-a-penny and they just got on with being Daleks, and it's very refreshing. And there's nothing more iconic than the Doctor crouching down in a dingy corridor, watching as the lower part of a Dalek casing trundles past the camera – those moments possess a kind of race memory effect in any audience member over 35 that sends a pleasurable shiver down the back of your spine … This was old-school *Doctor Who* – and I'm not talking about the '70s. "Daleks in Manhattan" evoked the classic black and white days of Hartnell and Troughton with the breathless style and pace of new *Who*. Alongside "The Shakespeare Code", Helen Raynor's script goes to the top of the pile as amongst the best modern *Doctor Who* has to offer.' Mark Wright, *The Stage* website, 22 April 2007.
- 'While it is great to see glinting metallic cylinders gliding around the set again, there is something rather stilted and artificial about the proceedings here. The acting is all a touch too broad, with everyone behaving like they've walked straight out of a 1930s musical: wisecracks, Brooklyn accent and all. Odd that this series can make the distant galaxies, lost in time and space, seem convincing, but can't quite pull it off when it comes to depicting our own planet – less than a century ago.' Alkarim Jivani, *Time Out*, 18 April 2007.
- 'Occasionally, the new series of *Doctor Who* has struggled with the pacing of the episodes and the lacklustre "Daleks in Manhattan" is a perfect example. The sheer burden of expectation associated with Dalek stories doesn't help our appreciation, but the flaws are glaring. The episode feels very two-paced and jarringly uneven. The scenes involving the Daleks and their fiendish plans are mostly absorbing and contain a brave new direction with their self-analysis

and dialogue. The cliffhanger is also particularly stunning thanks to the wonderfully designed Dalek Sec/human hybrid. However, away from their experimentation, the Doctor and Martha's exploration of a New York in the midst of the Great Depression is rather tedious ... The sequences in and around the sewers and the theatre feel rather dragged out and inconsequential and leave us itching for the Daleks to come back on screen. The character of Tallulah is simply painful. It's a nice, quaint idea to have a showgirl embroiled in the extraterrestrial plot, but she serves no real purpose apart from spluttering highly contrived dialogue and displaying irritating traits.' Ben Rawson-Jones, Digital Spy website, 21 April 2007

## FAN COMMENT

- 'Amazingly, Dalek Sec isn't afraid to follow the logic to where it leads him: the Time Lords are gone; the Daleks are essentially gone. This means that the most successful race in the history of the universe is – wait for it – humanity! If only he can splice the Dalek genome onto the human race, then perhaps the Daleks might survive. And while we can argue with his methods, give him points for deciding that the Daleks might just have to embrace the human values of love and tolerance, even though the human's capability for war is something Dalek Sec more readily understands. Speaking as a fan who has watched the Dalek character evolve (or, rather, firmly establish and re-establish itself) over 44 years, this is a watershed moment. That any Dalek would think, for a half second, of stepping outside its shell, is damn impressive, and the Doctor agrees. The question is: is my knowledge as a fan giving me an insight into the Daleks that casual viewers don't have? Or do casual viewers get the fact that this is a major change in Dalek character by witnessing with shock as the Doctor agrees to help Mr Sec with his plan?' James Bow, Bow James Bow website, 29 April 2007.
- 'As in "Gridlock", New York is used as a *Lexx*-like representation of Heaven and Hell. While the Empire State Building – or Dalek Empire State Building, perhaps – stretches to the heavens, the diabolical Daleks inhabit the underworld with their latest "sub-human" slaves where, almost echoing "Aliens of London", "Daleks in Manhattan" has its own, considerably less cute, pig men. Not quite sure what that is trying to say in a story that goes out of its way to avoid mentioning the racial tension of an America less than half a century after the civil war, and still 30 years before the civil rights movement. In between, again, the ordinary humans find themselves trapped in a limbo: the motorway in "Gridlock", the Hooverville shanty-town in Central Park here.' 'Millennium Dome', Millennium Elephant blog, 23 April 2007.
- 'Will the other Daleks reject [the Dalek Sec Hybrid]? Can they conceivably have any reason not to? They can't behave like Tallulah who upon seeing the transformed Laszlo does not reject the man she once knew. She embraces the changed man because she can still recognise him beneath the bestial appearance. The episode plays subtly with the animal and human condition, with bestial mindlessness and human reason, with constructed bodies and natural forms. It echoes well the Gothic romance of *The Phantom Of The Opera* and the fairy-tale psychology of *Beauty and the Beast*. All this benefits from

some lovely performances from Miranda Raison and Ryan Carnes as the seemingly doomed lovers.' Frank Collins, Outpost Gallifrey Reviews, 7 May 2007.

- 'No other show in the history of television does "utterly barmy" quite like *Doctor Who* – and pull it off. Were it any other programme, the disparate elements of "Daleks in Manhattan" would seem like the silliest thing in the world. And that's just the title. Straight off, we're back in the good old Reithian tradition of 1960s *Who*, disguising subtle history lessons for all as popularist science fiction. Before this episode, I had never heard of Hooverville or really thought about the Empire State Building being built at the same time as the Depression. Well, you learn a little something every day, don't you? ... This instalment was barmy indeed. It was *Doctor Who* meets *Chicago*, complete with song and dance number, which I would [bet] will be released on the next Murray Gold album. Pig men, Daleks, songs, art deco and yet more in a long history of stupid people helping the Daleks ... The one word that sums up this episode for me is Fun. Fun, Fun, Fun, with a capital F.' Simon Fox, Outpost Gallifrey Reviews, 7 May 2007.

## ANALYSIS

Helen Raynor reportedly watched a number of the 1980s Dalek stories as part of her research for writing 'Daleks in Manhattan'/'Evolution of the Daleks' – her debut script commission for *Doctor Who*, although she has been one of the series' script editors since its return in 2005 and has also written for *Torchwood* – and the fruits of that work can be clearly seen in the transmitted episodes. 'Revelation of the Daleks' (1984) seems to have been a particular influence: its idea of a new breed of Daleks being created from lifeless human bodies is echoed here; its concept of a hybrid consisting of a one-eyed human head transplanted into a transparent Dalek casing is essentially reprised, but in reverse, with a one-eyed Dalek head transplanted onto a human body; and its shots of the Daleks gliding around the tunnels of their underground lair on the planet Necros are recalled in the scenes of them moving through the Manhattan sewers. The notion of different Dalek factions clashing over genetic distinctions, explored in both 'Revelation of the Daleks' and 'Remembrance of the Daleks' (1988), also becomes significant in the latter stages of Raynor's story. The Daleks' use of subservient drones to do their bidding, in the form of mind-controlled human duplicates in 'Resurrection of the Daleks' (1984) and, delving rather further back into *Doctor Who* history, the Robomen in 'The Dalek Invasion of Earth' (1964) and the Ogrons in 'Day of the Daleks' (1972) and 'Frontier in Space' (1973), likewise serves as a precedent for their creation here of the Pig-Slaves (humorously nicknamed 'Hogrons' by some fans).

'Daleks in Manhattan' in fact has a very 'traditional' *Doctor Who* feel to it. Its status as the first half of a two-parter means that it can afford to take a little more time than usual over plot development, giving it a pace more akin to that of a typical classic series story; and the script's aforementioned nods to past Dalek episodes are not its only familiar-seeming elements. The obvious *The Phantom of the Opera* undertones to the theatre-centred romance between Tallulah and the part-converted Laszlo, along with the scenes set in sewers that can be accessed via the theatre, recall the acclaimed 'The Talons of Weng-Chiang' (1977) (which also features a pig-brained – but not pig-faced – homunculus). The way Raynor draws on this and other literary and cinematic sources – including H G Wells's novel *The Island of Dr Moreau* (Macmillan, 1896), concerning a deranged scientist's attempts to transform beasts into men through a kind of vivisection; vintage horror films such as *Frankenstein* (Universal Pictures, 1931), in which a monster manufactured from body parts is placed on an operating table suspended from a laboratory ceiling and animated by power from a lightning strike; and the fairy tale-inspired TV series *Beauty and the Beast* (CBS, 1987-1990), in which the Beast lives in tunnels beneath New York – is reminiscent of the approach taken in many classic series stories, most notably during the phenomenally popular 1975-1977 period. The Dalek Sec Hybrid bears a passing resemblance to Scaroth from 'City of Death' (1979) and even to the Monoids from 'The Ark' (1966). Memories of classic era Dalek episodes are further evoked by the reuse of established terms such as 'Dalekanium'[52] and 'rels'[53] (although curiously there is no 'Exterminate!'); by the visual similarity between the Daleks' circular-screened computer here and those seen in their earliest stories; by the use of the familiar 'heartbeat' sound effect; by Nicholas Briggs's use of a slightly more 'old school' Dalek voice style this time around; and by the inclusion in Murray Gold's incidental music of some nods to Roger Limb's 'Revelation of the Daleks' score and some decidedly retro-sounding stings that could almost have come from one of the 1960s Dalek movies starring Peter Cushing. And, more generally, the scenes of Daleks and Pig-Slaves pursuing the Doctor and his friends through the sewers recall the many chases through tunnels, corridors and indeed sewers that became a staple ingredient – in fact almost a cliché – of the classic series.

What the original *Doctor Who* could never have pulled off successfully, however, is setting a whole story in 1930s New York. For evidence of that, one need only compare the very convincing top-of-the-Empire-State-Building shots in 'Daleks in Manhattan' with the decidedly unconvincing ones in the third episode of the early Dalek potboiler 'The Chase' (1965) – and that first visit by the Daleks to this iconic setting (which Russell T Davies has amusingly theorised could have prompted them to return there when they made their emergency temporal shift at the end of 'Doomsday') wasn't even set in the past but in the then present day. That producer Phil Collinson was able to find sufficient money within the budget to allow for the series' first ever American location shoot – albeit on a limited scale – is really quite extraordinary, and the story makes the most of the opportunity to show off the city's most famous attractions: the Statue of Liberty, Broadway, the Empire State Building and Central Park, all are present and correct. The title 'Daleks in Manhattan' is an excellent one in this respect, because – like that of the

---

[52] Dalekanium is the metal out of which the Daleks' casings are made, as first revealed in 'The Dalek Invasion of Earth' (1964) – not to be confused with Dalekenium, a type of explosive capable of destroying Daleks, as featured in 'Day of the Daleks' (1972). In two other stories, 'Remembrance of the Daleks' (1988) and 'Dalek', the Daleks' casings have been said to be made of bonded polycarbide armour, which suggests that Dalekanium is a form of bonded polycarbide.

[53] The rel is a Dalek unit of time, apparently just longer than a second, first used in the two 1960s movies – *Dr. Who and the Daleks* and *Daleks Invasion Earth: 2150 AD* – and adopted in the TV series in 'Doomsday'.

movie *Snakes on a Plane* (New Line Cinema, 2006) – it neatly encapsulates the story's central premise in the simplest and most direct terms possible; and, let's face it, 'Daleks in Cardiff' just wouldn't have had quite the same ring to it (although an idea for a story entitled 'The Daleks in London' was briefly considered for inclusion in the 1972 season, before it was decided to make 'Day of the Daleks' instead).

Once again the Mill deserve enormous praise for their contribution to the production, as their excellent CGI work combining the New York-recorded plate shots with the UK-recorded foreground shots – and substituting appropriate period details for any more modern pieces of architecture that would otherwise be visible – plays a crucial part in creating the impression that the Doctor really has taken Martha back in time to the Big Apple as it was over 75 years ago (which is a nice idea, following on from the New New York setting of the previous episode). The UK-recorded interiors, both location and studio, also match seamlessly with the exteriors. The scenes set within the Lorenzi Theatre are particularly impressive, capturing very effectively the feel of a 1930s Broadway (or is it off-Broadway?) music hall, complete with a vintage-sounding song and dance number – 'My Angel Put the Devil in Me', actually a new composition by Murray Gold – performed as part of a 'New York Revue' by Tallulah, taking centre stage in her bright white angel costume, and a company of showgirls with devilish red outfits and fans. The inclusion of a musical routine like this is something of a first for *Doctor Who*, but it fits in nicely with the drama (although what exactly Martha is trying to do when she makes her way across the stage is anyone's guess) and is very well directed and choreographed, too, complete with a couple of Busby Berkeley-style kaleidoscopic touches nicely appropriate to an early 1930s setting, lending the episode a colourful, glamorous quality.

Beneath the surface sheen of New York, however, lies a darker reality – both literally in the sewers where the Pig-Slaves lurk and metaphorically in the grimness of the economic Depression that gripped the USA, and then spread to much of the rest of the world, in the wake of the Wall Street stock market crash of October 1929. It was apparently Raynor who came up with the idea of setting part of the action in Hooverville – one of many such shanty towns, derisively named after President Herbert Hoover, that were set up by the unemployed and homeless in communities across the country – this having not been part of the initial brief she was given by Russell T Davies; and although it does introduce a slight anachronism, in that the Central Park Hooverville was not actually established until 1931, a year after the story is set, it is to the writer's credit that she chose to highlight the stark contrast in circumstances between the rich and the poor in the city, giving this ostensibly fantastical story a more serious subtext. This is not least because, while it most obviously recalls other Depression-era tales such as John Steinbeck's landmark novel *The Grapes of Wrath* (The Viking Press, 1939), it also effectively invites the viewer to reflect upon the marked social inequality that still persists in the USA today, in Martha's time, as can be witnessed for instance in the situation in New Orleans in the wake of Hurricane Katrina.

The other real-life concern that hangs like a pall over the drama is the aftermath of the First World War (1914-1918) – or the Great War, as it was generally referred to at the time – in which many of New York's adult male population would have fought. These veterans include both Hooverville's *de facto* leader Solomon and the

Daleks' human overseer Mr Diagoras (whose role here is similar to that of the Controller in 'Day of the Daleks'). These two men have responded to their experience of the conflict in their own individual and contrasting ways; the former by demonstrating an innate authority and wisdom worthy of his Biblical namesake, whose celebrated 'judgment' [54] is neatly referenced when Solomon settles an argument between two men over a loaf of bread by breaking it in half and giving a piece to each, and the latter, who may well have been named after the ancient Greek poet Diagoras the Atheist, by developing an uncompromising determination to survive and succeed, even at the cost of his own humanity – as proves to be quite literally the case at the episode's conclusion. The two men are thus placed in direct opposition to each other as character types – in fact, they could almost be seen as human representations of the opposing principles of the Doctor and the Daleks, likewise survivors of a terrible conflict, the last great Time War – and this is carried through into the design of their respective costumes, the compassionate, humane Solomon's brown suit and long coat resembling the Doctor's own attire and the hard-nosed, uncaring Diagoras's sharp black suit reflecting Dalek Sec's black casing.

These allusions to the privations of the Depression and the War help to ground the story in reality, and allow for some thought-provoking questions to be raised. Solomon's comment concerning the construction of the Empire State Building, 'How come they can do *that* and we got people starving in the heart of Manhattan?' is a particularly interesting one, because it touches on issues that are, by *Doctor Who* standards, unusually political. Is Solomon merely pointing out the irony of a society being on the one hand capable of hugely impressive achievements but on the other hand unable to provide the basic necessities of life for millions of its poorest members, or is he actually expressing disapproval of money being spent on such an ambitious enterprise when it could be used instead to provide social aid to the residents of Hooverville? If the latter were the case, it would suggest that he had an essentially socialist outlook on the situation, out of step with that of most ordinary US citizens of his era. The typical capitalist viewpoint would be that, with its creation of thousands of jobs directly, and perhaps tens of thousands indirectly, the Empire State Building project was just the sort of endeavour that held out the greatest hope of relief for people in Solomon's position. This was clearly the attitude of the next US President, Franklin D Roosevelt, who between 1933 and 1938 initiated a series of 'New Deal' initiatives that centred around tackling poverty not by making social security payouts – although a limited form of social insurance was introduced during that period – but by creating thousands of new jobs on public works projects; and debate still rages today over whether this was an effective and appropriate approach to tackling the Depression, or whether it was actually counterproductive and delayed an economic turnaround. Certainly for many of those in Hooverville, finding work would have been the number one priority, and being forced to accept 'handouts' from soup kitchens and the like

---

[54] In the Biblical tale, in 1 Kings 3:16-28, King Solomon resolves a dispute between two women over which of them is the mother of a certain baby by threatening to cut it in two and give half to each of them; when one of the women protests and agrees to give up her claim, he knows that the she must be the true mother, because she would not allow the baby to be harmed.

would have been seen as deeply shaming. The harsh reality, though, was that there were never enough jobs in construction work for all those who wanted them, and not everyone was physically capable of doing such work.

Further evidence of Solomon's left-wing tendencies comes in the scene where he effectively acts as a spokesperson for his fellow Hooverville residents, almost in the manner of a union official, when Diagoras visits the camp and offers work, supposedly clearing a collapsed sewer tunnel, at the rate of 'a dollar a day'. Particularly given that he is a Black man, Solomon's scathing description of this as a 'slave wage' also raises the issue of race. He has previously told the Doctor and Martha, 'I will say this about Hooverville: we are a truly equal society; Black, White, all the same, all starving.' Again this is a sentiment that would have been seen at the time as distinctly left-wing, if not Communist; it does explain, though, why no-one in Hooverville makes an issue of Martha's race (whereas at the theatre Tallulah appears to allude to it when, thinking that the Doctor is romantically involved with Martha, she describes him as a 'forward-thinking guy'), if not why her obviously expensive clothes and highly conspicuous jewellery fail to attract any undue attention.

Also telling in terms of its political slant is the scene in which a group of labourers baulk at the demand that new work on the Empire State Building's mast be completed that night, and Diagoras tells them: 'You don't get it. If you won't work, I can replace you like that!' It is hard not to see this as a comment by Raynor on the way that high unemployment leaves workers vulnerable to exploitation. Could it be that her memories of growing up in Wales during the era of the miners' strike had a bearing on this aspect of the story? *Doctor Who* has arguably always had a left-leaning political perspective, or at least a liberal one, but never before has this been quite as explicit as it is here.

Possibly the best scene of the entire episode, though, is the one (reportedly added into the script by Davies during rewrites) that has Diagoras and Dalek Caan looking out from the Empire State Building over the vista of New York, with the following dialogue:

> **Dalek Caan:** 'This day is ending. Humankind is weak. You shelter from the dark. And yet, you have built all this.'
> **Diagoras:** 'That's progress. You gotta move with the times, or you get left behind.'
> **Dalek Caan:** 'My planet is gone. Destroyed in a great war. Yet versions of this city stand throughout history. The human race always continues.'
> **Diagoras:** 'We've had wars. I've been a soldier myself, and I swore then I'd survive. No matter what.'
> **Dalek Caan:** 'You have rare ambition.'
> **Diagoras:** 'I'm gonna run this city, whatever it takes. By any means necessary.'
> **Dalek Caan:** 'You think like a Dalek.'
> **Diagoras:** 'I'll take that as a compliment.'

This sort of exchange, in which a Dalek converses rather than simply rants, is one of the great innovations of Davies's version of *Doctor Who* when it comes to the presentation of the Doctor's greatest foes, and adds enormously to their believability and menace. Dalek Caan's comments here also echo the Doctor's reaction on first seeing a Dalek in the sewers: 'They survived. They always survive, while I lose everything.' This cleverly suggests that the Daleks view humanity in much the same way as the Doctor views the Daleks, and again adds depth to their depiction.

It is not only the Daleks who are well-handled in this episode but all the human protagonists as well. The characterisation is excellent throughout, and the tension of the drama is leavened by some nice moments of humour, particularly from Tallulah: her 'I know some guys are just pigs, but not my Laszlo' line is darkly comic, considering what has actually happened to Laszlo; and her assumption that the Doctor's lack of romantic interest in Martha indicates that he is 'into musical theatre' is also very amusing.

Undoubtedly one of the episode's biggest talking points is the scene at the end where the Dalek Sec Hybrid creature emerges from its casing as if breaking free from a kind of metallic chrysalis, in a shot somewhat reminiscent of the rising up of the Cyber Controller from its tomb in 'The Tomb of the Cybermen' (1967). This is an astonishing and truly bizarre image ... but sadly its impact on debut transmission will have been severely diminished for most viewers by the fact that the creature had already been unveiled on the front cover of that week's *Radio Times* (the first of three editions to include a free packet of *Doctor Who* stickers). That Davies actually co-operated with *Radio Times* in presenting this 'exclusive' is a huge surprise. He has generally shown himself to be very astute when it comes to the public promotion of the series, and his normal policy of maintaining tight secrecy over the details of forthcoming storylines, while it can be frustrating for some fans and has arguably sometimes been taken too far, has proved to be a wise one. Here, though, he has gone to the opposite extreme, and effectively spoiled what could potentially have been not only one of the series' strangest cliff-hangers ever (which it certainly is), but also one of its most jaw-dropping; and it is difficult not to see this as an uncharacteristic blunder.

Another problem with the Dalek Sec Hybrid is that it looks far more impressive and credible in still images than it does on screen. The depiction of tentacled creatures is something that it has always been a struggle for *Doctor Who* to pull off convincingly, and while the well-rendered CGI Dalek mutant is a rare exception to the rule – and the scene where it sucks Diagoras into its casing is both scary and repulsive – the prosthetic head-piece worn by actor Eric Loren in the episode's closing moments never looks anything other than artificial, chiefly because the animatronic movement of the – disturbingly phallic – tentacles is far too limited and inflexible to appear realistic. This is not something for which Neill Gorton and his Millennium FX company can really be held at fault, however, as all effects techniques have their inherent limitations; arguably the mistake here lay more in the decision to attempt this with an animatronic appliance in the first place. To be fair, though, it is difficult to see how else the creature could have been realised affordably within the series' budget, so perhaps this is one of those cases where it just has to be accepted that what is presented on screen is the best that could possibly have been achieved, albeit that it is less than perfect. Having said that, though, this episode is certainly not one of the series' finest hours from a make-up point of view as, although the Pig-Slaves are very well executed, Laszlo's part-pig, part-human features are far from convincing; the tusks in particular look like the sort of thing one might find as a cheap novelty in a joke shop (and also, incidentally, prevented actor Ryan Carnes from speaking properly, in consequence of which all his dialogue had to be re-recorded in a separate session in Los Angeles on 13 March 2007 and dubbed in post-production).

These, though, are just isolated missteps in what is otherwise a highly impressive and expensive-looking production; and, following on from his excellent work on Series Two's 'The Impossible Planet'/'The Satan Pit', James Strong again shows himself to be one of the very best directors on the new *Doctor Who*. All in all, 'Daleks in Manhattan' makes for a thoroughly enjoyable opening half to this two-part story, delivering on the promise of its title and setting up a lot of intriguing questions that will hopefully be answered in the concluding instalment. What is the green blob that the Doctor finds in the sewer? Will there be a happy ending to the romance between Tallulah and Laszlo? What exactly are the Daleks aiming to achieve with their 'final experiment'? Why do they need to have the work on the Empire State Building's mast completed with such urgency? And, perhaps most tantalising of all, what impact will the arrival of the Dalek Sec Hybrid have on the situation?

Roll on 'Evolution of the Daleks'!

# 3.05 – EVOLUTION OF THE DALEKS

Writer: Helen Raynor
Director: James Strong

DEBUT TRANSMISSION DETAILS

BBC One
Date: 28 April 2007. Scheduled time: 6.45 pm. Actual time: 6.44 pm.

BBC Three
Date: 29 April 2007. Scheduled time: 8.00 pm. Actual time: 8.00 pm.

Duration: 46' 29"

ADDITIONAL CREDITED CAST

Miranda Raison (Tallulah), Ryan Carnes (Laszlo), Hugh Quarshie (Solomon), Andrew Garfield (Frank), Eric Loren (Dalek Sec), Earl Perkins (Man # 1), Barnaby Edwards, Nicholas Pegg, David Hankinson (Dalek Operators), Nicholas Briggs (Dalek Voices), Paul Kasey (Hero Pig Man), Ian Porter (Hybrid).

Daleks created by Terry Nation.

PLOT

The Daleks' 'final experiment' involves replacing the human DNA of the most intelligent of the Hooverville abductees with a human-Dalek DNA mixture, thus perpetuating the Dalek race in a new form. The other three Cult of Skaro members rebel against the Dalek Sec Hybrid when he enlists the Doctor's help to increase the human component. They substitute pure Dalek DNA for the mixture, just before a predicted gamma radiation strike from the Sun, conducted through Dalekanium panels attached to the mast of the Empire State Building, provides the power needed to initiate the process. The Doctor ascends the mast and places his own body in the path of the gamma radiation, causing Time Lord DNA to be added to the mixture. In a climactic showdown, the Dalek Sec Hybrid is exterminated when he throws himself in the path of a Dalek ray intended for the Doctor, and Dalek Thay and Dalek Jast are destroyed in a shoot-out with their new army, who – owing to the newly-introduced Time Lord element of their DNA – have started to question orders. Dalek Caan triggers the remote destruction of the army as a failed experiment and then performs an emergency temporal shift away from the New York of 1930. The Pig-Slaves have a natural life span of only a few weeks, but the Doctor manages to stabilise Laszlo in his new half-human, half-pig form, and the Hooverville residents agree to take him in.

## QUOTE, UNQUOTE

- **Solomon:** 'Daleks. Ain't we the same? Underneath, ain't we all kin? See, I just discovered this past day that God's universe is a thousand times the size I thought it was. And that scares me, oh yeah, terrifies me right down to the bone. But surely it's got to give me hope. Hope that maybe, together, we can make a better tomorrow. So I beg you, now, if you have any compassion in your hearts, then you'll meet with us and stop this fight. Well, what do you say?'
  **Dalek Caan:** 'Exterminate!'
- **Dalek Jast:** 'You will die, Doctor, at the beginning of a new age.'
  **Dalek Thay:** 'Planet Earth will become New Skaro.'
  **Doctor:** 'Oh, and what a world, with anything just the slightest bit different ground into the dirt. That's Dalek Sec. Don't you remember? The cleverest Dalek ever and look what you've done to him. Is that your new empire? Hmm? Is that the foundation for a whole new civilization?'

## CONTINUITY POINTS

- The Doctor surmises that the emergency temporal shift performed by the Cult of Skaro at the end of 'Doomsday' must have 'roasted up' their power cells, leaving them vulnerable. ('Time was, four Daleks could have conquered the world,' he says, in what may be an in-joke reference to the fact that four Dalek props were commonly used to represent an entire army in the classic series, in stories such as 'Day of the Daleks' (1972).)
- The Dalek Sec Hybrid says, 'We tried everything to survive, when we found ourselves stranded in this ignorant age. First we tried brewing new Dalek embryos, but their flesh was too weak.' This explains the green blob that the Doctor found in the sewers in 'Daleks in Manhattan' and confirms that the Daleks can in principle reproduce asexually, as indicated in previous stories such as, in particular, 'The Power of the Daleks', where a Dalek 'production line' is seen at work in one of their spaceships, crash-landed on the planet Vulcan. The form of the Dalek embryo in 'Daleks in Manhattan'/'Evolution of the Daleks' recalls that seen in 'The Power of the Daleks'.
- It is confirmed here that the main part of the story takes place on 1 November – the young Hooverville resident Frank points to this date on a sheet of revisions to the Empire State Building's architectural plans and refers to it as 'today'. The showdown in the theatre takes place after midnight, in the early hours of the following morning.

## PRODUCTION NOTES

- 'Evolution of the Daleks' was made with 'Daleks in Manhattan' in Block 4 of production on Series Three.
- This episode had the working title 'Hooverville'.
- The themes of genetic manipulation that come to the fore in this episode were inspired by the Daleks' fictional origins as the result of a genetic experiment on their home planet, Skaro. Writer Helen Raynor also had in mind literary

sources such as H G Wells's 1896 science fiction novel *The Island of Dr Moreau*. She saw 'Daleks in Manhattan'/'Evolution of the Daleks' as being about the genesis of a new type of Daleks, with the Dalek Sec Hybrid fulfilling the role taken by Davros in 'Genesis of the Daleks' (1975) but with a vision to 're-humanise' the Daleks in ways that would benefit them. The Dalek Sec Hybrid was thus conceived as an almost Messiah-like visionary whose aim would be to lead the Daleks out of the darkness of defeat and near-extinction toward a brighter future.

- Actor Eric Loren sought advice from Dalek voice artist Nicholas Briggs, asking him to record all the Dalek Sec Hybrid's lines on a computer, so that he could hear how a Dalek would say them. He then incorporated aspects of Briggs's Dalek intonation into his performance as the Hybrid.
- The song 'Happy Days are Here Again' is featured again, on the radio that the Doctor uses to attack the Daleks at the beginning of the episode.
- The scenes featuring the Empire State Building's mast were shot on 22 and 23 November 2006 – *Doctor Who*'s forty-third anniversary – using a scale replica, over 20 feet tall, constructed at Cardiff Heliport. The short scene from the end of the episode, where Frank tells the Doctor, Martha, Tallulah and Laszlo that the Hooverville residents have agreed to take Laszlo in, was done earlier in the shoot, on 8 November, in the park behind Cardiff Castle.
- The Dalek alarm sound effect heard when the Doctor uses his sonic screwdriver in the theatre to alert the Daleks to his presence there was reused from 'Destiny of the Daleks' (1979).
- A shot intended for 'Evolution of the Daleks' and included in the Series Three trailer at the end of 'The Runaway Bride', showing a Pig-Slave charging at a Hooverville resident who is trying to cock a gun, was omitted from the episode as transmitted.

OOPS!

- The Doctor says 'This planet hasn't even split the atom yet,' but in fact physicist Ernest Rutherford (1871-1937) split the atom in work carried out between 1917 and 1919 – a fact actually referred to by Professor Lazarus in the following episode, 'The Lazarus Experiment'.
- Dalek Sec says, 'Consider a pure Dalek – intelligent but emotionless,' and the Doctor replies, 'Removing the emotions makes you stronger – that's what your creator thought, all those years ago.' This is incorrect: the Daleks' creator, Davros, removed all their *positive* emotions, such as love and compassion, but left in place their *negative* emotions, such as hate and anger; they have actually always shown themselves to be highly emotional creatures.

PRESS REACTION

- 'Better than the first half, this concluding chapter is still a bit hit-and-miss. Sec's emerging humanity is predictable, if undeniably effective – the Doctor is shocked at his plans to breed out the Dalek need to conquer, which is their fundamental "Dalekness" – and he never quite convinces. The *idea* of him is fascinating, but the execution is a little daft and unsurprising.' Jes Bickham,

*DeathRay* Issue 2, July 2007.

- 'Oh dear. It's difficult to say where the fault lies, as there's no one element – Helen Raynor's script, James Strong's direction or Russell T Davies's shopping list of plot elements – that's noticeably flawed, but this soufflé has slumped as it's come out of the oven.' Anthony Brown, *TV Zone* Issue 216, Summer 2007.
- 'In the risible "Evolution of the Daleks", it was claimed that the Daleks could "evolve" (meaning, in context, improve and increase their numbers) by implanting Dalek DNA into the empty shells of human beings who'd had their minds wiped ... For famously talented genetic scientists, the Daleks seemed surprisingly unfazed by the fact that the resulting creatures – who, as far as they were concerned, would now be 100 percent Dalek – looked entirely human, but seemed to expect that their behaviour and attitudes would be entirely Dalek. In scientific terms, this makes no sense at all: even starting to unpick all the errors would make an evolutionary theorist weep. The story only makes sense if you interpret it instead in religious terms, and replace the word "DNA" with the word "soul". In other words, *Doctor Who* has joined the cultural pantheon that understands so little of the concept of evolution that it might as well be an act of God after all.' John Binns, *TV Zone* Issue 216, Summer 2007.

## FAN COMMENT

- 'Why in God's name does the Doctor go along with Sec's nutty plan to produce the hybrids? Yes, it's all very Doctorly to allow even his deadliest enemies a chance at redemption, but to plunge into this, taking Sec's word that the humans can't reclaim their humanity and that they'll be a force for peace and love and light (or whatever), without even taking a second to think about the implications, is mad. Not only is it moronic: after all the Doctor's been through to eradicate the Daleks, it's utterly unbelievable. Redirect the Daleks down a new evolutionary path: sure. Do it on the spur of the moment taking a Dalek's word for it that it's for the best: are you kidding? And that's not the worst of it. In one of the least Doctorly scenes ever, the Doctor begs the Daleks to kill him if [they] will spare the others. Granted, the Doctor's a little bit overwrought due to his past history with the Daleks, but that's absolutely no excuse. First of all, giving up and leaving everyone else to face the Daleks once he's been offed is about as probable for the Doctor as proposing to one of his companions. And secondly, the Doctor isn't remotely daft enough to entertain even for a nanosecond the notion that sacrificing himself would make the Daleks spare as much as a sausage. This seriously tries our patience.' Uncredited reviewer, Androzani website, May 2007.
- 'Unfortunately, there's one chronic story problem inherent throughout – as Helen Raynor's scripts follow the Daleks as if they were regular characters, we know the broad outline of what their plan involves from very early in the first episode, but the Doctor and Martha spend the entire story catching up. This leads to long, long scenes where the heroes are trying painstakingly to work out plot points that are old news to the audience. This problem is exacerbated by certain plotlines having to go slowly to allow space for [others] to catch up. For instance, Martha's journey to the top of the Empire State Building to

discover the Dalekanium – which the Daleks ordered to be attached in the previous episode – slows to a crawl to allow time for the Doctor's plot to catch up to the point where he can rejoin her in time. It's an annoying story problem so basic it's surprising no-one caught it at an early stage in development.' Mark Clapham, Shiny Shelf website, May 2007.

- 'Much as I disliked last week's *Who*, I loved this week's, and strangely it's for the same reasons. It made no sense, it didn't follow any ideas up and it threw new ideas into the pot (or old, for those of us who've been about since the old days) just to throw them straight out again. We had humans being instilled with the Dalek Factor, internecine dissent, clearly signposted self-sacrifice and the Doctor grimacing while he's showered with blue sparks – all straight swipes from the Dalek tales of yore. It worked best as a piece of no-brainer fun, though. Being able to admire the brilliance of the Mill in turning Cardiff into '30s New York and the craftsmanship of the sets helped distract from the extremely derivative plot. The acting was universally good, especially from Eric Loren. The idea of the Daleks rejecting the continuation of their species at the cost of their ingrained creed was a good one. I feel that maybe it would've been thrown into sharper relief if more had been made of the Dalek-Humans. Perhaps their earlier experiments would've made a more effective retinue than the Pigmen. Once again, so many elements, so little time ...' Nick May, Shockeye Online website, May 2007.

- 'I had concerns after last week that this two-parter was a little too traditional, but "Evolution of the Daleks" was a mish-mash of the worst classic *Who* had to offer. We got runaround plotting – was there any need for everybody to run to Central Park other than [to] kill off [Solomon]? One mediocre battle later and everybody is back in the Empire State Building. We got poor characterisation: only two seasons on from the Doctor's palpable terror in "Dalek" and [he] is inviting the pepperpots to exterminate him. And, even more out of character, they don't. We got awful dialogue: if Daleks had moustaches to twirl, they'd do it to accompany melodramatic nonsense like, "Now we will destroy our greatest enemy, the Doctor." We got silly monsters: Eric Loren's lisping Hybrid was just bizarre. And we got a family show unsure how to strike the right tone. The pigs in the lift were gloriously funny; seconds later, their corpses were sprawled gruesomely across the floor. And a fundamentally very dark story about xenophobic hate seems an incongruous home for Freema's and Miranda Raison's "jolly hockey sticks" reading of "Dalekanium!"' Simon Kinnear, Shockeye Online website, May 2007.

ANALYSIS

Back in the middle of the last century, story writers who knew little about science but who wanted to provide an esoteric, scientific-sounding explanation for something would commonly resort to 'computers'; which no doubt seemed impressive at the time, when few people had ever actually seen a real computer let alone used one, but has now become almost laughably dated. Today, the equivalent all-purpose buzz-word seems to be 'DNA'. A good example of this from a little earlier in Series Three comes in 'The Shakespeare Code', when the Doctor identifies the Carrionites' voodoo-doll-like figurine as a 'DNA replicator'; a silly attempt at rationalisation, and really the only jarring line in the whole script, not only because it is at odds with the story's central premise of the creatures using the power of words rather than human scientific principles to achieve their ends, but also because the idea that the replication of someone's DNA might impart the ability to attack them physically is, frankly, ludicrous. 'Evolution of the Daleks' sadly suffers from the same problem, but to a far worse extent, because in this case it is not just a single, fairly inconsequential element that relies on a deeply unscientific 'DNA' explanation but, it transpires, the entire plot.

The central misconception here seems to be that changing people's DNA leaves them physically unaffected but somehow alters the way their minds work. So the Daleks believe that by removing their experimental subjects' human DNA and replacing it with a human-Dalek DNA synthesis taken from the genetic template of the Dalek Sec Hybrid, they will create an army of people who still look the same but who think and act like a cross between a human and a Dalek. Then, when the Dalek Sec Hybrid enlists the Doctor's help to strengthen the human component, and the other three members of the Cult of Skaro rebel against this and replace the DNA mixture with pure Dalek DNA, they assume that this will cause the members of their new army to think purely like Daleks. Finally, when the Doctor adds in Time Lord DNA to create a new mixture, by somehow managing to 'transmit' it (a ridiculous idea in itself) from the top of the Empire State Building to the Daleks' underground base along with the energy from a gamma radiation strike, the end result is a new 'species' of people who think like a cross between a Dalek and a Time Lord. This is all as absurd as it is convoluted.

Not only that, but it still leaves some important questions unanswered. How are the experimental subjects able to retain their intellectual capacity – clearly an important consideration for the Daleks, as they selected only those of higher intelligence from amongst their abductees – if the process begins with their minds being wiped, so that, as the Dalek Sec Hybrid says, 'Everything that they were has been lost'? Why exactly did the Daleks need to attach Dalekanium casing panels to the Empire State Building's mast, rather than simply use cables to transmit the power? And why does the Dalek Sec Hybrid show compassion for Solomon and the other Hooverville residents when this is clearly not something that Diagoras felt in the first place? If it had been Solomon who had been used in the creation of the Dalek Sec Hybrid, then this might make more sense, but it is difficult to see why being combined with Diagoras should cause Dalek Sec's outlook to be so radically altered, given that Dalek Caan has previously told Diagoras, 'You think like a Dalek', and Diagoras has taken this as a compliment.

The farrago of bad science doesn't end with the 'DNA' nonsense, either. The whole business of the gamma radiation strike is totally misconceived. Gamma radiation is a form of high-energy electromagnetic emission that can cause serious damage to living tissue, and that can be blocked only by heavy shielding, such as lead plate or thick concrete. An animated diagram displayed at one point on the Daleks' computer screen suggests that not only New York but the whole of one side of the Earth is about to be bombarded with gamma radiation from the Sun, and yet when the strike occurs, it is night-time in New York, meaning that that side of the Earth must be facing away from the Sun, and the only visible consequence is a powerful bolt of lightning – a completely different form of radiation – that hits the Empire State Building's mast; and the people of New York – and presumably of the rest of the Earth too – remain completely unaffected.

When watching a series such as *Doctor Who*, it is obviously necessary to make certain allowances for dramatic licence, but there is a limit to how far this can be stretched before the suspension of disbelief becomes simply impossible. 'Evolution of the Daleks' is perhaps the worst case since *Doctor Who* returned in 2005 of an episode with a plot that relies on a complete distortion of basic scientific facts. That the production team should be so careless over the scientific aspects of stories when they obviously go to great pains to ensure the accuracy of other aspects, such as the period detail of the historical setting here (although one obvious anachronism is that none of the workers or Hooverville residents is seen smoking; an activity presumably now considered unsuitable for family viewing!), is both surprising and disappointing, and would no doubt have infuriated the series' principal creator, Sydney Newman, who was always so keen to ensure that it had some educational merit and promoted an understanding of science.

'The Evil of the Daleks' (1967) actually takes a far better approach to telling a story in which the Daleks try to make humans think and act like they do. This involves the Daleks monitoring human test subjects in order to find the Human Factor – the mental essence of humanity – and then using that knowledge to determine the absolute opposite, the Dalek Factor, and spread it throughout all of Earth's history.[55] By focusing on the plausible (albeit vaguely expressed) idea of mental conditioning rather than the patently spurious one of changing people's characters by altering their DNA, it succeeds in positing a credible threat while at the same time allowing the Daleks to remain true to their commitment to racial purity. The new twist in Helen Raynor's story is to have the Dalek Sec Hybrid recognising the limitations inherent in Dalek thinking – similar to the way their creator Davros identified the drawbacks of their slavish reliance on logic in 'Destiny of the Daleks' (1979) – and consequently deciding to create a new human-Dalek hybrid race that will no longer strive for universal supremacy; an idea that challenges the very nature of the Daleks. But as soon as the other three members of the Cult of Skaro respond to this challenge by baulking at the plan and redirecting the 'final experiment' toward creating pure Daleks in human form, the story really becomes just a variation on the same theme as 'The Evil of the Daleks', complete with a conflict between different Dalek factions at the end – only not as good.

This may be to some extent symptomatic of a more general difficulty that writers face in finding new things to do with the Daleks after some 43 years of fairly frequent appearances. Dalek stories have traditionally tended to fall into one of three broad categories: first, those in which they serve as a metaphor for fascists in general or the Nazis of the Second World War in particular (examples include 'The Mutants'[56] (1963/64), 'The Dalek Invasion of Earth' (1964) and 'Day of the

---

[55] Given that the idea of water being drained into a hole in the Earth's crust in 'The Runaway Bride' is repeated from 'The Underwater Menace', that the shots of the Judoon yomping across the Moon's surface in 'Smith and Jones' strongly recall the advance of the Cybermen in 'The Moonbase' and that 'Gridlock' features the return of the Macra from 'The Macra Terror', one has to wonder if, when formulating his ideas for Series Three, Davies was for some reason feeling nostalgic about 1967, the year when all these classic series *Doctor Who* stories were transmitted.

[56] Also known as 'The Daleks'.

Daleks' (1972)); secondly, those that involve them trying to acquire additional capabilities or changing their own nature, sometimes resulting in factional conflict (examples here include 'Planet of the Daleks' (1973), 'Destiny of the Daleks' and 'Revelation of the Daleks' (1984)); and thirdly, those that eschew any attempt at a deeper subtext and concentrate on depicting them as a race of ruthless destroyers and conquerors (such as 'The Chase' (1965), 'The Daleks' Master Plan' (1965/66), and 'The Power of the Daleks' (1966)). There are also a few stories, such as 'Genesis of the Daleks' (1975) and 'Remembrance of the Daleks' (1988), that have aspects of more than one of these three types, but by and large the categorisation holds true. The new, Russell T Davies-led series may have added into the mix the novel factor that the Daleks have been almost wiped out in the last great Time War, so that the few that remain are essentially engaged in a struggle for their race's survival, but nevertheless their stories have still tended to fall into one or another of the three established categories: 'Dalek' is a 'category two' story, because it involves a lone Dalek changing its nature after absorbing Rose's DNA (that buzz-word again) and becoming so internally conflicted that it ultimately commits suicide; 'The Parting of the Ways' is also inherently a 'category two' story, because the Emperor has created a new army using human rather than Dalek DNA (there's that word again), causing them all to feel – as the Doctor astutely observes – incredible self-loathing; and 'Doomsday' is essentially a 'category three' story, because it focuses on the Daleks' attempt to defeat the Cybermen in battle and take over the Earth.

This is not to say that there is no scope remaining for new ground to be broken in Dalek stories; but it requires brilliant imaginative writing to pull it off. Good examples of this from Davies's own stories are the inclusion of the startlingly original idea of the Daleks worshiping their Emperor as a god in 'The Parting of the Ways', which cleverly recognises the fact that modern warfare tends to be less about responding to the threat of fascism and more about dealing with the consequences of religious fundamentalism; and the introduction of the Cult of Skaro as a new, more 'free thinking' group of individually-named Daleks in 'Doomsday'. It is this sort of inspired inventiveness that seems to be lacking in 'Evolution of the Daleks', which falls squarely into the 'category two' type.

In short, whereas in 'Daleks in Manhattan' Raynor's story comes across initially as an affectionate homage to classic series *Doctor Who*, with its many nods to popular episodes of that era, in 'Evolution of the Daleks' it starts to seem simply derivative. Aside from the innovation of the Dalek Sec Hybrid – which is undeniably astonishing, in all its B-movie glory – it has little to offer that is original in terms of ideas. Even viewers who have little or no knowledge of *Doctor Who* prior to its 2005 revival will surely experience a sense of *déjà vu* here. The Daleks' use of human DNA to perpetuate their existence is an idea explored previously, as already noted, in 'The Parting of the Ways'; the abduction of homeless people for conversion into a formidable army has also been seen before, in 'Rise of the Cybermen'/'The Age of Steel', and the way they march along in unison once the army is mobilised echoes the 'Cyber-stomp' of their counterparts in that story; Diagoras's enforced assimilation into the Dalek Sec Hybrid recalls John Lumic's unwilling conversion into the Cyber Controller, also in a base situated within a famous landmark, in the same story; the Daleks' status as the last survivors of a once-powerful race again brings to mind the earlier new series Dalek stories as well as the situation of the Empress of the Racnoss in 'The Runaway Bride', of the Face of Boe in the trilogy of stories ending with 'Gridlock' and indeed of the Doctor himself as the last of the Time Lords; and the exciting scene of the Doctor ascending the Empire State Building's mast prior to a 'lightning' strike essentially repeats, on a grander scale, that of him climbing the Alexandra Palace transmitter at the end of 'The Idiot's Lantern'.

Its terrible science and its unoriginal ideas are, unfortunately, not the only shortcomings that 'Evolution of the Daleks' has. Whereas in 'Daleks in Manhattan' the story is very well-constructed, has great pace and energy and is punctuated by a number of more thought-provoking scenes such as the one between Diagoras and Dalek Caan looking out over New York, here it just seems to fall apart. The three principal guest characters – Diagoras, Solomon and Tallulah – who were so very well established in 'Daleks in Manhattan' are all essentially wasted here. Diagoras is already gone before 'Evolution of the Daleks' begins, having been absorbed into the Dalek Sec Hybrid at the close of the previous episode; Solomon is killed early on, albeit in a very good scene where he makes a *Star Trek*-style appeal to the Daleks for peace and co-operation between species and, in a darkly humorous moment, is immediately exterminated for his pains; and Tallulah, although teamed up with Martha, is given virtually nothing to do. In fact, the story would be little changed if Martha and Tallulah were simply to remain in Hooverville for the duration of this episode and rejoin the Doctor just before the end. Their infiltration of the Empire State Building (with the young man Frank; a supporting role nicely played by Andrew Garfield) and examination of its architectural plans to determine what the Daleks have altered is really just padding, and crawls along at a snail's pace; the viewer can only groan in frustration when they pause to have a discussion of Martha's relationship with the Doctor, complete with the latest in the long succession of references back to Rose (although she is not actually named this time) that have definitely outstayed their welcome by this point in the series.

The impression one gets here is of a writer really struggling with her material, and despite having introduced a lot of very interesting ideas, ultimately not being able to pull the story together into a coherent whole. One thing for which Raynor cannot be held at fault, though, is the highly contrived way that the action returns to the Lorenzi Theatre for the final showdown between the Cult of Skaro, its newly-created army and the Doctor. Raynor originally wrote this scene to take place as a battle on a New York street, which would have been far more logical and effective, recalling the mob shootouts often associated with cities of the Depression era – a nice allusion to which is that the army members' weapons are gangster-style Tommy-guns with Dalek adaptations – but this was ultimately ruled out on cost grounds in favour of the much cheaper option of relocating it to the already-featured Theatre setting. This is regrettable, because it makes the action seem literally theatrical, complete with a 'special effect' explosion as the Daleks make their entrance on stage, as if through a trapdoor; although, having said that, for anyone who has seen one of the *Doctor Who* plays, such as *The Curse of the Daleks* (1965/66), *The Ultimate Adventure* (1989) or *Evil of the Daleks* (2006), there is something strangely nostalgic about the sight of Dalek Thay and Dalek Jast trundling across the Lorenzi stage to confront the Doctor in the auditorium. Easily the most remarkable aspect of this scene, though, is the fact that – for reasons best known to themselves – the two Daleks have brought the Dalek Sec Hybrid with them. Back in 'Smith and Jones', the Doctor, commenting on the two solid-leather

Slabs, said 'Someone's got one hell of a fetish', but that line would have been even more appropriate here. The image of a sharp-suited, one-eyed monster with multiple phalluses around his head being led along in chains by the Daleks like a gimp is way beyond bizarre, and really quite mind-boggling. First the boyfriend of a Jewish showgirl gets part-converted into a pig, then a Dalek gives birth, and now the Daleks indulge a previously-unsuspected penchant for BDSM: perhaps I was wrong to suggest that Raynor's story lacked originality. It is in weird, disquieting, even slightly twisted touches such as these that 'Daleks in Manhattan'/'Evolution of the Daleks' is at its most distinctive and memorable in narrative terms, arguably taking *Doctor Who* further than it has ever been before toward 'exploitation cinema' territory – albeit in a 'family friendly' way!

Another such touch comes quite early on in 'Evolution of the Daleks', when the Doctor almost begs the Daleks attacking Hooverville to exterminate him, shouting: 'Then do it! Do it! Just do it! Do it!' There have been many occasions previously in the series when the Doctor has been seen to be willing to sacrifice himself for the greater good, but here he seems just reckless, almost as if he has a death wish. Has his earlier realisation that his oldest and most terrifying enemies always survive while he loses everything – his fellow Time Lords, his home planet and even, most recently, Rose – disturbed him to such an extent that it has actually robbed him of the will to go on fighting, or even made him suicidal? That is certainly one interpretation that can be placed on the scene, and perhaps even the one most clearly suggested by the script and by David Tennant's electrifying performance; and it brings to mind the impression that the ninth Doctor sometimes gave of having been deeply traumatised by his experiences in the Time War. At the end of the story, however, when he confronts the one remaining Dalek, Dalek Caan, he says, somewhat surprisingly, 'Right now, you're facing the only man in the universe who might show you some compassion, because I've just seen one genocide; I won't cause another.' This is certainly not something that the ninth Doctor would have said to the lone surviving Dalek (or so he believed) in 'Dalek'; and it is difficult to imagine even the tenth Doctor having made such a pledge in Series Two, when in 'School Reunion' he told the Krillitanes' leader, 'I'm so old now; I used to have such mercy.' This suggests that the Doctor may be to some extent emerging from the dark frame of mind he has shown in some recent stories.

Do the Doctor's words influence Dalek Caan to some degree? Perhaps so, as rather than simply exterminate its race's greatest enemy, which would seem to be the obvious thing for it to do at this point, it performs an emergency temporal shift, as if afraid to stay and face up to the abject failure of the Cult of Skaro's 'final experiment' and the implication that the Dalek Sec Hybrid might have been right all along. This, though, does not explain why Dalek Caan left it until *after* Dalek Thay and Dalek Jast had been destroyed to trigger the deaths of the human-Dalek army, rather than doing so straight away when they stopped obeying orders … which must count as another minus point in scripting terms.

Dalek Caan's hasty departure, destination unknown, of course leaves open the possibility of a return appearance in Series Four (and producer Phil Collinson has more or less confirmed in the bbc.co.uk podcast commentary on 'Daleks in Manhattan' that the Daleks will be back every year for the foreseeable future), although one cannot help but think that by having only one of the creatures left alive at the end of the story – even fewer than last time! – the production team have really painted themselves into a corner here.

While Tennant's performance is (as usual now) the best of the episode, the other cast members all do good work too. Hugh Quarshie, who has a regular role as Ric Griffin in *Holby City* (BBC One, 1999- ), is excellent as Solomon; and Miranda Raison, who plays Jo Portman in the spy series *Spooks* (US title: *MI-5*) (BBC One, 2002- ), portrays Tallulah with an engaging quirkiness and an amusingly larger-than-life New York accent entirely appropriate to a Broadway showgirl character of this period. Eric Loren also turns in a great performance as the Dalek Sec Hybrid, in what must have been extremely uncomfortable circumstances, managing to give the creature a unique vocal inflection that neatly distinguishes it from his role as the human Diagoras in the previous episode.

Other aspects of the production continue to impress as well. James Strong's direction remains highly assured, and a particular highlight is the brilliant action sequence where the Daleks swoop down over Hooverville and attack the hapless residents, who are armed only with rifles; this is thrillingly spectacular stuff, with some more superb CGI work by the Mill. The Daleks' transgenic laboratory, with its ranks of human experimental subjects suspended on pallets from the ceiling, is also extremely well realised.

As ambitious and impressive as it may be from a production point of view, though, the unfortunate fact remains that 'Evolution of the Daleks' is really a bit of a mess from a scripting perspective; which is all the more disappointing given how very entertaining 'Daleks in Manhattan' was, and what great promise it held out for this concluding instalment. There is a really good story buried away in here – maybe, picking up on the Biblical connotations of the names of Solomon and Diagoras, and the 'angels and devils' subject of Tallulah's song, a couple more redrafts could have transformed it into an epic good-versus-evil struggle for sway over the future of humanity, losing some of the cod science and focusing more on the underlying themes – but sadly it never quite emerges.

# 3.06 – THE LAZARUS EXPERIMENT

Writer: Stephen Greenhorn
Director: Richard Clark

DEBUT TRANSMISSION DETAILS

BBC One
Date: 5 May 2007. Scheduled time: 7.00 pm. Actual time: 7.00 pm.

BBC Three
Date: 6 May 2007. Scheduled time: 8.00 pm. Actual time: 8.02 pm.

Duration: 43' 32"[57]

ADDITIONAL CREDITED CAST

Mark Gatiss (Lazarus[58]), Thelma Barlow (Lady Thaw[59]), Lucy O'Connell (Olive Woman[60]), Bertie Carvel (Mysterious Man).

PLOT

Professor Richard Lazarus aims to 'change what it means to be human' through his invention of a machine that rejuvenates people – starting with himself, at a reception held to demonstrate the process to potential investors. The Doctor's curiosity having been piqued by a TV news report, he and Martha attend the event, which has been organised by Martha's sister Tish in her new job as Head of PR at Lazarus Laboratories. Although Lazarus is indeed rejuvenated, the experiment has an unforeseen side-effect: it makes his DNA unstable, causing him to switch between his human form and a monstrous, scorpion-like evolutionary throwback. Lazarus ultimately seeks sanctuary in Southwark Cathedral, where Martha and Tish entice him up to the top of the bell tower, enabling the Doctor to blast the monster with sound waves from his sonic screwdriver and the church organ, resonated by the bell. The monster falls to the ground, where in death it transforms back into the human Lazarus, first in his rejuvenated form and then in his original

---

[57] The duration of the DVD version of this episode is 43' 05" due to the substitution of the different trailer at the end (see 'Production Notes').

[58] Full name given in dialogue as 'Professor Richard Lazarus'.

[59] First name given in dialogue as 'Sylvia'.

[60] Credited in *Radio Times* as 'Party Guest'. The description 'Olive Woman' derived from the character saying, in response to the Doctor's announcement that the reception guests are in danger, that the biggest risk they face is 'choking on an olive'.

elderly body.

## QUOTE, UNQUOTE

- **Doctor:** 'Using hypersonic sound waves to create a state of resonance; that's inspired.'
  **Lazarus:** 'You understand the theory then.'
  **Doctor:** 'Enough to know that you couldn't possibly have allowed for all the variables.'
  **Lazarus:** 'No experiment is entirely without risk.'
- **Doctor:** 'Hypersonic sound waves to destabilise the cell structure and then a metagenic program to manipulate the coding in the protein strands. Basically, he hacked into his own genes and instructed them to rejuvenate.'
- **Francine:** 'Martha, it's your mother. Please phone me back. I'm begging you. I know who this Doctor really is. I know he's dangerous. You're going to get yourself killed. Please trust me. This information comes from Harold Saxon himself! You're not safe!'

## CONTINUITY POINTS

- The Doctor returns Martha to her flat about 12 hours later than they left London at the end of 'Smith and Jones', although considerably more time has passed for them personally. The fact that he knows where her flat is suggests that she must have told him about it, or that he has learned its location in some other way, in events not seen in the televised episodes.
- Lazarus grew up in a tiny flat over a butcher's shop, which was destroyed in the Blitz in 1940. He was amongst the many local residents who sheltered in the nearby Southwark Cathedral's crypt during the bombing raids.
- The Doctor suggests that his ability to play the organ is something he picked up hanging around with the German classical music composer Beethoven (1770-1827).

## SAXON REFERENCES

- Mr Saxon is revealed to be a financial backer of Lazarus's experiment, and keen to attract investors for the new rejuvenation process – hence the reception to view the demonstration at the Lazarus Laboratories building.
- Martha's mother Francine is given information – or, more likely, misinformation – about the Doctor by a mysterious man at the Lazarus Laboratories reception; she later leaves a message on Martha's answerphone saying that the information comes from 'Harold Saxon himself' (the first time that Saxon's full name is revealed), implying that the man was an agent of Saxon's.

## PRODUCTION NOTES

- 'The Lazarus Experiment' was made with 'Gridlock' in Block 3 of production on Series Three.

- Interviewed for Issue 382 of *Doctor Who Magazine*, published in May 2007, writer Stephen Greenhorn explained how the initial ideas for his story were formulated: 'The basic brief for "The Lazarus Experiment" was "mad scientist", with the added stipulation that the story was set in contemporary London. When it comes to comic books, I'm certainly not as well read as Russell [T Davies], but I'm not exactly a stranger to them, and we discussed our favourite examples. Doctor Octopus from *Spider-Man* was an initial inspiration – and certainly influenced the naming of our villain – but the Green Goblin and even characters like the Hulk came up. Specifically, we were looking at that subcategory of the genre where a scientist involves himself in his own experiments, something goes wrong and he becomes something terrible. Also, I was thinking about films like *The Fly*, examples from literature like Jekyll and Hyde, and the Faust legend.' Greenhorn also wanted to contrast the human fear of ageing and death, which is Lazarus's primary motivation, with the more ambivalent view of longetivty taken by the Doctor from his perspective as a 900-year-old Time Lord.

- The original intention was that the climactic confrontation between the Doctor and Lazarus should take place in St Paul's Cathedral, with the building's famous dome amplifying the sound waves generated by the Doctor's sonic screwdriver, but this location proved unavailable, so the script was rewritten to move the action to Southwark Cathedral instead, with the bell fulfilling essentially the same function in the transmitted version as the dome did in the original. These interior scenes were actually shot on 3 and 4 October 2006 in Wells Cathedral in Somerset, the architecture of which is similar to that of Southwark Cathedral and which is nearer to the production team's Cardiff base. Surprisingly, given that the former was supposed to be representing the latter, the model seen in Lazarus's office is based on Wells Cathedral rather than Southwark Cathedral.

- It was initially thought that the old and young versions of Professor Lazarus might be played by different actors, but as soon as the possibility was raised of Mark Gatiss being cast, the production team were confident that he could do both – with, naturally, the aid of make-up for the old version. The prosthetics ultimately took three hours to apply each day; the wig was supplied by Gatiss himself (there having apparently been insufficient time for one to be specially made for the production), and had been previously worn by him as the character Mr Chinnery in the movie *The League of Gentlemen's Apocalypse* (Film4, 2005).

- Location recording for the scenes of the Lazarus Laboratories reception took place inside the Senedd – the Wales National Assembly building – in Cardiff over five nights on 5, 6, 9, 10 and 11 October 2006, and involved 55 extras as well as the principal cast members. Lazarus's rejuvenating machine was set up in the main foyer of the building. The exteriors of the venue were shot outside the National Museum in Cardiff on the evening of 16 October. The scene of the chase through the laboratory was shot on the evening of 17 October in a laboratory of the School of Biosciences at Cardiff University. The supply to the laboratory's gas taps had to be temporarily disconnected for the action where the Doctor opens all the taps in order to cause an explosion.

- Actress Thelma Barlow, best known for her remarkable 1971-1997 stint as Mavis Wilton in *Coronation Street* (ITV, 1960- ), accepted the role of Lady Thaw partly because she felt it was the nearest she could get to playing Shakespeare's Lady Macbeth – something she had always wanted to do – and partly because she thought her grandchildren, who are fans of the series, would never forgive her if she turned it down.
- Actor Mark Gatiss suggested that Lazarus, in his original elderly form, should have some dandruff on his shoulders, and also that his bow tie should be slightly askew. This was because he had noted these as being typical characteristics of elderly men he had seen at awards shows and the like. Later, while recording the Lazarus monster voiceover for the scene where it chases the Doctor, he ad-libbed the line 'Peek-a-boo', and it was decided that this should be left in.
- When Tish says 'I know the age thing's a bit freaky, but it worked for Catherine Zeta-Jones,' this is a reference to the marriage between the British actress and Hollywood star Michael Douglas, who is 25 years older – although the age difference between Tish and Lazarus would actually be about twice that!
- As the programme schedulers had decided that transmission of the following episode, '42', should be deferred by a week to make way for the live transmission of the *Eurovision Song Contest* final, a 'Coming Soon …' trailer for the remaining episodes of the series was added to the end of 'The Lazarus Experiment' in place of the previously-prepared 'Next Time …' trailer, followed by the caption 'Dr Who will return in two weeks'.[61] Unfortunately many casual viewers failed to realise this, and assumed that all the incidents shown in the trailer would be seen in '42' itself. The original 'Next Time …' trailer for '42' was subsequently made available for viewing by bbc.co.uk on the official *Doctor Who* website, and was reinstated in place of the 'Coming Soon …' trailer on the episode's 'vanilla' DVD release.

## UNFOUNDED PRE-TRANSMISSION RUMOURS

- Professor Lazarus would turn out to be the Doctor's arch-enemy the Master, and his machine a TARDIS.

## OOPS!

- Gugu Mbatha-Raw mistakenly delivers the line 'He was buying us time, Martha' as 'He was biding us time, Martha.'

## PRESS REACTION

- 'The Lazarus Experiment could almost be a metaphor for the revived *Doctor*

---

[61] This 'Coming Soon …' trailer was also made available to view on the 'red button' BBCi digital TV service – the purpose for which it had been originally prepared – at various times over the following fortnight.

*Who* itself. Much like Professor Lazarus (Mark Gatiss), the elderly show has been given new life courtesy of some youthful swagger, but at times it threatens to lose control, in thrall to its own monstrous success. So far this series, that's tended to mean big, boisterous adventures, with plenty of balls, but little in the way of soul. Somewhere along the way, the resonances that Russell T Davies identified in the first two series seem to have been lost amid the rumble of constant action, and the bang, bang, bang of the BBC buck. But the beast still has a human face, and sometimes the show turns out a thoughtful and balanced episode like this one. Concerning one man's misguided struggle to reverse the ageing process, "The Lazarus Experiment" mixes emotional drama with CGI spectacle in equal measure, and never seems heavy-handed with either.' Paul Collins, Dreamwatch SciFi website, 22 May 2007.

- 'It's hard to think of a *Who* episode that shows its hand earlier. By 16 minutes in, when the Lazarus-monster snacks on its first hapless victim, you know everything you need to know. After that it apes another template: a monster-on-the-loose B-movie that's unafraid to toss in a cliché as hoary as "turn on all the gas taps and blow it up!" And "defeating the menace with amplified sound" should go on the production team's list of banned clichés immediately – that's its *third* outing in the last six stories, so you'd have to have the memory of a concussed goldfish not to be struck by *déjà vu*. So yes, it's quite easy to reduce this story to a tick list of familiar old bobbins. And yet ... the experience of watching it is something quite else, thanks to the quality of the execution. It's slickly made, with horrendous deeds taking place in beautiful locations. The CGI monster is magnificent, possibly the production team's finest new creation – check out that scene where it scuttles along the floor *and* ceiling of a corridor. The script is played with gravitas and conviction; there isn't a single bad performance, but Mark Gatiss's icy, aloof turn as the crypto-fascist Lazarus is the stand-out.' Ian Berriman, *SFX* website, 5 May 2007.

- 'It's an armchair critics viewpoint to say this, but sometimes it's felt as if "guest writers" on the new *Who*, entrusted with one of Russell T Davies's shopping list briefs, have been asking themselves "What would Russell do if he were writing this?", whereas "The Lazarus Experiment" gives the impression that Stephen Greenhorn asked himself, "What can I do with this within Russell's framework?" A subtle difference that's given us an episode that's recognisably *Who*, but also subtly refreshing.' Anthony Brown, *TV Zone* Issue 216, Summer 2007.

- 'Mark Gatiss knocks it out of the park. His Lazarus is beautifully played: venal, power-hungry and yet ultimately human, raging against the dying of the light and holding on to life by any means necessary. This is counterpointed superbly by the Doctor's line about living forever meaning you end up alone. At first glance, this is familiar, by-the-numbers *Doctor Who*. Dig deeper, though, and it's a wise, sad gem of an episode.' Jes Bickham, *DeathRay* Issue 2, July 2007.

## FAN COMMENT

- 'I have to admit that I really wasn't that thrilled by the last Dalek adventure, so came to this week's episode with little enthusiasm. I mean, if you can't score highly with the Daleks, what hope for a simple tale of mad scientists and monsters? Thankfully, this week was, for me at least, the kind of *Doctor Who* I fell in love with all those years ago. Its simplicity was the key to its success. Experiment goes wrong, monster on the loose. Bingo! As with "Smith and Jones" and "The Shakespeare Code", this was an enjoyable romp. Good Saturday evening television. It was scary, fast and fun.' John Paul Green, Behind the Sofa website, 6 May 2007.

- 'Right from the concise opening teaser – with its nice nod to "Aliens of London"'s "12 hours" mistake and the illogic of the Doctor knowing how to get to Martha's flat – to the charming coda that sees the time-travellers reach some sort of understanding about "the other woman", "The Lazarus Experiment" ticks pretty much all the fan-boy boxes whilst providing a neat and literate variation on this show's fundamental theme: what it means to be human. Writer Stephen Greenhorn's debut may lack some of the knowing winks of his more *Who*-literate contemporaries, but on the evidence here that's no bad thing. And he's certainly well-versed enough to know that *Doctor Who* works best with a small group of well-defined characters in a confined setting. "The Lazarus Experiment" may start out as time-honoured, mad-scientist-meddles-with-nature guff, but before you can say "base under siege", there's a horrible monster about and more panicked running than [in] a dozen "[Horror of] Fang Rock"s.' Sean Alexander, Behind the Sofa website, 6 May 2007.

- '"The Lazarus Experiment" has a clarity that is admirable. Stories of scientific experiments gone wrong, from *Frankenstein* to *The Fly*, have a very clear structure and strategy, and Stephen Greenhorn wisely kept to the tradition. They are tales of hubris and intellectual vanity, and in Richard Lazarus we get an excellent example of the type, played by Mark Gatiss with a believable mix of haughty contempt and elegiac sadness. And the grotesque appearance of his mutated form was a triumph of using modern technology to create something that's walked straight out of our most primal nightmares. Better still, Greenhorn teased out wonderful parallels with the Doctor's situation, both in the loneliness of the long distance Time Lord and the danger he potentially poses to those he cares for. Arc-heavy episodes are always a danger in that the need to push the long-term story might hamper the demands of the standalone adventure, but the balance here was spot-on. Martha's family was drawn with a real flair for characterisation, especially Francine Jones' unexpected streak of cold steel, and the portents of what is to come were tantalising.' Simon Kinnear, Shockeye Online website, May 2007.

- 'The Doctor again gets to have a lot of his own emotional angst – comparing Professor Lazarus's experiment to Time Lord regeneration and talking about how living forever only guarantees one thing, that you'll just be there to watch everyone die and everything turn to dust. "Some people live more in 20 years than others do in 80" – another subtle shout-out to Rose? Martha continues to kick all kinds of ass, saving the day and calling the Doctor out on his "one more trip" excuse. He, of course, doesn't take much convincing – we know how lonely he is; he said so in this episode.' 'Crossoverman', LiveJournal blog, 6 May 2007.

## ANALYSIS

When the *Doctor Who* production team of the time decided to have the Doctor exiled to contemporary Earth from the start of the 1970 season, writer Malcolm Hulke lamented to script editor Terrance Dicks that this would restrict them to only two possible story types: 'alien invasion' and 'mad scientist'. As it turned out, he was quite wrong. The next few years actually saw the series presenting a remarkably varied run of stories, despite their mainly Earthbound settings; and while these featured plenty of alien invasions, only one of them involved what could be described as a mad scientist: 'Inferno' (1970), in which Professor Stahlman doggedly pursued a dangerous scheme to tunnel down to the centre of the Earth – an idea that Torchwood would later try with much greater success, judging from 'The Runaway Bride'. In fact, considering that they are fairly common in fantastical literature and cinema, mad scientist stories have been conspicuous by their scarcity in *Doctor Who*. Aside from one early example in 'The Underwater Menace' (1967), involving Professor Zaroff's scheme to drain ocean water through a fissure in the Earth's crust into the planet's molten core – again an idea echoed in 'The Runaway Bride' – it was really only during a brief period in the mid-1970s that such stories featured, perhaps because the series at that time started to draw heavily on literary and cinematic sources for its inspiration. Davros can certainly be considered a mad scientist, with his creation of the Daleks in 'Genesis of the Daleks' (1975); so can Professor Sorenson, with his scheme to mine a new power source from the universe of antimatter in 'Planet of Evil' (1975), a story influenced both by Robert Louis Stevenson's *Strange Case of Dr Jekyll and Mr Hyde* (Longmans, 1886) and by the movie *Forbidden Planet* (MGM, 1956); so too can Mehendri Solon, stealing body parts to build a new form for the evil Time Lord Morbius in 'The Brain of Morbius' (1976), a homage to Mary Shelley's *Frankenstein; or, The Modern Prometheus* (Lackington, Hughes, Harding, Mavor and Jones, 1818); and so can Harrison Chase, the deranged botanist in 'The Seeds of Doom' (1976), with its nods to John Wyndham's *The Day of the Triffids* (Michael Joseph, 1951).

In the revived series, John Lumic in 'Rise of the Cybermen'/'The Age of Steel' unquestionably qualifies as a mad scientist; perhaps not surprisingly, as he was intended to be to the new Cybermen what Davros was to the Daleks. 'The Lazarus Experiment' is, however, the first episode of this era to have been consciously conceived from the outset as a mad scientist story. Again the influence of *Strange Case of Dr Jekyll and Mr Hyde* is apparent here: the two different forms of Professor Lazarus after he has undergone his rejuvenation – young man and hideous monster – essentially mirror those of Stevenson's protagonist, the respectable scientist Dr Henry Jekyll and his savage *alter ego* Mr Edward Hyde, who likewise engage in a struggle for dominance in the wake of a failed experiment (in this case involving a potion). The gradual degeneration of the rejuvenated Lazarus, after he initially seems fine on emerging from his machine, also resembles the fate of the mad scientist character Seth Brundle in the David Cronenberg remake of the vintage horror film *The Fly* (20th Century Fox, 1986), in which a compromised teleportation experiment results in the man starting to exhibit insect-like tics and gradually taking on the physical characteristics of a fly.

Martha explicitly likens the tuxedoed Doctor to James Bond, and Lazarus recalls some of the larger-than-life villains, with their secret laboratories and advanced technology, presented in the novels and movies featuring Ian Fleming's famous spy character. In fact, the episode as a whole has something of a 'blockbuster' feel to it at times, with its impressive special effects, nick-of-time rescues, thrilling action set-pieces and overall high production values. Another obvious influence is mad scientists from comic book stories, such as Marvel's *Spider-Man* series, which has itself spawned a successful action movie franchise in recent years; by a curious coincidence, *Spider-Man 3* (Sony Pictures), released at the beginning of May 2007, even features a scene in which sound waves resonating within a church bell allow the hero, Peter Parker, to cast off an alien symbiote that has bonded with his suit, leaving him naked. It is no surprise to learn that at the episode's tone meeting, on 16 August 2006, Davies specifically cited the *Spider-Man* movies, and the Doctor Octopus mad scientist character in particular, as reference points for the production. The episode also bears some strong similarities to the horror film *The Relic* (Paramount Pictures, 1997), based on the novel by Douglas Preston and Lincoln Child, in which a monster representing aspects of human DNA that have lain dormant from evolutionary history goes on the rampage at a museum where a glitzy reception is taking place. The idea of 'devolved' monsters such as this was likewise central to the episode 'Genesis' from the seventh season of *Star Trek: The Next Generation* (Paramount, 1987-1994).

The final encounter between the Doctor and Lazarus in Southwark Cathedral meanwhile brings to mind the climax of Nigel Kneale's famous BBC serial *The Quatermass Experiment* (1953), and its Hammer movie remake *The Quatermass Xperiment* (1955), in which rocket scientist Professor Quatermass confronts a man-turned-monster menace in Westminster Abbey; a source openly acknowledged in the episode's title (although Davies has claimed that this is coincidental, and that the title was chosen – in preference to the working title 'The Madness of Professor Lazarus' – simply because it sounded good). This, along with its contemporary setting, has led a number of commentators, and some of those who worked on it, to liken 'The Lazarus Experiment' to the stories of the early part of the third Doctor's era, which drew on similar sources (and which have in turn afforded inspiration for a number of other ninth and tenth Doctor stories); but its mad scientist character and the way it pays homage to a variety of literary and cinematic classics arguably means that it is equally, if not more, reminiscent of those of the fourth Doctor's most popular period.

The focus of Professor Lazarus's work, and the central theme of the episode, is ageing, and the possibility of reversing it. This recalls 'secret of eternal life' type stories such as H Rider Haggard's novel *She* (Longmans, 1887) and its various movie adaptations, which also influenced aspects of 'The Brain of Morbius'; and the Biblical story of Lazarus, a man who (according to John 11:41-44) was raised from the dead by Jesus, is obviously referenced both in the Professor's name and in the scene where he revives in an ambulance after apparently being killed, prompting the Doctor to comment, 'Lazarus. Back from the dead. Should have known, really.'[62] The Professor's cabinet – or 'sonic microfield manipulator', as the Doctor describes it – resembles the recreation generator from the classic series story

---

[62] 'The Lazarus phenomenon' is a recognised medical term for the situation where an apparently dead patient's heart spontaneously starts beating again after resuscitation attempts have been abandoned.

'The Leisure Hive' (1980), in which the fourth Doctor is at one point greatly aged owing to a malfunction caused by sabotage and then later returned to his normal state, and also the rejuvenation apparatus of Magnus Greel in 'The Talons of Weng-Chiang' (1977).

The way the Doctor's longevity affects him is something that has been explored previously in the new series, in particular in 'School Reunion' and 'The Girl in the Fireplace' in Series Two, which highlighted the heartache he feels as his human friends and companions age and die while he lives on. The melancholy of great age and experience is something that Sylvester McCoy was also particularly keen to bring out in his portrayal of the seventh Doctor, as he has noted in a number of interviews. This, then, is not new dramatic territory for *Doctor Who*, but writer Stephen Greenhorn, in his excellent debut script for the series, makes the issue more central to the drama than it has been in any previous story.

The link between age and physical attractiveness is neatly illustrated by the fact that Martha's sister Tish coldly rebuffs Lazarus's advances when he is an old man but is quite prepared to join him on the building's roof for a 'snog' once he is in his younger form, and similarly by the fact that, following his rejuvenation, Lazarus himself finds it repellent to be kissed by the elderly Lady Thaw, who appears to have been his partner for many years previously. The most significant scene from a thematic point of view, however, is the very well-written exchange between the Doctor and Lazarus in the Cathedral at the end. Here, Lazarus explains his motivation for devising his experiment: to ensure that he would never again have to face death as he did during the Blitz of the Second World War. 'Facing death is part of being human,' the Doctor tells him. 'You can't change that.' 'No, Doctor,' he replies. '*Avoiding* death, that's being human. It's our strongest impulse: to cling to life with every fibre of being. I'm only doing what everyone before me has tried to do. I've simply been more … successful.' The Doctor warns him, 'I'm old enough to know that a longer life isn't always a better one. In the end, you just get tired. Tired of the struggle; tired of losing everyone that matters to you; tired of watching everything turn to dust. If you live long enough, Lazarus, the only certainty left is that you'll end up alone.' This is thought-provoking stuff and, while it rather ducks the question of how humanity would have coped had Lazarus's experiment actually succeeded and not inadvertently scrambled his DNA (yes, it's another 'DNA' explanation, although perhaps a more scientifically plausible one than in 'Evolution of the Daleks'), it adds considerable depth to what might otherwise have seemed a fairly straightforward 'rampaging monster' story. It also emphasises again just how lonely the Doctor is, and recalls how he seemed 'tired of the struggle' and almost suicidal when facing the Daleks in Hooverville in 'Evolution of the Daleks'.

The effectiveness of this key confrontation between the Doctor and Lazarus also owes much to the quality of Richard Clark's direction, which as on 'Gridlock' is excellent throughout the episode, and to the intensity and commitment of the performances by David Tennant and Mark Gatiss – who, coincidentally, had both previously co-starred in a BBC Four remake of *The Quatermass Experiment* (2005). Gatiss is not only something of a *Quatermass* aficionado but also has an extensive history of involvement with *Doctor Who*, going back well before he contributed the scripts for 'The Unquiet Dead' and the *Quatermass*-influenced 'The Idiot's Lantern'. A long-time fan of the series, he has written four of the tie-in novels – *Nightshade*

(Virgin Publishing, 1992) (also a *Quatermass* homage), *St Anthony's Fire* (Virgin Publishing, 1994), *The Roundheads* (BBC Books, 1997) and *Last of the Gaderene* (BBC Books, 2000) – and two of the Big Finish audio dramas – 'Phantasmagoria' (1999) and 'Invaders from Mars' (2002) (the latter of which he directed as well). He was also one of the team behind three short spoofs produced for the BBC's *Doctor Who* Night of 1999, in one of which he briefly played the Doctor himself. Previously he wrote and appeared in the four video dramas in BBV's *PROBE* series – *The Zero Imperative* (1994), *The Devil of Winterbourne* (1995), *The Ghosts of Winterbourne* (1996) and *Unnatural Selection* (1996) – all of which featured the Doctor's former companion Liz Shaw, played by Caroline John, and, in new roles, numerous other actors associated with *Doctor Who*. Under the pseudonym Sam Kisgart (an anagram of his name), which he had previously used when writing a column for *Doctor Who Magazine*, he portrayed the Doctor's arch-enemy the Master in 'Sympathy for the Devil' (2003), one of the audio plays in Big Finish's *Doctor Who Unbound* strand. In addition, he narrated the second run of *Doctor Who Confidential* documentaries in 2006. Professor Lazarus is, however, his first *Doctor Who* role in the TV series itself, and his pleasure at getting this long-wished-for opportunity is quite apparent from the relish with which he approaches the part, bringing great conviction to the character in both old and young versions – and even, vocally, in monstrous form, after the Professor undergoes his painful metamorphosis.

The actor is aided in this by some excellent make-up – particularly the old-age prosthetics created by Neill Gorton's Millennium FX for the Professor's original, 76-year-old persona, which are highly detailed and realistic. The monster, although its features are distorted to the extent that they barely resemble Gatiss's own, is another superb piece of CGI work by the Mill (certainly by TV standards), and possibly the most extraordinary creature they have yet provided for the series. Their impressively convincing realisation of its scuttling, leaping movement makes it all the more regrettable that they were not given the chance to tackle the Empress of the Racnoss for 'The Runaway Bride', as that static, studio-built creation was nowhere near as effective. In design terms, the Lazarus monster is scorpion-like and somewhat reminiscent both of the creature in *The Relic* and of the fully-developed alien in the John Carpenter-directed horror movie *The Thing* (MCA/Universal Pictures, 1982), while the scenes of it pursuing the Doctor and his friends through the corridors and infrastructure of the Lazarus Laboratories building recall the cat-and-mouse chases through confined spaces of Ridley Scott's *Alien* (20th Century Fox, 1979) and perhaps even more so of David Fincher's *Alien³* (20th Century Fox, 1992), in the latter of which the CGI-realised Alien likewise scuttles along the ceiling at one point.

Perhaps not surprisingly, given these horror film similarities, some of the scenes involving the Lazarus monster are pretty scary – it is no wonder that the official *Doctor Who* website's 'Fear Factor' panel of young viewers gave it a high rating of 5 – and I would be surprised if the production team did not have at least some concerns that they might be pushing the limits of acceptability in a family programme. That said, these scenes drew no public complaints – or, at least, none that gave rise to any publicity – and indeed the revived *Doctor Who* as a whole has so far attracted remarkably little criticism of the kind that Mary Whitehouse and other self-appointed guardians of the nation's moral standards frequently directed at the classic series, over arguably far tamer material, particularly during the 1960s and 1970s. This has to be a tribute to the good judgment of Russell T Davies and his team, and perhaps also an indication of the extent to which public opinion has changed over the past 20-odd years, leaving groups like Whitehouse's National Viewers' and Listeners' Association (now re-branded MediaWatch) out in the cold.

'The Lazarus Experiment' is also notable for taking the relationship between the Doctor and Martha to its next level as, in the closing scene, the former finally abandons the idea of taking the latter on 'just one trip' in the TARDIS – which has already been stretched to three trips by this point – and fully accepts her as a *bona fide* companion, acknowledging that she was 'never really just a passenger' anyway. Martha again proves herself worthy of companion status during the course of the episode, which is perhaps the strongest yet for her character, as she shows admirable intelligence, spirit and self-assurance, taking the initiative on a number of occasions, using the sonic screwdriver (something Rose was never seen to do) and playing an active part in getting the reception guests out of the Lazarus Laboratories building and away to safety. Freema Agyeman rises to the occasion here too, giving her best performance as Martha to date, full of sassy energy and feistiness.

In addition, this is the first episode since 'Smith and Jones' to feature other members of Martha's family: specifically, mother Francine, brother Leo and sister Tish (whose name is now revealed to be short for Letitia). It consequently has certain parallels with 'Aliens of London', the Series One episode in which the ninth Doctor first took Rose back to visit her family (although, unlike with Martha, he overshot somewhat then, returning her not 12 hours after she left but 12 months). This can be seen particularly in Francine's distrust of the Doctor – which at one point leads her to slap him across the cheek, just as Jackie Tyler did in the earlier episode ('Always the mothers, every time' he comments ruefully) – and in the story's focus on a public incident that draws TV news coverage, as well as in its contemporary London setting. Martha's family are not yet as engaging a group of characters as Rose's – the formidable Francine in particular falls well short of the appeal of the much-missed Jackie – but it would obviously have been a mistake to try to make them too similar, and there is still clearly plenty of potential for development. This is especially true of Tish, who toward the end of the episode becomes almost a second companion as her bond with Martha leads her likewise to defy her mother and rush off after the Doctor, ultimately becoming involved in the climactic scenes in the Cathedral. That said, she remains very much in Martha's shadow, both metaphorically and literally in the way the director frames his shots, leaving no doubt which of them is the principal character; and although Gugu Mbatha-Raw gives an excellent performance in the role, she doesn't have quite the same star quality as Agyeman, reminding the viewer just what a great discovery and asset the latter is for the series.

Another significant aspect of 'The Lazarus Experiment' is the way it advances the 'Mr Saxon' story arc, which at this point starts to take on greater prominence. The revelation that the titular experiment is actually financed by Saxon suggests that more will be heard of this later on – as does the fact that the Lazarus Laboratories logo, which resembles Time Lord notation in style, can be seen on the ring worn by Saxon in the 'Coming Soon ...' trailer at the end of the episode – and the arrival on the scene of the mysterious man who convinces Francine that the Doctor is 'dangerous' for her daughter to be around no doubt foreshadows further trouble ahead. There is also the question of why Tish has been employed in such a responsible post, as Head of the PR Department for Lazarus Laboratories, when she apparently lacks the necessary experience – something that even Lazarus himself comments upon. Could it be precisely because she is Martha's sister ...? Certainly it seems no coincidence that the mysterious man is present at the reception, and he would appear to be well aware that Martha is the Doctor's companion.

One of the many positive aspects of Greenhorn's script is its excellent dialogue. This includes some nicely humorous touches, for instance in the initial meeting between the Doctor and Francine, and some fan-pleasing references back to past stories, such as when the Doctor says that something bad always happens when he wears his black-tie suit, as previously seen in 'Rise of the Cybermen'/'The Age of Steel'; when he comments that it took him longer than he expected to 'reverse the polarity' of Lazarus's machine, a phrase often associated with the third Doctor; and when he mentions he was present in London during the Blitz, as seen in 'The Empty Child'/'The Doctor Dances'. Martha's explanation that the Doctor gained access to the reception by virtue of being the 'plus one' on her invitation is also a neat reminder of the way the ninth Doctor accounted for Rose's presence at the Platform One reception in 'The End of the World' by saying that she was his 'plus one'. Notable too is the inclusion of a number of references to the works of poet T S Eliot (1888-1965); Lazarus at one point says, 'Between the idea and the reality; Between the motion and the act ...,' and the Doctor completes this quote from Eliot's famous work *The Hollow Men* (1925) (which concerns the futility and scarring impact of total war, as witnessed by Eliot in World War One and experienced by the Doctor in the Time War), with the words, 'Falls the Shadow'[63]; later, the Doctor comments that Eliot was right when he said, 'This is the way the world ends; Not with a bang, but a whimper' – another quote from the same poem; and his allusion to the Biblical figure Lazarus echoes Eliot's line, 'I am Lazarus, come from the dead' from *The Love Song of J Alfred Prufrock* (1915). The way the Lazarus monster's jaw breaks open when it roars could also possibly be a conscious visual reference to the line, 'The broken jaw of our lost kingdoms', from *The Hollow Men*.

The script does have a few less successful aspects as well. The inclusion of a 'false ending', where Lazarus appears to be dead only to rise again and seek sanctuary in the Cathedral, is a well-worn horror film cliché, and has the added disadvantage of making the Doctor seem a bit naïve for having failed to realise what would happen. Greenhorn misses a trick, too, by not having Lazarus actually seen reviving in the ambulance and attacking the crew, which could potentially have been a very tense and scary scene and have made this plot development seem a bit less contrived. 'The Lazarus Experiment' is also probably the worst case yet of an episode in which the sonic screwdriver is overused to such an extent, and credited with such multifarious, magic-wand-like powers, that it becomes somewhat ridiculous, not to say irritating. (The Doctor mentions it having a 'setting 54' at one point, but as he is never seen to adjust the device before using it, this

---

[63] There are also *Doctor Who* novels called *Falls the Shadow* (Virgin Publishing, 1994) by Daniel O'Mahony and *The Hollow Men* (BBC Books, 1998) by Keith Topping and Martin Day.

makes one wonder if he is somehow able to control it telepathically.) The lack of a proper explanation for what the Doctor actually does to defeat Lazarus at the end is also frustrating. Given that he mentions 'hypersonic sound waves' and has earlier identified the principle of Lazarus's experiment as the use of such waves 'to create a state of resonance', the intention is presumably to suggest that the sound waves he makes with the sonic screwdriver and the Cathedral's organ, resonating within the bell, interfere with the monster's metamorphosis in some way, causing it to fall, and also to revert to Lazarus's original elderly human form after it dies on hitting the ground. None of this is stated explicitly, though, and an alternative interpretation – and the one that would probably be inferred by anyone who missed that earlier, quickly-delivered summation of the Professor's process – is that the monster is simply overwhelmed by the loud and intense noise and loses its grip on the bell tower railing.

On the whole, though, the positive points far outweigh the negative, and 'The Lazarus Experiment' is a superbly-crafted, highly entertaining and at times even thought-provoking mid-series episode.

# 3.07 – 42

Writer: Chris Chibnall
Director: Graeme Harper

DEBUT TRANSMISSION DETAILS

BBC One
Date: 19 May 2007. Scheduled time: 7.15 pm. Actual time: 7.14 pm.

BBC Three
Date: 20 May 2007. Scheduled time: 8.00 pm. Actual time: 8.03 pm.

Duration: 45′ 29″

ADDITIONAL CREDITED CAST

Michelle Collins (Kath McDonnell), William Ash (Riley Vashtee), Anthony Flanagan (Orin Scannell), Matthew Chambers (Hal Korwin), Gary Powell (Dev Ashton), Vinette Robinson (Abi Lerner), Rebecca Oldfield (Erina Lessak), Elize Du Toit (Sinister Woman)[64].

PLOT

The TARDIS arrives on board a spaceship, the *SS Pentallian*, which is in imminent danger of destruction. The ship's engines have been sabotaged by crew member Hal Korwin, the husband of Captain Kath McDonnell, and it is only 42 minutes away from plunging into a nearby sun. Korwin has fallen under the influence of an alien entity; his eyes are glowing with a bright white light that vaporises anyone he looks at, and he begins systematically killing his six crewmates. While the Doctor assists McDonnell and the others, Martha joins crew member Riley Vashtee in trying to reach the controls of the auxiliary engines – which, owing to Korwin's activation of the ship's 'secure closure' procedure, can be accessed only via a series of 29 password-sealed doors. When Martha and Riley take refuge in an escape pod, Korwin launches it toward the sun, and the Doctor has to reach a recall switch on the outer hull of the ship in order to bring it back. This exposes him to the alien influence as well, and he discovers that the sun is actually a living being. By attempting to mine fuel from it using illegal technology, McDonnell has brought this crisis upon her own ship. McDonnell jettisons herself and Korwin from an airlock. Martha, Riley and the other surviving crew member, Orin Scannell, finally reach the auxiliary engine controls; as time runs out, they follow an instruction from the Doctor to jettison the plundered fuel, and the auxiliary engines start to

---

[64] The uncredited Voice of Countdown was Joshua Hill.

move the ship away from the sun-entity to safety.

## QUOTE, UNQUOTE

- **Martha:** 'What are you typing?'
  **Riley:** 'Each door's trip-code's the answer to a random question set by the crew. Nine tours back, we got drunk, thought 'em up. Reckoning was if we're hijacked, we're the only ones who know all the answers.'
  **Martha:** 'So you type in the right answer …'
  **Riley:** 'This sends a remote pulse to the clamp. But we only get one chance per door. Get it wrong, the whole system freezes.'
  **Martha:** 'Better not get it wrong then.'
- **McDonnell:** 'Korwin? What are you? Why are you killing my crew? What did you do to him? What have you done to my husband? You recognise me. Korwin, you know me. It's Kath, your wife.'
  **Korwin:** 'My wife?'
  **McDonnell:** 'That's right. You're still in there. I'm your wife.'
  **Korwin:** 'It's your fault.'

## CONTINUITY POINTS

- The Doctor adjusts Martha's mobile phone – which is a BenQ-Siemens EF81 model – using the sonic screwdriver, so that it can be used anywhere in time and space, describing this as a 'frequent flier's privilege'. Its screen displays the words 'Universal Roaming Activated', along with some Time Lord symbols and an Archangel logo. This is similar to the way the ninth Doctor modified Rose's phone in 'The End of the World', although in that case he inserted a new device into the battery compartment.
- Martha's phone number, as seen on the screen of her mother Francine's mobile phone when she calls her, is 07711911905. (Viewers who phoned this number after the episode was transmitted got a standard recorded message from the $O_2$ network voicemail service, stating that the mailbox was full – although this may possibly have been because others had beaten them to it and left messages first.)
- The action takes place in the vicinity of a sentient star in the Torajii system (originally to have been called the 'Peony System', after the flower, but renamed at a late stage of scripting after writer Chris Chibnall realised that this could be misheard as 'Penis System'), but no date is given on screen; advance publicity material suggested that the time period would be the 42nd Century – tying in with the title – but the writer and production team intended it to be the same as that of 'The Impossible Planet'/'The Satan Pit', which occurs in the year '43 K 2.1'; while it is uncertain how this relates to current dating conventions, if '43 K' stands for 43,000, it would mean that the episode is set around the 430th Century. The scenes with Martha's mother on Earth are said to take place on 'Election Day', and although no date is given, they are clearly set very shortly after 'Smith and Jones' and 'The Lazarus Experiment', i.e. probably around January 2008.
- Elvis Presley and the Beatles are said to have played 'classical music'. This

echoes a comment made by the Doctor's companion Vicki in 'The Chase' (1965): on seeing a clip of the Beatles playing one of their hits, she says, 'I didn't know they played classical music'.

- When fighting against the influence of the sun-entity, the Doctor warns Martha: 'There's this process, this thing that happens, if I'm about to die' – presumably a reference to his Time Lord ability to regenerate.
- At the end of the episode, the Doctor gives Martha her own TARDIS key, stating that this is another 'frequent flier's privilege'.

## SAXON REFERENCES

- Martha's mobile phone conversations with Francine are monitored by a sinister blonde-haired woman using a laptop computer bearing the same Archangel symbol previously seen on the 'Universal Roaming' screen on Martha's phone. The woman, who is accompanied by two black-suited men, states that Mr Saxon will be 'very grateful' to Francine for allowing this. She also expresses the hope that Francine has voted; Francine replies that she has, but is not prepared to say who for.

## PRODUCTION NOTES

- '42' was made with 'Utopia' in Block 7 of production on Series Three. These episodes were originally to have constituted Block 6 of production and been directed by Charles Palmer rather than Graham Harper.
- It was Russell T Davies's suggestion that the action of the episode should take place in real time.
- Chris Chibnall was ill with tonsillitis when writing the second draft of his script, and he subsequently injured his back in a fall downstairs at his home, necessitating him having subsequent script conferences by phone while lying in bed.
- Early drafts of the script had the Doctor making a spacewalk from one end of the ship to the other, but the additional effects work that would have been required in order to achieve this could not be afforded, so it was scaled down to the scene where he leans out of the airlock door to reach the escape pod recall switch.
- The writer and production team intended this episode to be similar in look and feel to Series Two's 'The Impossible Planet'/'The Satan Pit'. They briefly considered the possibility of the Ood from the latter story making a return appearance, but this idea was dropped at the ideas stage, before the first draft of the script was written. Later, when he was given the script on joining the production, director Graeme Harper expressed concern that the story was still too similar to the previous year's two-parter; further rewrites were then carried out in order to address this. Another concern of Harper's was to avoid making the spaceship interior scenes appear too similar to those in *Alien* (20th Century Fox, 1979), so he endeavoured to give them an 'oily, greasy' look in contrast to the gritty, low-light look of the movie.
- The character Ashton was originally to have been called 'Motta', but this was

changed as it sounded too similar to 'Martha'.

- Elize Du Toit's character, credited as 'Sinister Woman', was at one point to have been called 'Miss Dexter', according to a report in the *Sun* on 15 February 2006. In Latin, 'sinister' means 'left' and 'dexter' means 'right'.

- The spacesuit the Doctor wears is of the same design as but not identical to the one he had in 'The Impossible Planet'/'The Satan Pit', and red in colour rather than orange. The same boots and helmet were used as in the earlier story, but with modifications made to the helmet.

- The spaceship was originally to have been called the *Icarus* rather than the *SS Pentallian*. This was changed after the completion of recording when it was discovered that the Danny Boyle-directed, Alex Cox-scripted film *Sunshine* (Fox Searchlight Pictures, 2007), which would be released only a few weeks before '42' was transmitted, also features spaceships called the *Icarus I* and *Icarus II* journeying toward the Sun. The lines in '42' where characters used the name *Icarus* were redubbed in post-production, although an *Icarus* insignia can still be seen on the Doctor's spacesuit helmet.[65] The name *SS Pentallian* was coined by Russell T Davies, inspired by the (similar-sounding but differently-spelt) name of a transmat drive system, the 'pentalion drive', in 'Revenge of the Cybermen' (1975).

- Location recording took place mainly inside an old paper mill, owned by the St Regis Paper Mill Company, in Caldicot. This was in January 2007, and it was freezing cold; the cast had baby oil and water applied to their faces and the exposed areas of their bodies to make it appear that they were perspiring. The auxiliary engine control room scenes were shot at one of the series' regular locations, a disused glass works on the Trident Park industrial estate. Other scenes, including those involving the stasis chamber, were done in the Upper Boat studios.

- The stasis chamber construction was adapted from the MRI scanner featured in 'Smith and Jones'.

- Transmission of this episode was deferred by a week from the date originally intended, to make way for BBC One's live coverage of the *Eurovision Song Contest* final.

- Preview clips of the episode shown on *Totally Doctor Who* and, to accompany a David Tennant interview, on ITV1's *Parkinson* were minus Murray Gold's final incidental music, as this had not yet been dubbed onto the episode at the point when they were sourced.

- Guest star Michelle Collins appeared on the *BBC Breakfast* programme on 17 May 2006 to promote the episode. Two clips were shown, the second of which was a significant 'spoiler', revealing the twist that the sun was a living entity.

- On 12 May 2007, the bbc.co.uk *Doctor Who* website made available a short text prologue to this episode, recounting the experiences of Erina Lessak (with her surname misspelt Lissak, taken from early drafts of the script), one of the *SS Pentallian* crew members, as the ship's engines stop, the countdown to impact

---

[65] In Greek mythology, Icarus and his father Daedelus escaped from imprisonment by King Minos using artificial wings, but Icarus flew too close to the sun; the wax holding his wings together then melted and he fell to his death.

begins and the Doctor and Martha arrive. This piece was written by Joseph Lidster and illustrated with one of artist Peter McKinstry's concept paintings of the ship.

## UNFOUNDED PRE-TRANSMISSION RUMOURS

- The episode would be a homage to Douglas Adams's *The Hitchhiker's Guide to the Galaxy* series of radio serials and novels (also adapted into a TV serial and a movie, amongst other things), in which 42 is said to be the answer to the ultimate question of life, the universe and everything. (This rumour stemmed in part from a comment made jokingly by writer Chris Chibnall in an interview published in *Doctor Who Magazine* Issue 381.)

## OOPS!

- There are a couple of shots where the actors' breath can be seen, betraying the fact that although they are supposed to be in a very hot environment, it was actually extremely cold on location.

## PRESS REACTION

- 'I thought it was a triumph: a pacy, tense episode where even though you know that the Doctor isn't due for regeneration any time soon, you (well, at least, I) genuinely thought he was in real peril. For those who missed it, the Doctor and Martha found themselves on a grotty old spaceship heading for a collision with the sun, and they had just 42 minutes – the length of the episode – to avert disaster. Now this is where I sat up and thought: hang on a tick, this reminds me of a movie I saw a few weeks ago: Danny Boyle's magnificent *Sunshine*. That film is set aboard a spaceship heading for a collision with the sun, though the aim in this film is to save humankind and Earth, whereas in *Doctor Who* it was merely to save themselves. *Sunshine* had a graceful, almost poetically beautiful self-sacrifice to the sun; so too did this episode of *Doctor Who*. The sequence of Michelle Collins as the Captain locked in a balletic embrace with her husband as they are ejected from the ship to their deaths was as beautiful as anything in the gorgeous-to-look-at *Sunshine*. *Sunshine* had a malevolent Something mysteriously on the ship picking off crew members one by one. So too did *Doctor Who*. *Sunshine* portrayed the sun itself as something alive. So too did *Doctor Who*, though in a more literal sense … Is global warming, perhaps, making dramatists in London and Hollywood sit at their desks cogitating on the meaning of life, the universe and everything?' Kate Bevan, *Guardian Unlimited* blog, 21 May 2007.
- '*Doctor Who* has never really been about originality or scientific accuracy, it's how it's done that matters, and ["42" has] got Graeme Harper directing a nonetheless solid script. Not an episode anyone will ever love, but it's 41 minutes decently filled – with a real kicker in minute 42.' Anthony Brown, *TV Zone* Issue 217, July 2007.

## FAN COMMENT

- '[*Doctor Who*] is never going to be a "serious" sci-fi programme, so isn't it time to go even further the other way? Because once you've turned Trinny and Susannah into Playmobil androids with face-removing weaponry, there really isn't any turning back. But if we're specifically talking about "42", then let's bear this in mind: the real-time clock marks it out as an obvious parody of *24* (even if it cheats and skips several minutes halfway through), yet three-quarters of the people who watched this episode on first broadcast will never have watched *24*. "Love & Monsters" and "Kinda" may have left the children behind, but this is the first episode of *Doctor Who* that doesn't make any sense at all unless you're a smug, media-aware adult who's seen the specific source material. If you're unfamiliar with *24*, then it just looks like a bunch of mediocre actors running up and down corridors. And that's exactly what it is. A 42-minute sci-fi in-joke, not a real story at all.' Lawrence Miles, The Beasthouse blog, 19 May 2007.

- '"42" isn't really about heroes and villains (from its own point of view, the "monster" is swatting at annoying insects and just wants to be left alone), but people, just being human and doing the careless, idiotic things that people do, and fighting to extricate themselves from one dumb mistake that anyone could have made … And you don't need a great big tubthumping "The Ark In Space" speech to convey what down-to-earth humanity is all about; it's the little things like the silent "I'll save you." Or Martha not quite bringing herself to say goodbye to her mother. Or even the much-maligned pub-quiz door security; the equivalent of using your pet's name to secure your credit card. It's just such a whimsically "people" thing to actually do.' David Sanders, Behind the Sofa website, 22 May 2007.

- 'In the latest adventure, "42", the Doctor is up against two possessed men wearing bug-like helmets with a horizontal eye guard. It's *Doctor Who* versus the band Daft Punk, who posed for their publicity photos in similar helmets. I suspect this is an observation made elsewhere on the internet. In fact, I'll lay money on someone editing the episode to a Daft Punk song like "One More Time" or "Digital Love".' Dickon Edwards, Dickon Edwards website, 20 May 2007.

- 'Countdowns in *Doctor Who* are something of a cliché, but I think this is the first time it has formed the entire basis for an episode. It was like the scenes in "The End of the World" in Series One where [the ninth Doctor] had to get past giant fans to the conveniently inconveniently-placed "Save the Day" switch, only with a more elaborate obstacle course with added trivia questions, plus people talking in deep voices (always a sure sign of possession by an evil force in sci-fi land). The story was also something of a mishmash of genre clichés. It was obvious a mile off that the Captain would heroically sacrifice herself to help save the day, and ejecting her and the monster out of the airlock was straight out of *Alien*. On the plus side, I enjoyed seeing the Doctor being more vulnerable, and the idea of a sentient sun could have been interesting but was completely undeveloped. All told, an entirely generic but moderately entertaining runaround.' Caleb Woodbridge, A Journal of Impossible Things blog, 20 May 2007.

- 'The concept of having the Doctor separated from the TARDIS and forced into taking part in the events unfolding on screen is something that harks all the way back to the early days of the classic show … But the new hook is the "real time" concept being used for the story. It heightens the suspense … and drives the narrative forward, giving us a ticking time clock that the Doctor and the crew of the spaceship must beat or meet their ultimate demise. Along the way, there are some really great scenes from a character standpoint, including Martha being trapped in a life support pod and jettisoned off the ship, Martha calling home to her mother to say goodbye and the Doctor becoming possessed by the sun. Not to sound repetitive here, but David Tennant really delivers again this week as the Doctor. He's still got the energy of Series Two, but he's more controlled and less manic about it – and it shows in his performance. The scenes where the Doctor desperately tries to save Martha and then becomes possessed by the alien intelligence are some of the best work he's done on the show. And, for the most part, the supporting cast do a good job as well. A lot of them are there as cannon fodder for the possessed humans to kill off, but the few that do get some screen time come off well. The only exception is Michelle Collins as the ship's captain. It's hard to believe she's as tough as nails as the script would like us to believe.' Michael Hickerson, Slice of SciFi website, 21 May 2007.

ANALYSIS

A distress signal picked up by the TARDIS brings the Doctor to the aid of a spaceship crew who have unwittingly angered a powerful alien entity by plundering its domain for a new source of fuel. They find themselves in a desperate race against time as the spaceship is dragged back toward certain destruction, while one of the crew, infected by the entity, begins systematically killing his colleagues, his eyes glowing with unnatural energy. That's the plot of 'Planet of Evil' (1975); but what about '42'?

Okay, so that's a bit of a cheap joke. Let's start again. In the far future, an isolated human crew trapped in a grimy, industrial environment find themselves in a desperate race against time as they are pulled toward a star with strange properties. To make matters worse, one of their number comes under the influence of a powerful alien being and starts murdering the others, his eyes hideously transformed and his voice unnaturally deepened as he issues terrifying arcane threats. The Doctor and his companion, meanwhile, are cut off from the TARDIS and caught up in the struggle for survival. No doubt about it: 'The Impossible Planet'/'The Satan Pit' is one of the most exciting stories of Series Two.

All right, no more jokes. The point is, of course, that '42' is never going to win any awards for originality; in fact, it is probably the most derivative episode yet produced since *Doctor Who* returned to TV in 2005. The idea of presenting a story similar in style to 'The Impossible Planet'/ 'The Satan Pit' was fine in principle, but surely this should not have extended to reusing some of the same major plot elements? The threat posed to the SS *Pentallian* by the sun also recalls the danger aboard Platform One in 'The End of the World'. While it may be new to *Doctor Who*, even the concept of a sentient star is familiar from science fiction literature, having featured in stories going right back to Olaf Stapledon's *Star Maker*

(Methuen, 1937). Stanislaw Lem's *Solaris* (1961) and its film adaptations also explore some similar ideas, as does the movie *Sunshine* (Fox Searchlight Pictures, 2007). In addition, '42' bears a number of striking similarities to the episode 'Heroes and Demons' from the first season of *Star Trek: Voyager* (UPN, 1995-2001), in which Captain Kathryn Janeway (a possible source of inspiration for Captain McDonnell's first name) takes samples from a protostar for use as a new power source for her ship and inadvertently brings on board at the same time an alien entity that proceeds to transform many of her crew members, the crisis being eventually resolved when the samples are returned to the alien. (Could this plot also have been inspired by *Doctor Who*'s 'Planet of Evil'?) The idea of a spaceship at risk of destruction as it draws ever closer to a sun has also featured previously in the episode 'Meltdown' from the third season of another American science fiction series, *Farscape* (Sci Fi Channel, 1999-2003).

Its lack of new ideas and approaches is by no means the worst of the episode's problems, either. In order for a 'countdown to disaster' story like this to have maximum impact, it needs to be utterly convincing, so that the viewer is caught up in the urgency of the situation and feels almost a part of it. Sadly, that isn't always the case here, for two main reasons.

The first reason is that it is difficult to believe in the *SS Pentallian* as a realistic setting. It's just about possible to accept that the ship's heat shields have so far saved it from being burnt up, despite it being drawn ever closer to the sun-entity, and that its life support systems have kept the interior cool enough for the crew to survive (and in addition presumably protected them from being blinded by the intense light). It's also just about credible that the ship has a 'secure closure' procedure that, once activated, causes a series of 29 doors along the main corridor to become password-sealed, with the intention of thwarting hijackers. Rather less plausible, though, is the idea that the crew have no way of activating the auxiliary engines unless they can get to the front of the ship via all these sealed doors. It's also a bit too convenient – or inconvenient, from the characters' point of view – that the TARDIS becomes inaccessible almost immediately after the Doctor and Martha arrive, and that the sonic screwdriver can't be used to open the sealed doors, because they are 'deadlock sealed'; a trite phrase trotted out by the series' writers whenever they want to deprive the Doctor of his usual easy way out of a tricky situation (as witnessed prior to this episode in 'Bad Wolf', 'School Reunion' and 'Evolution of the Daleks', and with Sarah's sonic lipstick in *The Sarah Jane Adventures*: 'Invasion of the Bane'). One also has to ask what spaceship crew in their right minds would set the passwords to the doors in such a bizarre way – using the answers to 'pub quiz'-type questions, some of them known only to crewmembers who have since left – even allowing for the fact that they were drunk at the time. Admittedly this is bound to raise a smile from any viewer who has had the fairly common experience of setting a password, for instance on an internet shopping account, and then struggling to recall it a few weeks later; but I have yet to encounter any such system that seizes up completely if even a single incorrect entry is made. Then there is the matter of the escape pod. This is obviously intended to be used in the event of an emergency – such as might give rise to a secure closure situation – so, logically, it should be situated somewhere where it can be very quickly and easily accessed. Here, though, it is positioned part-way down the corridor of sealed doors. Worse still, the switch used to recall it if it is launched in error is actually placed *outside* the spaceship, on the hull! It seems this spaceship can only have been designed by a madman.

There are numerous other points in the script that stretch the viewer's credulity. Why does Captain McDonnell call her husband of 11 years by his surname, Korwin, even in life-threatening circumstances where she should surely dispense with any formality that might otherwise be warranted by his status as a member of her crew?[66] Why does Martha use her mother as her 'phone a friend' lifeline (to extend the quiz analogy[67]) – rather than, say, her sister or someone else who would be more likely to know about pop music – to get the answer to the password question about whether Elvis or the Beatles had the most pre-download number one singles? Why do the infected Korwin and Ashton both take the trouble to put on dark-visored welding helmets – making them look rather like the Cyclops character from Marvel Comics' *The X-Men* series – when walking about the ship if, as seems to be the case, they intend simply to wipe out their crewmates and have no need to hide their eyes?

Any one of these implausibilities on its own would not be seriously detrimental to the story, but taken together they have the effect of making the whole thing seem very contrived.[68]

The second reason for the story's failure to achieve its full potential relates not to Chris Chibnall's script but to the performances of some of the guest actors. Michelle Collins in particular is completely out of her depth as McDonnell. Director Graeme Harper, commenting on the casting of this former *EastEnders* star in the accompanying *Doctor Who Confidential* documentary, 'Space Craft', says that the intention was that McDonnell should come across as someone tough yet vulnerable. One suspects that he had in mind Sigourney Weaver's famous portrayal of Ellen Ripley in the *Alien* franchise, or possibly Linda Hamilton's depiction of Sarah Connor (whose trademark vest-and-combat-trousers outfit McDonnell's closely resembles) in the first two *Terminator* films. A good idea in theory, but unfortunately it doesn't come off in practice, as Collins' acting here is distinctly wooden and lacking in conviction. In fact, aside from Catherine Tate's dreadful performance in 'The Runaway Bride', this is probably the poorest showing by a major guest star in *Doctor Who* since the series was revived. To be fair, though, Collins is not altogether to blame, as she is simply miscast. Her main preoccupation in interviews about the role, and in the episode's bbc.co.uk podcast commentary, seems to be the fact that she was not allowed to wear make-up for it,

---

[66] The behind-the-scenes reason for this was that, as originally scripted, the name of the Captain's husband was 'Korwin McDonnell' rather than, as in the final version, 'Hal Korwin'.

[67] 'Phone a friend' is one of three lifelines that a contestant may use on the TV quiz show *Who Wants to be a Millionnaire* (ITV1, 1998- ).

[68] Some fans have cited as an additional implausibility the notion that the escape pod is drawn back to the spaceship by magnetic force. In fact, though, this could be done with magnets not much more powerful than those in current industrial use, which is well within the bounds of scientific possibility and certainly involves less of a leap of faith than accepting that – as is generally taken as read in TV science fiction stories – the spaceship clearly has artificial gravity and can move faster than the speed of light.

and there is a general feeling of self-consciousness about her performance on screen. The scene where McDonnell punches Ashton in the stomach and wrestles the upper part of his body into the stasis chamber is particularly unbelievable, because it is obvious that the actress is unaccustomed to being so physical (she actually had to take advice from a stuntman on how to throw the punch) and is simply too slight in stature to be capable of doing this.

Equally disappointing is Rebecca Oldfield in the relatively minor role of Erina Lessak, who never for one moment convinces as a tough cargo ship crew member. William Ash is also somewhat below par as Riley Vashtee, giving a performance that veers from strong at certain points to stilted at others. In the midst of all this, even Freema Agyeman is for once unconvincing in the delivery of some of her lines, although thankfully she is still excellent for the most part.

The one cast member who really shines (no pun intended) is – perhaps predictably – David Tennant. He is especially brilliant (ditto) in the scenes where the Doctor is trying desperately to fight off the sun-entity's murderous influence. This is a real highlight of the episode, and shows the Doctor being probably more openly scared than at any other point in the series' history. It is also a welcome corrective to the impression given in some other stories that, as a 'lonely god', he is almost invulnerable. The suggestion seems to be that the Doctor's greatest fear is of being possessed – of having his own identity supplanted by that of another, more malevolent being – which actually ties in quite nicely with the denouement of 'Planet of the Spiders' (1974), where the third Doctor finds himself unable to resist the mental control of the Great One and ultimately has to regenerate after returning to her lair to face this fear. His experiences aboard the SS *Pentallian* certainly seem to have had quite a profound effect on him, judging from the way he stands brooding in the TARDIS for a time at the end of the episode. The idea of the Doctor being possessed is a very unsettling one for the viewer as well, as his heroic presence normally serves as a reassurance against the dangers presented, and it is something that has been used only a few times previously in the series – perhaps most notably in 'The Invisible Enemy' (1977), in which the fourth Doctor falls under the influence of a sentient virus.

Another outstanding scene is the slightly earlier one where the Doctor and Martha find themselves separated from each other on opposite sides of facing windows as the escape pod is launched and moves gradually further and further away from the main ship. This is all the more effective for the fact that it recalls how the Doctor was separated from Rose at the end of 'Doomsday', ostensibly on opposite sides of the same wall but actually a whole universe apart; and there is something really rather eerie about the fact that Martha can only see and not hear the Doctor as he repeatedly shouts 'I'll save you' to her – again a superb piece of acting by Tennant, nicely conveying the Doctor's utter determination not to lose another companion – while she bangs desperately on the glass on her side of the divide. The impact of this sequence is further enhanced by the fact that – uniquely in new *Doctor Who* – it is completely devoid of incidental music and sound effects, emphasising the silence of space and the apparent hopelessness of the situation in which Martha and Riley find themselves.

This leads on to another excellent and highly emotional scene, where Martha, believing that she is about to die, again phones her mother back in London, effectively to say goodbye – although, understandably, she does not actually explain her situation to Francine, who in any case seems strangely preoccupied ... Agyeman is superb here, with some good material to get her teeth into, and it's her best scene of the episode. It's also useful in shedding further light on Martha's relationship with her mother, and on her feelings toward her family in general.

The periodic switching back to Earth for these sequences with Francine has both pros and cons. On the plus side, it provides a stark contrast to the action on the spaceship, putting this in a real-world context and highlighting in particular just how radically Martha's life has changed since she hooked up with the Doctor. It is also a clever means of allowing for the 'Mr Saxon' arc to be progressed even though this episode's main setting is far removed from contemporary Earth, as it transpires that, unbeknown to Martha, her calls are now being monitored, apparently with her mother's co-operation (although this is open to debate; it is possible she is under a degree of duress), by a sinister blonde-haired woman who tells Francine 'Mr Saxon will be very grateful' and alludes to the fact that voting is taking place in what is presumably a General Election. The downside is that, by taking the viewer out of the (almost literal) pressure cooker environment of the *SS Pentallian*, these sequences tend to break the build-up of tension as the countdown moves ever closer toward zero.

One of the most notable aspects of '42' is the fact that the action progresses in real time – an interesting and worthwhile departure for *Doctor Who*, as well as an obvious homage (also reflected in the episode's title) to the American thriller series *24* (Fox, 2001- ), each season of which recounts in real time the events of a single day in the life of anti-terrorist agent Jack Bauer (Kiefer Sutherland).[69] In fact, one almost wishes that the production team had gone the whole hog and had a digital clock superimposed in one corner of the screen throughout, counting down from 42 minutes when the Doctor and Martha emerge from the TARDIS to zero at the climax. Perhaps, though, this would have been too distracting, or would have caused too many problems in editing the episode to achieve satisfactory dramatic pacing; it is noticeable that the timing is actually 'cheated' at certain points – as indeed it is in *24* itself – meaning that the action is not *strictly* in real time.

There isn't much in the way of meaningful subtext to '42' – one can perhaps discern a basic 'concern for the environment' message in it, in that McDonnell is blamed for having caused the crisis herself through her illegal mining of the sun without regard for the damage it could potentially cause (although one has to question how she could reasonably have been expected to foresee that it was actually a living entity in the form of a sun, unless these are more common than has so far been suggested in the series) – but that's fine, as *Doctor Who* ought to present a wide variety of different types and styles of story, and it's good to have a straightforward thriller every now and again. The CGI effects work and other aspects of the production are well up to the series' usual high standards, making for some memorably powerful imagery, and Murray Gold's incidental music – which reuses certain elements of his score from 'The Impossible Planet'/'The Satan Pit' – is also very effective. The threatening 'Burn with me' phrase uttered be the infected crewmembers is a good touch, too, and will no doubt have been repeated in many playgrounds up and down the country in the days following the debut

---

[69] The first season of *24* is detailed in the book *A Day in the Life: The Unofficial and Unauthorised Guide to 24* (Telos Publishing, 2003) by Keith Topping.

transmission. The ever-energetic Harper is an ideal choice of director to handle an action-orientated episode such as this, and he brings a real sense of pace and urgency to the proceedings, making excellent use of the claustrophobic industrial location. It is just a pity that he wasn't able to coax rather better performances out of some of the guest cast, and particularly out of Collins.

While it certainly has its good points, '42' ultimately fails to live up to expectations, and I have to say that, for me, it just edges out 'Evolution of the Daleks' as the weakest episode yet of Series Three.

# 3.08 – HUMAN NATURE

Writer: Paul Cornell
Director: Charles Palmer

DEBUT TRANSMISSION DETAILS

BBC One
Date: 26 May 2007. Scheduled time: 7.10 pm. Actual time: 7.11 pm.

BBC Three
Date: 27 May 2007. Scheduled time: 8.00 pm. Actual time: 8.02 pm.

Duration: 45′ 03″

ADDITIONAL CREDITED CAST

Jessica Hynes[70] (Joan Redfern), Rebekah Staton (Jenny), Thomas Sangster (Tim Latimer), Harry Lloyd (Baines[71]), Tom Palmer (Hutchinson), Gerard Horan (Clark), Lauren Wilson (Lucy Cartwright), Pip Torrens (Rocastle), Matthew White (Phillips), Derek Smith (Doorman), Peter Bourke (Mr Chambers). [72]

PLOT

Attempting to shake off a family of aliens who have been pursuing him and Martha, the Doctor uses a Chameleon Arch device in the TARDIS to transform himself into a human. The TARDIS gives him the identity of John Smith, a teacher at a boys' public school in the England of 1913, with Martha acting as his housemaid. A complication arises when Smith falls in love with the school nurse, Joan Redfern – a possibility the Doctor failed to foresee. When the aliens track them down to the school, landing their invisible spaceship in a nearby field and using animated scarecrows to help them capture and take on the forms of four local people, Martha decides it is time for the Doctor to return – but the pocket watch into which his Time Lord persona was placed by the Chameleon Arch has been taken from Smith's room by one of the schoolboys, the strangely gifted Tim Latimer. The alien family eventually track Smith down to a dance in the village hall, where they try to compel him to change back into a Time Lord by threatening

---

[70] Known by her maiden name Jessica Stevenson during production; the actress was married to her long-time partner Adam, and began using his surname, between production and transmission.

[71] First name given as 'Jeremy' in dialogue.

[72] Two of the uncredited actors playing the Scarecrows were Ken Hosking and Ruari Mears.

the lives of Martha and Joan. Smith, however, has no idea what they are talking about …

QUOTE, UNQUOTE

- **Joan:** 'Quite an eye for the pretty girls.'
  **Smith:** 'Oh, no, no. She's just an invention. This character. Rose, I call her. Rose. She seems to disappear later on. Oh, that's the box. The blue box. It's always there. Like a … a magic carpet. This funny little box that transports me to faraway places.'
- **Martha:** 'Sometimes he says these strange things, like people and places you've never heard of, yeah? But it's deeper than that. Sometimes when you look in his eyes, you know, you just know that there's something else in there. Something hidden, right behind the eyes, something hidden away, in the dark.'
- **Baines:** 'Have you enjoyed it, Doctor? Being human. Has it taught you wonderful things? Are you better, richer, wiser? Then let's see you answer this: which one of them do you want us to kill? Maid or Matron? Your friend or your lover? Your choice!'

CONTINUITY POINTS

- The Doctor explains to Martha how the Family of Blood are able to follow the TARDIS through time and space: 'Stolen technology. They've got a time agent's vortex manipulator. They can follow us wherever we go. Right across the universe.' The Doctor's sometime companion Jack Harkness is a time agent from the 51st Century and has a similar device.
- The Doctor says that the Chameleon Arch (which has never featured before in the series) rewrites his biology and changes every cell in his body. He also states that he has 'set it to human', implying that he could potentially have used it to take on a different form instead. The reason for the device's presence in the TARDIS and the other aspects of its function – such as whether it works only on a Time Lord or is capable of rewriting the biology of members of other species as well – are left unexplained.
- The Doctor's pocket watch, used in the Chameleon Arch as a receptacle for his Time Lord persona, is engraved on both front and back: the symbols on the front are standard Gallifreyan script while the pattern on the back is a representation of the constellation of Kasterberous – the star system within which Gallifrey is located – and matches that seen on the back of the ankh-shaped TARDIS key used during the 1970s. The Doctor says in his recorded message to Martha that he has put a perception filter on the watch so that in his human form he won't think anything of it; in *Torchwood*, the presence of a perception filter is the reason why passers-by are unable to see the invisible lift in operation by the water tower fountain in the Roald Dahl Plass.
- In the first scene set in 1913, the morning newspaper that Martha, in her housemaid's guise, brings to John Smith with his breakfast gives the date as 'Monday November 10th'. Joan later says that she has known him for two months, suggesting that the TARDIS arrived in mid-September. Much of the

action of the episode takes place the following day[73], 11 November, leading up to the dance in the evening.

- John Smith states that he recalls being in 'the year of our Lord 2007'. In Martha's MySpace blog, she states that she and the Doctor first encountered the Family of Blood in Helsinki at the final of the Eurovision Song Contest 2007, the year before her own time. (This is an in-joke reference to the fact that transmission of this and all the other episodes following 'The Lazarus Experiment' was shifted back by a week to make way for BBC One's live coverage of that final.)
- John Smith's *A Journal of Impossible Things* contains handwritten notes and sketches of, amongst other things, the TARDIS interior, the sonic screwdriver, Chula gasmask zombies, a Dalek, the Moxx of Balhoon, Autons, K-9, a Clockwork Man, Rose Tyler, Cybermen, the TARDIS exterior, Slitheen and the pocket watch featured in this episode, and on one page, five of the Doctor's previous incarnations: the first, fifth, sixth, seventh and (most prominently) eighth – the first time that incarnations prior to the ninth have been depicted in the new series.
- The second time that the boy Tim Latimer briefly opens the Doctor's watch, he sees fleeting images of a Dalek, Cybermen, the Ood, the Werewolf, the Sycorax leader, the Empress of the Racnoss and the mutated Lazarus monster. (These are all clips from previous episodes.)
- John Smith's skilful use of a cricket ball to save a woman with a pram from being struck by a falling piano recalls the fact that the Doctor in some of his previous incarnations, including the fourth and, most notably, the fifth, has also used a cricket ball to help him get out of tight scrapes. It is possible that the Doctor learnt about cricket while exiled on Earth for a time during his third incarnation. The first Doctor appeared completely unfamiliar with the game when the TARDIS materialised at the Oval cricket ground during an England-v-Australia Test Match at one point during 'The Daleks' Master Plan' (1965/66).

PRODUCTION NOTES

- 'Human Nature' was made with 'The Family of Blood' in Block 6 of production on Series Three. These episodes were moved forward from Block 7 because the scripts were ready early, and consequently were directed by Charles Palmer rather than, as had originally been intended, Graham Harper.
- 'Human Nature' and the following episode, 'The Family of Blood', form a two-part story, based on writer Paul Cornell's *Human Nature* (Virgin Publishing, 1995) – one of the *New Adventures* range of original *Doctor Who* novels. The text of this has been made available to read or download free of charge as an e-book on the official *Doctor Who* website, along with comprehensive notes supplied by Cornell, including an account of how he approached the TV

---

[73] The date appears to have been chosen by writer Paul Cornell because 11 November is now noted as Armistice Day; the First World War ended on 11 November 1918.

adaptation. The novel was partly plotted by fellow *New Adventures* author Kate Orman; although she received no on-screen credit on the TV version, at Cornell's request she was paid a small fee by the BBC in recognition of her contribution to the original.

- It was Russell T Davies's idea to ask Paul Cornell to adapt his novel for the TV series, not because he specifically wanted to do an adaptation of a novel but because he regarded *Human Nature* as one of the finest *Doctor Who* stories ever written in any medium and realised that only a few tens of thousands of people would have read it in its original form – a very small number compared with the millions who would see the TV adaptation. Executive producer Julie Gardner and script editor Helen Raynor both read the book during pre-production of the TV version (neither of them having done so before), but Davies deliberately avoided re-reading it, so that he could look at Cornell's scripts with a fresh eye. The early drafts of the scripts departed quite significantly from the storyline of the book, but changes that Davies asked Cornell to make to them eventually resulted in them following it rather more closely.
- Susie Liggat received her first credits as a *Doctor Who* producer on 'Human Nature' and 'The Family of Blood'. This was because regular producer Phil Collinson was on holiday during the making of the story; he was credited for the first time as an executive producer instead. Liggat had previously produced *The Sarah Jane Adventures*: 'Invasion of the Bane' (2007).
- Helen Raynor did some work as script editor in the early stages of preparation of this story, but Lindsey Alford then took over and received the sole on-screen credit.
- Recording for this two-part story took place over five weeks, with a break for Christmas. Locations used included side rooms of Llandaff Cathedral, in the Llandaff area of Cardiff, for some of the Farringham School interiors, including the dormitory, recorded at the end of November 2006; a field in the Brecon Beacons for the landing site of the invisible spaceship; a 'mud farm' called Neil's Soils in Wentloog Road, Cardiff, for the First World War trenches; Treberfydd, a Victorian country house, also in the Brecon Beacons, for the school exteriors and remaining interiors; and the St Fagan's National History Museum in Cardiff for a number of settings, including the row of shops outside of which the piano falls and the village hall where the dance takes place. The St Fagan's scenes were taped toward the end of the shoot, in mid-December 2006 and early January 2007. The remainder of the interiors, including those in the Cartwrights' cottage, were then recorded at the Upper Boat studios. The interior of the aliens' spaceship was constructed on the *Torchwood* Hub set, which was not at that point in use on the spin-off. The crew encountered terrible weather on location, and David Tennant was ill with a bad cold during the last week of recording, which eventually wrapped (save for a few pick-up shots done later on) on 11 January.
- Farringham School for Boys was named after the town of Faringham in Oxfordshire, where Paul Cornell is based.
- John Smith's *A Journal of Impossible Things* was created for the production by artist Kellyanne Walker, incorporating text provided by Paul Cornell. Walker was asked to create the impression that Smith wasn't a great artist, and that

these were notes and drawings he had jotted down quickly in order to record his dreams. Additional pages from the book viewable on the official *Doctor Who* website included a full double-page spread of the entry relating to the Doctor's previous incarnations, showing sketches of all ten Doctors. The Latin phrase 'Maius intra qua extra' written on one page means 'What is inside is greater than what is outside' – presumably relating to the TARDIS, although in the original novel *Human Nature* (unlike in this TV adaptation) it was also the school motto and was said to refer to books.

- The idea of an invisible spaceship featured previously in the untransmitted story 'Shada' by Douglas Adams, production on which had to be abandoned before completion at the end of 1979 due to industrial action within the BBC. The rationale for the ship's invisibility was the same in that case as in this: it saved the production the cost of having to create a spaceship exterior model or set.
- The actors playing the Family of Blood decided in rehearsals that they would try never to blink in the scenes where their characters were possessed.
- Smith states that his parents were called Sydney and Verity. These names were added to the script by Russell T Davies as a tribute to Sydney Newman, the principal creator of *Doctor Who*, and Verity Lambert, the series' first producer.
- Joan's comment that Smith has a 'girl in every fireplace' is a reference to the Series Two episode 'The Girl in the Fireplace', presumably written about by Smith in his journal.
- Smith tells Joan Redfern that he learnt to draw in Gallifrey – the name of the home planet of the Time Lords – and when Joan asks if this is in Ireland, he tentatively agrees. Gallifrey has been assumed to be a place in Ireland on a number of previous occasions in the series, going back to 'The Hand of Fear' (1976) and including also 'The Invisible Enemy' (1977) and 'Arc of Infinity' (1983).
- It was Russell T Davies's idea that the Doctor's Time Lord persona should be held in a pocket watch; in Paul Cornell's original novel, the device used for this purpose was a cricket ball.
- Over the first few scenes at the school, a boys' choir – from Thorpe House School in Buckinghamshire – can be heard singing the hymn 'To Be A Pilgrim'. The lyrics of this were written by John Bunyan (1628-1688) for the second part of his *The Pilgrim's Progress* in 1684 and adapted by the Rev Dr Percy Dearmer (1867-1936) for the *English Hymnal* in 1906, at which time composer Ralph Vaughan Williams (1872-1958) set the lyrics to the traditional Sussex melody 'Monk's Gate'.
- Actress Jessica Hynes, in an interview publishing in the *Guardian* on 25 May 2007, said of the character of Joan: 'She's magnificent. Intelligent, kind, good, and unaffected. She's liberated in a way that women today, shackled by their self-obsessions, aren't. Women now define themselves through their lifestyle, by their shoes and sofa throws. One hundred years ago, women defined themselves much more by their character and their interests.'
- In the scenes where Latimer briefly opens the watch, three voices are heard. The first is that of David Tennant as the Doctor, while the other two are supplied by crowd artistes frequently used by sound editor Paul McFadden.

The lines they speak are split up, overlaid and not fully audible in the transmitted version, but were scripted as follows:

> **Doctor:** Space ... and time ... Eternity and infinity within the vortex. The secret lies within. I'm trapped, I'm caged inside the cold and the metal and the dark, but waiting, always waiting. Contained, encircled, enclosed, the neverending circle goes round and round and round. Awaiting release. The power within, the power of a Time Lord, such a precious prize, protect me. I will return. I am returning, even now. And the human will fall.
>
> **Woman:** The Family is coming, the Family has picked up the scent, the time is not right... Timothy. Timothy? Hide us, hide me, hide it from harm. You have been chosen, boy. You stand as protector, against the dark and the cold. Reach out, boy, reach out with your mind ...
>
> **Wise Man:** Gallifrey, in the constellation of Kasterborous, galactic coordinates ten zero eleven zero zero by zero two from galactic zero centre. There stood the Citadel, before the fall, before the Last Great War of Time itself, home of the mighty Panopticon. All gone now, all fallen into dust. Atoms on the solar winds ...
>
> **Doctor:** Time Lord. You are not alone ...
>
> **Woman:** Shine with the light and the power and the majesty, the light of time and space and infinite fire, burn with the light, burn and turn, accept its wisdom.
>
> **Wise Man:** The children of Skaro and Cybernetic men made manifest, the blood and fire of the Racnoss Empire, slaughtered in the Great Purge of the Fledgeling Wars, flesh and bone of the Sycoraxic clan ...
>
> **Doctor:** Keep me hidden, keep me away from the false and empty man, the danger is coming, the danger is so close, hold me tight, keep me close and quiet and safe ...
>
> **Woman:** Darkness is coming, darkness is so close, they walk upon the Earth with the faces of men and women and children but their hearts are so old, so cold ...
>
> **Wise Man:** This is the last of Gallifrey, the last of the Time Lords, the last of that wise and ancient race ...

UNFOUNDED PRE-TRANSMISSION RUMOURS

• Paul Cornell's Series Three story would be called 'The Life and Loves of a Sea Devil'.

OOPS!

• A large white lorry of modern design can be seen driving along a road in the distance in the first shot of the scene where the boys are training with the machine gun.

## PRESS REACTION

- 'There's a general view … that television isn't what it used to be. We are bombarded by cheap reality shows, twee Sunday night dramas, cookery, property, wife swaps and diminished opportunities for children's drama. Yep, sometimes watching television can be a real chore. And then along comes something that restores your faith, that brings home all the things that are great about this most frustrating of mediums and reminds us … how lucky and privileged we are to have huge talent in front of and behind the cameras making television. That happened on Saturday night watching "Human Nature", the first of a two-part *Doctor Who* story. Not only is "Human Nature" the best piece of *Doctor Who* I've ever seen (and I've been there through thick and thin), it ranks up there with the best television drama I've ever seen … There's nothing duff in this episode. Not one off-note performance, wasted shot or fluffed line of dialogue. And as always, there has to be praise for David Tennant. Once again, he takes us in ever more surprising directions, and with his showing here as Smith, you realise there are some very definite choices layered into how he plays the Doctor.' Mark Wright, *The Stage* website, 28 May 2007.
- 'Two years ago, in "Father's Day", Paul Cornell's first script for the series, there was a moment where a bride and groom talked of meeting waiting for a taxi, when the Doctor admitted, with a hint of regret, "I could never have a life like that". This two-parter spins off from that moment, giving us a chance to contemplate how very different the Doctor is from us ordinary mortals. It's a story that has been told before, of course. This is an adaptation of *Human Nature*, Cornell's seventh Doctor spin-off novel, published way back in 1995. Always held in high regard by fans, it was voted the best *Doctor Who* book ever by readers of *Doctor Who Magazine*. It should come as no surprise, then, that the TV version is a solid-gold classic. Five stars doesn't really do it justice.' Ian Berriman, *SFX* website, 2 June 2007.

## FAN COMMENT

- '"Human Nature" is definitely a more sophisticated, adult look at *Doctor Who*, and Paul Cornell's much revered novel will now be a much revered set of episodes in this show's history. It's one of those magical things where [everything] works – the characters, performances, the writing, the history of the Time Lord, the essential creepiness and imminent disaster and Murray Gold's superb scoring. It's possibly the best episode of the series yet and definitely the most ambitious.' Shawn Lunn, Doctor Who Online website, 22 June 2007.
- 'In the utterly depressing sixth season of *Buffy the Vampire Slayer*, there is a story called "Normal Again", where we see an alternative perspective that has Buffy in a sanatorium suffering from catatonia, and under the delusion that her dreamworld of Sunnydale exists and that she is a super-hero there. The particular horror of the episode is that it treats this possibility as totally

plausible – in fact I think that it goes too far, because it plays its final scene in the "Buffy is mad and dreaming it all" world, suggesting that that is the world that is "real". The thrust of the "Human Nature" pre-titles [scene] is playing with a similar idea: is it possible that the whole of *Doctor Who* is just a dream in the mind of Mr Smith? Except that the opening has already explained that it is not. Nothing wrong with a fast paced opening scene, but I'd have just saved the explanatory exposition for later on, when Martha goes to the TARDIS halfway through.' 'Millennium Dome', Millennium Elephant blog, 29 May 2007.

- 'David Tennant discussed on the *Doctor Who Confidential* episode accompanying "Human Nature" how he approached Smith as a completely new character, and he certainly seems very different [from] and yet in some ways very similar to the tenth Doctor. I was worried that the character taking on a human aspect would not be noticeable given how very human he already is, but Cornell confounded my expectations by using the less desirable aspects of humanity to highlight Smith's human nature. His attitude during the Officer Training Corps sequence, for example, extolling the virtues of the gun practice and allowing Tim to be punished, was shocking for those used to the Doctor's heroism and sense of right and justice, and showed us effectively just how different a man he is. True, this is also in the book, but somehow the contrast with the tenth Doctor is greater than it was with the darker, more manipulative seventh. Tennant was terrific all the way through, from this ruthlessness right through to his touching romance with Joan.' Paul Hayes, Outpost Gallifrey website, 12 June 2007.

ANALYSIS

I suggested back in Chapter Two that the 2005 revival of *Doctor Who* would probably never have come about had it not been for the *New Adventures* range of novels put out by Virgin Publishing between 1991 and 1999, and that the two share essentially the same ethos. Never has this latter point been more apparent than in Paul Cornell's 'Human Nature'/'The Family of Blood', which is a fairly faithful adaptation of his award-winning *New Adventures* novel *Human Nature* and yet fits so perfectly into the TV series that it could easily have been written specially for it; indeed it could almost be said to be a quintessential new series story.

This has to be the starting point for any discussion of 'Human Nature'/'The Family of Blood': although the TV series has often drawn inspiration – occasionally quite heavy inspiration – from other sources, this is the first time that it has ever presented an explicit adaptation of a *Doctor Who* story from another medium, or indeed of any other story of any kind. Yes, Rob Shearman's 'Dalek' was commissioned on the strength of his earlier 'Jubilee' (2003) from the Big Finish audio CD range, and Tom MacRae's 'Rise of the Cybermen'/'The Age of Steel' was sufficiently influenced by 'Spare Parts' (2002) from the same range that an on-screen thanks credit was warranted for its writer, Marc Platt. In both those cases, however, although the same basic ideas were used as a starting point, the stories derived from them were really quite dissimilar, with different settings, different characters and even different underlying themes. That is not true of 'Human Nature'/'The Family of Blood', which has not only the same central premise as the novel – specifically, the premise of the Doctor taking on human form – but also the same setting around a pre-First World War English boys' school (albeit moved back a year, from 1914 to 1913), most of the same characters, and even many of the same individual scenes (or variants of them, at least). So the Doctor has now had essentially the same adventure twice, in two different incarnations (seventh and tenth respectively), with two different companions (Bernice and Martha) and in two different media (novel and TV story).

This inevitably raises the thorny issue of canonicity; which is closely related to that of story continuity. Much attention always seems to be devoted to these issues within *Doctor Who* fandom. At the root of this lies the simple and uncontroversial fact that when people are being told a story, they like and indeed expect it to be internally consistent. In TV drama terms, what this means at its simplest is that if, say, a character is established to be a vegetarian, then viewers will not expect to see him tucking into a beef sandwich just a few scenes later, and may even lose interest altogether, as they will find it hard to maintain belief in the situation being presented. Where the drama is not a one-off play but a multi-episode series, then the same thing generally applies across the whole series: if a character asserts that he is a vegetarian in the first episode, then viewers will expect that to hold true for all the subsequent episodes too – unless, of course, something happens in the interim to convert him to eating beef! It can thus be seen as part and parcel of writers' and, more especially, producers' jobs to ensure that the stories they present pass what might be termed the 'beef test'. But just how far does this need to be taken? Where a series lasts for many years, for instance, does it always remain incumbent upon the producers to ensure that the latest episodes do not contradict things said or done in the earliest ones, even though very few viewers will actually recall the latter (unless, of course, they have seen them only recently on DVD ...) and even though it might be detrimental to the telling of a good story? And where, as in *Doctor Who*'s case, the series gives rise to tie-in stories in other media – novels, audio CD dramas, comic strips and so on – should the respective producers be expected to ensure that these too maintain consistency with what has been established in the TV episodes, and vice versa, and indeed with each other as well?

Where *Doctor Who* is concerned, there are doubtless some fans, if few in number, who would answer a resounding 'Yes' to all these questions; but most – and probably most general viewers too, if they cared to give the matter any thought – would tend to take a more flexible and pragmatic attitude, confining their expectations of consistency to just certain of the Doctor's adventures and accepting that others may diverge and be contradictory. In other words, the great majority are inclined to draw a line between those adventures that they consider authentic – and thus supposed to be coherent – and those that they regard as apocryphal. Precisely where they draw that line is clearly down to individual preference, and varies from one person to another, although in many cases it seems to be between the stories seen in the TV series – both classic and new – and those presented in other media; and one suspects that this is broadly the stance taken by the current producers of the TV series as well, although – perhaps wisely – they have never made any official pronouncement on the subject, beyond saying that the new series is a continuation of the classic series and the 1996 TV Movie. (In fact, in Issue 356 of *Doctor Who Magazine*, Russell T Davies wrote that he was 'usually happy for old and new fans to invent the Complete History of the Doctor in their heads, completely free of the production team's hot and heavy hands'.) The further away the line is drawn from what might be considered the 'core' stories of the TV series, the more difficulty – or, depending on how one looks at it, fun – a fan is likely to have in trying to come up with theories to reconcile all the apparent contradictions, such as those presented by the various different adventures involving Shakespeare in the TV series, novels, audio plays, comic strips and the like, as discussed in the 'Analysis' section on 'The Shakespeare Code'.

Another way of looking at all this, though, given that the concept of parallel universes is well established within the series itself, is to assume that stories told in different media take place in different fictional universes. This affords a means of reconciling even major contradictions – such as the fact that the seventh Doctor's companion Ace is killed off in the Marvel comic strip series but not in the Big Finish audio CD range or in the original novels series – without recourse to any more convoluted theories. It is an idea that has actually been suggested within some of the tie-in stories themselves, including *The Gallifrey Chronicles* (BBC Books, 2005) in the Eighth Doctor Adventures novels range and 'Zagreus' (Big Finish, 2003) in the audio CD range.

A further possible overarching solution is to regard any apparent discrepancies between stories as a consequence of damage done to the timelines in the last great Time War, and of the fact that the Time Lords are no longer around to keep order. As the Doctor himself says of the time disruption inadvertently created by Rose in 'Father's Day': 'There used to be laws stopping this kind of thing happening. My people would have stopped this. But they're all gone.' Are we now effectively in a 'post-canon' era, when anything goes, and the Doctor can quite conceivably live through the same adventures more than once? Perhaps so. This superficially attractive way of viewing things does have a major downside, though, in that it is effectively at odds with the whole idea of stories needing to be internally consistent: even if there were multiple failures of the 'beef test' within a single episode, this could be simply explained as a consequence of the lingering effects of the Time War – which might take a lot of pressure off the writer, but would arguably make it scarcely worthwhile for the viewer (or listener or reader, depending on the medium) to commit time and effort to following the plot.

In case I appear to have gone off at a complete tangent here, it should be noted that the relevance of this canonicity issue was certainly not lost on either Davies or Cornell in the discussions that led to the commissioning of 'Human Nature'/'The Family of Blood'. On the contrary, Davies initially feared that Cornell might turn down an invitation to adapt his novel for the TV series, on the basis that a new version of the same story could be thought to 'invalidate' the original – and even, perhaps, all the other *New Adventures* as well, by effectively forcing fans to regard them as non-canonical. Cornell also recognised that some dedicated *New Adventures* fans might be troubled about or even hostile to the notion of the novel being adapted for the TV series. Questioned about these concerns in an interview for Issue 382 of *Doctor Who Magazine*, he noted: 'Russell's qualms were that he thought I wouldn't want to do it because, in that wonderful noun that we've turned into a verb, it would "unbound"[74] *Human Nature* the book from the show's continuity, and I can see that – but I'm not going to turn down the chance to do this story in a different way, and it doesn't mean that the book stops existing. And I think the differences between the two will act as such an interesting index of the needs of the two different media and of where we are in the two different years ... I think it does probably put some kind of stake through the heart of the novel continuity, in that I think it's unlikely that the Doctor would run into the same set of people twice ... There's no bigger fan of the *New Adventures* than me, you know. I think they were the heart and soul of *Doctor Who* for so long. Fans do find intricate and lovely ways of dealing with that "continuity" stuff, and I hope they'll do so for me. And anyway, it's quite romantic and lovely in a way that the same terrible, tragic thing happens to him a couple of times.'

This 'terrible, tragic thing' all stems from the fact that the Doctor fails to consider the possibility that, when in human form, he might fall in love. In one way this seems rather strange, given that he fell in love with Rose Tyler even as a Time Lord, but really it just goes to show that, even after all these years, humans and their emotions are still, literally, alien to him – one consequence of which is, of course, his apparent obliviousness to Martha's feelings towards him. This feeds into what has by this point turned out to be the key theme of Series Three: what it means to be human. The Judoon spend most of their time in 'Smith and Jones' trying to distinguish between humans and non-humans; Shakespeare is described by the Doctor in 'The Shakespeare Code' as 'the most human human there's ever been'; 'Gridlock' is set in an era when are there no 'pure blood' humans left and the race has survived through cross-breeding with other species; 'Daleks in Manhattan'/'Evolution of the Daleks' is all about the differences between human thought and Dalek thought; Professor Lazarus in 'The Lazarus Experiment' wants to 'change what it means to be human'; and '42' involves people losing their human identity when they are possessed by a powerful alien sun-entity. It is in 'Human Nature'/'Family of Blood', however, that this theme is given its fullest and profoundest treatment, through the central device of the Doctor himself becoming human.

The same basic story could no doubt have been told using just about any period setting, or even perhaps a present-day one, but the decision to base it around a pre-First World War boys' school – in both the novel and its TV adaptation – was a very astute one on Cornell's part. The mores of this time and place dictate that Joan Redfern and John Smith will act with traditional English reserve and decorum; Joan may be more worldly-wise than John, having already had and lost one husband, but she is not about to seduce him or lead him off to bed, as might be the case in a more liberal era. This allows for a gentle and charming courtship to take place as their relationship develops to the point where John can pluck up the courage to invite Joan to accompany him to the dance in the village hall. Giving Martha a job as John's housemaid at the school was an equally inspired idea, in this case unique to the TV version, as it means that she is placed right in the thick of things and yet in a position where she can only stand by and watch as the romance blossoms. As

---

[74] This term derives from Big Finish's *Doctor Who Unbound* audio series, which presents alternative takes on *Doctor Who* and is explicitly designed not to be consistent with the TV show's continuity.

she so eloquently puts it, 'You had to go and fall in love with a human – and it wasn't me.'

Another benefit to the story of giving it this particular historical setting lies in the viewer's knowledge that – as Martha is aware, and as John has foreseen in his *A Journal of Impossible Things*; a wonderful notion, very well realised – the horrors of the War lie just a few months in the future, and are likely to claim the lives of most if not all of the pupils in the school. A sense of foreboding hangs like a pall over the drama, and it is disquieting to see the boys being trained in the use of a Vickers machine gun. Participation in cadet activities of this sort is in fact still fairly commonplace in British public schools even today, and would have been more or less compulsory in one like Farringham in 1913 (although rifles would generally have been used rather than a machine gun; in the novel, Rocastle states that he has been loaned the machine gun for a month by 'the Regiment', but this additional exposition was no doubt deemed unnecessary for the TV version). The script cleverly incorporates a number of references to past conflicts – John is seen teaching a class about the Battle of Waterloo of 1815; he later lends Tim Latimer a book about the Siege of Mafeking from 1899 to 1900 during the Second Boer War (in a scene slightly reminiscent of the one where the Doctor's granddaughter Susan borrows a book on the French Revolution from history teacher Barbara Wright in the series' very first episode, 'An Unearthly Child' (1963)); the headmaster, Rocastle, expects the pupils to regard the firing range targets as 'tribesmen from the Dark Continent' and expresses the hope that Latimer will one day have a 'just and proper war' in which to prove himself; Joan says that her husband Oliver died at the Battle of Spion Kop, which also took place during the Second Boer War, in January 1900; and the doorman at the village hall is collecting money for veterans of the Crimean War of 1853 to 1856. The effect of all this is to suggest how the established view of warfare based on experience of past battles has left the general population of England completely unprepared for the new and very different type of combat that is about to engulf Europe over the next four years, as glimpsed by Latimer in a brief vision of an incident from his future where he and another of the boys, Hutchinson, appear to be on the point of being killed by a falling shell in the trenches. There is a real sense of history being at a turning point here, with the cosy, time-honoured traditions and class distinctions of England, as effectively embodied in Farringham School, about to be swept away forever in the first major conflict of the 20th Century.

This, along with the imagery of the dark-suited schoolboys and the teachers in their mortarboards and gowns, evokes memories of James Hilton's famous novel *Goodbye, Mr Chips* (1934) and its various film and TV adaptations, in which the impact of the War on the life of the public school where the title character teaches is an important element of the story, as is the way that he is affected when he falls in love with a woman he meets in the wake of an accident. A more direct source of inspiration for Cornell's story, however, seems to have been R F Delderfield's novel *To Serve Them All My Days* (Hodder & Stoughton,1972), adapted for a BBC TV serial in 1980, which not only has a similar setting and explores many of the same ideas but also describes pupils undergoing military training and sees the central teacher character, David Powlett-Jones, marrying a nurse.

Martha's understanding of what is to come the following year makes her perhaps a little more sympathetic than she would otherwise be toward some of the schoolboys such as Hutchinson and Baines, with their arrogance and their racism (an historical reality that it is good to see being reflected here, in a rather more direct way than in 'The Shakespeare Code' and 'Daleks in Manhattan'/'Evolution of the Daleks'). It also no doubt helps that, as she intimates to her friend and fellow housemaid Jenny, she believes that she will soon be leaving this place and resuming her travels in time and space with the Doctor; an expectation that is, however, called starkly into question when she discovers that the aliens who have been pursuing them have somehow tracked them down.

The idea that the Doctor has taken on human form specifically in order to hide from these aliens is new to the TV version: in the novel, his motivation was more vaguely expressed in terms of simply wanting to experience and thus better understand what it is like to be human. Similarly, the depiction of the aliens as a family of telepathically-linked 'bodysnatchers' who take on the forms of four local people – Baines, a farmer named Clark, the young girl Lucy Cartwright and Jenny – is different: in the novel, although likewise a family, they are shapeshifters called Aubertides. These changes enhance the story, because they give the aliens the clear motivation (fully elucidated in 'The Family of Blood') of wanting to obtain the life of a Time Lord in order to extend their existence beyond their normal lifespan of about three months, and preferably forever. Distinctive touches such as their referring to each other as 'Son of Mine', 'Mother of Mine' and so on, tilting their heads on one side in unison and literally 'sniffing out' their victims, also help to make these a memorable new group of adversaries for the Doctor.

Another new element for the TV version are the creepy scarecrows that are somehow animated by the aliens to become their 'foot-soldiers'. The initial shot of a lone scarecrow that suddenly moves on its wooden support out in a field recalls the (seemingly motiveless) adoption of a scarecrow disguise by the Doctor's arch-enemy the Master in 'The Mark of the Rani' (1984), although the 'wave' gesture it makes appears to be a homage to the distinctive move made by the scarecrow in Dennis Potter's acclaimed *The Singing Detective* (BBC One, 1986). The idea of 'living scarecrows' has quite a long history in popular fiction, possibly the most well-known example being the rather-less-threatening Worzel Gummidge character created in 1936 by writer Barbara Euphan Todd (1890-1976) and brought to TV in a successful ITV series in the 1980s by third Doctor actor Jon Pertwee. The idea has also featured before in *Doctor Who* tie-ins: most notably the second Doctor's final *TV Comic* adventure, 'The Night Walkers' (1969), in which a group of animated scarecrows are revealed to have been sent by the Time Lords to trigger the Doctor's regeneration; and *The Hollow Men* (1998), a seventh Doctor novel by Keith Topping and Martin Day in BBC Books' Past Doctor Adventures series, in which scarecrows fashioned from the bodies of the dead stalk the country lanes around the village of Hexen Bridge. Scarecrows were, in addition, intended to appear as monsters in the planned movie *Doctor Who Meets Scratchman*, aka *Doctor Who and the Big Game*, which fell through around 1980 when fourth Doctor actor Tom Baker and his associates found themselves unable to raise the necessary finance to put it into production. 'Human Nature'/'The Family of Blood' is, though, the first *Doctor Who* story on TV to feature animated scarecrows, and they serve as another excellent new monster for the series, particularly as a hook for younger viewers in what is otherwise an unusually adult-orientated story.

Charles Palmer's direction here is absolutely superb, equalling if not bettering his work on 'Smith and Jones' and 'The Shakespeare Code', and the production values are exceptionally high in every respect. There is the occasional flaw – for instance, unlike with the equivalent device in the novel, no explanation is given as to why the Doctor's pocket watch cannot be retained in the TARDIS or put somewhere else for safekeeping, rather than being left lying around, albeit protected by a perception filter; and the scene where John Smith uses a cricket ball and some handily-arranged building materials and milk churns to save a woman pushing a pram from being struck by a falling piano is not only a little too 'cartoonish' in conception to be fully in keeping with the overall tone of the piece (it is unclear why the piano is being lifted in the first place, and one can almost imagine the situation having been set up by Wile E Coyote as a trap for the Road Runner; no doubt the piano is an Acme model) but is also marred somewhat by the fact that the only time the woman and the piano are ever seen together in the same shot is after the incident is over, so that the viewer never gets a clear sense of where they are in relation to each other beforehand. These shortcomings are few and far between, however, and for the most part, both script and production are hard to fault.

The guest roles are all very well cast, and the actors without exception give superlative performances. Jessica Hynes – best known, under her maiden name Jessica Stevenson, as one of the creators, writers and stars of the comedy series *Spaced* (Channel 4, 1999-2001) – strikes just the right note as the mature yet vivacious Joan Redfern; Harry Lloyd – Will Scarlett from BBC One's end-of-year fill-in for *Doctor Who*, *Robin Hood* (2006- ) – is great as Jeremy Baines, particularly with his wonderfully lopsided look after he becomes Son of Mine; child star Thomas Sangster – now actually 17 years old but still looking quite a bit younger – is compelling as the strangely gifted Tim Latimer; and even those in less central roles, such as Rebekah Staton as Jenny and Pip Torrens as Rocastle, acquit themselves extremely well.

As good as all these guest performers are, though, the real acting honours in this episode once again go to David Tennant, who is absolutely outstanding in his dual role, somehow succeeding in making John Smith seem completely different from the Doctor – the distinction being seen at perhaps its starkest in the incident where he blithely permits the other boys to give Latimer 'a beating' – while at the same time skilfully conveying the impression that he still has residual elements of his former, Time Lord persona remaining within him, set to break through in his dreams.

This is also an excellent episode for Freema Agyeman as Martha who, having been given the responsibility of looking after the Doctor in his human form, plays an unusually proactive and independent part in the action, particularly after the Doctor starts to fall for Joan – a possibility he failed to anticipate in the raft of instructions and contingency measures he left for her in his recorded message in the TARDIS, which is currently hidden away on emergency power (to avoid being detected by the aliens) in a local barn. By the end of the episode, it is actually starting to look as if Martha may have bitten off rather more than she can chew, as the action builds to an excellent cliffhanger that leaves the viewer wondering how on Earth she and her friends can possibly get out of their predicament, raising anticipation still further for the conclusion of events in the story's second instalment.

# 3.09 – THE FAMILY OF BLOOD

Writer: Paul Cornell
Director: Charles Palmer

## DEBUT TRANSMISSION DETAILS

BBC One
Date: 2 June 2007. Scheduled time: 7.10 pm. Actual time: 7.11 pm.

BBC Three
Date: 3 June 2007. Scheduled time: 8.00 pm. Actual time: 8.02 pm.

Duration: 42' 59"

## ADDITIONAL CREDITED CAST

Jessica Hynes (Joan Redfern), Rebekah Staton (Jenny), Thomas Sangster (Tim Latimer), Harry Lloyd (Baines), Tom Palmer (Hutchinson), Gerard Horan (Clark), Lauren Wilson (Lucy Cartwright), Pip Torrens (Rocastle), Matthew White (Phillips), Sophie Turner (Vicar). [75]

## PLOT

Martha manages to seize of one of the Family's guns and hold them off so that everyone can get away from the village hall. The Family attack the school, and Smith and the headmaster, Rocastle, organise the pupils to defend it with their cadet force weapons, shooting down the scarecrow soldiers. Martha, Smith and Joan then take refuge in a nearby cottage, where Latimer comes to them to return the pocket watch containing the Doctor's Time Lord persona. Although distraught at giving up his human life and future with Joan, Smith ultimately makes the courageous decision to change back into the Doctor. The Doctor then proceeds to deal with the Family by placing them in various types of eternal imprisonment. He and Martha depart in the TARDIS, leaving Joan to grieve the loss of Smith and Latimer to face his destiny as a soldier in the trenches of the First World War.

## QUOTE, UNQUOTE

- **Smith:** 'You're this Doctor's companion. Can't you help? What exactly do you do for him? Why does he need you?'
  **Martha:** 'Because he's lonely.'

---

[75] Two of the uncredited actors playing the Scarecrows were Ken Hosking and Ruari Mears.

**Smith:** 'And that's what you want me to become?'

- **Latimer:** 'I've seen him. He's like fire and ice and rage. He's like the night and the storm in the heart of the sun …'
  **Smith:** 'Stop it.'
  **Latimer:** 'He's ancient and forever. He burns at the centre of time and he can see the turn of the universe.'
  **Smith:** 'Stop it! I said, stop it!'
  **Latimer:** 'And … he's wonderful.'
- **Joan:** 'He was braver than you, in the end, that ordinary man. You chose to change; he chose to die.'

## CONTINUITY POINTS

- Son of Mine says of the scarecrows: 'I made them myself … molecular fringe animation, fashioned in the shape of straw men.' This may explain why there are so many of them, and also why they all look virtually identical, whereas real scarecrows tend to differ markedly in appearance.
- The aliens give their full name – the Family of Blood – for the first time in this episode, in the scene where they confront the headmaster, Rocastle, outside the school.
- When Latimer asks why the pocket watch spoke to him, Smith, drawing on the Doctor's thoughts, says, 'Oh, low level telepathic fields. You were born with them. Just an extra synaptic engram, causing ...' This accounts for Latimer's unusual mental abilities.
- Most of the action of this episode takes place on the night of 11 November 1913, with the Doctor and Martha departing presumably the following day. In the scene in the trenches, Latimer tells Hutchinson that he will save him, as he promised 'all those years ago'. As this is presumably a reference back to the events of 'The Family of Blood', it would suggest that the scene is set toward the end of the First World War, probably in 1917 or 1918. It is unclear in what year the final scene at the war memorial is set; if it is in 2008 – as Martha indicates in her (not necessarily reliable) MySpace blog – then Latimer would be around 110 years old, making him one of the oldest men in Europe. However, his appearance would indicate that he is rather younger than that, and the vicar seems to be holding the Alternative Service Book (ASB), which was not generally in use after December 2000. Given that women were first ordained in the Church of England in 1987, this suggests that the scene actually occurs sometime between 1987 and 2000, making Latimer somewhere between about 90 and 100 years old.
- The unbreakable chains in which the Doctor imprisons Father of Mine were 'forged in the heart of a dwarf star'. Dwarf star alloy was first mentioned in *Doctor Who* in 'Warriors' Gate' (1980), where it was described as the only material dense enough to trap time sensitives, and has also featured in a number of the tie-in novels. How exactly this causes Father of Mine to live forever in his imprisonment, as is implied, is unclear.

## PRODUCTION NOTES

- 'The Family of Blood' was made with 'Human Nature' in Block 6 of production on Series Three. These episodes were moved forward from Block 7 because the scripts were ready early, and consequently were directed by Charles Palmer rather than, as had originally been intended, Graham Harper.

- The scene where the Doctor and Martha say goodbye to Tim Latimer and depart in the TARDIS was shot in the same field used for the landing site of the Family's invisible spaceship. The episode's closing scene was shot at a real war memorial on the green outside Llandaff Cathedral in Cardiff.

- It was Russell T Davies's suggestion to include the scarecrows in the story. After initially resisting the idea, writer Paul Cornell quickly warmed to it. The bodies were the responsibility of costume designer Louise Page. The heads meanwhile were handled by Neill Gorton and his Millennium FX company, and their design was based in part on the look of Tim Burton's film *The Nightmare Before Christmas* (Touchstone Pictures, 1993); eight heads were made in total, but only seven of these were actually used in the production.

- The hymn 'To Be A Pilgrim' is again heard in this episode, over the scene where the schoolboys fire their guns at the advancing scarecrows.

- David Tennant's old-age make-up, for the scene where John Smith sees a vision of a potential future life with Joan, took about four hours to apply, although the scene itself took only about a quarter of an hour to record.

- The words spoken by the vicar at the end of the episode are from the third and fourth stanzas of Laurence Binyon's poem 'For the Fallen' (1914) (with a few words from the end of the fifth stanza briefly audible out of sequence at the start), which feature as part of the standard Remembrance Service in the Church of England – although they were never in fact included in the Alternative Service Book from which the vicar appears to be reading, suggesting that she may have slipped a piece of paper into the book with these words on.

- A number of shots included in the 'Next Time ...' trailer at the end of 'Human Nature' are not actually seen in 'The Family of Blood', having been removed during editing. These include Martha saying 'Save us!' to Smith and Smith replying 'I am not the Doctor!' – both of which were also featured in the 'red-button' Series Three trailer made available prior to transmission of 'Smith and Jones' – plus a shot of the Doctor loosening his tie in front of the mirror.

- Sections of Latimer's description of the Doctor – 'He's fire, and ice, and rage ...' – were included not only in the 'Next Time ...' trailer at the end of 'Human Nature' but also in the 'red button' Series Three trailer and the 'Coming Soon ...' trailer at the end of 'The Lazarus Experiment'. In the latter two cases, however, the sound was treated electronically to lower it in pitch, creating the impression that an older person was speaking.

- The idea underlying the unusual design of the hand-held ray-guns used by the Family was that each would consist of a metal casing with a worm-like alien creature fitted within: when the trigger was pressed, the creature would spit out the energy ray.

## UNFOUNDED PRE-TRANSMISSION RUMOURS

- The Family of Blood would be vampires or Plasmavores. (As it is never made clear exactly why they call themselves by that name, it is just possible that this rumour could actually be true.)
- The Doctor would have children with Joan and, because these would be half-Time Lord, this would explain why, in 'Gridlock', the Face of Boe told him 'You are not alone'.
- The Family of Blood would have some connection to the Face of Boe, because their names both have the initials 'FOB', and this would also relate in some way to the Doctor's 'fob' watch.

## OOPS!

- There is a continuity error in the scene where Daughter of Mine confronts Rocastle in the school courtyard: the balloon she is holding is tied to her left hand in some shots but to her right hand in others.
- Son of Mine says that his sister, trapped in 'every mirror', is visited by the Doctor 'once a year, every year', which implies that the Doctor looks in a mirror only once a year. (Implausible though this might seem, it could explain why the ninth Doctor is interested to see the shape of his ears when he looks in a mirror in 'Rose', despite other evidence suggesting that it has been quite some time since he regenerated from the eighth Doctor.)

## PRESS REACTION

- 'The period of 1913 is presented absolutely fantastically in this cracking two-part story. Everything, from the actors right down to the subtleties of accent and décor, feels so tangibly right. There are many sweet moments, especially for long-[standing] fans as we see a couple of subtle nods to the series' past. Then when the aliens turn up in search of their Time Lord prey, things just get better, and the scarecrows – though slightly Auton-ish in concept – look very haunting as they lumber through the night. The main star on the "baddie" front, however, is Harry Lloyd's Baines, whose possessed youth is an enjoyable force to contend with.' Anthony Lamb, *TV Zone* Issue 217, July 2007.
- 'As the Family of Blood continue to hound the unwitting John Smith for his Time Lord DNA, they resort to violence of a terrorist magnitude to flush him out, revelling in the sport of the hunt. This is an England one year away from war, and we've already had scenes of the schoolboys training as cadets. Now they are forced into battle, albeit against an army of scarecrows, but bullets still fly, straw bodies are cut to pieces and tears flow freely down the faces of the boys who in the space of a minute had to become men. This battle sequence is beautifully shot by Charles Palmer, counterpointed by the lonely figure of Smith in the background, rifle raised, but unable to fire. The Doctor never uses guns, but not for reasons of cowardice. Is John Smith a coward? Possibly, but it disgusts him to see these boys fighting, and [he] leads them away from the school to safety. Is the distance between this human man and the Doctor not as far as we're led to believe?' Mark Wright, *The Stage* website, 3 June 2007.

## FAN COMMENT

- 'I thought that it was wonderfully ironic that the reason [why] the Doctor was hiding was [that] he was being merciful to the poor misguided creatures pursuing him. The Doctor is now a lot like David Banner in *The Incredible Hulk* in that you do not want to make him angry, you really would not like him when he is angry. This of course is the direct antithesis of Terrance Dicks's "never cruel or cowardly" description of the Doctor. The Family of Blood have pushed the Doctor so far that he inflicts upon each of them punishments that are incredibly cruel and cowardly, because each one picks on the basic nature of the victim and amplifies it. Father of Mine is the muscles of the organisation, so he is imprisoned in a method that defeats his strength; Mother of Mine is the strategist looking for others' weaknesses so she is imprisoned in a cage that will never weaken; Daughter of Mine is the spy and is trapped in a mirror, forever looking out on the world; whilst Son of Mine, the technician, is trapped forever in a technical bubble. If these punishments are not cruel and unusual, I don't know what is.' John Campbell Rees, The Journal of the Browncoat Cat website, 5 June 2006.

- 'The main point of controversy [arising from] "The Family of Blood" is not the Doctor's fragility or "human frailty" but the fact that by condemning the Family to "hell" the Doctor, for the first time, behaves like a vengeful Old Testament God. I can't imagine Tom Baker's Doctor believing in this kind of "revenge", and I for one find it disturbing that the Doctor thinks condemning living things to "eternal torment" is better than life imprisonment or even killing them … My son, unprompted, after the episode said that he thought what the Doctor had done to the Family was worse than death because it would never end. It clearly affected him and made him think. I think he found it a bit disturbing. This may be a good thing and I [recognise] that [some] fans get upset because [they think that] the Doctor is no longer a moral figure. I don't personally agree with this – I think he now has a "different" morality; one that is more akin [to] the *Daily Mail*'s … "vengeful" idea of morality. What the Doctor did is worse than [what] the "life should mean life" school [advocate] if you think about it. In other words, the Doctor is morally moving away from his "liberal" values and turning into a "hanger and flogger" arguably.' Michael Proctor, Outpost Gallifrey forum, 9 June 2007.

- 'Cornell's script is just as damning of the Doctor as it is forgiving, and for exactly the right reasons. The Doctor doesn't come across as completely likeable, because he's lost his innocence long ago … probably even before the [Time] War, [being] willing to put the individual after the big picture, and having been corrupted by his own knowledge and personal responsibility. This should not be used to excuse the Doctor's final defeat of the Family completely, however, because that itself is evidence just as much as anything of the Doctor's moral ambiguity. At the end of the day, the Doctor chooses to imprison them for eternity, rather than kill them. And is that right? The Doctor has always had a failing of being unable to kill in cold blood, even if it's "justified", so he chooses to grant their wish, in imprisoning them – and embrace the irony of the moment. Despite this, … his choice is fundamentally flawed, as it's one thing to imprison someone in mortal form, it's quite another to torment them [with an] immortal existence of boredom. This indicates, disturbingly, that he's angry that, after such mercy to them on his part, they could be able to cause such death and suffering, and angry at himself for not having seen that.' 'Dingdongalistic', Dingdongalistic Reviews website, 4 June 2007.

- 'After a flurry of activity, Paul Cornell gradually brings back "Human Nature"'s emotional resonance and embeds it into the action, to produce – in the sequence of tearful cadets seeing off an army of scarecrows – something tense, moving and utterly compelling. Better yet is what happens when things calm down. It was obvious that nothing could happen until Timothy turned up with the watch, but what I hadn't anticipated was how unhappy John Smith would be about it. The following stand-off is not merely as good as anything I've ever seen in *Doctor Who*, it is up there with the best television ever. Genuinely philosophical (there are shades of *Solaris* in the existential dilemma of the fictional construct who yearns for reality) and gut-wrenchingly sad (driven by an extraordinary, totally un-Doctor-like performance from David Tennant), it is sheer brilliance.' Simon Kinnear, Shockeye Online website, June 2007.

- 'Tennant paints us a picture of John Smith. The very nervous tics of the man are different, stretching his face into contortions as he tries to reshape his inner thoughts to take in the changes to his world. This is a scarred, smart, sympathetic man: terrified of the responsibility as much as desperate at the loss he is being asked to [suffer]; fast enough to realise that, whatever he means to anyone else, the return of this "Doctor" means the end of his own separate identity, effectively his death. There's a fourth-wall-breaking irony here as John Smith is a "written character" who knows that his existence will end when the writer decides that his story is over ... The Nottingham reference[76] is not a *Robin Hood* in-joke at Harry Lloyd's (Will Scarlett's[77]) expense, but more likely refers to Lemuel Gulliver, born at his father's small estate in Nottingham, who met the Doctor in "The Mind Robber" [1968]. Mr Smith, like that Gulliver, does not realise at the time that he is a fictional character.' 'Millennium Dome', Millennium Elephant website, 5 June 2007.

- '[The scene at the war memorial] was the moving moment of the whole episode for me. It was beautifully scripted. The last time I saw a mainstream programme touching on this subject so movingly was *Blackadder Goes Forth* when the troops went over the top of the trench, the music stopped, and the field of fire turned into a field of poppies. I will be honest, I had tears in my eyes tonight. This whole storyline was one of personal sacrifice be it John Smith's/the Doctor's or the soldiers'. What an amazing story. Wonderfully acted and superbly brought to the screen. The parallels between [John Smith's] own question of why he could not have the life he wanted and that of the millions of people during the First World War who must have just wanted the same from life, love and happiness but had their worlds destroyed instead, was wonderfully woven in the story. The scenes in the trenches gave a palpable feel of the sheer destruction and hellish chaos that ensued.' Emma Jane Shepherd, david-tennant.com website, June 2007.

---

[76] John Smith is said in the story to have grown up in Nottingham.

[77] Harry Lloyd plays Will Scarlett in the BBC One series *Robin Hood* (2006- ).

## ANALYSIS

One of the big puzzles implicit in 'Human Nature' – why has the Doctor taken the seemingly rather cowardly step of hiding from this particular group of aliens, instead of facing and defeating them as he has many other, surely more powerful adversaries in the past? – is resolved at the end of 'The Family of Blood' in a completely unexpected way. It turns out that he has hidden not in order to save himself, but in order to be kind to the aliens. Specifically, he has tried to allow them the opportunity to live out their natural, albeit short, lives without having to face his wrath. When that wrath is ultimately turned on them, it is to shocking effect, as he gives them the immortality they craved by trapping them in various kinds of 'living death' – recalling how those who sought immortality were turned into immobile living statues by Rassilon, one of the founders of Time Lord society, in the series' twentieth anniversary story, 'The Five Doctors' (1983). This touches on some of the same themes as 'The Lazarus Experiment', in that the latter also involves someone trying to extend his life way beyond its normal span, but arguably shows a harder, more pitiless edge to the Doctor's character than ever before, following up on the indications of a darker side to his nature in his destruction of the Racnoss at the conclusion of 'The Runaway Bride' (a clip of which is seen when Latimer briefly opens the Doctor's pocket watch to warn off Daughter of Mine) and belying his apparent readiness to be more merciful in his treatment of Dalek Caan at the end of 'Evolution of the Daleks'. Here, we see the full implications of him being a 'no second chances' sort of man, as he describes himself in 'The Christmas Invasion'.

One of the great things about Paul Cornell's script for this episode is that it poses some very thought-provoking questions that go right to the heart of the Doctor's nature, yet offers no easy answers. On one view, it would have been better for all concerned had the Doctor dealt with the Family in the first place. That way, as Joan suggests, they would never have come to the England of 1913, and the deaths of many innocent people would have been avoided. Was his decision to hide from the Family a cowardly one after all, in that it effectively sought to absolve him of moral responsibility for their fate, ultimately at the cost of a great deal of death and suffering for others? Admittedly he was not to know that his plan would fail and that the Family would track him down to his hiding place, which was actually decided on not by him but by the TARDIS (and was arguably a very poor choice at that, with so many people, and particularly children, in the vicinity), but there must always have been a risk that that would happen; and this points up a more general truth that – just as Francine was told by agents of the mysterious Mr Saxon in 'The Lazarus Experiment', and as Rose was warned by her internet contact Clive way back in 'Rose' – killing and destruction tend to follow the Doctor wherever he goes. And if it really was his intention to be kind to the Family, would it not have been preferable for him to have simply kept them imprisoned in the TARDIS until they died of natural causes a short time later, rather than have left them in situations of cruel torment forever more? Is his harsh treatment of the Family at the end of the story to some degree an act of vengeance on his part, on account of their having deprived him of the kind of normal human life that – as he said in his ninth incarnation back in Cornell's 'Father's Day' – he thought he could never lead? Had the Family not succeeded in tracking him down, and had he not consequently been forced to make the painful decision to revert to being a Time Lord, would he actually have chosen to remain in human form as John Smith and live out the remainder of his life with Joan, getting married, having children and ultimately dying as an old man, as seen in their – very moving – shared vision of a potential future together? If so, then what would have become of Martha? There is sufficient food for thought here to occupy the viewer's mind for a long time after the closing credits have faded away.

The idea of the Doctor taking on human form slightly recalls that of superheroes adopting human *alter ego*s or even giving up their powers in order to live among mortals, as featured in a number of comic book stories and perhaps most notably in the movie *Superman II* (Warner Brothers, 1980), in which Superman first hides behind his usual alias of Clark Kent and then actually becomes human in order to start a full relationship with his girlfriend Lois Lane. The idea is treated with far greater sophistication in 'Human Nature'/'The Family of Blood', however, and actually puts the viewer rather more in mind of Martin Scorsese's controversial film *The Last Temptation of Christ* (Universal Pictures, 1988), toward the end of which Jesus is seen to be tempted by Satan with a vision of life as an ordinary human being, complete with a wife and family – a possibility that Jesus eventually rejects in favour of sacrificing himself on the cross. John Smith's status as the metaphorical human 'son' of the Doctor – the 'lonely god', as he is described by implication in 'New Earth' – who resists temptation and sacrifices himself in order to save humanity, clearly echoes the Biblical story of Christ; and this is carried through into the imagery of the scarecrows, and ultimately Son of Mine, suspended on their cruciform supports out in the fields. It is also a clear example of the wider 'hero's journey' or monomyth archetype as described by Joseph Campbell in his book *The Hero with a Thousand Faces* (Princeton University Press, 1949), to which Russell T Davies specifically alludes in *Doctor Who Confidential*.

The fated romance between Joan and John, and the courageous, self-sacrificing decision that John eventually makes to go back to being the Doctor, take the series into some of the most intensely emotional territory it has yet explored. Jessica Hynes and David Tennant are again terrific here. Tennant in particular continues to shine with his brilliant portrayal of two very different yet connected characters. The contrast between the two is neatly illustrated in the scene where John takes back his pocket watch at the Cartwrights' cottage and, for just a few seconds, starts to speak as the Doctor would. The sudden switch from one character to the other, and then back again, as if at the press of a button, is superbly done, and leaves the viewer full of admiration for the actor's skill. For Joan, however, the contrast is most starkly highlighted in the heartrending scene where the Doctor returns to the cottage after consigning the Family to their fates. His alien detachment, so different from Smith's human warmth, is strikingly apparent here, as he answers simply 'No' when she asks if he will change back (echoing his response to Rose in the 2005 *Children in Need* special when she asks if he can reverse his regeneration), and then as he proceeds to invite her to accompany him on his travels in the TARDIS, utterly failing to grasp why she is so distraught, as well as showing himself once again to be completely insensitive to the feelings of the – fortunately absent – Martha, who has earlier admitted that she loves him. The Doctor's protestation that he still carries his human persona within him and is capable of all the same things that Smith was rings rather hollow, and Joan's cold dismissal of him – 'You can go' –

seems entirely justified in the circumstances.

The days of the Doctor being portrayed as an unambiguously heroic figure, whose actions could never be considered cruel or cowardly (a celebrated phrase coined by classic series script editor, writer and novelist Terrance Dicks and previously quoted with approval by Cornell), are now well and truly behind us, it would seem; the *Doctor Who* universe is no longer a place of moral certainties, as was arguably the case back in the old days, and this added degree of sophistication is yet another debt that the new series owes to the tie-in novels. Where 'The Family of Blood' perhaps breaks new ground is in the suggestion that, as he silently turns and walks away from Joan, leaving her to her grief, the Doctor actually realises how profoundly he has misread the situation, and how incapable he is of experiencing love in human terms. This begs the question, is he really oblivious to Martha's feelings for him, or has he simply chosen to give that impression, recognising his inability to respond in kind and fearing the pain he could cause, both for her and for himself, if he were to become involved with her to the same extent as he did with Rose? Is he, in other words, hiding himself from Martha, just as he tried to hide from the Family? He certainly seems very happy to go along with her subsequent, none-too-convincing pretence that she told him she loved him simply as part of her efforts to persuade him to reassume his Time Lord persona.

The other themes established in 'Human Nature' are also developed further in 'The Family of Blood'; in particular, the looming horror of the First World War continues to figure significantly in the drama. There is some fantastic dialogue here. 'War is coming,' Baines – or, rather, Son of Mine – tells the headmaster, Rocastle. 'In foreign fields, war of the whole wide world, with all your boys falling down in the mud. Do you think they will thank the man who taught them it was glorious?' 'Don't you forget, boy,' Rocastle replies, 'I've been a soldier. I was in South Africa. I used my dead mates for sandbags; I fought with the butt of my rifle when the bullets ran out; and I would go back there tomorrow, for King and country!' Son of Mine then promptly turns his gun on the accompanying teacher, Phillips, and disintegrates him, the alien weapon effectively acting as a metaphor for all the tanks and other modern war machines that will make the First World War so different from the conflict that Rocastle experienced in South Africa; and the rattled headmaster turns tail and runs back inside the school. Later, the family send destruction raining down on the local village, in a grim foreshadowing of the remorseless bombardment of the trenches in the coming conflict.

The sequences in which the pupils are assembled behind a barricade in the school courtyard and required to put their gun training into practice against a real enemy, causing them visible fear and distress, are deeply affecting, and not in the least undermined by the fact that the targets are merely animated scarecrows rather than people – particularly as they do not fully grasp this until afterwards. The only slight oddity about this scene is that, given that the scarecrows are not alive in the first place, it is difficult to understand why the bullets should have any effect on them. I was half expecting that, having been shot down, they would suddenly rise up and start lolloping forward again, until perhaps someone hit upon the idea of setting them alight; but that would possibly have been a little *too* scary for younger viewers, and would certainly have lessened their impact as a metaphor for the hapless young troops who would be mown down by gunfire in the fields of Europe in the years to come.

Tim Latimer's recognition of the pointlessness of the battle in the courtyard again marks him out as different from the other pupils, and his response of, 'Oh yes, sir, every time,' when the older boy Hutchinson calls him a coward – although it is not, in fact, cowardice that causes him to run back to the school building, but the awareness that the pocket watch he took from Smith's room may afford him a way to help – recalls the ninth Doctor's decision to be a coward rather than a killer – 'Coward, any day' – when challenged by the Dalek Emperor in 'The Parting of the Ways'. Smith's own inability to bring himself to fire his rifle at the scarecrows, and his realisation that it is wrong for the boys to be using guns like this, is a key moment for his character, attesting to the essential goodness seen in him by Joan.

Scenes of guns being fired in a public school perhaps inevitably recall the sequences of armed rebellion by similarly attired schoolboys in a similar setting in Lindsay Anderson's cult film *if ...*(Paramount, 1968), which deals with some of the same themes of English values and traditions. However, whereas *if ...* has a pro-revolution agenda and invites consideration of the idea that 'There's no such thing as a wrong war', 'Human Nature'/'The Family of Blood' depicts conflict in a far more negative light. While it would be wrong to suggest that the story preaches a straightforward anti-war message – in fact, on the contrary, it suggests that it can sometimes be right to make a stand and fight for the greater good – it certainly comes across as a damning indictment of the First World War, with all its senseless and futile slaughter – and Cornell has confirmed in interviews that this was indeed his intention.

The brief scene of Latimer with Hutchinson in the trenches some years later plays out just like his vision in 'Human Nature'; but with the benefit of that foresight, he is able to get them out of the path of the falling shell and save their lives. Over the start of this, David Tennant speaks the following poignant words: 'In June 1914, an Archduke of Austria was shot by a Serbian, and this then led, through nations having treaties with nations, like a line of dominoes falling, to some boys from England walking together in France, on a terrible day.' This is the episode's second use of a 'narration' device – the first having come a few minutes earlier with Son of Mine delivering a monologue about the fates of the four Family members – and is something of a rarity for *Doctor Who*. In fact, I can think of only three other instances previously in the series where characters have effectively recounted aspects of the plot directly to the audience: the first at the start of 'The Deadly Assassin' (1977), the second at the start of the TV Movie (1996) and the third, Rose's reflection on the day she 'died', in 'Army of Ghosts'/'Doomsday'. In this particular case, it is unclear if it is the Doctor who is talking, or John Smith giving one of his history lessons, or even – given that the words are really just spoken rather than acted – Tennant himself addressing the audience, in the manner of a documentary voiceover (albeit in an English accent rather than his natural Scottish one). It is, at any rate, a highly effective departure from the norm.

Immediately following this comes a great little coda scene in which the Doctor and Martha look on respectfully from a distance as a now-elderly Latimer, seated in a wheelchair and with numerous medals adorning his chest, attends a modern-day Remembrance Service at a war memorial – with a woman vicar officiating, as if to emphasise the extent to which society has changed since 1913. This is another emotionally-charged moment, guaranteed to have many a viewer wiping a tear from the eye, and serves also to highlight the true significance of Armistice Day for those members of the audience – particularly, perhaps, the younger ones – on whom this may hitherto have been lost. Also notable – and possibly indicative of a shift in Cornell's attitudes since he wrote the novel in 1995 – is the fact that the Doctor and Martha wear conventional red poppies, whereas in the equivalent passage in the novel, the poppy worn and dropped by Dean (which is Tim's surname in the original), and then picked up and affixed to his jacket by the Doctor, is white – the 'pacifist's poppy', denoting not only remembrance of the dead but also hope of an end to all wars – in light of the fact that, in this version, Dean's involvement in the War was not as a soldier but as a member of the Red Cross.

The terrible weather that Charles Palmer and his team encountered on location may have made it a difficult and unpleasant shoot at times – as a number of those involved have since recalled in interviews – but it actually works very much to the benefit of the production, giving it a suitably 'wintry' look. This is well illustrated by the scene where the Doctor and Martha bid farewell to the young Latimer outside the TARDIS: the fact that this is played out in torrential rain, with the three actors clearly getting soaked, is so unusual and striking that it makes the whole thing seem somehow more 'real', and complements perfectly the ominous tenor of their discussion about the forthcoming War. The aforementioned scene in the trenches also benefits greatly from the fact that the two actors, Thomas Sangster as Latimer and Tom Palmer (no relation to the director) as Hutchinson, are obviously bedraggled and wallowing in mud, as soldiers in that situation would often have been in reality.

The only really weak scene in the episode – indeed, in the whole two-part story – is the one where the Doctor enters the Family's spaceship and, pretending still to be John Smith, causes it to self destruct by 'accidentally' falling against a particular combination of buttons and levers. Not only is this extremely corny and at odds with the overall tone of the production, but the idea that the Doctor can disguise his Time Lord nature just by using 'a simple olfactory misdirection', which he describes as 'an elementary trick in certain parts of the galaxy', tends to undermine the whole premise of the story, because it suggests that he could have hidden from the Family without needing to turn himself into a human at all.

This rather ill-judged scene aside, it is actually quite difficult to write about 'Human Nature'/'The Family of Blood' without ultimately resorting to reeling off a long succession of superlatives. Just as *Human Nature*, in its original version, is one of the most notable and highly-regarded *Doctor Who* novels ever to have been published, so its small screen adaptation can be counted one of the very best TV stories ever to have been produced, and an outstanding piece of drama by any standards.

# 3.10 – BLINK

Writer: Steven Moffat
Director: Hettie Macdonald

## DEBUT TRANSMISSION DETAILS

BBC One
Date: 9 June 2007. Scheduled time: 7.10 pm. Actual time: 7.09 pm.

BBC Three
Date: 10 June 2007. Scheduled time: 8.00 pm. Actual time: 8.01 pm.

Duration: 43' 42"

## ADDITIONAL CREDITED CAST

Carey Mulligan (Sally Sparrow[78]), Lucy Gaskell (Kathy Nightingale[79]), Finlay Robertson (Larry Nightingale), Richard Cant (Malcolm Wainwright), Michael Obiora (Billy Shipton), Louis Mahoney (Old Billy), Thomas Nelstrop (Ben Wainwright[80]), Ian Boldsworth (Banto), Ray Sawyer (Desk Sergeant).[81]

## PLOT

Four Weeping Angels – aliens who kill by sending their victims back in time and absorbing the energy of their lost futures, and who are transformed into statues when in the sight of any other living creature – are inhabiting a run-down house called Wester Drumlins in 2007. They have sent the Doctor and Martha back to 1969, and are now trying to gain access to the TARDIS to feed off the energy within. A young woman named Sally Sparrow visits Wester Drumlins and comes across the first of a series of messages left by the Doctor in 1969 specifically for her to find in 2007. Trying to get to the bottom of this mystery, Sally is aided by her

---

[78] Credited as simply 'Sally' in *Radio Times*, to avoid giving away in advance the fact that this episode is based on the *Doctor Who Annual 2006* story 'What I Did on My Christmas Holidays' by Sally Sparrow.

[79] Kathy's full married name and dates of birth and death, as recorded on the headstone at her and her husband's grave, are 'Katherine Costello Wainright (1902-1987)' – the birth date being a false one chosen by her after she was transported back in time from 2007 to 1920.

[80] Ben's full name and dates of birth and death, as seen on the headstone, are 'Benjamin Wainright (1897-1962)'.

[81] The Weeping Angels were played, uncredited, by Aga Blonska and Elen Thomas; in scenes where more than two appeared, the others were dummies.

friend Kathy Nightingale, who is sent back to 1920 by the Weeping Angels; by a policeman, DI Billy Shipton, who is sent back to 1969, where he picks up a message from the Doctor that he eventually delivers to Sally as an old man in 2007, on the night of his death; and Kathy's brother Larry. Kathy and Larry eventually succeed in sending the TARDIS back to the Doctor and Martha – which was the aim of the Doctor's messages – leaving the Weeping Angels stuck in the cellar of Wester Drulims, looking at one another in a circle. A year later, Sally meets the Doctor in the street outside a shop that she and Larry are running. Realising that this is at a point in the Doctor's life before he encounters the Weeping Angels at Wester Drumlins, she gives him a folder of information that will tell him what to do when he gets trapped in 1969 in order to extricate himself from the situation by leaving messages for her to find in 2007 – thus completing a temporal paradox.

## QUOTE, UNQUOTE

- **Doctor**: 'Tracked you down with this. This is my timey-wimey detector. Goes ding when there's stuff. Also, it can boil an egg at 30 paces. Whether you want it to or not, actually, so I've learned to stay away from hens. It's not pretty when they blow.'
- **Doctor:** '"The Lonely Assassins" they used to be called. No-one quite knows where they came from, but they're as old as the universe, or very nearly, and they have survived this long because they have the most perfect defence system ever evolved: they're quantum locked; they don't exist when they're being observed. The moment they're seen by any other living creature, they freeze into rock. No choice: it's a fact of their biology. In the sight of any living thing, they literally turn to stone. And you can't kill a stone. 'Course, a stone can't kill you either; but then you turn your head away, then you blink, and oh yes it can … That's why they cover their eyes: they're not weeping; they can't risk looking at each other. Their greatest asset is their greatest curse. They can never be seen. Loneliest creatures in the universe.'

## CONTINUITY POINTS

- Martha's MySpace blog states that it is in 2007 that she and the Doctor go to Wester Drumlins and get sent back in time by the Weeping Angels. Sally pays her first visit to the house later the same year, this date being confirmed both in the letter that Kathy sends her and, indirectly, in the Doctor's DVD message from 1969 (when he indicates that he is replying to Sally's words 38 years before she says them). It is before nightfall when she arrives, although the sky is overcast and there is heavy rain falling. She calls on Kathy at 1.00 am that night, and goes back to Wester Drumlins with her some time the next day. It is later the same day, following Kathy's disappearance, that Sally visits the police station and meets the young Billy Shipton, who tells her that abandoned cars have been turning up outside Wester Drumlins for the past two years – i.e. since 2005, which is presumably therefore when the Weeping Angels first arrived there. Not long after – with 'the same rain' still falling – she visits the old Billy in hospital. It is daylight outside when she arrives, and again when she leaves after Billy's death. It is unclear how long she is there in between, but as Billy refers to 'the night I die', it seems likely that she stays all night and leaves the following morning. It is just possible, on the other hand, that Billy dies shortly before dusk on the first day. It is after dark when Sally subsequently phones Larry – who appears to be on the point of leaving work, as he already has his jacket and bag on when he answers – and gets him to meet her at Wester Drumlins, where they eventually succeed in sending the TARDIS back to the Doctor. This action involving Sally probably therefore spans about two and a half days, although it is just possible that it could be only a day and a half. Sally meets the Doctor outside the DVD and book shop a year later.

- It is unclear how long the Doctor and Martha spend in 1969 while waiting to be rescued. It is long enough for Martha to have got a job as a shop assistant, and for the Doctor to have acted upon the information given to him by Sally, left the writing behind the wallpaper, filmed his message, met the young Billy Shipton, and so on, so it could be weeks or even months. In her MySpace blog, Martha says that it is 'a few weeks' and says that she and the Doctor rented a small flat.

- The newspaper being read by Ben when Kathy arrives in 1920 is an edition of the *Hull Times* dated '5th December 1920'. The lead story refers to a 'Storm', and there is also a news item headlined 'Hull FC to Face Hull Kingston Rovers …' – a reference to two rugby teams based in Hull. (Although there was indeed a *Hull Times* in 1920 – unlike today, when the main local newspaper in that area is the *Hull Daily Mail* – this copy was mocked up for the programme by BBC Wales Graphics.)

- There is a sign outside Wester Drumlins bearing the words 'Danger', 'Keep Out', 'Unsafe Structure' and, at the bottom, 'London District Council'. This implies that the story is set somewhere in London (although there is no such thing as a London District Council in our universe). The DVD shop is said to be in 'Queen Street'.

- It is unclear how the Weeping Angels move, as this is never seen in the episode. Possibly they simply fly – at one point a 'flapping wings' sound is heard just before one appears, and in another scene a pair of them move between two high vantage points on opposite sides of the road outside the police station, in the blink of Sally's eye. They are able to transfer the TARDIS from the basement of the police station to the cellar of Wester Drumlins, presumably by carrying it there a short distance at a time, whenever they are unobserved.

- The elderly Billy says that the Doctor told him in 1969 that if he were to meet Sally again at a point in her life prior to their initial encounter when he was a young man, this would result in the destruction of 'two-thirds of the universe'. It is possible that this was an exaggeration on the Doctor's part, to emphasise the harmful consequences of damaging the time lines.

- The Doctor tells Sally 'I'm rubbish at weddings, especially my own.' This could be a reference to the vision that he – or, more precisely, John Smith – had in 'The Family of Blood' of his potential future wedding to Joan Redfern, or to one or more weddings unseen in the TV series. In the tie-in novels, the Doctor gets married in Lawrence Miles's *The Adventuress of Henrietta Street* (BBC Books, 2001).

- Some fans have speculated that Kathy's third child, named Sally after Sally Sparrow, is the same Sally that Billy Shipton later marries. While this would be possible in terms of their ages, there is nothing in the episode itself to confirm it.

## PRODUCTION NOTES

- 'Blink' was made as a stand-alone Block 5 of production on Series Three, at the same time as other episodes (chiefly 'Human Nature'/'The Family of Blood'). Consequently David Tennant did only two days' recording in total for the episode, and many of the behind-the-scenes crew members were not those normally assigned to *Doctor Who*; a number had previously worked on *Torchwood*.
- Writer Steven Moffat had originally been due to contribute either a one- or two-part story earlier on in Series Three, but had been forced to pull out of this due to other commitments, principally on his serial *Jekyll* (BBC One, 2007). Feeling that he had messed the *Doctor Who* team around, he volunteered to write instead this year's 'Doctor-lite' episode – i.e. the episode in which, for scheduling reasons, the Doctor and his companion would be able to make only brief appearances. He actually welcomed the opportunity to write an episode with a diminished role for the Doctor, as he explained in an interview published in Issue 351 of *Starburst* in July 2007: 'The Doctor is great for the beginning and end of the story; at times I question how great he is for the middle, because he is so powerful, so know-it-all, and can be slightly diffusing of tension. Of course he's the big star and you have to give him big star moments, but the truth is that for you to experience wonder or fear you pretty much have to experience that through the other characters, because he is not feeling it a lot of the time.'
- A run-down house in Field Park Road, Newport, was used for the interior and exterior of Wester Drumlins, the shots of which was taped over several days from 23 November 2006, although the cellar scenes – some of the last to be recorded, at the beginning of December – were done in the Upper Boat studios. The shots of Sally reading Kathy's letter in the Cappuccino! coffee shop were taped at Oddverse Café, Charles Street, Newport on on 27 November. The scenes featuring the DVD shop were recorded at Diverse Records on the opposite side of the same street on 27 and 28 November. A house in Llanfair Road, Cardiff, was used for the scenes in Kathy's house, which were recorded on 1 December.
- The DVDs and posters seen in the shop – which initially bears a sign reading 'Bantos DVD Store – New, Second Hand and Rare' and then, a year later, one reading 'Sparrow & Nightingale – Antiquarian Books and Rare DVD's' (Sally and Larry having presumably bought out Banto, the previous owner, as some point in the interim) – are mock-ups prepared by BBC Wales Graphics, the use of genuine ones having been ruled out by the need to avoid unintentional advertising and possible copyright problems. The fictional titles include *Acid Burn*, *City Justice* and *Candy Kane*. Others pictured more clearly on the official *Doctor Who* website are *Breakfast in the Rain*, *Dance of Days*, *Civilization Zero*, *Angel Smile* (possibly an in-joke allusion to the Weeping Angels), *Falling Star*,

*One Oak County*, *My Best Friend's Boyfriend*, *Mean Teens* and *Shooting the Sun*. The small print on most of these is copied from a DVD of Quentin Tarantino's *Pulp Fiction* (Miramax Films/Buena Vista Pictures, 1994). The titles of the 17 DVDs owned by Sally – the only ones on which the Doctor's DVD Easter Egg extra is to be found – are never revealed in the story, for the same reasons.

- Wester Drumlins is an old address of writer Steven Moffat's from the 1990s.
- The costume and make-up for each Weeping Angel took about three hours to apply, and included polystyrene wings and latex arms and facial appliances.
- Fellow new series writer Mark Gatiss gave Steven Moffat a number of ideas for his script for this episode, particularly in relation to the trick that he uses to defeat the Weeping Angels at the end.
- At the time of this episode's debut transmission, the BBC had just introduced a new practice on all its TV channels of 'squeezing' a section of each programme's closing credits into a small box in the bottom right-hand corner of the screen, allowing for other, forthcoming shows to be trailed in the remaining picture area. This was done for 'Blink' in most regions of the UK (an exception being Northern Ireland) and provoked a considerable number of complaints from viewers, on the grounds that it detracted from the atmosphere of the episode, and also that it was unfair to those who had worked on it, as in many cases it meant that their credits were now too small to be legible. Although the practice was maintained for the following episode, 'Utopia', it was dropped for 'The Sound of Drums' and 'Last of the Time Lords', apparently in response to these viewer complaints.

## OOPS!

- Given that Martha has a mobile phone that works anywhere in space and time, as established in '42', and that Billy Shipton has Sally Sparrow's phone number with him when he is transported back to 1969, why doesn't one of them simply phone Sally and tell her what to do; or, come to that, phone Martha's sister Tish or another member of her family and ask for help? (Perhaps Martha left her phone in the TARDIS to recharge?)
- The spelling of of Ben's and Lucy's surname on their gravestone – 'Wainright' – is inconsistent with that given in the closing credits – 'Wainwright'.
- The elderly Kathy's voice-over as Sally sits and reads her letter in the Cappuccino! coffee shop does not quite match the words seen on the page. For instance, whereas the voiceover says, 'You would have liked Ben – he was the very first person I met in 1920', the letter reads, 'You would have liked Ben – I wish you could have met him.'

## PRESS REACTION

- 'The series continues its satisfying descent into the dark, with a brilliant episode that owes more to the old-fashioned traditions of thriller writing than to whizz-bang science fiction. As in the episode starring Peter Kay in Series Two, the Doctor barely features here, dispensing wisdom via the occasional TV set to the heroine, played by Carey Mulligan with just the right mix of intelligence and incredulity. What grips from the outset is the set-up, which weaves elements of the classic haunted-house story with a paradoxical time-travel tale that's as good as anything Hollywood can produce. All this, and monsters, too. Blink and you'll miss them. But they won't miss you.' James Jackson, *The Times*, 9 June 2007.

- 'One thing that should surely bind Britain together next week is what every small child will be doing in public squares after watching tonight's *Doctor Who*. The brilliantly back-on-form third series follows up last week's tear-jerking classic by giving David Tennant and Freema Agyeman most of the episode off – but unlike previous Doctor-light episodes, "Blink" is a blinking cracker. It's partly thanks to the lovely Carey Mulligan (she played sweet Ada in *Bleak House*), who stars as a sparky young woman called Sally Sparrow who would make the perfect new TARDIS companion except ... ah, well, that's the twist. Some knowing gags about ITV and DVD extras are crammed into a script by Steven Moffat (based on a story in the [2006] *Doctor Who Annual*, fact fans) which manages to also create spooky new villains based on a traditional playground game. If the nation's children aren't playing at Blink by next week, I'll eat my sonic screwdriver.' Andrea Mullaney, *Scotsman*, 8 June 2007.

- 'Steven Moffat has combined the horror and science fiction genres with skill and seeming ease to perfectly fill the one episode format ... and has also paid a huge compliment to the audience by treating them as intelligent. His script requires some thought and is masterfully put together, with some interesting science fiction ideas that have some sense to them! And a round of applause for him having the Doctor speak the same words on two occasions, but in two different conversations!' Jan Vincent-Rudzki, *TV Zone* Issue 217, July 2007.

## FAN COMMENT

- 'Let me ask you a question: how many times in recent years have you watched a stand-alone episode of a big sci-fi show and walked away from it thinking, "Man, that was brilliant"? Seriously – it can't be more than once or twice. Maybe a few episodes of *The X-Files*, or *Star Trek: The Next Generation*, possibly some *Babylon 5* or *Battlestar Galactica*. Well, I'm really not overstating things when I say that "Blink" was one of the best stand-alone episodes of any sci-fi show I've watched in years, let alone a great episode of *Doctor Who*.' Martin Conaghan, TV Squad website, 26 June 2007.

- 'Blooming blinking brilliant! That was the verdict on this latest episode of *Who*. An absolutely cracking story, simple and yet really effective in all the right ways. Steven Moffat pulled out all the stops to present something scary and creepy, and the direction and acting combined to make it totally riveting from beginning to end.' David J Howe, Howe's Who website, 12 June 2007.

- 'I loved the spooky *Scooby Doo*/[*Buffy the Vampire Slayer*]-type house. This episode really played well on some good primeval fears. The tension was maintained throughout, but also with the good mixture of *Doctor Who* humour ... Another primeval fear is that of loneliness, which featured heavily in this episode. Even the Angel assassins were lonely as they could never be with their own kind because they would freeze in time. It is a life of exile for all concerned. The message was though, peculiarly, one of hope, because the humans who were sent back in time all managed to adapt and live full lives.

This is something our Doctor can never have: normality. So I actually take it as hope that no matter what happens, we have the potential to adapt and the most extraordinary thing we can do is be "normal", The script was absolutely excellent and [the] acting [of the] usual high calibre from all concerned. This episode is the epitome of the *Doctor Who* philosophy. Wonderful entertainment, though I am not sure it was for all the family. I think there may have been a few nightmares last night across the land!' Emma Jane Shepherd, david-tennant.com website, 10 June 2007.

- 'You could go on about "Blink"'s brilliance, I think, but to simply sit here and list everything that was great about it – the way the Angels killed, the Doctor's brief appearances, Billy the policeman, the creepy old house, the final meeting at the end – would just end up boring everyone. There are little complaints you can make, or at least small issues to raise. Why did the Angel bung a rock at Sally at the start? And why, as casting director Andy Pryor points out on the MP3 commentary, thus making me feel less clever than I had done five minutes previously, don't they just close one eye at a time instead of blinking? Minor quibbles, though – and easily excused in such a fine episode.' Paul Hayes, Behind the Sofa website, 10 June 2007.

- 'One thing that I really like about Steven Moffat's story, here, which I think may be a trait of his writing, is that his characters get involved in extraordinary things, but they remain ordinary people. They may panic or freak as ordinary people would, but then they bear up and do extraordinary things, showing off a resilience that many of us just hope we have. Steven Moffat's characters are fundamentally at peace with themselves; this may be partly the result of Moffat's willingness to play with the fourth wall, but it still makes these characters quite compelling indeed … Moffat may have set about to write a thriller, but it's the elegance of his writing that leaves me flabbergasted. *Doctor Who* may be a show with a time machine in it, but Moffat is one of the few writers to write a real story about time travel. It is effortless, but carefully measured. Moffat's humour balances the moments of fright and it makes the characters human. All of the plot developments confound Sally, and the viewer, but with the resolution, you can see Moffat in the background, guiding all of the elements with the precision of a choreographer. And for all of the scares, this is a story about a young woman triumphing against adversity, surrounded by sympathetic, ordinary people who help her along the way. It's also the best episode of this season so far. Quite possibly the best episode of *Doctor Who*, ever.' James Bow, Bow James Bow website, 11 June 2007.

## ANALYSIS

Hot on the heels of a pair of episodes adapted from an old *Doctor Who* novel comes one based on a short story, *'What I Did On My Christmas Holidays'* by *Sally Sparrow*, contributed by writer Steven Moffat to the *Doctor Who Annual 2006* (Panini, 2005). In this case, though, the adaptation is a much looser one; but for the fact that its lead character has the same name, Sally Sparrow, 'Blink' might almost be considered a completely different story from the original, albeit one that has the same basic premise of the Doctor being trapped in the past and leaving a series of messages for Sally to find in the present day in order to get her to send the TARDIS back to him – an idea probably inspired by a scene in the final episode of the sitcom *Goodnight Sweetheart* (BBC One, 1993-1999) in which the lead character, the time-hopping Gary Sparrow, leaves a message under some wallpaper in 1945 for his future wife to read in 1999.[82] As it is, though, the reuse of the same basic story and character – albeit that she is about ten years older in the TV version – has to be considered another nail in the coffin of the idea of a coherent *Doctor Who* canon; or, at least, of one extending beyond the TV series.

Moffat had a lot to live up to following his award-winning 'The Empty Child'/'The Doctor Dances' in Series One and his outstanding 'The Girl in the Fireplace' in Series Two (and while I greatly disliked his *Comic Relief* spoof 'The Curse of Fatal Death' (1999), I have to admit that I tend to detest *Doctor Who* spoofs in general, so that's probably more my problem than his). Thankfully, 'Blink' doesn't disappoint in the slightest; the script is well up to his usual exemplary standard, and again shows him to be a huge asset to the series' regular writing team.

One of the defining characteristics of Moffat's work is the suberb structuring of his stories, which often make use of a non-linear narrative or some cunningly concealed twist that means that the viewer is unable to see the full picture until the very end, leading to an unexpected and highly satisfying resolution. This is often demonstrated to great effect in the brilliant *Coupling* (BBC Two/BBC Three, 2000-2004) – which Moffat both created and wrote, and which has to be one of my favourite comedy series of all time – and, although it can sometimes leave the impression that the structure is almost the star of the show, it is an approach that works particularly well in *Doctor Who*, which naturally lends itself to stories involving the clever manipulation of time. 'Blink' in fact relies on just about the most outrageous time paradox yet presented in the series, as the Doctor, in order to save himself and Martha from being trapped in 1969, causes Sally Sparrow to assemble what amounts to a set of instructions for him, which she then hands to him in his own personal past, which he then follows, and which he thereby causes her to assemble for him … This is mind-bogglingly circular, turning the normal principle of cause and effect on its head in what science fiction fans refer to as a 'predestination paradox', but somehow it seems perfectly logical and acceptable in the context. As the Doctor explains, in a wonderfully off-the-wall piece of dialogue, 'People assume that time is a strict progression of cause to effect, but actually, from a non-linear, non-subjective viewpoint, it's more like a big ball of wibbly-wobbly … timey-wimey … stuff.'

'Blink' is clearly set up to be the 'Doctor-lite' episode of Series Three, but actually the Doctor plays a rather bigger role here than he did in Series Two's 'Love & Monsters', and a scarcely less prominent one than he did in 'Human Nature'/'The Family of Blood', which for the most part saw David Tennant

---

[82] The *Torchwood* episode 'Captain Jack Harkness' also uses a very similar idea, with Toshiko leaving a series of messages in 1941 for her colleagues to find in 2007, but this was written after Steven Moffat's *Doctor Who Annual* story featuring Sally Sparrow, and so cannot have been an influence on it. It is more likely that 'Captain Jack Harkness' and the Sally Sparrow story had a common source of inspiration in the *Goodnight Sweetheart* episode.

playing not the Doctor but his human alter-ego John Smith. Although Tennant carried out only two days' recording in total on 'Blink', his screen time is extended beyond what that would normally allow by the ingenious device of having the Doctor communicate with Sally mainly via a DVD Easter Egg extra, parts of which are replayed numerous times in various different contexts during the course of the action. This is a very clever idea, and typical of Moffat's skilful incorporation into his stories of elements that will strike a chord with genre fans – who are well used to seeking out such Easter Eggs on their DVD purchases – but also be accessible and intriguing to the general viewing public. Another nice contemporary reference comes when Sally's friend Kathy suggests that their two surnames, Sparrow and Nightingale, are very fitting for a pair of 'girl investigators', and Sally replies 'Bit ITV': a reference to the fact that the ITV network has screened a number of series with such teams; most notably *Rosemary & Thyme* (2003-2006), about a pair of middle-aged women gardeners who frequently find themselves acting as amateur sleuths. An amusing in-joke aimed specifically at *Doctor Who* fans comes when DI Billy Shipton comments that the police box impounded beneath the police station isn't a real one because 'the phone is just a dummy and the windows are the wrong size' – inconsistencies between the new series TARDIS prop and the original police box design having been a source of controversy amongst some fans, particularly on the Outpost Gallifrey online forum. When, shortly afterwards, Billy is transported into the past, this perhaps inevitably recalls the plight of the (apparently) time-displaced DCI Sam Tyler played by John Simm in the hit drama series *Life on Mars* (BBC One, 2006-2007), although that is really where the similarity between the two ends.

The 'haunted house' story is a staple of genre fiction in all media – including children's cartoons, as acknowledged when Kathy's brother Larry comments to Sally 'You live in Scooby Doo's house'; a reference to the spooky adventures presented in *Scooby Doo, Where Are You!* and its follow-ups (CBS/ABC/The WB/CW, 1969- ) – so it is something of a surprise to realise that this is only the second time that *Doctor Who* has ever ventured into this territory on TV, the first having been in 'Ghost Light' (1989). [83] The deserted and dilapidated Wester Drumlins house makes for a very atmospheric setting, and lends a real creepiness to scenes such as the one where Kathy's grandson, Malcolm Wainwright (or is it 'Wainright'? – see 'Oops!' above), arrives at the front door to give Sally a letter from his grandmother – very similar to the incident toward the end of *Back to the Future II* (Universal Pictures, 1989) where Marty McFly receives a letter from 'Doc' Brown trapped in 1885 – and Sally, discovering that her friend has disappeared from the room next door, is initially unwilling to accept the horrifying implication that she has somehow been transported into the past.

The real scares in this story, though, come not from the spooky old house but from the Weeping Angels that inhabit it – the most significant new element distinguishing 'Blink' from its *Doctor Who Annual* forerunner. These creatures are not only some of the most frightening ever to grace *Doctor Who* but also some of the most well-conceived, being based around not just one highly original and imaginative idea – which would be achievement enough for most writers – but

---

[83] A brief interlude in the 'Journey Into Terror' episode of 'The Chase' (1965) was also set in a 'haunted house' exhibit.

two. First, there is their method of dispatching their victims not by killing them outright but by sending them back into the past. 'The only psychopaths in the universe to kill you nicely,' says the Doctor. 'No mess, no fuss. They just zap you into the past and make you live to death. Rest of your life, used up, blown away in a blink of an eye. You die in the past, and in the present they consume the energy of all the days you might have had. All your stolen moments. They're creatures of the abstract; they live off potential energy.' Secondly, there is the fact that these 'Lonely Assassins', as they were apparently once dubbed, are 'quantum locked'; that is, they can move only when no-one is looking, and become stone statues if observed, even by one another. This is a real masterstroke on Moffat's part, drawing inspiration from the Medusa myth [84], 'moving statue' stories, the traditional children's games of Statues [85] and 'out-staring' contests [86] while also ingeniously referencing aspects of quantum physics – specifically, the idea that one cannot determine both the position and the momentum of a particle at the same time, as implied by Heisenberg's uncertainty principle, and the idea that an event 'crystalises' only when observed, as most famously elucidated in the Shrödinger's cat 'thought experiment' – to create one of the most effective and memorable alien races to have featured in *Doctor Who*, or indeed in telefantasy more generally.

A particularly notable aspect of this is that the Weeping Angels are never seen to move by the viewer even when they are out of sight of the characters in the story. The clear implication is that it is the viewer's observation of them that renders them immobile in these shots – a neat metatextual touch – although the reason why they fail to catch Sally when she is not looking at them is more likely to be that they actually want her to lead them to the TARDIS; which would also explain why they effectively present her with the key. The icing on the cake comes in the scene at the end of the episode where it is suggested that the statues one sees in everyday life, outside churches, in town centres and so on, could all potentially be Weeping Angels. [87] Although the sequence of statue images would perhaps have benefited from being shortened somewhat, to focus on those with an ugly, gargoyle-type appearance and lose those that are obviously nothing more than innocent representations of notable historical figures and the like, the underlying idea is simply wonderful. This is the stuff of which childhood TV memories are

---

[84] In Greek mythology, the Medusa is a female-formed character, the sight of which turns the observer to stone; an idea reversed in 'Blink'. In the classic series *Doctor Who* story 'The Mind Robber', the Doctor and his companions encounter the Medusa in the Land of Fiction, but escape by causing it to look upon its own reflection, turning it into a statue.

[85] This game, otherwise known as 'Grandma's Footsteps', involves one child, sometimes referred to as the 'curator', standing a little way off from a group of others with his or her back turned to them. The others have to advance upon and try to touch the curator, but whenever the curator turns around, they must stand immobile like statutes; if any of them are caught moving by the curator, they are either sent back to the start or eliminated from the game.

[86] These contests involve two opponents staring into each other's eyes, the loser being the one who blinks first.

[87] There are also two angel statues seen on the gateposts of the Bethlem Hospital in 'The Shakespeare Code'.

made, and the millions of children who have watched 'Blink' are surely guaranteed to be left with a certain apprehension of statues for many years to come – as indeed are many of the adult viewers too!

With the Doctor and Martha playing a diminished role in proceedings, it is even more important than usual that this episode – like 'Love & Monsters' – should have some strong performances from its guest cast members. This fortunately proves to be the case, with the excellent Carey Mulligan acquitting herself very well indeed in what is effectively the 'stand-in lead' role of Sally Sparrow, ably supported by Lucy Gaskell as Kathy Nightingale, Finlay Robertson as her brother Larry (short for 'Lawrence' – which, with his surname, would no doubt have got him nicknamed 'Florence' at school), and Michael Obiora and Louis Mahoney as the old and young versions respectively of Billy Shipton (Mahoney making his third appearance in *Doctor Who*, having previously played a newscaster in 'Frontier in Space' (1973) and spaceship crew member Ponti in 'Planet of Evil' (1975)). They are aided in this by the characteristically sharp dialogue and strong material that Moffat gives them to work with. A good example of this is to be found in the amusing scene where Sally pays an unannounced 1.00 am visit to Kathy's house and encounters Larry, presumably staying overnight there, walking around naked. Then there is the incident where, in a Freudian slip, Sally mistakenly gives her own surname as 'Shipton' when talking to Billy Shipton, then makes a hasty and embarrassed exit, repeatedly telling him not to look at her – presumably because she finds the prospect 'petrifying'. Another highlight is the affecting scene where Sally visits the elderly Billy in hospital and stays at his bedside to be with him during what he knows will be the final night of his life. Also excellent is the scene at the end where Sally finally meets the Doctor and realises that it is at a point in his life before he gets trapped in 1969 – the third instance of an 'out-of-sequence' meeting of this kind occurring during Series Three, the first having come with the Doctor's initial meeting with Martha in 'Smith and Jones' and the second with his brush with Queen Elizabeth in 'The Shakespeare Code'.

The characterisation is admittedly fairly broad – all we really get to learn about Larry is that he is a rather geeky guy who is into DVDs and the internet (following what has now become something of a pattern, given that the lead male guest character of Series Two's 'Doctor-lite' episode 'Love & Monsters' was also a geek, as was that of *Torchwood* Series One's 'regular-lite' episode 'Random Shoes'), and we never find out much at all about Kathy's life prior to her being sent back in time – but this is almost unavoidable in a story of only around 45 minutes' duration. We certainly get to know Sally and Larry well enough to be touched by the fact that they seem to have a hope of taking their relationship beyond mere friendship when, a year later, Sally finally solves the mystery of the Doctor's messages to her and is thus able to end her fixation on the events at Wester Drumlins.

Just about the only thing we do discover about Kathy's old life is that she apparently wasn't very happy with it, and that her transportation back to 1920 proved to be a blessing in disguise, as she fell in love, married, had children and, in short, found the 'new life' she had always wanted. This highlights the fact that the really terrifying thing about the Weeping Angels is not what they might do to you if they catch you – in the sense that being transported back in time is not as horrific a prospect as being instantly killed or, say, subjected to painful torment, and could even turn out to be a positive boon, as in Kathy's case – and certainly not their apparent inclination to resort to stone-throwing, as implied in a rather incongruous incident when Sally first enters Wester Drumlins, but their terrifying manifestation as they advance inexorably toward you in a series of motionless poses, their sharply-pointed teeth bared menacingly and their faces contorted in expressions of rage, as if revealed in a sequence of still images or perhaps the on-off illumination of a strobe light. This is superbly conveyed by director Hettie Macdonald, who does a great job throughout in what is her first but hopefully not her last contribution to *Doctor Who*, giving the whole thing a very filmic look. Kudos too to all those responsible for the excellent design and realisation of the Weeping Angels, the striking appearance of which is so crucial to their effectiveness; the prosthetic make-up is so good here that it is impossible to tell that they are actually not genuine statues but played by actors.

Will the Weeping Angels return in a future story? Although the four in the Wester Drumlins cellar seem to be stuck at the end of the episode, by virtue of them having been tricked into forming a circle and looking at one another, surely someone is bound to come along and move them eventually, or even simply turn out the light and thus release them (unless they can see in the dark, as is possibly the case) – or was it Moffat's intention to suggest that they are turned to stone permanently now? Perhaps this is something that is best left to the viewer's imagination, as it is hard to see how any sequel could better the original.

With the Doctor and Martha sidelined from the main action, 'Blink' could never be considered a typical *Doctor Who* story, but as 'Doctor-lite' episodes go, you couldn't hope for a finer one than this. And just remember, next time you see a statue: don't turn your back, don't look away, and don't *blink* ...

# 3.11 – UTOPIA

Writer: Russell T Davies
Director: Graeme Harper

<u>DEBUT TRANSMISSION DETAILS</u>

BBC One
Date: 16 June 2007. Scheduled time: 7.15 pm. Actual time: 7.14 pm.

BBC Three
Date: 17 June 2007. Scheduled time: 8.00 pm. Actual time: 8.01 pm.

Duration: 45' 58"

<u>ADDITIONAL CREDITED CAST</u>

Derek Jacobi (Professor Yana), Chipo Chung (Chantho), Rene Zagger (Padra[88]), Neil Reidman (Lieutenant Atillo), Paul Marc Davies (Chieftain), Robert Forknall (Guard), John Bell (Creet), Deborah Maclaren (Kistane[89]), Abigail Canton (Wiry Woman)[90].

<u>PLOT</u>

The Doctor briefly materialises the TARDIS in the Roald Dahl Plass in Cardiff in order to refuel with energy from the time rift there. His former companion Captain Jack Harkness, having detected the ship's arrival, clings on to its police box exterior when it leaves, and travels with it through the time vortex. Arriving on the planet Malcassairo in the year 100 Trillion, the Doctor, Jack and Martha explore, and narrowly escape being caught by the savage, cannibalistic Futurekind. They eventually find their way to an underground base, Silo 16, where the elderly Professor Yana and his insectoid assistant Chantho are trying to activate a rocket ship that will transport a group of human refugees to a mysterious 'Utopia', where they hope to find a way of surviving the imminent end of the universe. With the Doctor's help, they succeed in launching the rocket … but the Professor has a secret that even he has forgotten, as Martha realises when she sees that he owns a pocket watch identical to the one that the Doctor previously used to store his Time Lord persona while hiding from the Family of Blood in human form. The Professor opens the watch … and transforms into the Doctor's Time Lord arch-enemy, the Master. The Master electrocutes Chantho, but is shot by her in return as she dies.

---

[88] Surname given in dialogue as 'Shafe Cane'.
[89] Surname given in dialogue as 'Shafe Cane'.
[90] Not credited in *Radio Times*.

He locks himself in the TARDIS, where he regenerates into a new, younger form. He then dematerialises, leaving the Doctor, Jack and Martha stranded and apparently at the mercy of the rampaging Futurekind ...

## QUOTE, UNQUOTE

- **Doctor:** 'The ripe old smell of humans. You survived. Oh, you might have spent a million years evolving into clouds of gas, and another million as downloads, but you always revert to the same basic shape. The fundamental human. End of the universe and here you are. Indomitable, that's the word. Indomitable!'
- **Professor:** 'Time travel! They say there was time travel, back in the old days. I never believed ... But what would I know? Stupid old man. Never could keep time. Always late, always lost.'
- **Master:** 'Did you never think, all those years standing beside me, to ask about that watch? Never? Did you never once think, not ever, that you could set me free?'
  **Chantho:** 'Chan / I'm sorry / Tho. Chan / I'm so sorry! /'
  **Master:** 'You ... with your "Chan" and your "Tho", driving me insane!'
  **Chantho:** 'Chan / Professor, please ... /'
  **Master:** 'That is not my name! The Professor was an invention; so perfect a disguise that I forgot who I am.'
  **Chantho:** 'Chan / Then who are you? / Tho.'
  **Master:** 'I ... am ... the Master!'

## CONTINUITY POINTS

- At the end of the *Torchwood* Series One finale, 'End of Days', the sound of a TARDIS materialisation is heard in the Torchwood Hub and Jack disappears, leaving scattered papers in his wake. In 'Utopia', it is revealed that the TARDIS has actually materialised not in the Hub – as many fans assumed – but above it, in the Roald Dahl Plass, the sound having presumably carried down into the cavernous space below, perhaps through the entrance to the invisible lift that is sited there (a gust of air through which would also account for the scattered papers) or perhaps via a microphone system set up by Jack in conjunction with his 'early warning device' – which is linked to a jar containing the Doctor's hand, severed from his arm by the Sycorax leader in 'The Christmas Invasion'. Jack goes running out to the TARDIS, presumably exiting the Hub via the stairs leading up to the fake tourist information office at its front entrance (given that the lift leading to that entrance must already be in use by his Torchwood colleagues, who are seen to arrive in the Hub moments later, and that the other, invisible lift is obviously now blocked by the TARDIS). He has on his back a rucksack that is later revealed to hold the jar containing the Doctor's hand, which he must have picked up quickly on his way out. The haste of his exit may also account for some of the scattered papers.
- The Doctor notes when the TARDIS arrives in Cardiff that the time rift has recently been active. This ties in with events seen in the *Torchwood* episodes

'Captain Jack Harkness' and 'End of Days'. He also refers to having had 'trouble with the Slitheen' in this location, back when he was 'a different man' – i.e. in his ninth incarnation – as seen in 'Boom Town'. Martha does not appear to know what he means by this, or what Jack means subsequently when, on their arrival on Malcassairo, he comments that the Doctor has a new face. This suggests that at this point she is unaware of the Doctor's ability to regenerate.

- The TARDIS travels forward to the year 100 Trillion – the Doctor describes this as 'the end of the universe' and claims that 'not even the Time Lords came this far' (although he omits to explain why) – because it is trying to shake off Jack, who has clung on to its police box exterior at the point of dematerialisation. The Doctor explains that it reacts in this way because Jack is 'wrong': his immortality makes him a fixed point in time and space, which should not exist. It is uncertain whether Jack survives the trip through the vortex simply because he is immortal, or whether he is also protected by the TARDIS forcefield (in the same way as the arrow that is lodged in the TARDIS door when it leaves Elizabethan England at the end of 'The Shakespeare Code' remains undamaged when it arrives in New New York in 'Gridlock').
- By the year 100 Trillion, 'all the great civilisations have gone,' according to the Doctor, and 'all the stars have burned up, faded away, into nothing'. Jack theorises that the planet – later identified by the Professor as Malcassairo – must have 'an atmospheric shell' to make it habitable.
- Jack explains that he escaped from the Game Station in the year 200,100, where he was left by the Doctor at the end of 'The Parting of the Ways', by using his time agent's vortex manipulator – the device he wears on a strap on his wrist, which when operational gives him a rudimentary ability to travel in time.[91] (Contrasting this with the TARDIS, the Doctor says, 'It's like I've got a sports car and you've got a Spacehopper.'[92]) He arrived back on Earth in 1869, but the vortex manipulator burnt out and became 'useless' for further time travel. Jack eventually based himself at the time rift in Cardiff, knowing that the Doctor would return there at some point to refuel the TARDIS – as previously witnessed in 'Boom Town', when the rift was temporarily opened in 2006, causing an earthquake; an event that Martha, when talking to the Doctor at the start of the episode, recalls as occurring 'a couple of years ago', consistent with previous indications that she comes from 2008. (It may or may not be a coincidence that 1869 is another of the years in which the time rift in Cardiff became active, as seen in 'The Unquiet Dead'.) Jack has had numerous opportunities to contact other incarnations of the Doctor during the period of almost 140 years that he has been living on Earth – he says that he has been following him 'for a long time' – but has had to wait for a version that 'coincided' with him – 'the right kind of Doctor', as he previously put it in *Torchwood* – presumably to avoid damage to the time lines.

---

[91] The Family of Blood used a stolen vortex manipulator to pursue the Doctor and Martha through time and space to the England of 1913 in 'Human Nature'.
[92] A toy, particularly popular in the 1970s, consisting of a large, heavy rubber balloon, usually orange in colour, with two handles protruding from the top, which a child would sit on top of, holding the handles, and bounce along.

- The Doctor implies that human evolution is cyclical, and that although our race may sometimes take on different forms over the course of millennia – including clouds of gas and computer downloads – it always reverts to its 'fundamantal' original shape. This recalls how, in 'Gridlock', the Macra are said to have 'devolved' rather than evolved.
- The Professor explains that the planet Malcassairo was home to Chantho's race, the Malmooth, before his group of humans took refuge there. Chantho says that she is believed to be the last of her species, and that the abandoned city outside was where their 'conglomeration' lived.
- The Doctor admits that he 'ran away' from Jack on first realising, in 'The Parting of the Ways', that he had become immortal. He explains that Rose resurrected Jack, following his extermination by the Daleks, using the power of the time vortex. 'No-one's ever meant to have that power,' he says. 'If a Time Lord did that, he'd become a god; a vengeful god. But she was human; everything she did was so human. She brought you back to life, but she couldn't control it. She brought you back forever. That's something, I suppose. The final act of the Time War was life.'
- Jack says that on one or two occasions during the 1990s, while he was stranded on Earth, he went back to the estate where Rose lived and watched her growing up. He refrained from saying hello, however: 'Time lines and all that.'
- The Professor says that he has had an insistent drumbeat sounding inside his head throughout his whole life. He admits that his title is an affectation, notes that there hasn't been such a thing as a university for 'over a thousand years', and says that he has spent his life 'going from one refugee ship to another'. Later, when Martha asks him where his pocket watch came from, he replies: 'I was found with it … an orphan in the storm. I was a naked child, found on the coast of the Silver Devastation, abandoned, with only this.' It is uncertain how much of this is true and how much of it is simply a false memory supplied by the Chameleon Arch that made him human, like the false memory that the Doctor's human *alter ego* John Smith had in 'Human Nature'/'The Family of Blood' of having grown up in Nottingham. In 'The End of the World', set in the year 200,000, the Face of Boe is also said to be from the Silver Devasation; this may be in the Isop Galaxy (like the planet Vortis, visited by the first Doctor in 'The Web Planet' (1965)), given that in 'Bad Wolf' the Face of Boe is stated to be the oldest inhabitant of that galaxy. The Professor has been on Malcassairo for at least 17 years: Chantho tells Martha that that is how long she has been serving him.
- The Professor's pocket watch is identical to the one seen in 'Human Nature'/'The Family of Blood', save for the addition of a chain. It likewise has a perception filter on it, rendering it inconspicuous. This suggests two possibilities: first, that it simply looks the same, and that all Chameleon Arches use such a component; secondly, that it is in fact the self same watch, which the Master somehow managed to acquire at some point, possibly centuries after the Doctor gave it to Tim Latimer as a gift toward the end of 'The Family of Blood'. The former explanation would beg the question why Chameleon Arches – which are presumably the product of Time Lord, or at least alien, technology – should use a component that looks exactly like an ordinary pocket watch from 20th Century Earth, and that can indeed be used to tell the

time, or so it would seem from the scene in 'The Family of Blood' where Latimer uses it to identify the moment when a particular shell is about to fall in the First World War trenches. The latter explanation, on the other hand, would beg the question why the Master needed to use the pocket watch rather than some other similarly-shaped device within the Chameleon Arch that transformed him. When Martha tells Jack, 'But it's not a watch; it's this Chameleon thing,' the Doctor says, 'No, no, no, no, no. It's this … it's this … thing, this device; rewrites biology; changes a Time Lord into a human.' Martha then says, 'And it's the same watch.' This exchange of dialogue seems to make the former explanation more likely, as the implication in 'Human Nature' is that the Chameleon Arch can in principle rewrite the Doctor's biology into any form, but that he has 'set it to human'; if it is indeed the same watch, this might explain why the Master has become human too, rather than taken on some other alien form – unless the setting of the species is done purely in the Arch itself, with the watch simply acting as a receptacle for the subject's Time Lord persona and playing no other part in the process. Another possibility is that the Doctor and the Master owned a matching pair of the watches, from their childhood days when they were friends.

## SAXON REFERENCES

- Martha recognises the Master's voice following his regeneration. Although she does not put a name to it, this would be known to her as Harold Saxon's voice, which she would have heard on TV broadcasts etc in view of Saxon's status as a prominent politician.

## PRODUCTION NOTES

- 'Utopia' was made with '42' in Block 7 of production on Series Three. These episodes were originally to have constituted Block 6 of production and been directed by Charles Palmer rather than Graham Harper.
- Writer Russell T Davies's starting point in developing his script for this episode was the Master's fob watch, as he explained in an interview published in Issue 384 of *Doctor Who Magazine* in July 2007: 'I had to create a character who could easily wear a fob watch without it looking odd, to hide it from the viewer in plain sight for the first 30 minutes or so. Therefore, the vaguely formal, Edwardian dress beame a necessity, which then made me think, "Oh, he's going to look a little bit like William Hartnell's Doctor" – so we told [costume designer] Louise Page that. "Hartnell him up, Louise!" Like that's a Gallifreyan default. I liked the analogy, so I kept pouring in and adding detail – give him a faithful female companion, give him a home that's full of old junk and technology – but really that was all afterthought; it all stemmed from the fob watch.'
- John Barrowman's name appears in the opening titles of this episode (and the two subsequent ones) after David Tennant's and Freema Agyeman's; the first time in the new series that three people have been credited in this way.
- John Barrowman performed Jack's leap onto (supposedly) the TARDIS himself, declining the offer of having a stuntman stand in for him. It was done

using a trampet (i.e. a small trampoline).

- Some of the extras playing the Futurekind were bikers with genuine piercings. In most cases, however, the piercings were fake magnetic ones.
- Director Graeme Harper originally intended to shoot the scenes of the planet surface on some moorlands in the Trefil area of Wales, but this was ruled out on cost grounds in favour of a much closer quarry location, Argoed Quarry near Llantrisant, where recording – hampered by heavy rain – took place in mid-February 2007. A different site, Wenvoe Quarry, previously used for 'The Impossible Planet'/'The Satan Pit', was the venue for recording of the scenes of the Silo 16 exterior. The sentry tower outside was adapted from the construction representing the mast of the Empire State Building in 'Evolution of the Daleks'. Silo interiors were shot in the same disused glass factory on the Trident Park industrial estate that had been used several times before as a location for the series. The Professor's laboratory, however, was a studio set. Some of the control panels in this were designed and arranged to give them a slight resemblance to a classic-series-style TARDIS console, possibly suggesting that the Master's TARDIS had been cannibalised in their construction.
- The production team had the idea of approaching Sir Derek Jacobi to play Professor Yana after producer Phil Collinson bumped into him in a restaurant and the actor said how much he would like a role in *Doctor Who*.
- A number of flashback clips are seen in this episode: these are from 'The Christmas Invasion' (the Doctor losing his hand in the fight with the Sycorax leader), 'The Parting of the Ways' (Rose resurrecting Jack), 'Human Nature' (the Doctor explaining the pocket watch to Martha) and 'Gridlock' (the Face of Boe delivering his final message to the Doctor).
- It was not generally known that this was to be the first of a three-part story, rather than a stand-alone episode, until it was mentioned on the edition of *Totally Doctor Who* aired the day prior to its debut transmission.
- An article published in the *Daily Mirror* on 22 June 2007 suggested that well-known actor Robson Green had been approached to play the Master before John Simm. Green was quoted as saying: 'They asked me to play the Master but I said no. The BBC couldn't drop me quick enough after *Rocket Man*[93] didn't work out, so I'm sticking with ITV for now.' This has not been independently corroborrated, however.
- The title 'Utopia' was first coined in 1516 by the lawyer, statesman and author Sir Thomas More (1478-1535) for his book about an imaginary island with a perfect social, legal and political system.
- The Professor's admission that his title is an affectation recalls the adoption of the same false title by the Doctor's companion Bernice Summerfield from the tie-in novel and audio ranges.
- The drumbeat heard by the Professor in his head recalls the bass-line of the *Doctor Who* theme music, as composed by Ron Grainer, but was actually specified by Russell T Davies because it was the rhythm of the bleeping sound

[93] *Rocket Man* was an unsuccessful BBC One series from 2005 in which Robson Green starred.

made by his alarm clock.

- The prop used for the Professor's pocket watch was the same one as seen in 'Human Nature'/'The Family of Blood', with a new chain supplied by costume designer Louise Page.
- The Malmooth's abandoned city was originally referred to as 'Coral City' in Russell T Davies's script and some early production designs, but not in the episode itself.
- It was planned to record a shot showing the TARDIS being lowered into the Professor's laboratory by a crane, but this was abandoned due to lack of time.
- The protective suit worn by the technician who gets vaporised in the radiation-filled room beneath the rocket was a costume previously used on *Torchwood*, in the hospital quarantine scene in the episode 'End of Days'.
- John Simm's part of the Master's regeneration sequence was recorded about a week after Derek Jacobi's, and the two actors never met on set. They both wore the same costume, without any alterations made to it.

OOPS!

- It is indicated in the story that the Futurekind can be distinguished from humans by the fact that they all have sharp, pointed teeth. In a couple of shots, however, it can be clearly seen that some of the extras playing the Futurekind have ordinary human teeth.
- In light of his later comment to the Doctor and Martha in 'Last of the Time Lords' that he was known in his youth as 'the Face of Boe', why does Jack not react in any way when, clearly within his earshot, Martha says to the Doctor, 'Think what the Face of Boe said; his dying words'? (Could it be that his youth is now such a distant memory for him, given his incredible longevity, that he does not immediately recall the details of it? If so, could Martha's remark in 'Utopia' be what triggers his memory of his one-time nickname and causes him to make mention of it in 'Last of the Time Lords?')

PRESS REACTION

- 'The opening 20 minutes of "Utopia" feels like a throwback to the more embarrassing moments in the series of old. An obvious quarry, shouty extras running around trying to look scary and a plot that doesn't make an awful lot of sense ([as] we're told that the last humans are being sent to a place called "Utopia", but surely the point of the end of the universe is that there's nowhere else to go?) – these all contribute to a sense of cheapness that is thankfully not typical of the modern incarnation of the show. At around the midpoint, the story picks up as the benevolent Professor Yana slowly begins to realise his true identity. After months of speculation, this is the dramatically satisfying reintroduction of the Master, and Derek Jacobi lends a considerable amount of dramatic weight to his dual roles as the humble Professor and the twisted embodiment of evil.' Jonathan Wilkins, Dreamwatch SciFi website, 26 June 2007.
- 'Hindsight makes it easy to say an actor of Derek Jacobi's calibre was never

likely to play a nondescript, benign scientist …, but Professor Yana's metamorphosis into that most famous of renegade Time Lords proves a Master-class (sorry) in handling a major reveal. First it's the sound of drums rattling around his brain; then the recognition of objects from his Time Lord past; and then the identity-masking watch that Martha recognises from "Human Nature"/"The Family of Blood", reawakening long-forgotten memories and that Roger Delgado laugh [sic]. It's a sequence of events destined to be played back and discussed for years.' Richard Edwards, *SFX* website, 16 June 2007.

## FAN COMMENT

- 'Jacobi is a top star turn, but Tennant also does some great work as the Doctor befriends the Professor, only to realise that he may be another Time Lord, descending into confusion and then horror as he finds he isn't alone, but that this other last Time Lord is the worst possible person to set loose on the universe. As Jacobi's Master regenerates, one would think there was nowhere still to go. Then John Simm jumps up in his place, and turns his performance right up to 11. Jacobi's Master was old, bitter, and sadistic, while Simm's is demented, chaotic and gleeful, hyperventilating as he bursts into life, stealing the TARDIS and leaving the Doctor stranded at the end of time. In a few minutes of screen time, Simm's Master is established as a major, highly entertaining threat. The confrontation between the two last Time Lords that plays out across the next episodes should be well worth the anticipation.' Mark Clapham, Shiny Shelf website, June 2007.
- 'Interestingly, "Utopia" assumes that you already know who the Master is. You know why the Doctor is so frightened when he realises, and the Master's glee at gaining the TARDIS, at finally finding himself again, is more threatening than it otherwise would have been. I'm not certain what casual viewers would make of it, though I expect that next week the Doctor will reveal just how dangerous he is. To be fair, [Russell T] Davies and Derek Jacobi as Professor Yana do what they can, portraying the Master as someone with absolute contempt for anyone other than himself and without any moral scruples. [David] Tennant also helps – if the Doctor is really that panicked by the Master's return, then the situation is serious. All this leads to the best cliffhanger yet, with the Doctor and his friends abandoned at the end of the universe and fighting off psychotic mutants whilst the Master is hurtling towards 21st Century Earth in the TARDIS. "Utopia" might start off on a shaky foot, but it ends powerfully and ultimately is a success.' 'Baron Scarpia', LiveJournal blog, 16 June 2007.
- 'A self-indulgent, yet completely validated nod to the past took place as Professor Yana opened his Gallifreyan watch, and long-term *Doctor Who* fans the world over were rewarded with the evil chuckle of Anthony Ainley and a snippet of Roger Delgado from "The Dæmons". It was a joy to behold, and I suspect that even at this point casual viewers were still watching as this unassuming man became the embodiment of eternal evil, as opposed to switching off in their droves because they felt excluded. This wasn't, "Look, it's the Master, this is for the fans, we don't care what you think" – instead it

was, "Look, the Doctor isn't the last Time Lord. There's another, and he is *bad!*" Climaxing on *that* cliffhanger, with an omnisexual, 200 year old time agent trying to stop a tribe of Futurekind heroes from ripping the TARDIS team to shreds as the old girl departed, was a Master-stroke, and having watched the last 12 minutes seven times, I suspect Series Three is going to get even better. Yes. Better.' Christian Cawley, Kasterborous website, 20 June 2007.

- '"Utopia" isn't so much an episode as it is a force of nature – *Doctor Who's* essence distilled into a powerful shot of creative juice that fires both the blood *and* the imagination. At its heart, it's pure and disposable set up ... but in the hands of Russell T Davies and Graeme Harper, it transforms into something *magnificent!*' Daniel Kukwa, Dopplegangland blog, 20 June 2007.

## ANALYSIS

Back in the days of the classic *Doctor Who* series, writers faced with the daunting prospect of scripting a six-part story – that is, coming up with enough material to fill almost two-and-a-half hours of screen time – would occasionally adopt the strategy of dividing the narrative into two segments, one consisting of two episodes and the other of four episodes, with a significant change of setting and/or characters at the transition point, giving an added impetus to the action part-way through and helping to keep things fresh and interesting. One of the clearest instances of this one-third/two-thirds structure is to be found in 'The Seeds of Doom' (1976), the first two episodes of which are set around a research base in Antarctica and the other four around an English country mansion, with certain characters appearing only in the former setting and certain others only in the latter. Another notable example – this time with the long and short segments transposed, giving a two-thirds/one-third structure – is presented by 'The Invasion of Time' (1978), the first four episodes of which see the Doctor resisting an attempted invasion of his home planet Gallifrey by the Vardans, and the remaining two episodes of which involve him trying to thwart an attack by the Vardans' secret overlords, the Sontarans – the arrival of the Sontarans forming an excellent shock revelation at the end of Part Four.

In scripting 'Utopia'/'The Sound of Drums'/'Last of the Time Lords' – the revived series' first three-part story, with roughly the same total duration as one of the classic series' six-parters – Russell T Davies has clearly chosen to adopt this tried and tested approach. Thus 'Utopia' – the one-third segment – has a completely different setting and different characters from 'The Sound of Drums'/'Last of the Time Lords' – the two-thirds segment – with a shock revelation separating the two. The downside of this as far as 'Utopia' is concerned is that, while on the one hand it seems quite self-contained, on the other hand it doesn't tell a complete story in its own right, the outcome of humanity's quest for Utopia in particular being left completely up in the air at this stage. It thus gives the impression of falling between two stools.

This episode's main narrative function is actually to set things up for the two that follow. It is consequently extraordinarily heavy on exposition (as attested to by the length of the 'Continuity Points' section above). Explanations – or in a few cases, from the viewer's perspective, reminders – are given for all manner of things, including: how Jack escaped from the Game Station following the events of 'The

Parting of the Ways' by using his time agent's vortex manipulator (which actually begs the question why he did not use this before to extricate himself from other perilous situations, such as being stuck on the Chula ship with a bomb in tow at the end of 'The Doctor Dances' or being exterminated by the Daleks in 'The Parting of the Ways'); what year he arrived in when he returned to Earth; how Rose survived the Battle of Canary Wharf and became trapped in a parallel universe; how Jack discovered that he had become immortal; what brought about his state of immortality; why the Doctor abandoned him on the Game Station in the first place; what has become of the human race by the year 100 Trillion (the choice of this ridiculously large and completely arbitrary number being another example of Davies's tendency sometimes to over-egg things, as discussed in relation to some of the earlier episodes); what the scattered groups of surviving humans are hoping to achieve by answering the mysterious summons to Utopia; how the Master managed to survive the last great Time War; and what the Face of Boe meant in 'Gridlock' when he told the Doctor 'You are not alone'. This is all conveyed through reams and reams of dialogue – an exception being the entirely visual, and highly effective, initial revelation of Professor Yana's true nature when Martha sees that his pocket watch is the same as the one the Doctor used in the Chameleon Arch in 'Human Nature'; although even this is subsequently explained through dialogue as well – and altogether it makes for an exceptionally talky episode.

Thankfully the dialogue is – as always from Davies – extremely well-written, and often very funny, and the explanations never feel at all forced. A particularly good example comes in the scene where Martha and Jack – making his much-anticipated and very welcome return to *Doctor Who* – exchange stories as they walk across the surface of Malcassairo, and the Doctor complains: 'You two! We're at the end of the universe, eh? Right at the edge of knowledge itself. And you're busy ... blogging!' Another real highlight is the sequence where the Doctor and Jack talk while on opposite sides of a radiation-proof door, as if it is only with the reassurance of a physical barrier between them that they feel able to open up to each other, discuss the divisive question of Jack's immortality and achieve a reconciliation. This is superb, edgy stuff, full of unspoken feeling, and wonderfully played by both David Tennant and John Barrowman, who deservedly gets his name added to the series' opening credits from this episode.

The fact remains, though, that with all this exposition going on, there isn't much time left for anything else. The only real action in the episode comes courtesy of the rampaging Futurekind –who, perhaps because their involvement is confined to this first third of the story, are accorded much less attention in the script than the elements that are being established for the remaining two-thirds. Professor Yana simply says, 'We call them the Futurekind, which is a myth in itself, but it's feared that they are what we will become, unless we reach Utopia.' It is unclear what exactly he means by this: is it the possibility of mutating or finally evolving into the Futurekind that the human race fears, or simply the prospect of descending to their level of savagery – and cannibalism – as the universe nears its end? Whichever is the case, it is apparent that not much thought has been devoted by Davies to the conception of the Futurekind, beyond an obvious desire to come up with a basic threat to the group of humans gathered within the Silo where Professor Yana is working on his rocket – although how these humans came to be on Malcassairo in the first place is another question, specific to this first third of the story, that is left unanswered, save for a vague reference to refugee ships.

In terms of appearance, the Futurekind obviously recall the leather-clad warrior gangs of the movie *Mad Max 2* (Warner Brothers, 1981) – an impression that would have been further strengthened had the production team proceeded with their original plan to give them quad bikes and motorbikes – but may also have been influenced in part by a similar-looking band of cannibalistic savages in the *Doctor Who* comic strip story *End of the Line*, first published by Marvel in Issues 54 and 55 of *Doctor Who Monthly* in 1981 (prior to the release of *Mad Max 2*) and reprinted by Panini in the *Dragon's Claw* collected edition in 2004. Like 'Utopia', *End of the Line* tells of a dystopian future where a desperate group of humans, hunted by the savages, have placed their trust in an elderly scientist – known in this case as 'the Engineer' – to save them by finding a way to gain control of a transport system – here an old train line rather than a rocket – that will carry them away to a utopia – 'the countryside' – that ultimately proves a false hope; it seems therefore that this may have been a source of inspiration not just for the Futurekind but for the episode more generally. (Given that a number of other elements of *End of the Line* are echoed in 'Gridlock' – see the relevant 'Analysis' section above – perhaps Davies had recently re-read the story at the time when he was formulating his plans for Series Three.) Another comic strip source may possibly have been a sequence in the story *The Stockbridge Horror*, first published in Issues 70 to 75 of Marvel's *Doctor Who Monthly* in 1982 and reprinted by Panini in its *The Tides of Time* collected edition in 2005, in which an elemental being clings on to the outside of the TARDIS as it travels through the vortex, just as Jack does at the start of this episode.

'Utopia' actually works best if viewed primarily as an origin story for the John Simm incarnation of the Master, introducing the character to viewers who have come fresh to the new series and reintroducing him to those who recall him from his earlier incarnations in the classic series. As Davies has noted in interviews, this approach of giving an established character a new origin story for the benefit of a mass audience who may be unfamiliar with the source material is often used in the cinema, particularly in movie adaptations of comic book sagas, which themselves effectively pioneered this type of story. Some prime examples of this are *Superman* (Warner Brothers, 1978), *Spider-Man* (Columbia Pictures/Sony Pictures, 2002), *Batman Begins* (Warner Brothers, 2005) and *Fantastic Four* (20th Century Fox, 2005). In 'Utopia', Davies effectively reboots the character of the Master by having him initially hiding in human form as the benign Professor Yana (who actually uses the term 'reboot' at one point, in reference to a computer), just as the Doctor previously hid as the mild-mannered John Smith in 'Human Nature'/'The Family of Blood', and then reassuming his true, evil persona as the episode approaches its climax. This idea may well have been influenced in part by Joseph Lidster's audio CD drama *Master* (Big Finish, 2003), which likewise serves as a new origin story for the Master and sees him initially living in human form as a man named John Smith (forcing the Doctor to adopt a different alias for once) with no memory of his evil past, and then having his true nature reawakened; a scenario that itself clearly owes a debt of inspiration to Paul Cornell's original novel *Human Nature* (Virgin Publishing, 1995).

Even though the fact that the Master would be featuring in Series Three was almost as poorly-kept a secret as the appearance of the Dalek Sec Hybrid in 'Daleks in Manhattan', it having been mentioned in numerous advance press reports, it was not generally known that 'Utopia' was to be the episode in which he would make his return, and the way Davies achieves this revelation via the device of the pocket watch is a stroke of real inspiration, and something that the viewer just doesn't see coming. It neatly explains why the Doctor mistakenly believed himself to be the last of the Time Lords, finally makes sense of the Face of Boe's dying message – the initial letters of the four words 'You are not alone' being brilliantly revealed to spell out the Professor's name – and leads up to what must surely be one of the very best episode endings in the entire history of the series, as the restored Master regenerates and steals the Doctor's TARDIS. The way that Davies brings so many different, and hitherto apparently unconnected, plot threads together to create this incredibly dramatic cliffhanger is really quite wonderful, and gives 'Utopia' its *raison d'être*, as well as a place of huge significance in *Doctor Who* lore.

Another notable aspect of 'Utopia' is the casting as Professor Yana of Sir Derek Jacobi, one of Britain's finest and most distinguished thespians, still perhaps best known for his remarkable portrayal of the title character in the classic serial *I, Claudius* (BBC One, 1976); a character who, notably, was afflicted by the sound of horses' hooves pounding continuously in his head – possibly a source of inspiration for the sound of drums in the Professor's head. This is not, in fact, the first time that Jacobi has played the Master: he previously took the role (or an android version of it, at least) in the flash-animated adventure 'Scream of the Shalka', written by Paul Cornell and made available to view in six instalments on the official *Doctor Who* website in 2003. [94] He has another prior *Doctor Who* connection, too, having played the lead role of Martin Bannister, an elderly scriptwriter whose identity starts to become confused with that of the Doctor, in Robert Shearman's audio CD drama 'Deadline' (Big Finish, 2003), part of the *Doctor Who Unbound* range. 'Utopia', however, sees him gaining his first credit on the TV series itself – and thus fulfilling what was apparently a long-time ambition of his. His performance as the Professor is simply superb, bringing a real warmth and dignity to the character and making it entirely credible that the Doctor should strike up an instant rapport with this endearing and resourceful old man. Equally if not more impressive is his skilful playing of the scene where the Professor opens the pocket watch and transforms into the Master, an evil glint suddenly appearing in his eyes and a new steeliness in his manner. This is a truly spine-chilling moment – although still perhaps not *quite* as astonishing as the similar incident in 'The Family of Blood' where John Smith suddenly switches to the Doctor and then back again in the space of a few seconds; which is testament to the sheer brilliance of Tennant's performance in the latter scene, as indeed throughout Series Three. Jacobi has only a couple of minutes of screen time as the Master before he regenerates, but is so gloriously arrogant and delightfully malicious in the role that

---

[94] The canonicity of 'Scream of the Shalka' is an even more problematic issue than usual for a tie-in story, owing to the fact that it features an 'alternative' ninth Doctor portrayed by Richard E Grant – although some fans have argued that as the one line of dialogue that appears to identify him as the ninth incarnation is clearly a reference to something that happened in his past, he could actually be a post-tenth incarnation Doctor.

one wishes it could have been a lot longer.

John Simm, by contrast, is alarmingly over-the-top in his brief debut as the new incarnation of the Master, giving considerable cause for concern as to his suitability for the role. This concern will thankfully prove to be unfounded in 'The Sound of Drums'/'Last of the Time Lords', and Davies has since attributed the character's bizarre behaviour at the end of 'Utopia' to the effects of 'regeneration trauma', as has been previously seen to afflict the Doctor in the aftermath of some of his own regenerations; but one is tempted to wonder if this was not really just a case of Simm misjudging his performance here, and refining it, perhaps with the benefit of further direction and advice, before going on to record the other two episodes.

Amongst the other guest cast members, two in particular stand out. The first is young John Bell, winner of the *Blue Peter* competition for a viewer to take an acting part in the series, who is genuinely impressive in the role of Creet and really rather puts to shame one or two of the professional actors playing the adult human refugees, whose performances might be charitably described as indifferent. The second is Chipo Chung, who does an excellent job in the difficult role of the Professor's faithful insectoid companion Chantho – whose status as the last survivor of her race recalls that of the Doctor as the last (or so he believed) of the Time Lords. The actress copes admirably well with the highly unusual speech pattern that Davies has chosen to give the character – which involves her prefacing every utterance with 'Chan' and following it with 'Tho' (something that producer Phil Collinson initially thought was a repeated typo in the script) – and also with the heavy prosthetic appliances and other make-up that she is required to wear. This makes it all the more unfortunate that the prosthetic appliances themselves are far too obvious, and really rather poorly done. While the contributions that Neill Gorton and his Millennium FX team make to *Doctor Who* are generally of an extremely high quality, this is the fourth instance in Series Three of them turning out a less-than-fully-effective piece of work – the other three being the hag-form Carrionites in 'The Shakespeare Code', the pig-augmented Laszlo in 'Daleks in Manhattan'/'Evolution of the Daleks' and the Dalek Sec Hybrid, also in the latter story – which suggests that they may on occasion have been overstretched, or else been given insufficient time and resources to achieve successfully everything that was being asked of them. In other respects, though, the production values on 'Utopia' are fortunately well up to the series' usual, very high standards.

Director Graeme Harper is back on top form on this episode, too, having disappointed slightly on '42', particularly in his handling of the guest cast members. He succeeds here in creating an atmosphere of mounting tension and excitement as the action builds toward its thrilling climax, and in giving this truly dystopian future a suitably apocalyptic feel. His handling of the regeneration sequence – the second he has directed, as he was previously responsible for the change-over from the fifth Doctor to the sixth in 'The Caves of Androzani' (1984) – is also excellent. It obviously follows the template of the regeneration from the ninth Doctor to the tenth in 'The Parting of the Ways' – a good idea on Davies's part, as it makes it absolutely clear what is happening, even for viewers unfamiliar with the classic series – but is much better realised, and the Master actually looks quite demonic as the transformation occurs and he unnervingly screams.

If one can get past Simm's performance, the Master's dialogue in the post-regeneration scene is actually very amusing. His line 'Why don't we stop and have a nice little chat while I tell you all my plans and you work out a way to stop me, I *don't* think' humorously recalls the way that, in the classic series, the Master's schemes were often foiled when the Doctor caught him monologuing – to use the apt description of this type of cliché coined in the movie *The Incredibles* (Buena Vista Pictures, 2004). The only slight mystery here is why the Master makes a point of picking up and taking with him into the TARDIS the jar containing the Doctor's severed hand.

There are a number of other very nice incidental touches for the fans to spot in the episode. One example is the Doctor's description of the human race as 'indomitable', echoing a celebrated line from the classic series story 'The Ark in Space' (1975). Another is the way he gives a wave and says 'Hello!' to Martha at one point, when she expresses amazement at his having grown a new hand, recalling a similar exchange between the ninth Doctor and Rose in an early scene in 'Rose'. Then there is the use on the soundtrack, just before the Professor opens his pocket watch, of brief audio snippets of two of the earlier Masters, Roger Delgado (delivering a line from 'The Dæmons' (1971)) and Anthony Ainley (giving his trademark chuckle), in a last-minute addition by Davies (the omission of a similar clip of Eric Roberts' Master apparently being due purely to the fact that the BBC does not own full copyright to the TV Movie in which he played the role).

But really 'Utopia' is all about that last ten minutes or so, as the Master regains his Time Lord form, regenerates into his new, 'young and strong' body and departs in the TARDIS, leaving Chantho dead and the Doctor, Martha and Jack apparently stranded at the mercy of the savage Futurekind. Never before has an episode of *Doctor Who* been so wholly geared toward setting up its cliffhanger, and while this has a downside in terms of its failure to tell a self-contained story, it certainly has the very positive effect of building up huge anticipation for the two remaining instalments to come.

# 3.12 – THE SOUND OF DRUMS

Writer: Russell T Davies
Director: Colin Teague

## DEBUT TRANSMISSION DETAILS

BBC One
Date: 23 June 2007. Scheduled time: 7.15 pm. Actual time: 7.15 pm.

BBC Three
Date: 24 June 2007. Scheduled time: 8.00 pm. Actual time: 8.00 pm.

Duration: 46' 16"

## ADDITIONAL CREDITED CAST

Alexandra Moen (Lucy Saxon), Colin Stanton (President[95]), Nichola McAuliffe (Vivien Rook), Nicholas Gecks (Albert Dumfries), Sharon Osbourne (Herself), McFly (Themselves), Ann Widdecombe (Herself), Olivia Hill (BBC Newsreader)[96], Lachele Carl (US Newsreader)[97], Daniel Ming (Chinese Newsreader)[98], Elize Du Toit (Sinister Woman)[99], Zoe Thorne, Gerard Logan, Johnnie Lyne-Pirkis (Sphere Voices)[100].[101]

## PLOT

The Doctor and his companions get back to 21st Century Earth courtesy of Jack's vortex manipulator device, which the Doctor has managed to repair. They find to their amazement that the Master, having arrived back 18 months before them in the TARDIS, has just been elected Prime Minister in the guise of Harold Saxon, with his wife Lucy at his side. They are forced into hiding as the Master brands them suspected terrorists. The Doctor rigs up a personal perception filter for each of them, and they are able to make their way unnoticed onto a UNIT sky ship, the *Valiant*, which is to be the venue for a 'first contact' meeting set up by the Master with a supposedly benign alien race called 'the Toclafane', who appear as floating metal spheres. The US President takes charge of the event, but is assassinated by

---

[95] Full name given in dialogue as 'Arthur Coleman Winters'.
[96] Not credited in *Radio Times*.
[97] Not credited in *Radio Times*.
[98] Not credited in *Radio Times*.
[99] Not credited in *Radio Times*.
[100] Not credited in *Radio Times*.
[101] Leo's partner Shonara was played uncredited by Channon Jacobs.

the Toclafane when they arrive. The Master then assumes control and, at a prearranged time, the sky breaks open, allowing six billion Toclafane to stream down to the Earth and begin decimating the population. The Master uses his laser screwdriver augmented by technology developed by Professor Lazarus to age the Doctor through 100 years, severely weakening him. Jack is taken prisoner, but Martha escapes from the *Valiant* using the vortex manipulator.

## QUOTE, UNQUOTE

- **Jack:** 'The moral is, if you're going to get stuck at the end of the universe, get stuck with an ex-time agent and his vortex manipulator.'
- **Master:** 'This country has been sick. This country needs healing. This country needs medicine. In fact, I'd go so far as to say that what this country really needs, right now … is a Doctor.'
- **Master:** 'The Time Lords only resurrected me because they knew I'd be the perfect warrior for a Time War. I was there when the Dalek Emperor took control of the Cruciform. I saw it. I ran. I ran so far. Made myself human so they would never find me, because … I was so scared.'
- **Doctor:** '[Gallifrey] was beautiful. We used to call it the Shining World of the Seven Systems, and on the continent of Wild Endeavour, in the mountains of Solace and Solitude, there stood the citadel of the Time Lords. The oldest and most mighty race in the universe, looking down on the galaxies below, sworn never to interfere, only to watch.'
- **Master:** 'And so it came to pass that the human race fell, and the Earth was no more, and I looked down upon my new dominion as Master of all and I thought it … good.'

## CONTINUITY POINTS

- Most of the action of the episode takes place on the day following the General Election, which Martha states is only four days after she met the Doctor. This implies that the Election Day scenes involving Francine in '42' take place three days after the events of 'Smith and Jones' and two days after those of 'The Lazarus Experiment'. The Toclafane arrive at 8.00 am the following day.
- The Doctor repairs Jack's vortex manipulator using his sonic screwdriver, and he and his companions then use it to get back to 21st Century Earth from Malcassairo. Due to the Doctor's revamping of it, it subsequently functions as a teleport as well.
- *Sunday Mirror* journalist Vivien Rook says of Harold Saxon, '18 months ago, he became real. This [photograph] is his first honest-to-god appearance, just after the downfall of Harriet Jones. And at the exact same time, they launched the Archangel network.' Since Harriet Jones's downfall did not occur until sometime after Christmas 2006 – when, as Prime Minister, she ordered the destruction of the Sycorax spaceship ('The Christmas Invasion') – this could be taken to imply that 'The Sound of Drums' is set no earlier than 18 months after that, i.e. no earlier than June or July 2008. This, though, would not tie in with earlier indications that the General Election takes place around January 2008. Another possible interpretation of Rook's statement, and one that seems more

likely to be correct, is that Saxon 'became real' six months or so before he made his 'first honest-to-god appearance' as seen in the photograph; after all, it would surely have taken him at least six months of behind-the-scenes work to create the Archangel network before he could 'go public' with it and officially launch it. This would suggest a timeline as follows:

**Summer 2006:** The Master first arrives on Earth, establishes himself as Harold Saxon (or becomes 'real' in Rook's terms) and starts to work toward the creation of the Archangel network – while also secretly making trips back and forth between Earth and Utopia, in the two time zones locked into the TARDIS co-ordinate systems by the Doctor, to set up the invasion by the Toclafane.

**December 2006:** The Sycorax spaceship appears over London and is destroyed on the orders of Prime Minister Harriet Jones, leading the Doctor to start rumours about the state of her health. These rumours quickly lead to her downfall.

**Spring 2007:** Harold Saxon makes his first ('honest-to-god') public appearance and joins the Government as the Minister responsible for launching the Archangel network (as stated by Rook in a video message to Torchwood). This subsequently causes most of the population to believe his fictional biography.

**Summer 2007:** Harold Saxon at some point becomes Minster of Defence, and contributes to the design of the *Valiant*.

**Autumn 2007:** A General Election is called. This may or may not be due to the downfall of Harriet Jones a few months earlier, since which time Great Britain has presumably had a different Prime Minister (identity currently unknown; but this must be the Prime Minister that Jack speaks to over the phone in the *Torchwood* episode 'Greeks Bearing Gifts'), perhaps explicitly on a 'caretaker' basis. For some reason (also currently unknown), there is to be an exceptionally long interval of more than four months before the General Election actually takes place, during which time the country will be in considerable political turmoil. It is public knowledge that Harold Saxon is on course to be the next Prime Minister if his party wins the General Election, and one edition of the *Daily Telegraph* reports that he is leading 'the polls', presumably meaning the opinion polls, 'with 64 percent'. During this pre-Election period, 'ghosts' begin mysteriously appearing, and the Battle of Canary Wharf takes place; possibly it is this that causes the Election to be delayed.

**December 2007:** Harold Saxon, either in his capacity as Minister of Defence or as *de facto* leader of the Government pending the General Election, gives the order for the Racnoss's webstar to be destroyed when it appears over London on Christmas Eve. (Jack curiously states that this is when Saxon 'first came to prominence', but possibly the general public were previously distracted from political matters by the 'ghosts' and the sudden arrival of Cybermen all over the world, or possibly he means 'came to prominence' from Torchwood's perspective.) It is possible that Saxon subsequently resigns from the Government and sets up his own independent political party, the Saxon Party, if suggestions to that effect on the Vote Saxon website are to be believed. This would account for the 'Vote Saxon' posters seen in 'Smith and Jones', 'The Sound of Drums' and *Torchwood*'s 'End of Days' (given that such General Election posters would normally seek to persuade members of the public to vote for a particular party, rather than its leader).

**January 2008:** Martha meets the Doctor when the Royal Hope Hospital gets temporarily transported to the Moon. Four days later, the General Election takes place and Harold Saxon becomes Prime Minister, apparently leading a Government of national unity, with Cabinet members drawn from all political parties. (This may perhaps be why Rook refers to him at one point as 'a modern Churchill', Winston Churchill having also led a Government of national unity during the Second World War.)

- The Master appears to recall everything that he experienced as Professor Yana – just as the Doctor appeared to remember his time as John Smith at the end of 'The Family of Blood'. He knows who Martha and Jack are, and is aware that Jack is immortal. His prior knowledge of Martha would also account for his attempt to trap the Doctor by manipulating members of her family, ensuring that Tish gained employment (for which she was not fully qualified) first at Lazarus Laboratories, as seen in 'The Lazarus Experiment', and now, just a couple of days after Lazarus's death, as an aide at 10 Downing Street, and also securing the help of Francine to monitor Martha's phone calls, as seen initially in '42'.

- When the Master, as Harold Saxon, arrives for the first – and last – meeting of his Cabinet (who are said to have 'gone into seclusion' after he murders them), he mentions 'Downing Street rebuilt'. This refers to the fact that the street was destroyed by a missile in 'World War Three'.

- The logo of Magpie Electricals – the TV sales company introduced in 'The Idiot's Lantern' – is briefly visible on the back of the TV set in Martha's flat.

- Referring to an incident in the Time War, the Master says: 'I was there when the Dalek Emperor took control of the Cruciform. I saw it … I ran. I ran so far, made myself human so they would never find me because … I was so scared.' The implication of this seems to be that he fled from the Time War in a TARDIS, complete with a Chameleon Arch like the one seen in the Doctor's ship in 'Human Nature'. If this is so, it leaves open the question of what subsequently became of the Master's TARDIS. It is possible that, as Professor Yana, he cannibalised its systems to aid in the construction of the rocket on Malcassairo; some of the control panels in his laboratory, as seen in 'Utopia', slightly resemble an old-style TARDIS console. The possibility remains, however, that the Doctor's TARDIS is not, after all, the only one still in existence.

- The Doctor explains that Time Lord children[102] are taken from their families at the age of eight to enter the Academy, and that their initiation involves looking into the Untempered Schism – shown as a kind of circular portal on the surface of Gallifrey, with the Seal of Rassilon on the ground before it – which is 'a gap in the fabric of reality through which could be seen the whole of the vortex'. He says that, in reaction to this, 'some would be inspired, some would run away … and some would go mad,' clearly implying that the Master was one of those who went mad, and that he himself was one of those who ran. (The Master will later confirm, in 'Last of the Time Lords', that it was at his initiation that he first heard the sound of drums in his head.) This recalls the Doctor's comment to Jack in 'Utopia' about what would happen if a Time Lord were actually to absorb the vortex: 'If a Time Lord did that, he'd become a god; a vengeful god.'
- The Doctor says that when the TARDIS was stolen by the Master on Malcassairo, he used the sonic screwdriver to 'fuse the co-ordinates' and lock them 'permanently', so that the ship could thereafter travel only backwards and forwards between the year 100 Trillion and the last place it landed – which was Cardiff around February 2008, as seen at the start of 'Utopia' – give or take a maximum of 18 months. Clearly the Master has been unable to overcome this limitation, and it is left unclear in 'The Sound of Drums' whether or not the Doctor will be able to do so subsequently. The TARDIS's systems are seen here to have been cannibalised by the Master to create a 'paradox machine', the precise purpose of which the Doctor is unable to deduce at this stage. The familiar cloister bell warning sound, first heard in 'Logopolis' (1981), rings out repeatedly inside the ship.

---

[102] The question of how Time Lords reproduce has been the subject of much debate within *Doctor Who* fandom. Some of the tie-in novels, most notably Marc Platt's *Lungbarrow* (Virgin Publishing, 1997), maintain that Gallifrey was cursed with sterility by its one-time ruler the Pythia, so that children could no longer be born naturally; instead, new Time Lords were subsequently woven in genetic looms, each loom being linked to a 'house' – the equivalent of a dynasty – comprised of numerous 'cousins'. There were thus no longer any 'true' children on Gallifrey, although some might have emerged from the looms in a form that, to human eyes, would resemble a child, and might have been referred to as such (and certainly, as *Lungbarrow* confirms, educated as such). According to this history, the Doctor is special, because he was effectively 'born twice'. He was originally a mysterious entity called the Other, who may not even have been native to Gallifrey, but after sacrificing himself by throwing himself into the looms, was reborn as the Doctor – the only Time Lord to have a navel – in the House of Lungbarrow. The Other's grand-daughter, Susan, the last child to be born naturally on Gallifrey, was subconsciously recognised by the Doctor and joined him on his travels when he left in the TARDIS. The curse of sterility was later broken (and may possibly have been only propaganda to start with) when the Doctor's one-time companion Leela married the Time Lord guard Andred and fell pregnant. This strand of continuity is advocated by some fans but dismissed by others. There is nothing in 'The Sound of Drums', or elsewhere in the TV series, that either confirms or directly contradicts it.

- The Doctor explains that the signal generated by the 15 satellites of the Archangel network (which has the same rhythm as the drumming in the Master's head) has been exerting a subtle hypnotic influence on the world's population. This explains why those in the UK voted for Harold Saxon in the General Election, and also why he himself previously failed to sense that there was another Time Lord present on Earth, as he should have done 'way back'. He creates personal perception filters for himself and his two companions by specially adapting their TARDIS keys – 'three pieces of the TARDIS, all with low-level perception properties, because the TARDIS is designed to blend in; well, sort of' – to work in conjunction with a second, low-level, signal generated by the Archangel network. He describes the effect of a perception filter by saying: 'It's like when you fancy someone, and they don't even know you exist; that's what it's like.' Seeing how Martha reacts to this, Jack says 'You too, huh?' This appears to suggest that, like Martha, Jack has unreciprocated romantic feelings toward the Doctor. A possible alternative explanation is that he is likening Martha's situation to Rose's, as he recalls it from when he last saw the Doctor and Rose together at the end of 'The Parting of the Ways'; this is made less likely, however, by the fact that on Malcassairo he appeared to be aware of the Doctor's feelings toward Rose.

- Although the US leader who takes charge of the first contact meeting with the Toclafane is generally referred to simply as 'President Winters' – and the Master describes him to Lucy as 'the last President of America' – in the scene where he addresses the Toclafane on the bridge of the *Valiant* he says, 'My name is Arthur Coleman Winters, President Elect of the United States of America and designated representative of the United Nations'. 'President Elect' is a formal term used to describe someone who has won a Presidential election, these being held once every four years in November (in 2004, 2008, 2012 and so on in our universe), but has not yet been sworn into office, this taking place the following January. During this period, the incumbent President remains in charge. Taken at face value, Winters' self-description as 'President Elect' would thus seem to suggest that he is not in fact the President, but will become so shortly, and that the episode is set sometime during the November to January period – which, if one assumes that there is a US Presidential election in 2007 in the *Doctor Who* universe as opposed to 2008 in ours, would tie in with other indications that the action takes place in January 2008 (see the suggested timeline above). Against this, however, it seems distinctly odd that the President Elect, rather than the President, should be entrusted with such an historic duty, even as a designated representative of the United Nations, given that the President Elect has no constitutional standing. In addition, a plane transporting the President Elect should not be referred to by the call sign 'Air Force One', as mentioned in a news report in the episode, as that designation is reserved for aircraft carrying the President. One possible explanation that presents itself is that Winters is not only the President Elect but also the existing Vice President, and has at the same time been appointed Acting President for some reason – possibly incapacity on the part of the incumbent President. If this scenario were correct, Winters would be Vice President, Acting President and President Elect all at the same time, and might just conceivably refer to himself as 'President Elect', given that the office of President is obviously more senior than that of Vice President or even Acting President. This seems rather far fetched, however, and another, perhaps more likely, explanation is that Winters intends to say 'elected President' but, in the stress of the moment, and possibly having only just taken office within the last few days, simply garbles his words (as real US Presidents have been known to do even in our universe ...). This would mean that in the *Doctor Who* universe – taking into account evidence from the tie-in stories as well as from the TV series – the succession of US Presidents is as follows (with, as suggested above, the elections taking place in different years than in our universe):

Jan 1994 – Jan 1998: President Bill Clinton[103]
Jan 1998 – Jan 2002: President Tom Dering[104]
Jan 2002 – Jan 2004: President Bruce Springsteen[105]
Jan 2004 – Jan 2008: President George W Bush[106]
Jan 2008: President Arthur Coleman Winters[107]
Jan 2008 – Jan 2013: President Chuck Norris[108]

---

[103] See the novels *Option Lock* (BBC Books, 1998) and *Interference* (BBC Books, 1999).

[104] See the novels *Option Lock* (BBC Books, 1998) and *Interference* (BBC Books, 1999). In *Option Lock*, Dering recalls the election having taken place the previous year, probably meaning 1997, as the action of this book is set in 'the present day' according to its publicity material, i.e. probably in 1998. He is said to have defeated Clinton in the election, and so is probably a Republican.

[105] See the novels *Eternity Weeps* (Virgin Publishing, 1997) and *Interference* (BBC Books, 1999). Becomes President after retiring from the music business. Orders nuclear attacks on Turkey and the Moon in 2003 in an attempt to stop the spread of an alien terraforming virus known as Agent Yellow.

[106] George W Bush is President in the *Doctor Who* webcast and audio CD drama 'Death Comes to Time' (2001), and aspects of his real-life Presidency such as the 'war on terror' and the Iraq war are referenced in the novel *Trading Futures* (BBC Books, 2002) and the audio CD drama *Unregenerate!* (Big Finish, 2005). It has to be assumed that Springsteen's term of office is cut short for some reason – probably related to the events of *Eternity Weeps*, which he may not have survived – and a new election held in November 2003, resulting in Bush being sworn into office in January 2004. Given that Springsteen was probably a Democrat, if he did die in the events of *Eternity Weeps*, there may have been a short period during which his Vice President served as Acting President before Bush was elected.

[107] Assassinated by the Toclafane just a few days after taking office, at the end of January 2008.

[108] See the novels *Cat's Cradle: Warhead* (Virgin Publishing, 1992), set circa 2007-2009, and *Interference* (BBC Books, 1999). A very right-wing President, Norris ended immigration to the US and endorsed the establishment of Local Development laws that prevented the unemployed from leaving their local area to find work. It is assumed here that Norris was Winters' Vice President, became Acting President after his assassination and was then elected in his own right in a new election held in November 2008, taking office in January 2009 (in the same way that President Johnson succeeded President Kennedy following the latter's assassination in 1963).

Jan 2013 – Jan 2017: President Mather[109]

Dates unknown: President Schwarzenegger[110]

- Jack admits to the Doctor for the first time in this episode that he now works for Torchwood (as seen in *Torchwood*). He says, 'I swear to you, it's different, it's changed. There's only half a dozen of us now … The old regime was destroyed at Canary Wharf. I rebuilt it, I changed it, and when I did that, I did it for you, in your honour.' Jack is initially puzzled as to why he is unable to contact his Torchwood colleagues, and the Master says that he has sent them on a wild goose chase to the Himalayas.
- On arriving in Britain, President Winters tells the Master that the operation leading up to the first contact meeting with the Toclafane is now under the control of UNIT. UNIT – the United Nations Intelligence Taskforce – has featured numerous times in *Doctor Who* since making its debut in 'The Invasion' (1968). Its most recent appearance prior to 'The Sound of Drums' was in 'The Christmas Invasion', although it was also mentioned a number of times in *Torchwood*. The aircraft carrier *Valiant* is explicitly stated by Jack to be a UNIT ship. When it arrives for the 8.00 am first contact meeting with the Toclafane, the co-ordinates given for it (58.2° N, 10.02° E) suggest that it is hovering in international airspace somewhere over the Baltic Sea; a later shot of the Toclafane descending from above the ship down to the Earth below appears to confirm this. The Master is said to have contributed to the design of the ship. The bridge has a number of features that recall Time Lord motifs, such as circular patterns akin to the roundels on TARDIS interior walls and insignia reminiscent of Gallifreyan symbols.
- In an article written by Russell T Davies for the *Doctor Who Annual 2006* (Panini, 2005), it is stated that a significant event leading up to the last great Time War was an attempted Dalek-Time Lord peace treaty initiated by President Romana[111] under the 'Act of Master Restitution'. Fans have long theorised that this is a reference to events in the TV Movie (1996), in which the Daleks execute the Master but allow his remains to be taken back to Gallifrey by the Doctor. It is however possible that the phrase 'Master Restitution' could

---

This would probably mean that Winters and Norris are both Republicans, like Bush.

[109] Mather is President in the novel *Trading Futures* (BBC Books, 2002). No date is given in the novel itself, but circumstancial evidence from the text suggests that the action takes place circa 2010-2015.

[110] See 'Bad Wolf', where his first name is unspecified. Some fans have suggested that he is the former actor and Governor of California Arnold Schwarzenegger, but this seems unlikely as his Austrian nationality prevents him from running for President. Given that 'Bad Wolf' is set in the year 200,100, it is more likely to be a descendent of the actor or someone completely unrelated that is being referred to. It is not actually specified in the episode that the country of which Schwarzengger is President is the USA.

[111] Romana, companion to the fourth Doctor in the TV series, becomes President of the Time Lords in the tie-in novels and CD audio dramas.

also allude to the Time Lords' resurrection of the Master to fight in the Time War, as he describes in 'The Sound of Drums'.

- The Master has a laser screwdriver, in contrast to the Doctor's sonic screwdriver. He has incorporated into it a miniaturised version of Professor Lazarus's experimental device – the development of which he funded, as noted in 'The Lazarus Experiment'. He uses this in conjunction with the Doctor's genetic code, obtained from the severed hand that he took with him when he left Malcassairo in the TARDIS, in order to age the Doctor's body by '100 years'.

- The beginning of the Master's televised address from the bridge of the *Valiant*, 'Peoples of the Earth, please attend carefully ...' echoes his – rather wider – broadcast in the final episode of the classic series story 'Logopolis': 'Peoples of the universe, please attend carefully ...'

## SAXON REFERENCES

- The mystery of Harold Saxon is finally revealed in this episode.

## PRODUCTION NOTES

- 'The Sound of Drums' was made with 'Last of the Time Lords' as part of Block 8 of production on Series Three.
- For the first time in the second part of a multi-part story in the new series, the opening pre-titles sequence consists of new material rather than a montage of clips recapping the first part.
- The group Girls Aloud were reportedly invited to make one of this episode's celebrity cameo appearances, but were unable to do so due to a scheduling conflict.
- Russell T Davies had previously stated in interviews that he disliked the character of the Master and had no intention of bringing him back. This was partly to avoid spoiling the surprise of the character's eventual return, and partly a 'delaying tactic' as he had yet to figure out how to write the character in a way that would appeal to a 21st Century audience. He eventually realised that the key was to depict the Master as a literal madman; a clinically insane sociopath. He also decided to make him just as witty as the Doctor, so that the Doctor would no longer have all the best lines in each episode; a development that he reasoned would be unsettling both to the Doctor and to the viewer at home, and would heighten the drama of the story.
- In an interview published in the 18 June 2007 edition of the listings magazine *TV and Satellite Week*, John Simm explained how he had come to be cast as the Master: 'I'd been talking to BBC producer Julie Gardner, who is responsible for both *Life on Mars* and *Doctor Who*, quite a bit over the last year or so about the possibility of me appearing on the show. We were trying to find something for me to do in *Doctor Who*. When they came up with the role of Harry Saxon I thought it was perfect ... Russell T Davies came up to Manchester where I was [recording] *Life on Mars*, and we had a top-secret midnight meeting in a

hotel[112] after a night shoot. Russell described what was going to happen and I was like, "Yes, absolutely, I'll do that."'

- The Master's opening of his televised address from 10 Downing Street with the words 'Britain, Britain, Britain,' is a homage to the comedy series *Little Britain* (BBC Three/BBC One, 2003-2006), in which the same phrase is regularly used in narration delivered by fourth Doctor actor Tom Baker, who has occasionally expressed a wish to return to *Doctor Who* in the role of the Master. This scene features brief flashback clips from 'Aliens of London', 'The Christmas Invasion', 'Army of Ghosts', 'Doomsday' and 'The Runaway Bride'.

- John Simm was initially keen to play the Master with a goatee beard, akin to that worn by Roger Delgado and Anthony Ainley in the role in earlier eras. This idea was seriously considered and discussed at length before it was eventually dropped.

- The journalist character Vivien Rook was based on real-life journalist Jean Rook (1931-1991), who was similar in appearance. Sometimes known as 'the First Lady of Fleet Street', she once in the mid-1970s wrote a newspaper article – now infamous amongst long-time *Doctor Who* fans – attacking the series' then script editor Robert Holmes under the pretext of interviewing him.

- A brief clip from 'Utopia' is used as the Doctor recalls fusing the TARDIS co-ordinates when the Master stole the ship.

- The US newsreader played by Lachele Carl has previously featured in 'Aliens Of London', 'World War Three' and 'The Christmas Invasion'. A video clip accessible via the spin-off website Who is Doctor Who? (www.whoisdoctorwho.co.uk) gives her name as Mal Loup – a French translation of 'Bad Wolf'.

- The headline of the Chinese TV news report about Harold Saxon's announcement concerning his plan to greet the Toclafane translates as 'Western Lies'. The report itself roughly translates as indicating that the Chinese government have declared it illegal to watch the British broadcast; and the newscrawl running across the bottom of the screen repeats this. The Chinese accent of the actor who plays the newscaster is reportedly very unrealistic.

- The costume of the young Master seen in the retrospective sequence of his initiation on Gallifrey was based on those of the Time Lords featured in 'The War Games' (1969). This was at the suggestion of uncredited script editor Gary Russell. The adult Time Lords' collars were three slightly adapted originals from 'The Deadly Assassin' (1976), borrowed by costume designer Louise Page from the Doctor Who Museum in Blackpool. The look of Gallifrey itself – complete with twin suns in the sky, as mentioned in 'Gridlock' – appears to have been inspired in part by a concept painting of the planet in what is referred to as the 'Leekley bible', a leather-bound document prepared in conjunction with a subsequently-rejected script by John Leekley for what ultimately became the TV Movie (1996), as documented in Gary Russell's book *Regeneration* (HarperCollins, 2000). The image of Gallifrey depicted on the cover of the audio CD drama *Neverland* (Big Finish, 2002) also appears to have

---

[112] The Malmaison Hotel.

been inspired by the same painting.

- The Untempered Schism on Gallifrey resembles, and may have been inspired by, a similar device used by the Time Lords in the comic strip story *The 4-D War*, published by Marvel in Issue 51of *Doctor Who Monthly* in 1981. Another influence may have been the Total Perpective Vortex in Douglas Adams's *The Hitchhiker's Guide to the Galaxy* saga.
- Flashback clips from 'The Lazarus Experiment' are used in the scene where the Master uses his laser screwdriver to age the Doctor.
- The prosthetic make-up used for the elderly version of the Doctor in this episode was different from that seen in 'The Family of Blood', owing to the far greater ageing that he had supposedly undergone.
- The televised press conference by 'Harold Saxon' that the Doctor and his companions see in the opening pre-titles sequence was recorded at Cardiff's Millennium Centre. As in 'Aliens of London'/'World War Three', Hensol Castle in Wales was used for the interior shots of 10 Downing Street, which were recorded in mid-February 2007. The brief scenes in the American students' flat, with Toclafane smashing through a window, were also recorded here. The brief location scene of Leo and his family in Brighton was shot in Penarth in Wales.
- The official *Doctor Who* website notes that the name 'Toclafane' is a rough French translation of the phrase 'Fool the fan'. Whether or not this was intentional on Russell T Davies's part is uncertain.
- The dance music track played by the Master at the end of the episode is 'Voodoo Child', a single first released in Australia in 2005 by the group Rogue Traders, taken from their album of the same year, 'Here Come the Drums' (Sony BMG).
- Two spin-off websites were created by bbc.co.uk to promote this episode: Vote Saxon – at www.votesaxon.co.uk – and Harold Saxon – at www.haroldsaxon.co.uk. The former presented graphics of various 'Vote Saxon' posters, video clips of references to Saxon in previous *Doctor Who* episodes and a poll where the user could vote either for or against Saxon. The latter replicated the video and web pages seen on Saxon's personal website by the Doctor, Martha and Jack in 'The Sound of Drums' itself. Following transmission of 'Last of the Time Lords', the Vote Saxon pages were taken down and the web address redirected to the Harold Saxon site. (See also 'Press Reaction' below for comments by Adam Sherwin, media correspondent of *The Times*, on this online promotional activity.)

## UNFOUNDED PRE-TRANSMISSION RUMOURS

- The Gallifrey flashback sequence would show the Doctor as a young man, with footage of first Doctor actor William Hartnell from one of his film roles incorporated and adapted using CGI.
- Elisabeth Sladen would make a cameo appearance as Sarah Jane Smith, being taken into custody by Saxon's 'men in black'.

OOPS!

- In the opening scene where the Doctor, Jack and Martha first arrive back in London by teleport, there is an obvious continuity error: in one shot, Martha initially puts her hands to her stomach and forehead respectively and then lowers them to her sides; in the next shot, they are back on her forehead and stomach again.
- A council vehicle with a distinctively Welsh logo of a red dragon on the front is seen in one of the location scenes where Martha drives to her parents' house through what are supposedly London streets.
- In the scene where the Doctor, Martha and Jack, having seen themselves branded as suspected terrorists in a TV news bulletin, start to run, the laptop computer that Jack is carrying switches from his left hand to his right hand and back again between shots.
- It seems highly unlikely that the Master could have taken Professor Lazarus's process, perfected it, succeeded in reversing its effect (so as to age the subject rather than rejuvenate) and managed to incorporate it in miniaturised form in his laser screwdriver, all in the space of the three days since Lazarus gave his first public demonstration of his device. (Perhaps the Master was working on the process in parallel, using the Professor's interim results as he went along?)

PRESS REACTION

- 'He has blogged his manifesto, taken over YouTube and submitted to grillings on Bebo. Tonight *Doctor Who* viewers will finally meet the mysterious Harold Saxon after his emergence from one of television's most intricate web campaigns. After three months of sophisticated "viral" promotion that has spread through dozens of networking websites, the Saxon character will be revealed as the latest *Doctor Who* villain … Mr Saxon is already a familiar figure for "Whovians", thanks to the BBC's web campaign, which has exploited popular social networking websites. As younger viewers drift from television to the net, the BBC has to ensure that hits such as *Doctor Who* now have a life far beyond a once-a-week slot in the schedules. A "Vote Saxon" website has promoted the candidate's policies – national renewal with a tough line on illegal aliens – and featured Mr Saxon's interviews with outlets including the BBC's *Politics Show*. The character has answered questions about his plans for Britain on the Bebo and MySpace networking websites, and antiSaxon sites have warned "voters" that he is a dangerous demagogue who will destroy the world. A link was even posted on Hazel Blears' Labour deputy-leadership website. BBC trailers featuring Mr Saxon have been posted on YouTube and "remixed" by fans, attracting thousands of views. The campaign culminated in a "General Election" on Thursday night. Opinion polls were published daily and fans signed up for SMS messages updating them on the result. The BBC hopes to inspire an interest in Parliamentary politics among apathetic teenagers. More than 50,000 fans voted, with Saxon-sceptics winning by 55 percent to 45 percent.' Adam Sherwin, *The Times*, 23 June 2007.
- 'The second part of this fiendishly involved story by Russell T Davies involves

John Simm masquerading as the Prime Minister. His style is presidential and he treats the Cabinet with contempt. His policies may lack substance, but everyone voted for him because, as Martha Jones ... says: "He always sounded good – like you could trust him." The first intimation of trouble ahead comes when the PM tells the nation: "I have been contacted. I have a message for humanity from beyond the stars." Ring any bells?' David Chater, *The Times*, 23 June 2007.

- 'Life on Mars's fabulous John Simm plays the Master, rocking a winning combo of pantomime camp and total psychotic fury. It's often genuinely unnerving – like watching Keyser Söze[113] play Widow Twanky. The moment when Simm ripped open the sky, and dropped six billion Toclafane on the Earth – like when they release the Lottery balls, but with genocide – was absolutely thrilling.' Caitlin Moran, Times Online website, 30 June 2007.

## FAN COMMENT

- 'The Master is not just another *Who* baddy, he is supposedly the Doctor's nemesis, his equal in all matters except [that] where the Doctor is good and devoted to saving people (hence the name), the Master is evil and devoted to dominating them. At a time when the Doctor was played by a 51 year old man who was very much a traditional action hero, it made sense for the Master to be an older and more traditional monomaniacal villain. However, David Tennant's Doctor is young, hip, attractive and has a marked tendency to gurn. Given that this is who the Doctor is at this time, it makes perfect sense for his evil reflection to be just as attractive, just as hip and just as prone to gurning. In Simm's Master, [Davies] has created a perfect foil for his own Doctor ... The episode [also] contains some interesting politics. "The Christmas Invasion" featured Harriet Jones firing upon a retreating alien battleship: a clear reference to Mrs Thatcher's decision to destroy the Belgrano during the Falklands war despite the fact that the ship had exited the area of engagement. "The Sound of Drums", by contrast, seems to be far more internationalist in its politics, with Saxon initially going out of his way to antagonise, mock and generally annoy the American President, who uses the UN charter to justify taking over something that he had no right to take over. Clearly, the portrayal of the Americans wielding international law because it suits their vanity to do so is a reference to the highly suspect justification of the invasion of Iraq on the basis of the ceasefire that ended the Gulf War. Equally, one suspects that Saxon's antagonistic attitude towards the Americans is a reference to the widely held belief that Tony Blair was George W Bush's "poodle", deployed to put a multilateral sheen on what was clearly an illegal and unilateral war.' Jonathan McCalmont, SF Diplomat website, 25 June 2007.
- 'The bulk of "The Sound of Drums" was some serious amount of fanwank, but wow it was fun. To paraphrase the Doctor, 57 fanfic authors just punched the air. I hear those were the exact same Time Lord collars from "The Deadly Assassin" [1976]. That dome was gorgeous, and the fact that the Time Lords

---

[113] The villain from the movie *The Usual Suspects* (PolyGram Filmed Entertainment / Gramercy Pictures, 1995).

have a door into the temporal vortex just sitting on a beach somewhere is wonderful. I like that there was a Black Time Lord in canon as well. Makes me a little giddy, considering how much I enjoyed Don Warrington's turn as Big Finish's Rassilon.[114]' J Salem, Behind the Sofa website, 2 July 2007.

• 'Having spent almost three series being perfectly circumspect about "the mythology", carefully layering in everything on a need-to-know basis, letting the viewer's imagination fill in the gaps, not even bothering to mention the Doctor's home planet for two years, [Davies now gives us something] like ... one of those YouTube montages that edit together old episodes to evoke the Time War or the eighth Doctor's regeneration ... Except with a much vaster budget and a modicum of taste ... You can imagine the glee in Russell's face as he tapped away until three in the morning, wired on caffeine, as 40-odd years of watching the show poured through his fingertips, finally letting rip doing absolutely everything that potential novelists at Virgin and BBC Books and scriptwriters were told not to do. No resurrecting of old villains, no continuity references and absolutely, definitely no flashbacks to the Doctor's days at the academy, unless we say you can ... But ... somehow, magically, it's entirely possible that he managed to reintroduce all of this mythology and still make it play for fans and non-fans alike. I would imagine if I was ten years old, the Gallifrey flashback here would have been like the appearance of the Time Lords at the close of "The War Games" [1969], vital elements of the Doctor's past suddenly made real.' Stuart Ian Burns, Behind the Sofa website, 23 June 2007.

## ANALYSIS

As Russell T Davies has noted, if one puts any surname containing the letter 'a' after the title 'Mister', the result is bound to contain an anagram of the word 'Master'. Nevertheless, given that in the classic series the identity of the Master, and even of the actor portraying him, was sometimes concealed behind an anagrammatical alias, such as 'Gilles Estram' (Gilles Master) for the character and 'James Stoker' (Master's Joke) for actor Anthony Ainley in 'The King's Demons' (1983), it is an amazing, and really rather pleasing, coincidence that the name 'Mister Saxon' should be an anagram of 'Master No. Six', with John Simm portraying the sixth version of the Master to have been seen on TV to date.

The full rundown of the six versions is as follows:

1. Roger Delgado ('Terror of the Autons' (1971) to 'Frontier in Space' (1973))
2. Peter Pratt ('The Deadly Assassin' (1976)) and Geoffrey Beevers ('The Keeper of Traken' (1981))
3. Anthony Ainley ('The Keeper of Traken' (1981) to 'Survival' (1989)) and Gordon Tipple (TV Movie (1996))
4. Eric Roberts (TV Movie (1996))
5. Derek Jacobi ('Utopia' (2007))
6. John Simm ('Utopia' (2007) to 'Last of the Time Lords' (2007))

---

[114] Rassilon, one of the founders of Time Lord society, is played by Black actor Don Warrington in the *Doctor Who* audio CD dramas produced by Big Finish.

Alternatively, as one intriguing fan theory would have it, and given that there is presumably no reason why the Doctor and the Master, as two time travellers, should always meet 'in sequence' from their own individual perspectives (unless this was one of the Time Lords' Laws of Time …?), it might be:

1. Roger Delgado ('Terror of the Autons' (1971) to 'Frontier in Space' (1973)) and Gordon Tipple (TV Movie (1996))
2. Eric Roberts (TV Movie (1996))
3. Peter Pratt ('The Deadly Assassin' (1976)) and Geoffrey Beevers ('The Keeper of Traken' (1981))
4. Anthony Ainley ('The Keeper of Traken' (1981) to 'Survival' (1989))
5. Derek Jacobi ('Utopia' (2007))
6. John Simm ('Utopia' (2007) to 'Last of the Time Lords' (2007))

Whichever of these alternatives is correct – and this question is greatly complicated if one considers also the tie-in stories in other media, some of which, such as John Peel's novel *Legacy of the Daleks* (BBC Books, 1998), would seem to confirm the former, others, such as David A McIntee's novel *First Frontier* (Virgin Publishing, 1994), would seem to support the latter, and others still are difficult to reconcile with either – it is certain that the Master has had at least 11 other incarnations not seen on TV. The Pratt/Beevers, Ainley, Tipple and Roberts versions are all explicitly indicated to be different physical manifestations of the same, thirteenth incarnation; having already used up the maximum 12 regenerations normally allowed to a Time Lord (as established in 'The Deadly Assassin'), the Pratt/Beevers version steals the body of a Trakenite named Tremas (another anagram) in order to become the Ainley version, and the Tipple version transforms into a snake-like mutant and then takes over the body of a human ambulance driver named Bruce in order to become the Roberts version. The Delgado version could actually be any one of the Master's 13 standard incarnations, although David A McIntee's novel *The Dark Path* (Virgin Publishing, 1997) would seem to imply that he is the first – and if he is any other than the thirteenth then, under the fan theory, the Tipple incarnation seen at the start of the TV Movie would have to be moved onto a separate line in the list, making Simm the seventh version rather than the sixth.

What none of this explains, of course, is how the Master ends up in 'Utopia' in the Jacobi incarnation, hiding in human form on Malcassairo, with his ability to regenerate obviously restored and intact. This is dealt with fairly cursorily in 'The Sound of Drums', when the Master says: 'The Time Lords only resurrected me because they knew I'd be the perfect warrior for a Time War. I was there when the Dalek Emperor took control of the Cruciform. I saw it. I ran. I ran so far. Made myself human so they would never find me, because … I was so scared.' To this, the Doctor replies 'I know' – which could be simply an expression of sympathy and understanding, or could alternatively suggest some prior knowledge of the Master's role in the Time War, which might perhaps explain why, in 'Utopia', he appears to guess straight away the identity of the Time Lord whose essence is contained within the Professor's watch. It is left unspecified how and in what circumstances the Time Lords 'resurrected' the Master, but perhaps when doing so they gave him a whole new regeneration cycle – something that he had previously sought to obtain from them in 'The Five Doctors' (1983), and that was clearly therefore within their power to bestow. At any rate, the lack of any detailed explanation for the Master's survival is very much in keeping with the precedent established during the 1980s, when it was generally the case that no hint at all would be given as to how he had managed to extricate himself from the seemingly fatal situation in which he had been left at the end of his previous encounter with the Doctor.

I have to admit that, prior to seeing 'The Sound of Drums', I had considerable reservations about the wisdom of Russell T Davies's decision to bring back the Master. The original version portrayed by Delgado in the 1970s was great, and hugely popular with the general viewing public, but that was arguably due as much to the brilliance of the actor's performance, and to his perfect chemistry with Jon Pertwee, as to the appeal of the Master *per se*. I've never really understood why the production team decided to resurrect the character in a new, deformed version in 'The Deadly Assassin' in 1976 – it's not as if the series' format actually *requires* the Doctor to have an 'arch-enemy', after all – and it just didn't quite work for me. Less palatable still was the Ainley version introduced in 1981, owing both to the over-the-top, pantomime-villain-like performance the actor was generally required to give in the role (contrary, it seems, to his own wishes) and to the appallingly bad material he was frequently afforded in the scripts, the combined effect of which was to completely devalue the character. *Doctor Who Magazine*'s Clayton Hickman summed this up perfectly in his editorial in Issue 384, dated 25 July 2007:

> I'm a self-confessed Dalek fanatic, and the Cybermen have a similar iconic lure, but when I was watching *Doctor Who* as a boy, the Master just didn't cut it for me – he seemed like a bit of an idiot, to be honest. Remember, dear reader, this was back in the 1980s, so for me the Master was Anthony Ainley in a toupee, dressed in crushed black velvet, "heh-heh-heh"-ing his way around the universe in the regular TARDIS set except painted matt black. Plus, of course, he could return from the dead at any moment, without the faintest whiff of an explanation, and had plans so ridiculous they boggled even my young mind.

Although criticised by many fans, for reasons I've never quite been able to fathom, Roberts' take on the role in the TV Movie of 1996 was much more successful to my eyes, being deliciously villainous, wonderfully camp and, at times, startlingly violent; but that was only a one-off appearance, and did little to redress the way the character had been mishandled during the previous decade.

Thankfully, by the end of 'The Sound of Drums', the skilfulness of Davies's scripting and the brilliance of Simm's portrayal have firmly re-established the Master as a viable character in a new, emphatically modern mould, perfectly matched to David Tennant's Doctor. The most problematic aspects of the Ainley Master's plans in stories such as 'Time-Flight' (1982), 'The King's Demons' and 'The Mark of the Rani' (1984) were their apparent motivelessness, irrationality and (certainly in universal terms) sheer triviality; here, Davies responds to the challenge of rehabilitating the character by giving him a reason for his actions that not only makes perfect sense of his schemes as Harold Saxon but also, rather wonderfully, provides a sort of retrospective justification for the craziness of some of his past exploits, as

Hickman observed in his *Doctor Who Magazine* editorial:

> [This] brings us full circle to John Simm, and his hilariously
> bonkers take on the character. Another Master to love – at last!
> And what thrills me the most is that now we have an explanation
> for the Master's constant failure and ludicrous plans – the drums
> were obviously much louder on those days. *Duh-du-du-DUM* –
> 'Ow! Ooh, I know, I'll go and mess up Magna Carta.[115] Heh-heh-
> heh ...'

In other words, by virtue of some clever retconning (as science-fiction fans would
term it), it now becomes apparent that, from a very early age, the Master has been
completely and utterly insane. As the Doctor explains: 'Children of Gallifrey are
taken from their families at the age of eight, to enter the Academy. Some say that was
where it all began, when he was a child. That's when the Master saw eternity. As a
novice, he was taken for initiation, stood in front of the Untempered Schism – that's a
gap in the fabric of reality through which could be seen the whole of the vortex. We
stand there, eight years old, staring at the raw power of time and space, just a child.
Some would be inspired, some would run away ... and some would go mad.' This
wonderfully evocative speech, spoken over a stunningly-realised retrospective
sequence of the young Master, flanked by more senior Time Lords, gazing into the
Untempered Schism on the surface of Gallifrey – the first glimpse that viewers have
had of the Doctor's home planet in the new series, or indeed at all since 'The Five
Doctors' – supplies just the sort of imaginative and plausible backstory that the
Master has really always needed but has previously lacked (leaving aside one or two
attempts made in the tie-in ranges to remedy essentially the same shortcoming; in
particular in the novel *The Dark Path* and the audio CD drama *Master* (Big Finish,
2003)). Admittedly the Doctor has never had a specific reason for going around the
universe doing good, as opposed to evil, but somehow that hasn't seemed to matter.
The Master's malevolent plans, by contrast, have always felt contrived and
unbelievable, and that is what is finally addressed here. It adds the last, crucial
element to the new origin story meticulously set up by Davies in 'Utopia', and makes
all the difference in terms of the credibility of the character and the integrity of the
drama.

The Simm incarnation is truly a Master for the 21st Century: witty, energetic,
unpredictable, disco-music-loving – and totally psychotic. His gleeful frivolity in
scenes such as the one where he happily watches an episode of *Teletubbies* (BBC One,
1997-2001) on TV – mirroring an incident in 'The Sea Devils' (1972) where he watches
an episode of the earlier children's series *Clangers* (BBC One 1969-1974) – is hilarious;
and when he shows the same sort of childlike delight while indulging in casual
slaughter, such as in the sequence where journalist Vivien Rook is killed by the
Toclafane as he and Lucy Saxon repeatedly check on the progress of the carnage from
beyond a soundproof door, it really becomes quite chilling as well. That the Master

---

[115] This is a reference to the Master's scheme to prevent the signing of the Magna
Carta – an English charter issued by King John in 1215 and now regarded as an
important legal document in the history of the development of democracy – in 'The
King's Demons' (1983).

has at his side this archetypal attractive-yet-ruthless 'politician's wife', beautifully portrayed by Alexandra Moen, is really just the icing on the cake, topping off a fantastic reinvention of the character.

The relationship between the Master and Lucy at times recalls that between the Joker and Harley Quinn in *Batman: The Animated Series* (Fox, 1992-1995), and can also arguably be seen as a sort of dark, distorted reflection of that between the Doctor and Rose Tyler. When Rook tries to persuade Lucy to betray Saxon, she replies 'I made my choice' – echoing what Rose says in 'Doomsday' when the Doctor tries to persuade her to leave him and join her family in the safety of the parallel universe. The Master, having entered the room unnoticed by Rook, then refers to Lucy as 'My faithful companion', reinforcing the impression that the bond between them is similar to that between the Doctor and his companion. Later, on the *Valiant*, in another very amusing touch, he produces a paper bag and offers Lucy a jelly baby (which she eats with relish), borrowing one of the fourth Doctor's most famous traits (although the second Doctor was actually the first to offer jelly babies to his friends, in 'The Three Doctors' (1972), and the eighth Doctor also did so in the TV Movie). In fact, as the episode progresses, it starts to seem that Lucy is, in her own way, almost as twisted and sadistic as the Master himself. She certainly seems to share in his delight at the chaos he unleashes, even doing a little dance as the Toclafane stream down to Earth to the strains of an upbeat dance track, 'Voodoo Child' by Rogue Traders; the latest example in the series, and possibly the most effective yet, of a piece of fun pop music being used to counterpoint terrible events unfolding on screen, as for instance when John Lumic's men play Tight Fit's 'The Lion Sleeps Tonight' (1982) to drown out the sound of people screaming while being converted into Cybermen in 'Rise of the Cybermen'.

A particular highlight of the episode is the scene where the Doctor and the Master first talk to each other via Martha's mobile phone. There is a curious intimacy to this conversation – in fact, it might not be going too far to say that there is an almost erotic quality to it; an impression reinforced when the Master playfully enquires of the Doctor 'Are you asking me out on a date?' – recalling how in some of their earlier encounters, in stories such as 'The Claws of Axos' (1971) and 'Colony in Space' (1971), they seemed at times to have an unspoken bond that far exceeded the Doctor's loyalty to his human friends, occasionally even leading the latter to fear that the two Time Lords might join forces and abandon them. It throws an interesting light on the Doctor's feelings toward Rose and his other recent human companions when he says to the Master, 'I've been alone ever since [the end of the Time War], but not any more. Don't you see; all we've got is each other.' This closeness between these two supposed enemies is one reason why, back in the 1980s, there arose amongst fans a popular theory that they might secretly be brothers – an idea that, in an excellent in-joke, Martha actually puts to the Doctor in 'The Sound of Drums'. The Doctor's reply, 'You've been watching too much TV', obviously refers to the cliché of secret family relationships being sensationally revealed in soap operas and the like – although, for those fans determined to cling on to the theory, it is worth noting that he does not explicitly deny it.

The Master's scheme to become Prime Minister by subjecting the British electorate to a sort of mass hypnosis using the Archangel satellite network recalls his frequent use of hypnosis to achieve his ends in the classic series, and also John Lumic's use of the mobile phone network to control the population in 'Rise of the Cybermen'/'The

Age of Steel' (and more obliquely the role played by mobile phone signals in the defeat the Bane in *The Sarah Jane Adventures*: 'Invasion of the Bane'). Davies's main source of inspiration for this, however, appears to have been the two-part story 'Meet John Doe'/'Lois and Clarks' (1997) from season four of *Lois and Clark: The New Adventures of Superman* (ABC, 1993-1997), in which a recurring villain named Tempus secures the Presidency of the USA in exactly the same way; the likelihood that this was a significant influence is further strengthened by the fact that in his debut appearance, in the season two episode 'Tempus Fugitive' (1995), Tempus also travels back in time from a place called Utopia to try to rewrite history. The idea of Harold Saxon putting out a fake biography, which is initially widely believed despite containing many inaccuracies, may have been inspired by the fact that, notoriously, the very same thing was done by real-life politician and thriller writer Jeffrey Archer when he began his career.

Davies seems to have an uncanny knack of timing his writing of this kind of politically-flavoured story to perfection. Just as, by a happy coincidence, 'Aliens of London'/'World War Three', with its scenes of chaos in 10 Downing Street and oblique allusions to the Iraq war, was transmitted during a General Election period, so 'The Sound of Drums', with its depiction of Harold Saxon becoming the new Prime Minister, was seen by viewers in the very week that, in the real world, Tony Blair handed over the reins of power to Gordon Brown – whose first statement to the media outside 10 Downing Street had a number of uncanny similarities to Saxon's first televised address from inside the same building. What's more, a Conservative MP then swiftly defected to the Labour Party, and Brown stunned the establishment by offering Ministerial posts to a number of people from outside his own party, just as in this episode Saxon populates his Cabinet with defectors from other political camps – whom he then proceeds to murder in a gas attack, in one of the most memorable demonstrations of his total lunacy to be found in the entire story.

It is actually difficult not to see Harold Saxon as, to some degree, a satirical representation of Tony Blair, with his insincere smile, sanctimonious manner, soundbite-over-substance policy-making and New Labour-style suit. Davies has made light of such suggestions, but then he could hardly confirm them without risk of attracting criticism for bringing real-life politics into a family show (any more than the series' production team of the time could confirm that Helen A in 'The Happiness Patrol' (1988) was a satirical depiction of the then serving Prime Minister Margaret Thatcher, although they have since admitted that this was indeed the case). Certainly one can detect subtle hints of Blair's familiar mannerisms at times in Simm's performance, such as in his aforementioned televised address from 10 Downing Street (and particularly so in the full version of this viewable on the Harold Saxon website), and it is almost inconceivable that this was not intentional on the actor's part. Viewed in this light, the scenes where Saxon cheekily goads the US President (or is it President Elect? – see 'Continuity' above), who is muscling in under cover of the UN, and ultimately brings about his death-by-Toclafane, can perhaps be seen as providing a kind of fantasy wish fulfilment for those viewers who are of the opinion, quite commonly held in the UK, that the relationship between Blair and real-world US President Bush was altogether too close for comfort.

In terms of style, 'The Sound of Drums' takes *Doctor Who* into the territory of the urban thriller. Martha's flat being blown up by a time bomb (presumably intended as a 'calling card' by the Master, similar to the booby trap bombs he left for the Doctor in

'Terror of the Autons' (1971)); Francine and Clive being seized by heavily-armed police officers under the direction of Saxon's sinister female operative and 'men in black'; Martha racing to the scene in her little Vauxhall Corsa car, with the Doctor and Jack crammed in the passenger seats, only to be fired upon and forced to speed away again; the Master tracking them through the city via CCTV cameras, and having the TV stations issue bulletins branding them as suspected terrorists; the three fugitives being forced to hide in an abandoned warehouse, eating bags of chips that Martha has sneaked out to buy. This rapid succession of starkly realistic incidents would not seem out of place in a high-tech espionage drama, and is really quite unlike anything seen in *Doctor Who* before – a degree of innovation that is admirable in itself – although, as is often the case, there are precedents for it to be found in the tie-in novels ranges. Even relatively minor bits of business such as Jack making cups of tea with a teabag in Martha's kitchen as the Doctor finishes researching Harold Saxon on the internet help to ground the story in instantly recognisable reality and give the drama an exciting immediacy. The sense of realism is further enhanced by the series' latest, and by now almost obligatory, set of celebrity cameo appearances – in this instance by Sharon Osbourne, McFly and Ann Widdecombe – and by the device, as used in a number of other contemporary Earth stories, of having aspects of the action covered in authentic-looking TV news reports of various nations. Then there are the undertones of political intrigue as the US President arrives in England in his personal aircraft, identified by its traditional call sign Air Force One, to be met by the Prime Minister on the runway, recalling familiar images from many real-life international summits.

Events take a rather more fantastical turn when the action switches to the *Valiant*, revealed to be a huge aircraft-carrier-cum-military base hovering in the sky – a secret headquarters of *James Bond*-movie-supervillain proportions. Following on from his creation of a Captain who cannot die, this strongly suggests that Davies is being influenced by the classic Gerry Anderson series *Captain Scarlet and the Mysterons* (ITV, 1967-1968), whose title character is likewise indestructible and which similarly features a large, skyborne aircraft-carrier headquarters, known in this instance as Cloudbase. The Toclafane are also very similar in appearance to another Gerry Anderson creation, the Zeroids from *Terrahawks* (ITV, 1983-1984) – although, with their knife-like weapons extended, they equally recall the flying silver spheres from the cult horror movie *Phantasm* (AVCO Embassy Pictures, 1979) – giving a nice added frisson to the episode for those who recall those old series. Another possible source of inspiration for the *Valiant*, given Davies's love of comic books, is the Helicarriers used by the titular organisation in the *S.H.I.E.L.D.* series (Marvel Comics, 1965- ).

All this is really rather wonderful, and brilliantly directed by Colin Teague, making his *Doctor Who* debut (although he has previously worked on both *Torchwood* and *The Sarah Jane Adventures*). 'The Sound of Drums' is by no means perfect, though. The idea of the Doctor, Martha and Jack managing to get back to London in 2008 using Jack's vortex manipulator, rapidly repaired by the Doctor, is rather implausible, particularly given that they were in so distant a future on Malcassairo that not even the Time Lords had ventured that far. More seriously, coming directly after a very exposition-heavy episode in 'Utopia', 'The Sound of Drums' again sees the Doctor and his companions spending a great deal of their time sitting around talking about and explaining things (and continuity-related things at that – at times this seems almost like a throwback to the 1980s) rather than actually doing things.

They are, indeed, rendered literally inconspicuous after the Doctor rigs up a perception filter for each of them using their respective TARDIS keys – an idea possibly inspired by the 'somebody else's problem field' concept thought up by Douglas Adams and featured most prominently in his book *Life, the Universe and Everything* (Pan Books, 1982) – which effectively sidelines them from the principal action and leaves the Master as the story's main protagonist. This gives the episode a rather unbalanced feel, almost as if the Master has become the main star of the show.

The viewer then gets a foretaste of what is to come in the following episode when the Master eventually sees through the Doctor's perception-filter deception and – in a nice pay-off to the link with 'The Lazarus Experiment' established by Tish's unqualified employment first at the Lazarus Laboratories facility and now at 10 Downing Street – uses the fruits of Professor Lazarus's work to incapacitate his adversary by ageing him through 100 years. Naturally he would not want to actually *kill* the Doctor, as this would leave him without his perennial 'sparring partner' and give him no-one to gloat to – which he seems intent on doing here, having gone to great lengths to trap the Doctor and bring him to the *Valiant* apparently for this very purpose, despite having recognised at the end of 'Utopia' the dangers of monologuing – but causing him humiliation is obviously quite a different matter. Having said that, why being aged just 100 years should render the Doctor *quite* so feeble and helpless is unclear, given that he was aged 500 years in 'The Leisure Hive' (1980) to much less crippling effect, and that his first incarnation must have been several hundred years old at the point when the series began and he seemed to get by just fine, albeit with the odd ache and pain. Perhaps, though, the Master means 100 Gallifreyan years and they are a lot longer than Earth years …

The regrettable marginalisation of the regulars detracts only slightly, though, from what is otherwise a thrilling and highly memorable cliffhanger, as the Toclafane arrive on Earth through a tear in the sky and all hell breaks loose. There are some jaw-droppingly spectacular CGI shots here, particularly when Martha uses Jack's vortex manipulator to escape from the *Valiant* and teleport down to Earth, where the Toclafane are busy carrying out the Master's instruction to decimate the population; and great credit must go to the Mill for making these sequences so effective. There is, admittedly, a slight sense of *déjà vu* about the shots of London under attack, as they are not too far removed from those of the Cybermen and the Daleks battling it out in the city in 'Doomsday', but they are just about different enough to avoid this seeming like merely a repeat of the situation in the Series Two finale.

As thematically-rich, epic and exciting as this episode is, though, it is of course – and even more self-evidently so than 'Utopia' – only one-third of an ongoing narrative, rather than a complete story in its own right, so the final verdict on Series Three's climactic three-part conclusion will have to await 'Last of the Time Lords' …

# 3.13 – LAST OF THE TIME LORDS

Writer: Russell T Davies
Director: Colin Teague, Graeme Harper[116]

<u>DEBUT TRANSMISSION DETAILS</u>

BBC One
Date: 30 June 2007. Scheduled time: 7.05 pm. Actual time: 7.05 pm.

BBC Three
Date: 1 July 2007. Scheduled time: 7.00 pm. Actual time: 7.02 pm.

Duration: 51' 29"

<u>ADDITIONAL CREDITED CAST</u>

Alexandra Moen (Lucy Saxon), Tom Ellis (Thomas Milligan), Ellie Haddington (Professor Docherty[117]), Tom Golding (Lad), Natasha Alexander (Woman), Zoe Thorne, Gerard Logan, Johnnie Lyne-Pirkis (Sphere Voices)[118].[119]

<u>PLOT</u>

One year after the Toclafane's arrival, the Master rules the world, and millions of its inhabitants have died. Martha, protected by her perception filter, has been travelling from continent to continent on a secret mission. Returning to England and meeting up with a resistance group, she is taken to see a scientist called Professor Docherty. With the Professor's help, a Toclafane is captured, and Martha learns the dreadful truth: these creatures are the last survivors of humanity from Utopia, reduced to electronically-augmented heads in metal spheres and brought back in time to wipe out their ancestors, while their own continued existence is protected by a paradox machine constructed by the Master in the Doctor's TARDIS. The Master meanwhile has been using slave labour to build huge fleets of rockets with which he plans to attack neighbouring alien civilisations and establish a new Time Lord empire. Professor Docherty betrays Martha, who is captured by the Master and brought back to the *Valiant*. This, though, was all part of her plan. As instructed by the Doctor before she left a year earlier, she has been spreading a message around the world, telling everyone to say the Doctor's name

---

[116] Uncredited.
[117] First name given in dialogue as 'Alison'.
[118] Sphere Voices not credited in *Radio Times*.
[119] The hospital nurse to whom Martha speaks over the phone was played uncredited by costume supervisor Linda Bonaccorsi.

simultaneously at the point when the countdown to the launch of the Master's rockets reaches zero. When they do so, the Doctor is restored and able to defeat the Master. Jack destroys the paradox machine, causing time to roll back to the point just before the Toclafane's mass arrival on Earth, thus erasing the past year for all but those present on the *Valiant*. Lucy shoots the Master and, in preference to living out the rest of his life as the Doctor's prisoner, he refuses to regenerate and dies. Martha bids farewell to the Doctor, having decided to stay with her family and resume her career, but promises she will see him again. The Doctor departs, and is astonished when the TARDIS control room is suddenly breached by the prow of the famous ocean liner *Titanic* ...

## QUOTE, UNQUOTE

- **Master**: 'Once the empire is established and there's a new Gallifrey in the heavens, maybe then it stops. The drumming. The never-ending drumbeat. Ever since I was a child. I looked into the vortex. That's when it chose me. The drumming; the call to war. Can't you hear it? Listen; it's there now, right now. Tell me you can hear it, Doctor. Tell me.'

- **Martha**: 'I travelled across the world, from the ruins of New York, to the fusion mills of China, right across the radiation pits of Europe, and everywhere I went, I saw people just like you, living as slaves. But if Martha Jones became a legend, then that's wrong, because my name isn't important. There's someone else. The man who sent me out there; the man who told me to walk the Earth. And his name ... is the Doctor. He has saved your lives so many times, and you never even knew he was there. He never stops, he never stays, he never asks to be thanked, but I've seen him. I know him. I love him. And I know what he can do.'

- **Martha:** 'The thing is, it's like my friend Vicky. She lived with this bloke. Student house, they lived. There were five of them, all packed in. And this bloke was called Sean, and she loved him. She did. She completely adored him. Spent all day long talking about him.'
  **Doctor:** 'Is this going anywhere?'
  **Martha:** 'Yes! 'Cause he never looked at her twice. I mean, he liked her, but that was it, and she wasted years pining after him. Years of her life. 'Cause whilst he was around, she never looked at anyone else. And I told her, I always said to her, time and time again, I said, "Get out". So this is me, getting out.'

## CONTINUITY POINTS

- The scene immediately after the episode's opening credits consists of an announcement, over a computer screen graphic, aimed at passing space travellers: 'Space lane traffic is advised to stay away from Sol 3, also known as Earth. Pilots are warned, Sol 3 is now entering terminal extinction. Planet Earth is closed. Planet Earth is closed. Planet Earth is closed ...' Sol 3 was a name established for Earth in the classic series, initially in 'The Deadly Assassin' (1976).
- Martha recalls having met Shakespeare, as seen in 'The Shakespeare Code'.

- During his year in control of the Earth, the Master has arranged for the building of thousands of rockets that he intends to use to wage war on alien civilisations and create a new Time Lord empire. The entire south coast of England has been converted into shipyards where slave workers toil on the rockets' construction, using scrap materials from broken up cars, houses and the like. Martha says: 'You should see Russia. That's Shipyard No. 1. All the way from the Black Sea to the Bering Strait, there's 100,000 rockets getting ready for war.' The Master has also had giant statues of himself erected in numerous places, and even had his face carved into Mount Rushmore, the monumental granite sculpture of the heads of four former US Presidents located in South Dakota.
- The Master says that his laser screwdriver has isomorphic controls, meaning that only he can operate them. In the classic series story 'Pyramids of Mars'(1976), the Doctor states that his TARDIS has isomorphic controls, but he could simply be lying in order to deceive the evil Sutekh; certainly in subequent stories a number of other people are also seen to be able to operate the ship.
- The Master reminds the Doctor of their previous encounters involving the Axons – as seen in 'The Claws of Axos' (1971) – and the Sea Devils – as seen in 'The Sea Devils' (1973). He also refers to the Doctor having 'sealed the rift at the Medusa Cascade single-handed'; an incident not depicted in the TV series. The Doctor later mentions both the Axons and the Daleks.
- Professor Docherty, who works in 'a repair shed, nuclear plant seven', mentions the TV show *Countdown* (Channel 4, 1982- ) and says, 'It's never been the same since Des took over. Both Deses.' This refers to the fact that following the death of the original presenter Richard Whiteley in 2005, the show has been presented first by Des Lynam and secondly by Des O'Connor. The Professor also says, 'Whoever thought we'd miss Bill Gates?', referring to the famous American entrepreneur and chairman of Microsoft.
- It is revealed in this episode that the human race's final quest to find a way to survive the end of the universe in 'Utopia' was unsuccessful. Martha is told by a captured Toclafane: 'There was no solution. No diamonds. Just the dark and the cold.' The Master also notes of his visit to Utopia: 'You should have seen it, Doctor. Furnaces burning. The last of humanity screaming at the dark.' The human race became the Toclafane, and were then brought back in time to the 21st Century by the Master, who constructed a paradox machine in the Doctor's TARDIS so that they would be able to destroy their own ancestors without also cancelling out their own existence – a type of situation sometimes described as a 'grandfather paradox', as referenced by Martha on arriving in Elizabethan England at the start of 'The Shakespeare Code'.
- Martha tells Professor Docherty that both UNIT and Torchwood have been studying the Time Lords for 'years' (which may refer in part to the time the third Doctor spent working with UNIT during his third incarnation, when together they foiled a number of the Master's schemes), and that the end product of this research is a weapon, incorporating four phials of different coloured chemicals, that can kill a Time Lord outright. She claims that it is this weapon that she has been travelling the world to assemble. This, though, is simply a fiction, and a cover-story for her true plan, which she keeps

concealed, knowing that Professor Docherty will betray her to the Master out of concern for her son.

- While 'Destiny of the Daleks' (1979) suggests that a Time Lord can decide to regenerate at any time, as the Doctor's companion Romana selects a new body apparently at will, 'Last of the Time Lords' is the first story to indicate that a Time Lord can choose *not* to regenerate when his or her body is fatally injured.

- In the scene toward the end of the episode where Martha phones Thomas Milligan at the hospital where he works, a whiteboard on the wall behind Milligan shows what appears to be a chart divided into monthly columns on which figures have been entered up to October. Some fans have taken this to suggest an October dating for this scene and thus, by extension, for all the scenes prior to the arrival of the Toclafane and after the rolling-back of time, contrary to other indications that the General Election takes place in January 2008. It is possible however that the schedule shows projected targets for several months ahead, rather than results that have already been recorded, and this seems altogether too ambiguous a piece of evidence to form the basis of any conclusions.

- At the end of the story, Jack decides to return to his responsibilities with Torchwood rather than resume travelling with the Doctor. The Doctor disables the time travel and teleport functions of his vortex manipulator before he goes.

- Jack tells the Doctor and Martha that as a 'poster boy' of the Boeshane Peninsula, where he grew up in the 51st Century prior to becoming 'the first one ever to be signed up for the Time Agency', he was referred to as 'the Face of Boe'. This, along with the fact that he cannot be killed, suggests that he will one day become the wise old creature seen in 'The End of the World', 'New Earth' and 'Gridlock', who is said to have lived for millions if not billions of years and finally dies of old age after giving up the last of his life force to save the population of New New York at the end of the latter episode (old age presumably being the one thing that can, in the end, cause him to expire). The Face of Boe's knowledge that the Doctor was not the last surviving Time Lord, and that the initial letters of the words in the message 'You are not alone' would spell out the name of the Master's human *alter ego*, Yana, would thus be explained by the fact that he had previously discovered these things as Jack in 'Utopia' – another example of a predestination paradox of the kind featured in 'Blink'. The fact that the Face of Boe is said to have given birth to children – a news report in 'The Long Game' states that he is pregnant with the 'Baby Boemina', and the text of the book *Doctor Who: Monsters and Villians* (BBC Books, 2005) indicates that he had six children in the 2001st Century, each of whom lived for his species' average lifespan of 40 years – would not necessarily rule this out, as Jack implies in the 'Everything Changes' episode of *Torchwood* that he was once pregnant, suggesting that this is something of which he is capable. There are, however, other possible interpretations of Jack's revelation at the end of 'Last of the Time Lords'.[120] It may be, for instance, that the people who called Jack 'the Face of Boe' in his youth were

---

[120] In the bbc.co.uk podcast commentary on this episode, Russell T Davies refers to Jack's comment as simply a 'theory' as to the Face of Boe's origins, although his fellow executive producer Julie Gardner then urges him to 'stop backpedalling'.

actually having a joke at his expense, which he failed to realise because he didn't know who the real Face of Boe was; although in the novel *The Stealers of Dreams* (BBC Books, 2005), Jack says that he once saw someone 'dressed up as the Face of Boe'. This therefore leaves open the possibility that Jack is not in fact the same Face of Boe as seen in the earlier trilogy.

- Before she leaves, Martha gives the Doctor her mobile phone (which he adapted in '42' to have universal roaming) and tells him: 'When that rings, you'd better come running, you got it? … I'll see you again, mister.'

## PRODUCTION NOTES

- 'Last of the Time Lords' was made with 'The Sound of Drums' as part of Block 8 of production on Series Three.
- Although he had been thinking about it for a long time in advance, Russell T Davies wrote the first draft of the script for this episode in only four and a half days.
- Graeme Harper was brought in to direct the last two days of recording on the episode, mainly covering the scenes involving Professor Docherty, owing to the fact that principal director Colin Teague had fallen down some stairs and injured his back (earning him the nickname 'Tumbling Teague' amongst the production team). Harper was not credited for this either on screen or in *Radio Times*.
- This is the longest 'regular' episode of *Doctor Who* to have been transmitted since the series was revived; only the Christmas specials have been longer. The production team obtained special dispensation from the BBC One schedulers for it to be given a longer-than-usual slot, as they were loathe to cut anything out to bring it down to the normal length. They did however prepare a different version with approximately six minutes edited out for overseas sales purposes. The full version will thus be seen only in the UK and on the series' DVD releases.
- A 'One Year Later' jump similar to that seen at the start of this episode occurs in 'Lay Down Your Burdens' Part II, the Season Two finale of the US science fiction series *Battlestar Galactica* (Sky One/Universal HD/SciFi Channel, 2004- ), first transmitted on 10 March 2006. Davies, however, had the idea independently and prior to that date; in the bbc.co.uk podcast commentary for 'Last of the Time Lords', he recalls that he was initially annoyed when he saw the *Battlestar Galactica* episode, but then thought: 'Well, it's only watched by 300,000 people; I don't care. No-one's gonna know!' A 'One Year Later' device is also used a little earlier in Series Three in 'Blink', but only just prior to the closing scene. Another series to have used a similar idea is *Alias* (ABC, 2001-2006), the third season of which opens two years after the end of the second.
- Incorporated in this episode are brief flashback clips from 'Utopia', 'The Sound of Drums' and 'Smith and Jones'.
- Russell T Davies originally came up with the idea for the Toclafane back during production of Series One of the new *Doctor Who*, as he told *Doctor Who Magazine* in an interview published in Issue 385 in August 2007: 'When the original deal to use the Daleks fell through in Series One, I gave the concept, then nameless, to Rob Shearman as the replacement villain [for "Dalek"], and

they would then have turned up *en masse*, from the end of the universe, in "The Parting of the Ways". And when we had no idea what to find at the bottom of the Satan Pit [in Series Two's "The Satan Pit"] – it took us a strangely long time to realise that it should actually be Satan! – then these cannibalised end-of-humanity spheres were suggested for all of ten minutes. Thank God I was able to save them for their proper place. I'm not sure what I would have done here otherwise!'

- The idea of the Master having giant statues of himself erected around the world was inspired by the former Iraqi dictator Saddam Hussein's predilection for commissioning statues of himself. This was one of Davies's starting points in developing the story.

- The production team debated for some time whether or not to include the scene of an unknown woman's hand retrieving the Master's ring from the ashes of his funeral pyre. It was eventually decided to do so, and the scene was added to the script at quite a late stage. The idea was to leave open a possible way for the Master to be resurrected at some point in the future – for instance by revealing that the ring contained the Master's DNA, allowing for him to be cloned – although Davies has claimed to have no intention of using the character again himself.

- Ten copies of the Master's ring were made, and after the completion of recording, some of these were presented as gifts to members of the production team, including producer Phil Collinson and director Colin Teague.

- The suggestion that Jack might be the Face of Boe was not planned from the outset; Davies added it to his script for this episode at quite a late stage.

- The scene were Martha arrives on the beach at the beginning of the episode was shot on a rat-infested beach at Whitmore Bay, Barry Island, to the south of Cardiff, on 12 March 2007. The Gallifrey flashback scenes were recorded at the same location. The brief scene toward the end where Martha gives a surprised Professor Docherty a bunch of flowers in a park was recorded in Gorsedd Gardens in Cardiff civic centre two days later. The action in the infrastructure of the *Valiant* was shot at the beginning of the month in a disused paper mill on Trident Park industrial estate, previously used as a location on a number of other stories, including 'Daleks in Manhattan'/'Evolution of the Daleks'. (This building has since been demolished.) The bridge of the *Valiant*, on the other hand, was a studio set, the design of which was intended to evoke the style of plush hotel reception areas. The street where Martha meets the resistance group, supposedly in the London Borough of Bexley, was actually South Luton Place in Adamstown, Cardiff. The Doctor's cliff-top confrontation with the Master was recorded in Vaynor Quarry, Merthyr Tydfil, on 8 March 2007, as were the night-time scenes involving the Master's funeral pyre. As originally scripted, the pyre was to have been built on a boat that the Doctor would send out to sea, as in a Viking leader's funeral, but this idea was dropped in rewrites in order to reduce costs.

- The music track played by the Master on the *Valiant* at the beginning of the episode is 'I Can't Decide' by the Scissor Sisters, track three (as correctly stated by the Master) from their album *Ta Dah!* (Polydor, 2006). This was one of Russell T Davies's initial inspirations for the story.

- 'Last of the Time Lords' was also a working title for an unmade *Doctor Who* feature film in the 1990s, scripted by Johnny Byrne.

- Certain plot elements of this episode appear to have been inspired by the comic strip story *The Glorious Dead*, published in *Doctor Who Magazine* Issues 287-296, in which the Doctor's companion likewise joins a resistance movement to foil the plans of a regenerated Master while the Doctor himself is incapacitated.

## OOPS!

- In the scene where Milligan and Martha lead a Toclafane sphere into a trap set by Professor Docherty, Milligan holds his gun in his right hand throughout the sequence, apart from in one shot where it inexplicably switches to his left hand.

## PRESS REACTION

- 'The days when the nation stopped as one and huddled round the TV set for a big event are supposed to be long gone. But, by surrounding the finale with ferocious secrecy and hitting the warp-factor promo button, there was an old school buzz [created] about the season-crescendoing episode of *Doctor Who*. So, did it live up to the hype? Well, almost. In truth last week's cliffhanger was the real doc's whatsits, with John Simm an instant legend as a maniacal Master with a weakness for camp disco. But this week, with David Tennant, who'd been whizzed through the centuries and turned into a wizened old man, forced to sit out much of the action under a shedload of make-up, the battle between good and evil felt only half joined. It was left to Freema Agyeman's Martha Jones to tackle both the labyrinthine plot and a scene-stealing Simm, and she made a fine fist of it, even carrying off a pretty lame twist – the world saved by the power of telepathic union … get outta here – without cracking up. But no sooner have we clutched Martha to our bosom than it looks like she's off, unable to bear the frustration of flying through time with a hottie with two hearts – neither of which beats for her. So, Doctor, who's next?' Keith Watson, *Metro*, 2 July 2007.
- 'Saturday night's episode just felt too epic, too rushed and the resurrection of the Doctor through that global telepathic network (Praise the Lord!) left me cold. Perhaps if there had been more of a back story it would have been credible. I have always thought that the programme has never been able to excel when attempting the epic in its old or new seasons. Give me the claustrophobic dread of the lighthouse in the "Horror of Fang Rock" [1977] over the "Last of the Time Lords" any day.' Stephen Brook, *Guardian Unlimited* website, 2 July 2007.
  'Don't get me wrong. I love Doctor Who as much as the next man. Unless of course that man is Russell T Davies, the writer/Doctor Who fanatic responsible for reviving one of TV's greatest icons and making it the most thrilling, intelligent piece of family entertainment around. But Saturday's series finale was a mess. Sure, it was challenging, fascinating … but a mess just the same. Just when the occasion demanded a sensational, emotional rollercoaster (such as the one Davies delivered for Billie Piper's departure as

Rose), he lost the plot. Literally. God knows what it was all about. It was overloaded with schoolboy science and hokum about Utopia, specifically the paradox machine in which the children of 100 trillion years in the future had been sent back in time to destroy their own past. (Huh?)' Jim Shelley, *Daily Mirror*, 3 July 2007.

## FAN COMMENT

- 'I think this season of *Doctor Who* has been extremely conscious of its status as the top-rating British family drama, and its resulting responsibilities. I think the writing asks itself about whether or not to use its powers for good or evil, and what both of those might involve … Martha leaving the TARDIS is meant to show that she has grown up in some way (or was grown-up already), but … I [don't] mean by this that [she] has put away childish things … Like the angels and the demons in "The Girl in the Fireplace", like the drawings in "Fear Her", like the Toclafane coming true for the Doctor (a childhood bogeyman – something that can break all your hearts), *Doctor Who* expressly says to us: "Those childhood stories? They're true. They contain truth." What does this mean? Well, first of all, it means the emotional reality of childhood experience is affirmed. It's not silliness, or something to be grown out of – it's real, and it matters. And so, at various places throughout this season, we are asked to consider what a responsibility this is. Whether or not we will use this power for evil. Whether or not we will tell lies. Which casts a new light on the Time Lords' spectacularly irresponsible Saturday teatime viewing: "Hey, kids, let's peer at the infinite!" … So what did that produce? Well, the Master for one. And the Doctor too – we can't have the angels without the demons, or vice versa. I also think that when we look at the Time Lord Academy … we are meant to be reminded of the boarding school in "Human Nature"/"The Family of Blood". And so we are meant to be reminded of the spectacularly irresponsible Edwardian storytelling that culminated in a generation of young men being sent to slaughter each other. However, there is a difference, perhaps, between the kinds of stories these two schools are telling their students. What the teachers are telling at the boarding school is the Old Lie ("Dulce et decorum est …"). What the Time Lords tell is the unleavened truth. Through which some are inspired, some go mad, and some run like hell and keep on running.' 'Altariel', LiveJournal blog, 2 July 2007.
- 'What is interesting about the paradox machine is that it, in effect, allows for a complete breakdown of the laws of narrative by bracketing [this] within a set of clearly demarcated criteria. In other words, the question the paradox machine poses is, does it make sense for a story to contain bits that intentionally don't make sense? Can a story explicitly defy the laws of logic and narrative and still not collapse in on itself? … I suspect that it can, seeing as there are two sets of laws here. First, there are the laws of logic and physics as they apply in the *Doctor Who* universe and secondly, we have the higher-order laws of narrative and logic that apply to all stories in such a way that [they] make sense. These higher-level laws are necessary, because without them you can have characters be married or dead one second but single or alive the next. These are the laws that set off alarms in your head when

characters start doing things they wouldn't normally do. In creating the paradox machine, [Davies] is saying that the plot of the final episode of Series Three will … make [no] sense, but it will make no sense for a reason that makes perfect sense (namely there's a machine that bends the rules of narrative logic). So, in effect, the first-level laws of narrative logic are shattered by the paradox machine, but the second-order laws remain intact because there's a reason why something will happen for no apparent reason.' Jonathan McCalmont, SF Diplomat website, 27 June 2007.

- 'There was much to enjoy in the episode, in particular how all the various strands of the series came together. Time Lords hiding as humans, loneliness, the power of words, the non-linear nature of time, even the Face of Boe joke/resolution, but somehow it all rang a little bit hollow. Unfortunately, the reset button was predictable and took away much of the tension of the episode. I also felt that the resolution, with the chanting of the Doctor's name, while it made thematic and even some kind of technobabble sense, was very cheesy. These leaps of logic and somewhat dodgy mysticism are always the least successful parts of *Doctor Who* for me. However, on reflection the plot wasn't my real source of dissatisfaction. What really disappointed me was the decision to have the Doctor either absent or not in his normal state for most of the episode. I really missed him. David Tennant's eyes as the old Doctor powerfully conveyed his despair and his vocal performance really sold the CGI Doctor, but it wasn't really enough. I am at loss to explain why you would cast two of the most charismatic and talented actors currently working today (David Tennant and John Simm), playing two of the most iconic characters in the history of the series, and then reduce their interaction down to about ten minutes.' Libby Aldrich, www.david-tennant.com website, July 2007.

## ANALYSIS

I don't know what word Russell T Davies used in his tone meeting for 'Last of the Time Lords' to sum up the feel he wanted it to have, but based on how it turned out, a good guess might be 'bleak' or maybe even 'depressing'. This doesn't necessarily make it a bad episode, of course, but I do find it a very dispiriting one. There are seven main reasons for this, and I'll take each of them in turn.

### 1. The ill-treatment of the Doctor

Former *Doctor Who* script editor Andrew Cartmel has often recalled how, during his time on the production team, he aimed to make the Doctor a more powerful and mysterious presence, because he felt that the stories of the previous few years had tended to have him being pushed around, locked up and generally ill-treated, and that this diminished the character and undermined the series more generally. I do not by any means agree with everything that Cartmel says, but in this case I think he was spot on. In 'Last of the Time Lords', the Doctor is not only pushed around and locked up, but kept as an old man, treated like a dog, punched, taunted (as for instance when the Master refers to him as 'Gandalf', the wizened magician from Tolkein's *The Lord of the Rings* saga), deprived of his ability to regenerate, aged still further, turned into a withered homunculus (something like a cross between

*Harry Potter*'s Dobby and *The Lord of the Rings*' Gollum), kept in a birdcage and, in short, utterly humiliated. It might perhaps be argued that this is just another case of the series being influenced by the *New Adventures*, in which the Doctor is sometimes subjected to a great deal of punishment. The difference, though, is that while he is indeed made to suffer severe physical and mental torment in certain of the novels – perhaps most notably some of those written by Kate Orman – he is never made out to be cowed or victimised in quite the same way as he is in 'Last of the Time Lords'. It is quite apparent what Davies was aiming to achieve here: he wanted to have the Doctor placed in a situation of extreme degradation so that, when he ultimately won through, it would seem all the more glorious and uplifting. But for the Doctor to be seen to be so thoroughly debased, and powerless to do anything about it, is demeaning and ultimately damaging to the character; and this is a huge mistake. Not only that, but David Tennant is effectively reduced to the status of a guest star in his own series, as John Simm takes centre stage and gets all the best lines and action – making this arguably the fourth 'Doctor-lite' episode of Series Three, after 'Human Nature', 'The Family of Blood' and 'Blink'.

Even when the Doctor does get restored to his normal state, the way it is done just doesn't feel right. The depiction of the Doctor as a god-like figure has been (oddly enough, given that Davies is an avowed atheist) a recurrent feature of the Tennant era. It began at the start of Series Two with the explicit description of him as a 'lonely god' in 'New Earth', and his assertion in the same story, 'I'm the Doctor, and if you don't like it, if you want to take it to a higher authority, there isn't one; it stops with me'; and it has continued in Series Three, most notably in 'Human Nature'/'The Family of Blood', with his Christ-like adoption of human form and subsequent self-sacrifice, and his meting out of cruel punishments to the Family in the manner of, as one fan reviewer put it, 'a vengeful Old Testament God'. In 'Last of the Time Lords', the Master at one point shouts to Martha, who is hiding out with a resistance group in a scenario reminiscent of World War Two dramas, 'What would the Doctor do?' – an obvious allusion to the 'What would Jesus do?' approach to decision-taking espoused by some modern Christians. Eventually the Doctor becomes in effect a god to the whole world, and is saved by – as the Master incredulously observes – the power of prayer. Not only does this rejuvenate him, and at the same time conveniently disintegrate his cage and give him back his old clothes, but it even temporarily transforms him into a glowing, angelic form that descends from on high, first to hover over the Master [121], dispensing force from his outstretched hand to deprive him of his laser screwdriver, and then to embrace and bestow forgiveness on him. One can, of course, rationalise all this in terms of the fiction of the series: it is well established in *Doctor Who* that the power of collective human emotion can be harnessed to affect the physical world as if by magic, as seen for instance in a previous Master story, 'The Daemons' (1971); and the power of words, and specifically of names, is

---

[121] Davies, quoted in *Doctor Who Magazine* Issue 385, says of this image: 'It's funny, but it was only after this scene was completed and finished that I remembered those scenes from "The Mind of Evil" [1971], where the Master's worst nightmare is an all-powerful Doctor, looming above him. And here he is! I suppose these things seep into my subconscious – it wasn't a deliberate reference, but now I've seen it, I'm happy if people think it is!'

highlighted in the earlier Series Three episode 'The Shakespeare Code'. The idea of the Doctor tuning in to the psychic network formed by the (aptly named, as it turns out) Archangel satellites, so that he can draw on the positive thought energy of the Earth's surviving population all saying his name simultaneously at the point when the Master's countdown reaches zero (although how the Doctor knew a year in advance that there was going to be a countdown is something of a mystery), is perfectly consistent with this rational, scientific world-view. The metaphorical intent nevertheless remains clear: the Doctor here takes on the aspect of a divine being.

This really is a case of going from one extreme to the other: first the Doctor is reduced to the level of a caged beast, then he is elevated to the status of a god. Neither of these is an appropriate way for the character to be depicted, in my view, and it is the episode's worst aspect.

2. The use of the 'reset button'

As soon as the caption 'One Year Later' appears on screen and it is revealed that the world has been devastated by the Toclafane, it becomes obvious that at the end of the story Davies will resort to pressing the 'reset button' and restoring things to how they were before the Master's scheme came to fruition. It is, to be fair, difficult to see what else he could have done, given that he wanted to tell this story; it clearly wouldn't have been viable, or in keeping with the series' ethos, for him to have left the planet in a shattered state post-2008 – particularly in view of the heavy reliance that *Doctor Who* now places on contemporary Earth as a setting. It does, though, make the whole thing a bit predictable – at least for science fiction fans familiar with the cliché (as used, for instance, in the movie *Superman* (Warner Brothers, 1978)), if not so much for the general viewing audience, given that this device has never really featured in mainstream TV drama. It also leaves a number of unanswered questions. If the destruction of the paradox machine takes everything back to the point just after the US President is killed and just before the Toclafane arrive *en masse* on Earth, then why does it not restore all the other dignitaries, TV crew members and others who were on the bridge of the *Valiant* at that time? Is their failure to reappear accounted for by the fact that the ship is at 'the eye of the storm', as stated by the Doctor by way of explanation for the fact that he and his friends on board are unaffected by the time reversal and so still retain their memories of everything that has happened? And does this 'eye of the storm' factor explain also why Martha went to such great lengths to get betrayed by Professor Docherty, captured by the Master and taken back to the ship? Certainly she must have had some good reason for doing this as, logically, her mission – to get the whole of the Earth's remaining population to speak the Doctor's name at the appointed time – would surely have worked just as well even if she had remained on the planet's surface. Had she not returned to the *Valiant*, would she have simply ceased to exist, like those aforementioned dignitaries, TV crew members and so on? What will be the political consequences of the assassination of the US President on the orders of the British Prime Minister, and of the latter's subsequent murder at the hands of his wife? What becomes of Lucy Saxon after she shoots the Master? Why is it that the TARDIS is back to normal at the end of the story, with no trace of the paradox machine remaining? Is the absence of the usual handrails around the console area supposed to indicate that, unseen by the viewer, the Doctor has taken time out to repair his ship, making some modifications in the process?

The redeeming feature of all this is that, precisely because everyone on board the *Valiant* is left unaffected by the time reversal, things are not *completely* reset, and the story is saved from being rendered totally redundant in dramatic terms: the terrible events that have occurred will still have a lasting impact on the Doctor, Martha, Jack, the Jones family (except, presumably, for Leo, who was never captured), Lucy Saxon and no doubt all the security guards and crew members who also happened to be on the ship at the time – not to mention, of course, the Master. This leads nicely on to the episode's highly dramatic closing events.

3. The fate of humanity

One thing that remains completely unchanged by Davies's use of the 'reset button' is that the ultimate fate of humanity, in the *Doctor Who* universe, is to become what the Master dubs 'the Toclafane' – electronically-supported, telepathically-linked severed heads encased within hovering, weapons-bedecked spheres, speaking and acting like wicked children and taking a gleeful pleasure in slaughter and destruction. 'Tell me the human race is degenerate now!' says the rejuvenated Doctor as he rises up to hover angel-like above the Master. Well, we may not be degenerate in the 21st Century, but we certainly seem to have become so by the time we reach the year 100 Trillion; and more savage even than the Futurekind it was feared we might become, as mentioned by Professor Yana. 'Human race; greatest monsters of them all,' says the Master, and it is difficult to disagree with him. This is a cruelly ironic outcome to the last, hopeful quest for Utopia. It surpasses even the notoriously downbeat conclusion of *End of the Line*, the comic strip story that may have partly inspired it (see the 'Analysis' on 'Utopia'), and strongly recalls the equally bleak scenario of the fifth Doctor audio CD drama 'Singularity' (Big Finish, 2005), in which humans from the far future, mutated and half-metal, travel back in time to try to take over the Earth and escape the end of the universe. It is an extraordinarily grim picture for Davies to paint of our race's final destiny, very much at odds with his usual optimistic take on humanity, and also gives a strange and unsettling last twist to the recurring Series Three theme of what it means to be human, leaving a very bitter aftertaste.

4. The underuse of Captain Jack

Following his introduction in 'The Empty Child'/'The Doctor Dances' back in Series One, Captain Jack Harkness, brilliantly portrayed by John Barrowman, quickly established himself as a very popular companion to the Doctor; and with the advent of *Torchwood*, he became one of only two to have been granted a spin-off show (the other, of course, being Sarah Jane Smith, played by Elisabeth Sladen, with *K-9 and Company* and *The Sarah Jane Adventures*). Many fans were disappointed that he did not return to *Doctor Who* in Series Two, as had originally been intended, but consoled themselves with the knowledge that he would be back in Series Three. There was, therefore, a huge amount of anticipation built up for the Captain's involvement in this closing three-part story … but sadly it turns out to be a bit of a let-down, not because of any failing on Barrowman's part, but because the character is terribly underused in the scripts. His best moments really come in 'Utopia', with the explanation of what happened to him after he was abandoned on the Game Station at the end of 'The Parting of the Ways' and the well-achieved reconciliation between him and the Doctor; 'The Sound of Drums' sees him given very little to do, and here in 'Last of the Time Lords' he spends most of the episode chained up aboard the *Valiant*, with just a failed escape attempt to pass the time before he finally comes into his own a little toward the end, when he destroys the paradox machine. The final revelation that he will apparently one day become the Face of Boe is an unexpected twist, and adds a new dimension to this aspect of the series' mythology, but leaves me rather cold, as it seems an inappropriate fate for the dashing Captain, and also begs the question how he could possibly end up as a huge face in a glass life-support tank simply through the process of ageing, which normally causes things to wither away rather than grow larger.

All told, the much-vaunted return of Captain Jack proves to be a disappointment; and one can only imagine that Barrowman must have found it so too. It has to be hoped that the character will be brought back again at some later date – it would be sad if this turned out to be his last ever appearance in *Doctor Who* – and that he will be given a rather bigger slice of the action next time around. In the meantime, thankfully, the Captain's many admirers will at least have Series Two of *Torchwood* to keep them happy.

5. The failure of the Jones family

One of the great success stories of Series One and Series Two was the way that Rose Tyler's 'extended family' – mother Jackie Tyler, boyfriend Mickey Smith and father (or alternative universe counterpart) Pete Tyler – went from being fairly minor supporting characters to playing quite a major role in the unfolding drama, leading up to the exciting resolution of their story arc in 'Army of Ghosts'/'Doomsday'. Excellent characterisation by Davies and his writing team and superb performances by the likeable and well-cast Camille Coduri, Noel Clarke and Shaun Dingwall combined to see these characters make a really important contribution to the overall appeal of the new *Doctor Who*. Their departure at the end of Series Two left a big gap to fill. Step forward, the Jones family ... except that, sadly, these newcomers have proved to be not a patch on their predecessors, and to show nothing like the same potential for further development.

It would obviously have been a mistake for Davies to have tried to introduce characters who were essentially copies of Jackie, Mickey and Pete, but that still left him plenty of scope to come up with a different yet equally appealing family group for Martha, and the Joneses really don't fit that bill. They are given probably their best opportunity to shine in 'Last of the Time Lords', but fail to rise to the occasion. Leo is conspicuous by his absence (save for a brief shot of him through the window of the family home at the end of the episode), owing to actor Reggie Yates having been double-booked by his agent so that he was unable to appear, as planned, in the opening beach scene (where it would have been revealed that he had joined the resistance but, due to his commitment to his partner and child, was unwilling to accompany Martha on her journey to find Professor Docherty); Tish, although again nicely portrayed by Gugu Mbatha-Raw, fails to deliver on the promise she showed in 'The Lazarus Experiment'; Clive, not so well acted by Trevor Laird, is given little to do but be chained up; and Francine, once more the most prominently featured of the group but invested with little likeability by Adjoa Andoh, is hard to feel sorry for, even when she is mistreated by the Master, given that she has previously been seen to betray Martha to him in both '42' and 'The Sound of Drums'. The implication that Francine and Clive get back together again as a couple at the end of the episode, despite Martha's conviction in 'The Sound of Drums' that this could never happen, is also very corny.

That the Joneses have not worked out as viable substitutes for the Tylers or as a successful group of supporting characters in their own right is something that it is probably too late for Davies to do anything about by this point, short of writing them out or sidelining them from now on; and their failure to come good in 'Last of the Time Lords' is another disheartening aspect of the episode.

6. The departure of Martha

Martha's personal journey from medical student in 'Smith and Jones' to saviour of the world in 'Last of the Time Lords' is a remarkable one, and in many ways mirrors that undertaken by Rose, out of whose shadow she is finally able to step. This demonstrates once again how travelling with the Doctor can transform the lives of his companions, and brings Martha's time in the TARDIS to a natural conclusion. After everything she has experienced, particularly over the past year of walking the Earth and telling people about the Doctor (an idea that recalls how, in the tie-in series *Dalek Empire* (Big Finish, 2001), the character Susan Mendes, known as the 'Angel of Mercy', travels around spreading a message of hope that contains a secret instruction to enslaved populations to rise up against the Daleks at a given signal), it makes perfect sense for her to want to leave at this point, to resume the life that was interrupted in 'Smith and Jones'. It would, in fact, be almost unthinkable for her simply to resume her travels with the Doctor as if nothing had changed. Her decision to go also allows the character to keep her dignity, which would have been at serious risk had she continued to pine after the Doctor when it was obvious that her love for him was not going to be reciprocated; and the scenes where they say goodbye to each other are beautifully written and acted. Davies has since stated in interviews that, for him, unrequited love is the key theme of Series Three, and that his writing out of Martha was actually motivated by the need to ensure that she broke out of that trap. But none of this alters the fact that, however appropriate it may be for the character, the sudden departure of a companion – especially one as appealing, charismatic and well-portrayed as Martha – is always going to be a real downer for the viewer; and on debut transmission there wasn't even the comfort of knowing that she would be appearing in Series Two of *Torchwood* and returning to *Doctor Who* at a later date, as that had yet to be publicly announced. This all contributes toward the sense that 'Last of the Time Lords' is a really depressing episode.

7. The demise of the Master

John Simm continues to shine as the Master in this concluding instalment, matching the brilliance of Davies's characterisation with the bravura of his performance. The sequence at the beginning where he dances his way onto the bridge of the *Valiant*, sweeps his wife around in his arms and kisses her, takes and spits out a mouthful of tea, mounts a set of steps to toll what is presumably a 'wake up' bell, and then pushes the aged Doctor around in his wheelchair, all to the strains of the Scissor Sisters' gloriously camp 'I Can't Decide' (which, amusingly, is just the sort of contemporary music track to which this action might be set on *Doctor Who Confidential*, were it not already there), is brilliantly conceived and staged, and one of the episode's most wonderfully off-the-wall incidents, recalling the style of Baz Luhrmann's movie extravaganzas *William Shakespeare's Romeo + Juliet* (20th Century Fox,1996) and *Moulin Rouge!* (20th Century Fox, 2001). Simm really steals every scene he is in – although, to be fair, this is made a lot easier for him by the fact that Tennant is for the most part either stuck in his wheelchair buried under heavy prosthetic make-up (which makes him resemble the aged form of David Bowie's character John in the horror movie *The Hunger* (MGM, 1983)) or else replaced by an ambitious but sadly very obvious and unconvincing CGI creation (a rare example of the Mill biting off more than they could chew).

This is a truly twisted and deranged Master. A particularly inspired touch, albeit another grim one, comes when his wife Lucy – again superbly portrayed by Alexandra Moen, radiant in a beautiful red 'gangster's moll' gown – appears at one point with her face marked and swollen. The obvious implication is that the Master has physically abused her, but what makes this all the more disturbing is that none of the other characters comments on it or even seems to notice, suggesting that it is a commonplace occurrence. A further indication of the Master's cruelty to Lucy comes when he openly relishes receiving a massage from a 'gorgeous' woman named Tania and says, 'You two should get to know each other; that might be fun', giving a subtle hint as to the kind of debauchery he might have been indulging in over the past year. It is noticeable that Lucy seems altogether more subdued and puppet-like in this episode than in 'The Sound of Drums', and is clearly no longer so enamoured of her husband, reinforcing earlier indications that her feelings toward him – whether positive or negative – have always been genuine rather than, as might conceivably have been the case, the product of hypnosis. These are great incidental touches that really help to impart depth to the character, and it is a pity they are not developed even further. Small wonder that Lucy is ultimately moved to shoot the Master, in a fitting, if somewhat predictable, denouement to their relationship (and indeed an instance of history repeating itself, after Chantho shot him in his previous incarnation in 'Utopia' – 'It's always the women,' as he puts it).

The idea of the Master having a human wife who ultimately betrays him could well have been drawn from David A McIntee's *Missing Adventures* novel *The Dark Path* (Virgin Publishing, 1997), the title of which even seems to be alluded to by Phil Collinson in *Doctor Who Confidential*: 'The Saxon Mystery'. In this novel, a Time Lord hitherto known as Koschei turns to the 'dark path' and becomes the Master after learning that his human companion and lover, Ailla, is really a spy sent from Gallifrey to monitor his behaviour (a backstory that is not necessarily contradicted by 'The Sound of Drums'/'Last of the Time Lords', as presumably he would not have begun his evil activities straight away after his mind became twisted by his looking into the time vortex at the age of eight; although the history recounted in the audio CD drama *Master* (Big Finish, 2003) – see the 'Analysis' section on 'Utopia' – is difficult to reconcile with either or these). That said, it has always seemed rather strange that the Master, in stark contrast to the Doctor, has never had a companion (apart perhaps from when young Chang Lee assists him for a short time in the TV Movie), so perhaps this was simply an obvious omission for Davies to rectify; and it seems entirely appropriate that the Master, in stark contrast to the Doctor, should be using his companion for sexual gratification. (At any rate, it seems clear that she is not simply the Master's 'beard' ...)

Lucy's betrayal of her husband proves to be a terminal one. Horrified by the idea of being kept prisoner in the TARDIS and looked after by the Doctor for the rest of his life (which, curiously, recalls his situation in the webcast story 'Scream of the Shalka' (2003)), the Master claims a final victory of sorts by refusing to regenerate, thereby allowing the bullet to kill him and leaving the Doctor utterly distraught at being placed once more in the position of being the sole survivor of his race, when it had seemed for a time that he was not after all destined to be the last of the Time Lords. It is, again, a very grim turn of events; and the grimness is compounded as the Doctor then proceeds to burn the Master's body on a funeral pyre at night – in a scene strongly reminiscent of Luke Skywalker's cremation of the remains of his father Anakin (or is it just the latter's Darth Vader armour?) in *Star Wars Episode VI: Return of the Jedi* – leaving only ashes behind ... plus the Master's ring. In an intriguing coda, the ring is then seen to be retrieved by the hand of a woman wearing red nail-varnish, to the accompaniment of evil laughter on the soundtrack, suggesting that there might still be a twist in the tale in some future story – an obvious homage to the ending of the film *Flash Gordon* (Universal Pictures, 1980), in which the ring of the apparently dead Ming the Merciless is retrieved in exactly the same way. The identity of the woman is left a mystery; one possibility is that it is Lucy – which could suggest that her shooting of the Master was pre-planned between them, and would leave the way open for her to make a well-deserved return appearance – but the hand actually looks to be that of a rather older person.[122] It remains to be seen what, if anything, will one day come of this ...

One thing that Davies certainly cannot be accused of is taking easy options. Having painstakingly introduced, established and developed a fantastic new companion, only to write her out again (for the time being) just a short time later and put himself effectively back at square one, he now seems to have done exactly the same thing with his brilliant new version of the Master. Is this really the last we will see of the Master, or will he, like Martha, be back again at some later date? And if he does return, will he again be played by John Simm, or will the part once more have to be recast? One thing is for sure: if he does return, he – or whoever has the task of writing the story – will be very hard pressed to come up with a new scheme that comes even close to being as grand, ambitious and evil as the one depicted in 'Utopia'/'The Sound of Drums'/'Last of the Time Lords'.

There is, then, a lot that is great about 'Last of the Time Lords'; chiefly, the excellent

---

[122] Russell T Davies states in the episode's bbc.co.uk podcast commentary that the hand is that of the Rani, a female renegade Time Lord seen in the classic series stories 'The Mark of the Rani' (1984) and 'Time and the Rani' (1986), but this is simply an in-joke, referring to an earlier erroneous press story, sparked by a spoof fan rumour, that the Rani would be appearing in Series Three. In behind-the-scenes terms, the hand was actually that of production manager Tracie Simpson.

treatment of Martha and satisfying resolution to her time as the Doctor's regular companion; the inspired characterisation by Davies and portrayal by Simm of a brilliant new, 21st Century version of the Master, perfectly matched to Tennant's wonderful Doctor; the impressive scale and ambition of the story and its production; and, last but not least, Moen's fantastic performance as Lucy Saxon. The fact remains, though, that all significant aspects of the episode, successful and unsuccessful alike, are extraordinarily dark in tone. In fact, I would go so far as to suggest that this is the darkest that *Doctor Who* has ever been on TV in its entire 44-year history. 'Last of the Time Lords' is consequently an episode that I find it far easier to admire than to actually like.

And yet ... just how dark does *Doctor Who* have to get before it becomes *too* dark? The official statistics show that – unlike the dedicated fans, whose reactions were decidedly mixed – the eight-million-plus members of the general viewing public who tuned in to the debut BBC One transmission of 'Last of the Time Lords' were hugely impressed by it: its excellent Appreciation Index (AI) figure of 88 was the joint highest of Series Three.[123] It would thus seem that, for its target family audience, this episode *wasn't* too dark.

Have some fans got so used to the idea that *Doctor Who* needs to be relentlessly bright, colourful and fun if it is to succeed in its flagship early Saturday evening slot – as Davies has so often asserted in the past – that they have allowed themselves to be completely wrong-footed by what would seem to be a quite radical change of approach by the showrunner? And will this change of approach be maintained in Series Four, or will it be eventually seen as just a temporary descent into darkness prior to a return to the much lighter tone that has generally characterised the revived series to date? Only time will tell; but before Series Four, there is another Christmas special to look forward to first. In a scene disappointingly similar to the one that ended 'Doomsday', 'Last of the Time Lords' concludes with the Doctor saying 'What?' three times in incredulity after a sudden and seemingly impossible intrusion into the TARDIS control room: this time, not by a runaway bride but by the prow of the famed, but doomed, ocean liner RMS *Titanic*. As the caption says, *Doctor Who* will return in 'Voyage of the Damned' ...

---

[123] See Appendix D for a full discussion of the Series Three ratings.

# SERIES OVERVIEW

Over the course of its first three series, Russell T Davies's *Doctor Who* has grown steadily bolder in ambition, broader in scope, greater in sophistication and, ultimately, darker in tone. This to some extent parallels the way the classic series developed over its first three seasons, from 1963 to 1966, not only in general terms but also in certain specifics: for instance, just as the new series stretched its format in its second year by including a strongly humorous episode, in the form of 'Love & Monsters', so too did the classic series, in the form of 'The Romans' (1964); and just as in its third year the new series has presented its longest and darkest story yet, in 'Utopia'/'The Sound of Drums'/'Last of the Time Lords', so too did the classic series, in 'The Daleks' Master Plan' (1965/66). Whether the changes that have occurred since 'Rose' are a good thing or a bad thing is obviously a matter of personal taste. I must admit I occasionally feel a pang of regret at the passing of the simpler, lighter pleasures of Series One, which in some ways seems almost like ancient history now, although it was actually less than three years ago as I write. On the whole, though, I would have to say that, for me, Series Three probably counts as the best to date.

Excellent though she has been, Freema Agyeman's Martha hasn't *quite* matched up to Billie Piper's Rose, but that's not really a fair standard by which to judge her, given that Rose rivals Sarah Jane Smith for the title of the most successful *Doctor Who* companion ever. Martha is certainly well up there with the likes of Frazer Hines's Jamie and Katy Manning's Jo Grant as one of the very best of the rest, and a huge asset to the series; so thank goodness she is being brought back for at least part of Series Four. David Tennant's Doctor, on the other hand, is second to none. I said back in the 'Analysis' section on 'The Runaway Bride' that it was too early at that point to make a final judgment on his standing in relation to his predecessors, but by the end of Series Three that is no longer the case: he really *is* the best the series has ever had. Tennant completely nailed the part in Series Three, avoiding the excessive goofing that occasionally marred his performance in Series Two and getting his portrayal of the last of the Time Lords absolutely spot-on throughout. Could any of the previous Doctors have risen to the challenge of a story like 'Human Nature'/'The Family of Blood' as effectively as he did? As great an admiration as I have for them, I would have to say probably not.

Although Series Three probably had a slightly higher proportion than Series One or Series Two of stories about which I had reservations – and in some cases, such as 'The Runaway Bride', '42' and 'Last of the Time Lords', quite strong reservations – this was compensated for by the sheer ambition it showed. If a story is going to be less than fully successful, I would far rather that be because it is trying too hard than because it is not trying hard enough. And some of the stories this year – such as 'Smith and Jones', 'Gridlock', 'Human Nature'/'The Family of Blood' and 'Blink' – have been right up there with the very best the new series has yet presented, and thus amongst the very best that *Doctor Who* has ever produced, full stop, in its entire 44-year history.

But what of the future? We now know that, although Martha will be returning for five episodes in Series Four, the Doctor's main companion, appearing in all 13 episodes, will be Catherine Tate's Donna Noble. This is not a prospect that fills me with joy. I well remember the terrible sinking feeling I got, back in 1986, on being told by someone over the phone that Bonnie Langford would be joining *Doctor Who* to partner Colin Baker's Doctor. These days we tend to learn of breaking news not over the phone but over the internet, but the feeling I got was exactly the same when, on 4 July 2007, I switched on my computer and read of Tate's imminent return to the series. Like Langford, Tate is best known for something other than her dramatic acting ability – in this case, for her work as a comedienne – and, again like Langford, she is the sort of performer who seems to have the unfortunate knack of causing extreme irritation to a sizeable minority of the general viewing public. I would consequently have had serious misgivings about her becoming a regular in *Doctor Who* even if I personally had greatly enjoyed her performance in 'The Runaway Bride' and felt that she worked well alongside David Tennant – which, as the perceptive reader will have gathered from the 'Analysis' section on that story, I most certainly did not. It is notable that, of all the Series Three episodes, 'The Runaway Bride' received the joint lowest Appreciation Index figure amongst general viewers and was also the lowest-ranked amongst fans in the Outpost Gallifrey forum polls.[124] If this was due to some extent to the 'Tate factor', then it does not bode at all well for Series Four.

It is not as if Davies did not have other, far better options open to him if he wanted to bring back an already-established character as a companion. Subject to the actresses' availability, he could for instance have chosen Carey Mulligan's excellent Sally Sparrow, or even perhaps (as was apparently suggested by producer Phil Collinson at one point) Alexandra Moen's wonderful Lucy Saxon, intent on making up for her past mistakes and becoming a reformed character – now wouldn't *that* have made for an fascinating new Doctor-and-companion dynamic! It seems highly likely, though, that Davies's decision to offer Tate a regular role in the series was motivated far more by her star-name status than by a desire to see Donna back *per se*; and if, as he and other production team members have suggested in interviews, the intention is that she and the Doctor should continue the Katharine-Hepburn-and-Spencer-Tracy-style 'screwball comedy' sparring that was attempted, and fell so flat, in 'The Runaway Bride', it raises the dreadful prospect of a return to the frequent 'bickering in the TARDIS' scenes that marred many of the Doctor-and-companion relationships of the 1980s. I very much hope that, in a year's time, I will be eating my words on this; but, as things stand, this looks to me to be the first really major, potentially ruinous, mistake that Davies has made since taking over the series.

Looking even further ahead, it was announced by the BBC on 3 September 2007 that there will be a year's gap between Series Four in 2008 and Series Five in 2010, bridged by four specials: the Christmas special in 2008, and three others – presumably including a further Christmas special – in 2009. David Tennant has signed up to appear in all these specials, but whether or not he will continue as the Doctor in Series Five is at present uncertain. Tennant has often joked about the fact that, ever since he joined the series, he has found himself repeatedly quizzed about

---

[124] See Appendix D for further details.

when he intends to leave. One can see how this might have disconcerted the actor, but the reason for it is quite plain: having experienced the shock departure of Christopher Eccleston after just one series, the viewing public are anxious not to lose another wonderful Doctor any time soon. In other words, the questions that have been put to Tennant have been motivated not by any desire to see him leave, but by a fear that he might do so. If the four specials for transmission in 2008/2009 do indeed turn out to mark the end of his tenure as the Doctor, it will be a crying shame, and a great blow to the series.

Similarly uncertain is how long Russell T Davies will remain as *Doctor Who*'s creative supremo. While on the one hand it is hard to believe that he would ever want to leave the series, given that he is such a huge, life-long fan of it, on the other hand, bearing in mind his status as one of the most highly respected and hugely influential creative talents working in the industry today, it seems unlikely that he will be prepared to pass up indefinitely the many opportunities he has for taking on exciting new projects. If he does decide to leave, how will the BBC respond? Will they consider a continuation of *Doctor Who* without Davies as unthinkable a proposition as, say, a continuation of *The X-Files* (Fox, 1993-2002) without Chris Carter, or a revival of *Buffy the Vampire Slayer* (The WB/UPN, 1997-2003) without Joss Whedon? Davies has, after all, fulfilled much the same role on the new *Doctor Who* as those American showrunners did on their own respective series, and this has been something of a first for British TV. He has obviously been the driving force behind the brilliant and hugely successful reinvention of *Doctor Who* for the 21st Century, and the BBC might simply take the view that it could not go on without him, raising the prospect of it being consigned to another lengthy period on hiatus. There is, on the other hand, a long tradition from the days of the classic series of new producers being assigned to *Doctor Who* from time to time and each making their own distinctive mark on it; and is it really conceivable that the BBC would be prepared to lose what has now become its flagship drama series, at the very height of its popularity?

It is possible, of course, that Davies and the BBC have already addressed this issue. Could it be that one aim – or perhaps even the main aim – of the 'gap year' in 2009 is to allow for a transition between Davies and a new showrunner? Rumour has it that Steven Moffat could be in the frame to take over from Davies at some point after the completion of work on Series Four. At the time of writing, however, this is still a matter for conjecture.

For now, perhaps it is enough simply to savour the many wonderful episodes that Davies and his team have already given us, and await with baited breath the Doctor's next adventure in 'Voyage of the Damned'.

# COMPLEMENT

# APPENDIX A
# DOCTOR WHO CONFIDENTIAL

It has long been fairly common practice for major feature film releases to be accompanied by dedicated 'making of' programmes specially prepared for TV broadcast, essentially for promotional purposes. It is, by contrast, very rare for a TV series to be accorded such a privilege, let alone for *every episode* of a series to be supported by its own individual behind-the-scenes mini-documentary. The first run of BBC Three's 30-minute-long *Doctor Who Confidential* programmes was consequently a pretty groundbreaking endeavour when transmitted back in 2005, giving a detailed insight into the production of each episode of the revived *Doctor Who*, and also into how it related to the classic series. Its second run, in 2006, saw it going from strength to strength, with even better coverage of all aspects of the making of Britain's favourite family drama series, and less reliance on clips from past eras.

By this point, although it was no longer perhaps quite so unique – for one thing, *Torchwood* had now been given its own equivalent companion series, *Torchwood Declassified*, produced by essentially the same team – *Doctor Who Confidential* was firmly established as one of BBC Three's top-rated programmes, and there was little doubt that it would be back to cover Series Three of *Doctor Who*. Following on from a special Christmas special edition entitled 'Music and Monsters' – transmitted for once on BBC One rather than BBC Three, and devoted to the staging of the 19 November 2006 *Doctor Who* concert in aid of the *Children in Need* appeal – the third series proper kicked off at the end of March, coinciding of course with *Doctor Who*'s own return. It continued to present the familiar mix of behind-the-scenes insights and interviews, with a new, extended episode length, as neatly summarised in the following description on the official programme website:

> *Doctor Who Confidential* is back for its third series, with unlimited access to all the backstage action and exclusive interviews with the key cast and crew. With its trademark fast-paced, music-led energy, the series has now been extended to 13 x 45 minute episodes, each with its own theme and narrated by Anthony Head. It's a real treat for *Doctor Who* fans and anyone eager to get up close and personal with the team that bring the nation's favourite Time Lord to our screens. *Confidential* airs on Saturday nights, on BBC Three, immediately after the BBC One transmission of *Doctor Who*.

This latest series broke new ground, too, most notably in 'A New York Story'/'Making Manhattan' – for which sufficient money was found in the budget to shoot some material actually in New York, without which it is quite likely that the *Doctor Who* team itself would have been unable to afford to record the spectacular plate shots of the city seen in 'Daleks in Manhattan'/'Evolution of the Daleks' – and also in 'Do You Remember the First Time?' – for which, in an inspired departure from the usual format, David Tennant served as guest director, talking to a number of prominent contributors to *Doctor Who* about their own love of the series.

In addition to the 'standard' programmes in their new, 45-minute slot – which, although most actually came in at closer to 40 minutes, made them almost as long as the episodes of *Doctor Who* they were actually covering – there were also, as in previous years, condensed versions, each roughly ten minutes long, prepared for shorter repeat slots, under the informal title *Confidential Cutdown*. Because these shorter edits omitted the contemporary music tracks featured in the full-length ones, it would again be these versions that would be lined up for inclusion in the *Complete Series* DVD box set due to be released in the autumn, in order to avoid potential music clearance problems and associated fees.

Producer Zoë Rushton, in a preview interview about the series for Issue 380 of *Doctor Who Magazine*, commented: 'Much like the main *Doctor Who* production, if there's one thing *Confidential* needs to do with every new series it's raise the bar even higher – be even more amibitious, and even more fresh and original – without jeopardising the reasons people love *Confidential* in the first place, of course!' Added series producer Gillane Seaborne: 'I know we say it every year, but we've got even more backstage stories than ever this year.'

This was no exaggeration, and throughout its third series, *Doctor Who Confidential* again proved to be essential viewing for anyone interested in getting the inside story on the grand and exciting production that is *Doctor Who*.


## MUSIC AND MONSTERS CREDITS

Narrated by: Anthony Head

Camera: Mat Bryant, Eric Huyton, Nick Jardine, Aled Jenkins
Sound: Kevin Meredith, Brian Murrell, Will Planitzer, Phil Turner

Concert Production Team

BBC National Orchestra and Chorus of Wales
Senior Producer: Tim Thorne
Orchestra Manager: Byron Jenkins
Chorus Manager: Osian Rowlands
Engineering Manager: John Eynon, Hugh Davidson
Camera Supervisor: Mike Goodman
Show Caller: Kate Salberg
OB Production Assistant: Sian Parry
Vision Mixer: Alison Bartrop
Concert Sound: Huw Thomas
Production Designer: Eryl Ellis
Lighting Director: Mark Henderson
Production Team Assistant: Carlie Smith
Production Manager: Jo Marks

Producer: Paul Bullock
Director: Rhodri Huw

Doctor Who Confidential Production Team

Rhian Arwel, Nicola Brown, Rhiannon Cooper, Will Dennis, Geoff Evans, Tors Grantham, Scott Handcock, Ailsa Jenkins, Claire Jones, Sam Jones, Donovan Keogh, Nathan Landeg, Stuart Laws, Jamie Lynch, Mark Procter, Edward Russell, Zoë Rushton, Natalie Street, Hannah Williams, Rob Wootton

Editor: Tom Appleby
Additional Editing: Dan Ablett
Colourist: Perry Gibbs
Dubbing Mixer: Damian Reynolds

Executive Producer for BBC Music: David M Jackson
Executive Producers for *Doctor Who*: Russell T Davies, Julie Gardner
Executive Producer: Mark Cossey
Producer and Director: Adam Page
Series Producer: Gillane Seaborne

BBC Wales


**SERIES CREDITS**

Narrated by: Anthony Head

PRODUCTION TEAM[125]

Location Director: Sarah T Davies (3.01, 3.02, 3.03), Mark Proctor (3.10)
Camera: Mat Bryant (3.01, 3.02, 3.03, 3.06), Andrew Clifford (3.01, 3.05, 3.10, 3.11), James Daniels (3.01, 3.03, 3.06, 3.08, 3.09, 3.11, 3.12, 3.13), Dewi Davies (3.01), Eric Huyton (3.01, 3.02, 3.06), Nick Jardine, Oliver Russell (3.01, 3.05, 3.06, 3.07, 3.08, 3.09, 3.10, 3.11), Paul Cox (3.02), Mark Thompson (3.02), Jaimie Gramston (3.04, 3.05), Richard Ganniclift (3.05, 3.07), Aled Jenkins (3.06, 3.12, 3.13), Stuart Brereton (3.10), Alastair Evans (3.12, 3.13)
Sound: Nat Reid (3.01, 3.02, 3.03), Gareth Meirion (3.01, 3.02), Kevin Meredith, Maz Tajiki (3.01, 3.05, 3.06, 3.07, 3.08, 3.09, 3.10, 3.11, 3.13), Phil Turner (3.01, 3.02, 3.07, 3.10), Tony Tasfield (3.02), Peter Jones (3.04), Mike Larini (3.04, 3.05), Jonny Stothert (3.05), Andrew Yarme (3.05, 3.07, 3.12), Brian Murrell (3.06, 3.09), Dafydd Parry (3.06), Paul Baker (3.12, 3.13), Sean Miller (3.12), Will Planitzer (3.12, 3.13)
Runner: Sam Jones (3.01, 3.02, 3.03, 3.04, 3.05, 3.06, 3.07), Scott Handcock (3.06, 3.07,

---

[125] Where an episode number (or more than one) appears in brackets after a person's name in the listing, this means that they were credited only on the episode (or episodes) indicated. Otherwise, the person concerned was credited on all 13 episodes.

3.08, 3.09, 3.10, 3.11, 3.12, 3.13)

Edit Assistant: Christopher Moore, Sam Jones (3.08, 3.09, 3.10, 3.11, 3.12, 3.13)

Junior Researcher: Claire Jones (3.01, 3.02, 3.04, 3.06)

Researcher: Nathan Landeg, Jamie Lynch, Claire Jones (3.07), James Goss (3.10)

Assistant Producer: Geoff Evans (all except 3.07), Hannah Williams (all except 3.13), Cat Chappell (3.11)

Additional Archive: Steve Roberts (3.07)

Production Team Assistant: Elaine Stephenson (3.01), Gavin Chappelle (3.02, 3.03, 3.04, 3.05), Alexandra Gibbs (3.03, 3.04, 3.05), Scott Handcock (3.04, 3.05), Amanda Buckley (3.06, 3.07, 3.08, 3.09, 3.10, 3.11, 3.12, 3.13)

Production Accountant: Elaine Stephenson (3.03, 3.04, 3.05, 3.06, 3.07, 3.08, 3.09, 3.10, 3.11, 3.12, 3.13)

Production Co-ordinator: Rhiannon Cooper (3.01, 3.03, 3.04, 3.05, 3.06, 3.07), Tors Grantham

Post Production Co-ordinator: Vickie Mansell

Production Manager: Kirsty Reid, Natalie Street

Production Executive: Paul Williams (all except 3.02)

Additional Editing: Sven Brooks (3.05), Rob Franz (3.08), James Brailsford (3.10), Marius Grose (3.13)

Editor: James Brailsford (3.01, 3.02, 3.04, 3.09, 3.12), Paul Kiff (3.01), Rob Mansell (3.01, 3.05, 3.08), Rob Franz (3.02, 3.03, 3.13), Dan Ablett (3.03, 3.10), Adam Mitchell (3.06), Simon Abrahams (3.06), Lizzie Minnion (3.07), Sven Brooks (3.11, 3.12, 3.13), Marius Grose (3.12), Fiona Pandelus (3.12)

Colourist: Jon Everett

Dubbing: Mark Ferda


Executive Producer for *Doctor Who*: Russell T Davies, Julie Gardner

Executive Producer: Mark Cossey

Edit Producer: Mark Procter (3.01, 3.02, 3.03, 3.11, 3.12), Rob Mansell (3.06), Hannah Williams (3.13)

Edit Producer and Additional Editing: Rob Mansell (3.04)


Producer and Editor: Rob Mansell (3.10)

Producer: Zoë Rushton (all except 3.05)

Produced and Directed by: Zoë Rushton (3.05), Geoff Evans (3.07), Ailsa Jenkins (3.08, 3.09)

Directed by: David Tennant (3.10)

Series Producer: Gillane Seaborne


BBC Wales


## EPISODE GUIDE

The episode durations quoted below are for the full versions as originally transmitted (not the shorter, *Confidential Cutdown* versions used for most subsequent repeat screenings). They may be a couple of seconds different from the timings of the complete programmes on the BBC's master tapes, as each episode tended to be cut into very slightly by the preceding and/or following continuity caption and announcement or programme trailer.

## 3.00 – MUSIC AND MONSTERS

DEBUT TRANSMISSION DETAILS

BBC One
Date: 25 December 2006. Scheduled time: 1.00 pm. Actual time: 1.00 pm.
Duration: 58' 35"

*Doctor Who Confidential* goes behind the scenes of the *Children in Need* musical celebration of *Doctor Who* performed at Cardiff's Millennium Centre on 19 November 2006.

## 3.01 – MEET MARTHA JONES

DEBUT TRANSMISSION DETAILS

BBC Three
Date: 31 March 2007. Scheduled time: 7.45 pm. Actual time: 7.45 pm.
Duration: 38' 44".

PUBLICITY BLURB

The Doctor's back, but now his time and space is shared with a brand new companion. By sheer courage and determination, she has wowed the Time Lord and been offered a place on board the TARDIS, and *Doctor Who Confidential* was backstage to see it all unfold. With extensive behind the scenes footage of this lunar adventure and interviews with Freema Agyeman (Martha Jones), David Tennant (the Doctor) plus head writer, Russell T Davies, *Confidential* examines the development of her character, the huge interest behind the casting of the new companion and invites you to ... Meet Martha Jones!

## 3.02 – STAGE FRIGHT

DEBUT TRANSMISSION DETAILS

BBC Three
Date: 7 April 2007. Scheduled time: 7.45 pm. Actual time: 7.46 pm.
Duration: 41' 55".

PUBLICITY BLURB

It's Martha's first trip in the TARDIS and what better journey than to Elizabethan England to meet William Shakespeare? The *Doctor Who* production team recreated some of the most breathtaking scenes to date and *Confidential* were there to capture every compelling moment. With extensive footage both in the studio and on location through the long nights at London's Globe Theatre, this episode of *Confidential* highlights how this visual feast was created.

## 3.03 – ARE WE THERE YET?

### DEBUT TRANSMISSION DETAILS

BBC Three
Date: 14 April 2007. Scheduled time: 8.25 pm. Actual time: 8.26 pm.
Duration: 40' 30".

### PUBLICITY BLURB
Set in New New York, far in the future with endless space-age motorways and more CGI than you can shake a stick at, the [recording] of 'Gridlock' was an almighty challenge for all involved. Confidential was on location and backstage in the green-screen studios to witness just how they shot some of this series' most complicated action sequences. Plus, 'Are We There Yet?' looks at how guest star Ardal O'Hanlon was transformed into his character Brannigan and we hear from David Tennant, Freema Agyeman and head writer, Russell T Davies, who look beyond the bleak script to find a true story of hope.

## 3.04 – A NEW YORK STORY

### DEBUT TRANSMISSION DETAILS

BBC Three
Date: 21 April 2007. Scheduled time: 7.25 pm. Actual time: 7.24 pm.
Duration: 39' 15".

### PUBLICITY BLURB

Writing fiction in a world of iconic landmarks, historical locations and amazing urban landscapes is hard work but someone's got to do it! 'Daleks in Manhattan' is set in 1930s New York and *Confidential* travels Stateside with writer Helen Raynor to capture some of her most notable inspirations, looking out at Manhattan, walking through Central Park, seeing exactly how people lived in tenement buildings in the '30s, and much more. We hear how she got her muse for this two-part visual extravaganza!

## 3.05 – MAKING MANHATTAN

### DEBUT TRANSMISSION DETAILS

BBC Three
Date: 28 April 2007. Scheduled time: 7.30 pm. Actual time: 7.31 pm.
Duration: 41' 10".

## PUBLICITY BLURB

How on Earth do you re-create 1930s New York in the heart of South Wales? *Confidential* travelled to Manhattan itself to find out. We discover just how it can be done when producer Phil Collinson and director of episodes four and five James Strong show us the New York locations they plan to reproduce and the atmospheres they intend to create. Also on location in Manhattan, visual effects supervisor Dave Houghton shows us exactly what they need to make Manhattan in Cardiff and, combined with insightful comments from the design team, *Confidential* takes you on a journey through the process of re-creating a whole new time and place told by the people who make it all happen.

### 3.06 – MONSTERS INC.

## DEBUT TRANSMISSION DETAILS

BBC Three
Date: 5 May 2007. Scheduled time: 7.45 pm. Actual time: 7.44 pm.
Duration: 43′ 35″.

## PUBLICITY BLURB

An episode of *Doctor Who* just wouldn't be the same without a monster to scare the living daylights out of you! The creation of such a beast is never easy – especially when it's purely computer generated! *Confidential* is on set throughout this chilling episode, spends some quality time with guest star Mark Gatiss and takes a look at some of the fantastic prosthetic and computer generated monsters created since the series made its welcome comeback in 2005.

### 3.07 – SPACE CRAFT

## DEBUT TRANSMISSION DETAILS

BBC Three
Date: 19 May 2007. Scheduled time: 8.00 pm. Actual time: 8.00 pm.
Duration: 41′ 00″.

## PUBLICITY BLURB

It's back into outer space for *Doctor Who*, and this time it's an adventure set entirely on a spaceship. Join *Confidential* as we gain exclusive access to *Doctor Who*'s art department and take you on a tour of the spaceship's sets and locations. *Confidential* also journeys back in time to show you some of the best off-the-wall spaceship designs seen in five decades. Guest star Michelle Collins discusses her role as the ship's captain, and how she felt performing stunts on her very first day on set. From models on wires to cutting edge CGI, this is a space craft extravaganza.

## 3.08 – ALTER EGO

<u>DEBUT TRANSMISSION DETAILS</u>

BBC Three
Date: 26 May 2007. Scheduled time: 7.55 pm. Actual time: 7.56 pm.
Duration: 42′ 35″.

<u>PUBLICITY BLURB</u>

With aliens in hot pursuit, the Doctor and Martha find themselves in 1913 England. *Confidential* is right beside them to delve deeper into the *alter ego* of the nation's favourite Time Lord. Amidst all the stiff upper lips, we follow the advancing 'aliens' and their army, with exclusive backstage footage of the mayhem caused as the outer-space enemies close in on their prey. [Recorded] almost entirely on location, *Confidential* was on-set with cast and crew in the winter wind, rain and mud for the nail-biting first episode of this two-part story. Features interviews with writer Paul Cornell, whose original novel forms the basis of 'Human Nature', David Tennant and Freema Agyeman.

## 3.09 – BAD BLOOD

<u>DEBUT TRANSMISSION DETAILS</u>

BBC Three
Date: 2 June 2007. Scheduled time: 7.55 pm. Actual time: 7.55 pm.
Duration: 43′ 00″.

<u>PUBLICITY BLURB</u>

With the Family of Blood breathing down the neck of the Doctor, time is running out. *Confidential* follows the action backstage as we glimpse a life more ordinary (for the Doctor) as well as a vision of the dark future ahead. The complexities of [recording] this powerful episode are revealed, as well as the logistics behind the explosive ending. Features interviews with head writer Russell T Davies, and Freema Agyeman on one of her toughest TARDIS assignments yet.

## 3.10 – DO YOU REMEMBER THE FIRST TIME?

<u>DEBUT TRANSMISSION DETAILS</u>

BBC Three
Date: 9 June 2007. Scheduled time: 7.55 pm. Actual time: 7.54 pm.
Duration: 43′ 54″.

<u>PUBLICITY BLURB</u>

This week, David Tennant directs his very own *Doctor Who Confidential*. TV's top

Time Lord has been given complete control to film his own very personal account of the making of *Doctor Who*. David takes a nostalgic voyage of discovery to find out the secret behind the success of *Doctor Who*.

### 3.11 – 'ELLO, 'ELLO, 'ELLO

<u>DEBUT TRANSMISSION DETAILS</u>

BBC Three
Date: 16 June 2007. Scheduled time: 8.00 pm. Actual time: 8.02 pm.
Duration: 41' 46".

<u>PUBLICITY BLURB</u>

*Doctor Who Confidential* says "ello, 'ello, 'ello' to everyone's favourite time agent, Captain Jack Harkness, who returns to the series this week. Left alone by the Doctor and Rose in Series One, we talk to John Barrowman about his return to the show – what it's like for him and his character to be back on *Doctor Who* and working with a new Doctor and companion.

### 3.12 – THE SAXON MYSTERY

<u>DEBUT TRANSMISSION DETAILS</u>

BBC Three
Date: 23 June 2007. Scheduled time: 8.00 pm. Actual time: 8.02 pm.
Duration: 41' 32".

<u>PUBLICITY BLURB</u>

It's back to earth with a bump for the Doctor and his companions as they come face to face with the infamous Mr Saxon, brought to life by *Life on Mars* star John Simm. Join *Doctor Who Confidential* in unravelling the mystery behind Saxon, with a detailed look at this character's journey, which surprisingly began way back in Series Two. The *Doctor Who* team use a number of locations to bring this story to life and we join them every step of the way, in making the first part of this massive series finale. John Simm also talks exclusively to *Doctor Who Confidential*, discussing how he prepared for the role as an enemy who is more than a match for the Doctor.

### 3.13 – THE VALIANT QUEST

<u>DEBUT TRANSMISSION DETAILS</u>

BBC Three
Date: 30 June 2007. Scheduled time: 7.55 pm. Actual time: 7.57 pm.
Duration: 43' 14".

## PUBLICITY BLURB

It's the end of an amazing series and *Confidential* goes behind the scenes of the nail-biting finale to Series Three as we see two enemies square up for a battle of valiant proportions. Features interviews with David Tennant, John Simm, Freema Agyeman, Russell T Davies, Julie Gardner and Phil Collinson as they reflect on the past series and what may be to come ...

# APPENDIX B
# TOTALLY DOCTOR WHO

The lively children's magazine programme *Totally Doctor Who* returned for a second series in 2007. As before, each episode aired initially on BBC One (apart from in the final week, when coverage of the Wimbledon tennis tournament on BBC One necessitated a move to BBC Two) as part of the CBBC strand. The first episode debuted on Monday 2 April, two days after *Doctor Who* returned with 'Smith and Jones', but the series was then switched to a Friday slot for the rest of the run, which consisted of a total of 12 episodes, one fewer than the first. Each episode had three repeat screenings: the first on the CBBC digital channel on Friday afternoon; the second on BBC Two on Saturday morning; and the third on CBBC on Saturday afternoon. (The actual time of transmission tended to vary from week to week.) The first episode also had an extra repeat, on CBBC on Sunday afternoon. There was a break of a week between the sixth and seventh episodes, owing to the similar break in *Doctor Who*'s own run.

Continuing as a presenter from the first series was Barney Harwood, a familiar face to children from numerous other CBBC shows. His original co-presenter Liz Barker having taken a break from TV work after giving birth to a new baby, Harwood was joined this time around by Kirsten O'Brien, whose involvement with CBBC stretches back to 1996 and who is well known for her one-time on-air partnership with the Otis the Aardvark puppet character and for her presenting of *SMart!*. The other big change for the second series was that *Totally Doctor Who* was now accorded studio space within *Doctor Who*'s main Upper Boat studios, giving the team much improved access to the cast and crew.

Regular features of the programme for the second series included: 'Who Goes There?', in which viewers would be challenged to recognise a popular *Doctor Who* monster purely from its silhouette, with mug and sweatshirt prizes on offer for a randomly-selected winner who wrote or e-mailed in with the correct answer; a competition to win a set of handprints and signatures made in clay by some of the series' guests, entrants being asked to send in correct answers to 12 quiz questions, one set in each programme; 'Team Totally', in which two teams of children – Team Time Lord (Alia, Sara and Cody) and, the eventual winners, Team TARDIS (Chris, Molly[126] and Daniel) – competed in a series of challenges that involved them trying their hands at various aspects of *Doctor Who*'s production, the promised 'money can't buy' main prize eventually being revealed to be (somewhat disappointingly, judging from the looks on the children's faces) a weekend visit to Blackpool to meet David Tennant and see him turn on the town's famous seasonal illuminations; 'The Infinite

---

[126] Full name Mollie Kabia; she had previously had an acting role as an unnamed 'Girl' character in the 'red button' digital *Doctor Who* mini-adventure 'Attack of the Graske', a fact not mentioned at any point in *Totally Doctor Who* and reportedly not revealed to her fellow contestants.

Quest', a new, flash-animated *Doctor Who* story, one short instalment of which was shown in each programme (see Appendix C for further details); and a brief preview clip of the following Saturday's new *Doctor Who* episode. The fourth and fifth episodes were notable for including inserts of O'Brien recorded on location in New York, including in the Empire State Building. The twelfth episode also took a rather different format than usual, presenting the studio final of the Team Totally contest.

The consensus of opinion amongst fans seemed to be that, with this second series, *Totally Doctor Who* had really hit its stride, making it a worthy, high-quality stablemate to *Doctor Who Confidential* and, of course, to *Doctor Who* itself, and a third must-see programme to enjoy each week.

## CREDITS

Presented by: Barney Harwood, Kirsten O'Brien
Set Design: Edward Thomas
Graphic Design: BDH
Title Music: Tim Baker
Additional Music: Mosquito Music
Animation: Firestep Ltd.
Animation Cast: David Tennant, Freema Agyeman, Anthony Head (2.01, 2.02, 2.10, 2.11, 2.12), Toby Longworth (2.01, 2.02, 2.11, 2.12), Liza Tarbuck (2.03, 2.04, 2.05), Tom Farrelly (2.03, 2.04, 2.05), Lizzie Hopley (2.06, 2.07, 2.08), Paul Clayton (2.06, 2.07, 2.08), Steven Meo (2.07, 2.08), Stephen Greif (2.09, 2.10), Dan Morgan (2.09, 2.10)
Lighting Director: John Walton
Sound Supervisor: Ian Johnson
Location Sound: Kevin Meredith (2.01, 2.04, 2.05, 2.11), Brian Ullah (2.02, 2.03, 2.06, 2.07, 2.08, 2.09, 2.10), Will Planitzer (2.08, 2.09)
Location Camera: Nick Jardine (2.01, 2.02, 2.03, 2.05, 2.06, 2.07, 2.08, 2.09, 2.11), Simon Cox (2.04), Aled Jenkins (2.08, 2.09), Peter Allihone (2.10)
Editor: Gareth Owens, David Peate
Dubbing Mixer: Mark Ferda (2.09, 2.11, 2.12)
Camera Supervisor: Andy Smith
Vision Mixer: Ann Thomas
Floor Manager: Richard Wyn Jones
Make-up: Sian Hicks
Props Assistant: Anna Coote (2.01), Corinna Everett (2.01, 2.02, 2.03, 2.04, 2.05, 2.07, 2.08, 2.09, 2.10, 2.11, 2.12)
Production Team: Rhian Arwel, Nicola Brown, Rob Wootton
Production Accountant: Elaine Stephenson
Post Production Co-ordinator: Vickie Mansell
Production Co-ordinator: Siân Parry
Researcher: Catrin Honeybill, Lucy Lutman
Assistant Producer: Dave Beardsell, Cat Chappell[127]
VT Director: Janet Midian (2.01, 2.02, 2.04, 2.05, 2.07, 2.08, 2.09, 2.12), Gerard Williams

---

[127] Credited as 'Catherine Chappell' on 2.01.

Studio Director: Jeanette Goulbourn
Production Manager: Kirsty Reid, Natalie Street (3.06, 2.08, 2.10)
Production Executive: Paul Williams
Executive Producer for *Doctor Who*: Russell T Davies, Julie Gardner
Executive Producer for CBBC: Gillian Scothern, Reem Nouss
Executive Producer: Mark Cossey
Produced by: Ros Attille
Series Producer: Gillane Seaborne

CBBC

## EPISODE GUIDE

The episode durations quoted below are for the episodes as transmitted. They may be a couple of seconds different from the timings of the complete programmes on the BBC's master tapes, as each episode tended to be cut into very slightly by the preceding and/or following continuity caption and announcement. Information on actual transmission times is unavailable for these programmes, but they invariably differed little from the scheduled times. Some of the guests listed below appeared in the *Totally Doctor Who* studio space at Upper Boat, while others where interviewed on location or in other recorded inserts.

### 2.01

DEBUT TRANSMISSION DETAILS

BBC One
Date: 2 April 2007. Scheduled time: 5.00 pm.
Duration: 28' 13".

Guests: actors David Tennant, Freema Agyeman and Reggie Yates, special effects supervisor Danny Hargreaves and storyboard artist Shaun Williams.

### 2.02

DEBUT TRANSMISSION DETAILS

BBC One
Date: 13 April 2007. Scheduled time: 5.00 pm.
Duration: 28' 09".

Guests: actors David Tennant and Freema Agyeman, prosthetics supervisor Rob Mayor, make-up artist Ros Wilkins, art department co-ordinator Matthew North and wire work co-ordinator Kevin Welch.

**2.03**

DEBUT TRANSMISSION DETAILS

BBC One
Date: 20 April 2007. Scheduled time: 5.00 pm.
Duration: 27' 59"

Guests: actors Freema Agyeman and Lenora Crichlow, showrunner Russell T
Davies and Foley artist Julie Ankerson.

**2.04**

DEBUT TRANSMISSION DETAILS

BBC One
Date: 27 April 2007. Scheduled time: 4.00 pm.
Duration: 27' 45"

Guests: actor Miranda Raison, writer Helen Raynor and choreographer Ailsa Berk.

**2.05**

DEBUT TRANSMISSION DETAILS

BBC One
Date: 4 May 2007. Scheduled time: 5.00 pm.
Duration: 28' 13"

Guests: actors Eric Loren and Freema Agyeman, voice artist Nicholas Briggs, Dalek
remote control operator Colin Newman and Dalek operator Barnaby Edwards.

**2.06**

DEBUT TRANSMISSION DETAILS

BBC One
Date: 11 May 2007. Scheduled time: 5.00 pm.
Duration: 27' 45".

Guests: actors Freema Agyeman, Gugu Mbatha-Raw, Adjoa Andoh and Trevor
Laird, *Doctor Who Adventures* magazine editor Moray Laing and VFX supervisor
Barney Curnow.

**2.07**

<u>DEBUT TRANSMISSION DETAILS</u>

BBC One
Date: 25 May 2007. Scheduled time: 5.00 pm.
Duration: 28' 15"

Guests: actor William Ash, special effects supervisor Danny Hargreaves and associate designer James North.

**2.08**

<u>DEBUT TRANSMISSION DETAILS</u>

BBC One
Date: 1 June 2007. Scheduled time: 5.00 pm.
Duration: 28' 10".

Guests: actors David Tennant, Freema Agyeman and Lauren Wilson, choreographer Ailsa Berk, art department co-ordinator Matthew North and voice director Gary Russell.

**2.09**

<u>DEBUT TRANSMISSION DETAILS</u>

BBC One
Date: 8 June 2007. Scheduled time: 5.00 pm.
Duration: 28' 00"

Guests: actors Tom Palmer and Freema Agyeman, stunt co-ordinator Crispin Layfield, stuntman Gordon Seed (David Tennant's usual stunt double) and second assistant director Anna Evans.

**2.10**

<u>DEBUT TRANSMISSION DETAILS</u>

BBC One
Date: 15 June 2007. Scheduled time: 5.00 pm.
Duration: 28' 07"

Guests: actor John Barrowman, monster actor Paul Kasey, special effects technician Charlie Bluett and Firestep animators Jon Doyle and Steve Maher.

**2.11**

<u>DEBUT TRANSMISSION DETAILS</u>

BBC One
Date: 22 June 2007. Scheduled time: 5.00 pm.
Duration: 28′ 13″

Guests: showrunner Russell T Davies, actors John Barrowman and Freema Agyeman, costume designer Louise Page and Futurekind actors Ken Hosking and Ed[128].

**2.12**

<u>DEBUT TRANSMISSION DETAILS</u>

BBC Two
Date: 29 June 2007. Scheduled time: 5.00 pm.
Duration: 27′ 46″

Guests: actors David Tennant and John Barrowman.

---

[128] Surname unknown.

# APPENDIX C
# THE INFINITE QUEST

'The Infinite Quest' is the fifth animated *Doctor Who* story to have been produced, following on from 'Death Comes to Time' (2001), 'Real Time' (2002), 'Shada' (2003) and 'Scream of the Shalka' (2003).[129] However, whereas those four earlier serials were made as webcasts for the official *Doctor Who* website, and in the first three cases were more audio dramas set to pictures than true animations, 'The Infinite Quest' was always intended for TV broadcast – initially as part of *Totally Doctor Who*, which financed its production – and ultimately for DVD release. It features far more sophisticated animation than even 'Scream of the Shalka' (which was at one point also intended for DVD release, although this was subsequently put on hold), and is certainly the most ambitious to date.

'Scream of the Shalka' was animated by the famous Manchester-based company Cosgrove Hall, as were the recreated versions of two currently-missing episodes of the classic series story 'The Invasion' included on its DVD release in 2006, and the two men mainly responsible for the work on both those projects were Steve Maher and John Doyle. Maher and Doyle then left Cosgrove Hall to set up their own animation house, Firestep Ltd, after being approached by the BBC to handle 'The Infinite Quest'. The project's Executive Producer Mark Cossey was subsequently quoted as saying of their work, 'I like the sophistication of their designs. They understood what we were looking for.' Firestep was also supported on the project by Kilogramme, another Manchester-based company, which created the 3D effects.

'We worked on so many great animations at Cosgrove,' noted Maher in an interview on the BBC website's Manchester pages, 'so to go from that to *Doctor Who* was great, seeing as it was our first job. I'm not a *Doctor Who* expert by any means, but John is a big fan – he has a full size TARDIS in his living room.

'John and I direct [the animation for "The Infinite Quest"] but about ten people have been involved all in all. It's just great to be a part of. There are so many great animators in Manchester and not just at Cosgrove. We're working with Jon Turner and Christian Jonson from Kilogramme, who are providing computer generated imagery for the series. They have done some incredible work for us.'

The story's writer, Alan Barnes, was very familiar with *Doctor Who*, having worked on *Doctor Who Magazine* for some five years in the 1990s and served as its editor in 2000-2001, and having also scripted numerous comic strip stories for the magazine and several audio CD dramas for Big Finish's *Doctor Who* tie-in ranges.

---

[129] The earliest serious attempt to make an animated series was in the early 1990s. This was to have been produced by Nelvana for the Canadian Broadcasting Corporation, but fell through after the completion by artist Ted Bastien of initial concept drawings, which he worked on for almost a year. Some of these drawings have since been made available to view online at: www.cbc.ca/planetofthedoctor/tb_gallery.html

The director, Gary Russell, had an even longer association with the series, having edited *Doctor Who Magazine* from 1991 to 1995, written numerous tie-in novels, factual books and comic strip stories, and been a mainstay of Big Finish's output from 1998-2006, contributing in a variety of capacities including producer, director, writer and actor. He is currently employed as a script editor at BBC Wales, contributing to *Doctor Who*, *Torchwood* and *The Sarah Jane Adventures*, and is writing a new series of *Doctor Who* comic book adventures for leading US publisher IDW. Voice recording for the story took place in two main sessions in January and early February 2007.

The majority of 'The Infinite Quest' was initially transmitted in 12 instalments, lasting approximately three-and-a-half minutes each, as one of the regular weekly features in the second series of *Totally Doctor Who* (see Appendix B). Omitted – rather strangely – was the story's ending, which would have made up a thirteenth instalment. The complete story then had its debut screening in omnibus form, with the ending included for the first time, on the morning of 30 June 2007, helping to build excitement for the Series Three finale of *Doctor Who* later that day. It was subsequently scheduled to be released on DVD on 5 November 2007.

**THE INFINITE QUEST**

Writer: Alan Barnes
Director: Gary Russell

DEBUT TRANSMISSION DETAILS

BBC Two
Date: 30 June 2007. Scheduled time: 10.30 am.

Duration: 46' 46"

CAST

David Tennant (The Doctor), Freema Agyeman (Martha Jones), Anthony Head (Baltazar), Toby Longworth (Caw/Squawk), Liza Tarbuck (Captain Kaliko), Tom Farrelly (Swabb), Lizzie Hopley (Mantasphid Queen), Paul Clayton (Mergrass), Steven Meo (Pilot Kelvin), Barney Harwood (Control Voice), Stephen Greif (Gurney), Dan Morgan (Locke/Warders).

PRODUCTION TEAM

Animation: Firestep
Production Designer: Edward Thomas
Sound Design: Doug Sinclair, Howard Eaves, Paul McFadden
Dubbing Mixer: Peter Jeffreys
Composer: Murray Gold
Music Arranger: Ben Foster
Production Runner: Scott Handcock
Production Accountant: Elaine Stephenson

Post-Production Co-ordinator: Vickie Mansell
Production Manager: Kirsty Reid
Production Executive: Paul Williams
Executive Producer for CBBC: Gillian Scothern, Reem Nouss, Jon East
Producer: James Goss, Ros Attille
Series Producer: Gillane Seaborne
Executive Producer: Mark Cossey
Executive Producer for *Doctor Who*: Russell T Davies, Julie Gardner

CBBC

PLOT

A run-in with the evil alien Baltazar in the 40th Century sets the Doctor and Martha on a quest to prevent him from capturing the *Infinite*, the legendary ancient spaceship of one of the Great Old Ones – from the same era as the Racnoss, the Nestenes and the Great Vampires – that can grant people their heart's desire. To locate the ship, they need four data chips. Baltazar's robotic pet bird Caw gives them the first, and they obtain the other three from, respectively, the pirate captain Kaliko, the lizard-like arms dealer Mergrass and escaped convict Gurney ... all of whom are mysteriously murdered. The murderer is Baltazar, newly released from prison on the icy planet Volag-Noc, which is where he first met his three victims. He has tricked the Doctor and Martha into tracking down the data chips on his behalf, following them by homing in on a brooch that Caw gave to Martha, which is actually Caw's chick, Squawk. Baltazar seizes the TARDIS, with Martha on board as his prisoner, and uses the data chips to direct it to the *Infinite*, which is now a crumbling wreck drifting in space. The Doctor follows, riding on the back of a now-grown-up Squawk. The *Infinite* appears to give Baltazar his heart's desire – a hoard of treasure with which he can buy himself a new ship and become the scourge of the galaxy once more – but it is really just an illusion, and the Doctor uses the sonic screwdriver to trigger the collapse of what remains of the ancient vessel. The Doctor and Martha leave in the TARDIS, while Baltazar is rescued by Squawk ... only to be taken back to prison on Volag-Noc.

# APPENDIX D
# RATINGS AND RANKING

Over the course of its first two series, the revived *Doctor Who* had proved to be not only a critical triumph and a winner with the fans but also, and no doubt more importantly from the BBC's perspective, a huge hit with the general viewing public in the UK, pulling in ratings that were both extraordinarily high and – taking into account distorting factors such as seasonal variations, public holidays and coverage of major sporting events – remarkably consistent. The number of viewers tuning in for a show is not, of course, the only statistical measure of its success: also important is the extent to which those viewers enjoyed it; and a measure of this is provided by the Appreciation Index (AI). In this respect, too, *Doctor Who* had performed amazingly well in its first two years, making it a rare example of a show that had achieved the highly-prized 'double whammy' of attracting a very big audience and keeping it highly entertained.

The question on many people's lips in the run-up to Series Three – the first without the popular Billie Piper as Rose Tyler – was: would *Doctor Who* be able to maintain this astonishing record of achievement, or would the viewing public's love affair with the series start to cool?

The table below shows what happened. It lists, for the BBC One and BBC Three debut transmissions of each of the 14 episodes (including the Christmas special): the estimated total number of viewers aged four and over (corrected and adjusted to include those who recorded the episode to watch within the week following transmission) in millions (RATING); percentage share of the total TV audience at the time of transmission (S); chart position amongst all programmes transmitted the same day on the same channel (D); overall chart position amongst all programmes transmitted the same day on all terrestrial channels (for the BBC One transmissions) or all digital channels (for the BBC Three transmissions) (D/O); chart position amongst all programmes transmitted the same week (Monday to Sunday inclusive) on the same channel (W); overall chart position amongst all programmes transmitted the same week (Monday to Sunday) on all terrestrial channels (for the BBC One transmissions) or all digital channels (for the BBC Three transmissions) (W/O); and the audience appreciation index as a percentage (AI). The entries marked n/k are not known, as the relevant data are unavailable.

| EPISODE | BBC- | RATING | S | D | D/O | W | W/O | AI |
|---|---|---|---|---|---|---|---|---|
| 'The Runaway Bride' | One | 9.35 m | 37% | 4th | 5th | 7th | 10th | 84 |
| | Three | 0.59 m | 3% | 3rd | 3rd | 5th | 20th | n/k |
| 'Smith and Jones' | One | 8.71 m | 41% | 1st | 1st | 4th | 9th | 88 |
| | Three | 1.00 m | 5% | 1st | 1st | 1st | 2nd | 90 |
| 'The Shakespeare Code' | One | 7.23 m | 37% | 1st | 1st | 4th | 14th | 87 |
| | Three | 1.04 m | 6% | 1st | 1st | 1st | 1st | 86 |
| 'Gridlock' | One | 8.41 m | 40% | 1st | 1st | 2nd | 7th | 85 |
| | Three | 0.83 m | 5% | 1st | 1st | 1st | 4th | 86 |
| 'Daleks in Manhattan' | One | 6.69 m | 36% | 1st | 1st | 6th | 18th | 86 |
| | Three | 1.13 m | 6% | 1st | 1st | 1st | 3rd | 84 |
| 'Evolution of the Daleks' | One | 6.97 m | 39% | 2nd | 2nd | 7th | 17th | 85 |
| | Three | 1.04 m | 5% | 1st | 1st | 1st | 3rd | 84 |
| 'The Lazarus Experiment' | One | 7.19 m | 39% | 1st | 1st | 5th | 12th | 86 |
| | Three | 0.98 m | 5% | 1st | 1st | 1st | 5th | n/k |
| '42' | One | 7.41 m | 37% | 1st | 1st | 5th | 16th | 85 |
| | Three | 0.88 m | 5% | 1st | 2nd | 2nd | 6th | n/k |
| 'Human Nature' | One | 7.74 m | 38% | 1st | 1st | 6th | 13th | 86 |
| | Three | 0.87 m | 5% | 1st | 1st | 1st | 3rd | n/k |
| 'The Family of Blood' | One | 7.21 m | 41% | 1st | 1st | 6th | 13th | 86 |
| | Three | 0.76 m | 4% | 1st | 1st | 2nd | 4th | 86 |
| 'Blink' | One | 6.62 m | 38% | 1st | 1st | 7th | 16th | 87 |
| | Three | 0.75 m | 4% | 1st | 1st | 1st | 6th | 90 |
| 'Utopia' | One | 7.84 m | 38% | 1st | 2nd | 4th | 14th | 87 |
| | Three | 0.82 m | 4% | 1st | 1st | 1st | 4th | 88 |
| 'The Sound of Drums' | One | 7.51 m | 40% | 1st | 1st | 4th | 11th | 87 |
| | Three | 1.09 m | 5% | 1st | 1st | 2nd | 2nd | 90 |
| 'Last of the Time Lords' | One | 8.61 m | n/k | 1st | 1st | 4th | 13th | 88 |
| | Three | 0.81 m | 4% | 1st | 1st | 2nd | 3rd | 88 |

Source for viewing figures: Broadcasters' Audience Research Board (BARB)
AI figures not sourced from BARB

The following table indicates how many viewers each episode attracted not only on its BBC One and BBC Three debut transmissions but also on its first BBC Three repeat – on the following Friday evening except in the case of 'Utopia', which was delayed by a week (owing to coverage of the Glastonbury music festival) and shown immediately before the equivalent repeat of 'The Sound of Drums' – giving an overall total viewing figure for the whole week.[130] (No figure is available, though, for the Friday repeat of 'The Lazarus Experiment'.) The figures for 'The

---

[130] General research into viewing figures has shown that the great majority of viewers who tune in for repeats are additional, i.e. that they have not already seen the programme on one or more of its earlier transmissions. Some sources suggest that the figure is at least 90 percent.

Runaway Bride' are not strictly comparable to those for the other 13 episodes as, being a Christmas special, it naturally had different transmission slots, and also an extra repeat on BBC One. Its four screenings were on Christmas Day 2006 on BBC One, 27 December on BBC Three, 29 December on BBC One and 2 January on BBC Three. The relevant figures are nevertheless included here for the sake of completeness, with the 'BBC One Repeat' column marked n/a – not applicable – in all other cases.

| EPISODE | BBC ONE DEBUT | BBC THREE DEBUT | BBC ONE REPEAT | BBC THREE REPEAT | TOTAL |
|---|---|---|---|---|---|
| 'The Runaway Bride' | 9.35 m | 0.59 m | 0.22 m | 0.46 m | 10.62 m |
| 'Smith and Jones' | 8.71 m | 1.00 m | n/a | 0.40 m | 10.11 m |
| 'The Shakespeare Code' | 7.23 m | 1.04 m | n/a | 0.53 m | 8.80 m |
| 'Gridlock' | 8.41 m | 0.83 m | n/a | 0.34 m | 9.58 m |
| 'Daleks in Manhattan' | 6.69 m | 1.13 m | n/a | 0.45 m | 8.27 m |
| 'Evolution of the Daleks' | 6.97 m | 1.04 m | n/a | 0.35 m | 8.36 m |
| 'The Lazarus Experiment' | 7.19 m | 0.98 m | n/a | n/k | n/k |
| '42' | 7.41 m | 0.88 m | n/a | 0.30 m | 8.59 m |
| 'Human Nature' | 7.74 m | 0.87 m | n/a | 0.36 m | 8.97 m |
| 'Family of Blood' | 7.21 m | 0.76 m | n/a | 0.33 m | 8.30 m |
| 'Blink' | 6.62 m | 0.75 m | n/a | 0.38 m | 7.75 m |
| 'Utopia' | 7.84 m | 0.82 m | n/a | 0.33 m | 8.99 m |
| 'The Sound of Drums' | 7.51 m | 1.09 m | n/a | 0.62 m | 9.22 m |
| 'Last of the Time Lords' | 8.61 m | 0.81 m | n/a | 0.52 m | 9.94 m |
| Average* | 7.55 m | 0.92 m | n/a | 0.41m | 8.88 m |

* Not including 'The Runaway Bride'
Source: Broadcasters' Audience Research Board (BARB)

The above tables indicate that leaving aside 'The Runaway Bride' – which has to be considered an exceptional case, as its viewing numbers, and indeed its percentage share and chart positions, are obviously affected by its status as part of a special schedule of Christmas programming – the average debut transmission rating for Series Three was 7.55 million on BBC One – which compares with 7.95 million for Series One and 7.71 million for Series Two – and 0.92 million on BBC Three – which compares with 0.58 million for Series One[131] and 0.63 million for Series Two. The average viewing figure for the BBC One debut transmissions is thus tending to decrease very slightly from year to year, but the average viewing figure for the BBC Three debut transmissions is tending to increase very slightly, meaning that the

[131] This figure, although it likewise relates to the regular Sunday evening repeat, is not strictly comparable, because the Series One episodes from 'World War Three' onwards actually had their debut BBC Three transmission in a late night Saturday slot. This attracted only 0.2 million viewers on average, but it is possible that it may have slightly reduced the audience for the Sunday evening screening.

combined total for the two is staying fairly constant at around the 8.4 million mark. This rises to around 8.8 million if one takes into account also the Friday evening BBC Three repeats.

Series Three has thus clearly maintained and reinforced *Doctor Who*'s position as a big-hitter in the ratings war, and one of the BBC's flagship drama productions, to the extent that it arguably now rivals the long-established soap opera *EastEnders* for pre-eminence. Its achievement in this regard is actually even more impressive than these figures alone would suggest, as while it has been enjoying unwavering popularity, the average viewing figures for TV programmes in general have been steadily falling, the multitude of channels now available leading to the total audience being spread ever more thinly between them. *Doctor Who* has not simply held its own, but has actually bucked this trend of declining viewing figures.

On BBC One, the highest rating for an individual Series Three episode (excluding 'The Runaway Bride') was 8.71 million for 'Smith and Jones' and the lowest was 6.62 million for 'Blink', giving a spread of 2.09 million. This compares with a high of 10.81 million, a low of 6.81 million and a spread of 4.00 million for Series One; and a high of 9.24 million, a low of 6.08 million and a spread of 3.16 million for Series Two (excluding 'The Christmas Invasion'). Taking into account all three transmissions that each Series Three episode had within its debut week (again excluding 'The Runaway Bride'), the overall total weekly viewing figures peaked at 10.11 million for 'Smith and Jones' and bottomed out at 7.75 million for 'Blink', giving a spread of 2.36 million. Thus, even more so than over Series One and Series Two – and significantly more so than over drama series in general – the viewing figures remained remarkably consistent over Series Three, with very little week-on-week variation, despite the numerous changes in the BBC One transmission time. This becomes even more apparent if one discounts the unusually high figure for 'Smith and Jones', which is in line with the well-recognised phenomenon that the first episode of any new series tends to benefit both from novelty value and from heavier advance publicity.

The average audience share on BBC One was 39%, with a high of 41% for 'Smith and Jones' and 'The Family of Blood' and a low of 36% for 'Daleks in Manhattan'. This compares with an average of 40%, a high of 45% and a low of 36% for Series One; and an average of 41%, a high of 45% and a low of 33% for Series Two. The average share on BBC Three was 5%, varying from a low of 4% to a high of 6%. This compares with an average of 4%, a low of 3% and a high of 5% for Series Two; equivalent figures are not available for Series One. (All these figures exclude the Christmas specials.) The audience share won by the BBC One debut transmissions was thus on average slightly down on that achieved in Series One and Series Two; but, as with the viewing figures, it was even more consistent over the course of the 13 episodes. Also following the pattern of the viewing figures, the average audience share for the BBC Three debut transmissions was slightly up on that for Series Two.

*Doctor Who* was almost always BBC One's top-rated programme on Saturday and amongst its top five for the week, and was without exception in the top 20 programmes across all channels for the week, with two episodes (or three if one includes 'The Runaway Bride') achieving a coveted top ten place. Only once was it bested by one of ITV1's Saturday programmes (one of the very successful *Britain's Got Talent* shows), and that went out in a slightly later time slot, not in direct competition. Similarly, *Doctor Who* was almost always the top-rated Sunday programme on BBC Three, and amongst the top five for the week (on a couple of occasions being knocked down a place by *Doctor Who Confidential*, which tended to have quite similar figures – see below), and invariably in the top ten across all digital channels for the week. This was essentially in line with the pattern established in Series One and Series Two.

The average AI figure on BBC One was 86 (compared with 82 for Series One and 84 for Series Two) and on BBC Three was 87 (compared with 86 for Series Two; no equivalent figure is available for Series One). Given that the average AI figure for all drama programmes broadcast by the BBC or ITV is 77, these are exceptionally good results; they also show a steady year-on-year improvement, indicating that the viewing public's enjoyment of *Doctor Who* has been growing with each successive run, from an already high base. It seems unlikely, though, that the figure can rise much further now, as it is already at an extraordinary and possibly unprecedented level for such a highly-rated drama series. The slightly higher figure for BBC Three is not unexpected: programmes with smaller ratings tend to get higher AI figures, as their audiences generally have a higher proportion of viewers who are predisposed to like them (as opposed to casual viewers who have tuned in more on a whim).

On BBC One, the highest AI figure was 88 for 'Smith and Jones' and 'Last of the Time Lords' and the lowest was 84 for 'The Runaway Bride'. This compares with a high of 89 and a low of 76 for Series One; and, coincidentally, figures identical to those for Series Two. On BBC Three, the highest was an outstanding 90 for 'Smith and Jones', 'Blink' and 'The Sound of Drums' and the lowest was 84 for 'Daleks in Manhattan' and 'Evolution of the Daleks' (with figures unknown for three episodes). This compares with a high of 91 and a low of 79 for Series Two; equivalent figures for Series One are not available. As with the viewing figures and audience share, therefore, the AI figures show a greater degree of consistency over the course of Series Three, with a spread of only four points for the BBC One transmissions as opposed to 13 in each of the previous two years, and the figures for the BBC Three transmissions showing a similar trend.

Based on the BBC One figures, the general viewing public's order of preference for the episodes, working downwards from favourite to least favourite, was:

1. = 'Smith and Jones'
1. = 'Last of the Time Lords'
3. = 'The Shakespeare Code'
3. = 'Blink'
3. = 'Utopia'
3. = 'The Sound of Drums'
7. = 'Daleks in Manhattan'
7. = 'The Lazarus Experiment'
7. = 'Human Nature'
7. = 'The Family of Blood'
11. = 'Gridlock'
11. = 'Evolution of the Daleks'
11. = '42'
14. = 'The Runaway Bride'

An indication of the relative merits of the episodes from the point of view of fans can be gleaned from the online episode polls conducted in the forum of the hugely popular Outpost Gallifrey *Doctor Who* website. Between around 3,500 and 5,300 voters participated in these polls, in which each episode was given a mark of between one and five, with five being the highest. The percentages in the table below have been calculated by adding together the total number of marks received by each episode (as of 30 July 2007) and dividing by the maximum that could have been achieved if everyone who voted had given the episode a five.

| EPISODE | FAN RATING |
|---|---|
| 'The Runaway Bride' | 71% |
| 'Smith and Jones' | 78% |
| 'The Shakespeare Code' | 78% |
| 'Gridlock' | 79% |
| 'Daleks in Manhattan' | 76% |
| 'Evolution of the Daleks' | 71% |
| 'The Lazarus Experiment' | 79% |
| '42' | 77% |
| 'Human Nature' | 94% |
| 'The Family of Blood' | 95% |
| 'Blink' | 93% |
| 'Utopia' | 90% |
| 'The Sound of Drums' | 84% |
| 'Last of the Time Lords' | 73% |

Based on these figures, the fans' order of preference for the episodes was:

1. 'The Family of Blood'
2. 'Human Nature'
3. 'Blink'
4. 'Utopia'
5. 'The Sound of Drums'
6. = 'Gridlock'
6. = 'The Lazarus Experiment'
8. = 'Smith and Jones'
8. = 'The Shakespeare Code'
10. '42'
11. 'Daleks in Manhattan'
12. 'Last of the Time Lords'
13. = 'The Runaway Bride'
13. = 'Evolution of the Daleks'

Unlike in previous years, this ranking does not correspond particularly closely to the one for the general viewing public (see above), athough certain episodes – 'Blink', 'Utopia' and 'The Sound of Drums' – come near the top in both, and certain others – 'The Runaway Bride' and 'Evolution of the Daleks' – come at or near the bottom in both. Perhaps the most significant point to note here is that, in common with the general viewing public, the fans clearly thought that the overall standard of the episodes was higher in Series Three than ever before, and that there was less to choose between them: the spread of the figures in the fan ranking – from a still-very-respectable low of 71 percent ('The Runaway Bride' and 'Evolution of the Daleks') to an extraordinary high of 95 percent ('The Family of Blood') – is four points less than for Series Two – which went from a low of 65 percent ('Fear Her') to a high of 93 percent ('Doomsday') – and one point less than for Series One – which went from a low of 68 percent ('Boom Town') to a high of 93 percent ('Dalek'). Paul Cornell's remarkable 'Human Nature' and 'The Family of Blood' would thus seem to be the most popular new series episodes to date amongst dedicated fans.

The full ratings statistics produced by BARB for the main BBC One transmissions (which go into too fine a level of detail to be worth reproducing in their entirety here) reveal three other points of particular interest.

First, *Doctor Who* consistently scored well above the average for drama programmes under a range of viewer response headings, including 'Made a special effort to watch', 'Watched with a lot of attention', 'High quality programme', 'Feels original and different', 'Would like to discuss', 'Liked the storyline' and 'Liked the characters'. The two main exceptions were 'Learned something new' and 'Programme was thought-provoking', under which headings the episodes tended to score around or just below the average for drama.

Secondly, the average number of children aged four to 15 amongst viewers for these BBC One transmissions (excluding 'The Runaway Bride') was 1.49 million, and the average share of the total children's audience an astonishingly high 59%, making *Doctor Who* by far the most popular TV programme amongst children each week. Boys outnumbered girls by an average of seven percentage points amongst viewers in this age range. In three cases – 'Gridlock', 'Daleks in Manhattan' and 'The Sound of Drums' – this disparity between the sexes was as high as 14 percentage points, although in two other cases – 'The Shakespeare Code' and 'The Family of Blood' – girls actually outnumbered boys, by six percentage points for the former and four percentage points for the latter, indicative of the fact that there was quite a wide spread in these figures.

Thirdly, where adult viewers were concerned, the position was reversed: there were consistently fewer men than women in the audience for the BBC One transmissions. Excluding 'The Runaway Bride', the average proportion of the total BBC One viewing audience (all ages) who were men was 49%, and the average proportion who were women was 51%. (For the BBC Three screenings, the average split was closer to even, although women still had a very slight edge.) Children aside, the series was most popular amongst those in the 35 to 44 age range, but had a good spread of viewers across all other age ranges as well. This belies the once-stereotypical image of the typical *Doctor Who* viewer as being a young male science fiction fan.

To conclude this section, set out below, for what it's worth, is this author's own ranking of the episodes, again working downwards from favourite to least favourite – although I should perhaps add that my views on this tend to change from time to time!

1. 'Gridlock'
2. 'Human Nature'
3. 'Smith and Jones'
4. 'The Family of Blood'
5. 'Blink'
6. 'The Shakespeare Code'
7. 'Daleks in Manhattan'
8. 'The Lazarus Experiment'
9. 'Utopia'
10. 'The Sound of Drums'
11. 'Evolution of the Daleks'
12. 'Last of the Time Lords'
13. '42'
14. 'The Runaway Bride'

DOCTOR WHO CONFIDENTIAL

The main ratings data for the debut transmissions of the third series of *Doctor Who Confidential* were as follows. (The terms in the heading have the same meanings as in the equivalent table above for *Doctor Who* itself.)

| EPISODE | RATING | SHARE | AI |
|---|---|---|---|
| 'Music and Monsters' | 1.50 m | n/k | n/k |
| 'Meet Martha Jones' | 0.81 m | 5% | 85 |
| 'Stage Fright' | 0.66 m | 4% | 85 |
| 'Are We There Yet?' | 0.58 m | 3% | 82 |
| 'A New York Story' | 0.49 m | 3% | 81 |
| 'Making Manhattan' | 0.59 m | 4% | 83 |
| 'Monsters Inc.' | 0.80 m | 5% | 83 |
| 'Space Craft' | 0.50 m | 3% | 80 |
| 'Alter Ego' | 0.71 m | 4% | 83 |
| 'Bad Blood' | 0.57 m | 4% | 81 |
| 'Do You Remember the First Time?' | 0.69 m | 4% | 82 |
| ''Ello, 'ello, 'ello' | 0.74 m | 4% | 85 |
| 'The Saxon Mystery' | 0.96 m | n/k | n/k |
| 'The Valiant Quest' | 1.02 m | n/k | n/k |
| **Average*** | **0.70 m** | **4%** | **83** |

* Not including 'Music and Monsters', which was transmitted on BBC One rather than BBC Three on Christmas Day 2006.
Source: Broadcasters' Audience Research Board (BARB)

The average rating amongst children aged 4 to 15 inclusive was 0.21 million, meaning that they made up 30% of the audience. The split between male and female viewers (all ages) was 53% to 47%.

These excellent figures – higher in some cases than for the BBC Three transmissions of *Doctor Who* itself – maintained *Doctor Who Confidential*'s record of success, the average viewing figure of 0.70 million for the debut transmissions representing a steady improvement on the second series' 0.63 million and the first series' 0.54 million. As in previous years, repeat screenings – generally in the *Confidential Cutdown* format – also drew significant numbers of additional viewers.

TOTALLY DOCTOR WHO

The main ratings data for the debut transmissions of the second series of *Totally Doctor Who* were as follows. (No AI figures were recorded for these programmes.)

| EPISODE | RATING | SHARE |
|---|---|---|
| 2.01 | 0.76 m | 8% |
| 2.02 | 0.69 m | 7% |
| 2.03 | 0.72 m | 7% |
| 2.04 | 0.55 m | 8% |
| 2.05 | 0.86 m | 8% |
| 2.06 | 0.83 m | 7% |
| 2.07 | 0.82 m | 8% |
| 2.08 | 0.70 m | 8% |
| 2.09 | 0.73 m | 8% |
| 2.10 | 0.92 m | 8% |
| 2.11 | n/k | n/k |
| 2.12 | n/k | n/k |
| **Average** | **0.76 m** | **8%** |

Source: Broadcasters' Audience Research Board (BARB)

Although ostensibly a children's programme, *Totally Doctor Who* actually had a bigger adult audience. The average number of viewers aged four to 15 was 0.27 million, while the average number of those aged 16 plus was 0.49 million, with the largest proportion of the latter group being in the 35 to 44 age range. On average, 55% of viewers (all ages) were men and 45% were women, with the equivalent figures for children alone being a little closer at 53% and 47% respectively.

The lower-than-usual viewing figure for the fourth episode is no doubt accounted for by the fact that it went out at 4.00 pm, an hour earlier than all the others; notably, its audience share at the time of transmission was still in line with the average.

The 0.76 million average viewing figure is identical to that achieved by the first series, while the 8% average share is a marginal improvement on the latter's 7%. This again put *Totally Doctor Who* in the same bracket as *Blue Peter* as one of CBBC's most successful programmes.

# APPENDIX E
# ORIGINAL NOVELS

During the period of the build up to and transmission of Series Three, BBC Books published a further six titles in their ongoing range of tenth Doctor hardback novels, plus another of the paperback 'Quick Reads' books following on from the previous year's successful *I Am a Dalek*. Summary details are as follows.

## 10: THE NIGHTMARE OF BLACK ISLAND

Writer: Mike Tucker
Publication date: 21 September 2006
Commissioning Editor: Stuart Cooper; Creative Director and Editor: Justin Richards; Production Controller: Peter Hunt; Cover designer: Henry Steadman

### PUBLICITY BLURB

On a lonely stretch of Welsh coastline a fisherman is killed by a hideous creature from beneath the waves. When the Doctor and Rose arrive, they discover a village where the children are plagued by nightmares, and the nights are ruled by monsters. The villagers suspect that ancient industrialist Nathanial Morton is to blame, but the Doctor has suspicions of his own. Who are the ancient figures that sleep in the old priory? What are the monsters that prowl the woods after sunset? What is the light that glows in the disused lighthouse on Black Island? As the children's nightmares get worse, the Doctor and Rose discover an alien plot to resurrect an ancient evil ... This book features the Doctor and Rose as played by David Tennant and Billie Piper in the hit series from BBC Television.

### NOTE

- Also released by BBC Audio on 6 November 2006 as an abridged audiobook CD set read by Anthony Head.

## 11: THE ART OF DESTRUCTION

Writer: Stephen Cole
Publication date: 21 September 2006
Commissioning Editor: Stuart Cooper; Creative Director and Editor: Justin Richards; Production Controller: Peter Hunt; Cover designer: Henry Steadman

### PUBLICITY BLURB

The TARDIS lands in 22nd Century Africa in the shadow of a dormant volcano.

Agri-teams are growing new foodstuffs in the baking soil to help feed the world's starving millions – but the Doctor and Rose have detected an alien signal somewhere close by. When a nightmare force starts surging along the dark volcanic tunnels, the Doctor realises an ancient trap has been sprung. But who was it meant for? And what is the secret of the eerie statues that stand at the heart of the volcano? Dragged into a centuries-old conflict, Rose and the Doctor are soon elevating survival to an art form – as ancient, alien hands practice arts of destruction all around them. This work features the Doctor and Rose as played by David Tennant and Billie Piper in the hit series from BBC Television.

NOTE

- Also released by BBC Audio on 6 November 2006 as an abridged audiobook CD set read by Don Warrington.

## 12: THE PRICE OF PARADISE

Writer: Colin Brake
Publication date: 21 September 2006
Commissioning Editor: Stuart Cooper; Creative Director and Editor: Justin Richards; Production Controller: Peter Hunt; Cover designer: Henry Steadman

PUBLICITY BLURB

Laylora – the paradise planet. A world of breathtaking beauty, where peace-loving aboriginals live in harmony with their environment. Or do they? The Doctor and Rose arrive to find that the once-perfect eco-system is showing signs of failing. The paradise planet has become a death trap as terrifying creatures from ancient legends appear and stalk the land ... Is there a connection between the human explorers who have crash-landed and the savage monsters? What secret lies at the heart of the natives' ancient ceremonies? And what price might one human have to pay to save the only home he has ever known? When a planet itself becomes sick, can there be a cure? The Doctor and Rose find themselves in a race against time to find out. This book features the Doctor and Rose as played by David Tennant and Billie Piper in the hit series from BBC Television.

NOTE

- Also released by BBC Audio on 6 November 2006 as an abridged audiobook CD set read by Shaun Dingwall.

## MADE OF STEEL

Writer: Terrance Dicks
Publication date: 1 March 2007
Creative Director: Justin Richards; Project Editor: Steve Tribe; Production Controller: Alenka Oblak; Cover designer: Henry Steadman

## PUBLICITY BLURB

Since its return to the screen in 2005, masterminded by Russell T Davies, *Doctor Who* has become a genuine phenomenon picking up countless awards, attracting huge audiences and selling lots and lots of books – over half a million so far. This latest adventure sees the Doctor pitted against one of his most famous adversaries – the deadly Cybermen. It is the first book to feature the Doctor's new companion Martha Jones and is sure to be snapped up by all fans of the show.

## NOTES

- A paperback in the 'Quick Reads' range launched by the National Literacy Trust charity on World Book Day 2006 with the stated aim to 'provide fast-paced, bite-sized books by bestselling writers for emergent readers, anyone who had lost the reading habit or simply wanted a short, fast read'.
- This was the first story featuring Martha to be made publicly available, predating her introduction in the TV series itself.

## 13: STING OF THE ZYGONS

Writer: Stephen Cole
Publication date: 19 April 2007
Creative Director: Justin Richards; Project Editor: Steve Tribe; Production Controller: Alenka Oblak; Cover designer: Henry Steadman

## PUBLICITY BLURB

The TARDIS lands the Doctor and Martha in the Lake District in 1909, where a small village has been terrorised by a giant, scaly monster. The search is on for the elusive 'Beast of Westmorland', and explorers, naturalists and hunters from across the country are descending on the fells. King Edward VII himself is on his way to join the search, with a knighthood for whoever finds the Beast. But there is a more sinister presence at work in the Lakes than a mere monster on the rampage, and the Doctor is soon embroiled in the plans of an old and terrifying enemy. And as the hunters become the hunted, a desperate battle of wits begins – with the future of the entire world at stake ... This work features the Doctor and Martha as played by David Tennant and Freema Agyeman in the acclaimed hit series from BBC Television.

## NOTES

- Features the Zygons from the classic series story 'Terror of the Zygons' (1976).
- Also released by BBC Audio on 2 July 2007 as an abridged audiobook CD set read by Reggie Yates.

## 14: THE LAST DODO

Writer: Jacqueline Rayner
Publication date: 19 April 2007
Creative Director: Justin Richards; Project Editor: Steve Tribe; Production Controller: Alenka Oblak; Cover designer: Henry Steadman

PUBLICITY BLURB

After a trip to the zoo, the Doctor and Martha go in search of a real live dodo, and are transported by the TARDIS to the mysterious Museum of the Last Ones. There, in the Earth section, they discover every extinct creature up to the present day – billions of them, from the tiniest insect to the biggest dinosaur, all still alive and in suspended animation. Preservation is the Museum's only job – collecting the last of every endangered species from all over the universe. And for millennia the Museum has been trying to trace one elusive specimen: the last of the Time Lords ... This work features the Doctor and Martha as played by David Tennant and Freema Agyeman in the acclaimed hit series from BBC Television.

NOTE

• Also released by BBC Audio on 2 July 2007 as an abridged audiobook CD set read by Freema Agyeman.

## 15: WOODEN HEART

Writer: Martin Day
Publication date: 19 April 2007
Creative Director: Justin Richards; Project Editor: Steve Tribe; Production Controller: Alenka Oblak; Cover designer: Henry Steadman

PUBLICITY BLURB

The *Castor*, a vast starship, seemingly deserted, spinning slowly in the void of deep space. Martha and the Doctor explore the drifting tomb, and discover that they may not be alone after all ... Who survived the disaster that overcame the rest of the crew? What continues to power the vessel? And why has a stretch of wooded countryside suddenly appeared in the middle of the craft? As the Doctor and Martha journey through the forest, they find a mysterious, fogbound village – a village traumatised by missing children and tales of its own destruction ... This title features the Doctor and Martha as played by David Tennant and Freema Agyeman in the acclaimed hit series from BBC Television.

NOTE

• Also released by BBC Audio on 2 July 2007 as an abridged audiobook CD set read by Adjoa Andoh.

# APPENDIX F
# ORIGINAL COMIC STRIPS

During the 12 month period covered by this book, *Doctor Who* fans could enjoy no fewer than three different comic strip series presenting new adventures for the tenth Doctor (and, for the last three months or so, his companion Martha Jones). The first of these was a regular feature in *Doctor Who Magazine*, which (under various different titles) had been home to a *Doctor Who* comic strip since 1979, and the other two appeared in relative newcomers, *Doctor Who Adventures* – a fortnightly comic aimed at a pre-teen audience – and *Battles in Time* – a fortnightly trading-card magazine pitched toward slightly older children. Listed below are details of the stories from each of these three titles in turn.

## DOCTOR WHO MAGAZINE

### THE FUTURISTS

Story and Art: Mike Collins
Inks: David A Roach; Colours: James Offredi; Lettering: Roger Langridge; Editors: Clayton Hickman and Scott Gray
Publication[132]: Issues 372-374; 16 August 2006, 13 September 2006, 11 October 2006

PLOT

The Doctor takes Rose to see Milan in the 1920s, but something is badly wrong: futuristic buildings suddenly break through into the city, displacing the old ones. Rose meets a woman named Altea Orsi, who loves a man named Giovanni, a member of the Futurist movement of artists and architects. The Doctor meanwhile finds a dazed soldier from ancient Rome in the otherwise deserted hall where the Futurists were holding a meeting, and from where the time disturbance seems to have originated. Of Giovanni there is no sign. The Doctor and Rose take Altea and the soldier back to the TARDIS, where the Doctor makes a grim discovery: according to the ship's instruments, they are the only ones left alive, and the Earth has been dead for centuries. Believing that the soldier 'swapped places' with Giovanni, the Doctor materialises the TARDIS in Britain at the time of the Roman Empire. Rose and Altea get captured by Roman troops, while the Doctor and the dazed soldier fall in with a group of native Britons who are resisting the oppressors. Recovering his wits, the soldier identifies himself as a conscript named Valente. He believes that Giovanni has been consorting with demons called the

---

[132] The publication dates given here for *Doctor Who Magazine* are those printed on the covers of the issues in question. The issues generally went on sale about a month earlier than the cover dates.

Hajor, and the Doctor determines to end this. Rose and Altea have meanwhile been locked up in an anachronistically modern prison, where the other women prisoners know Giovanni as a wizard. The Doctor and the resistance fighters infiltrate the prison, where the Doctor confronts the Legate in charge, to discover that he is being 'advised' by Giovanni. Suddenly Giovanni and the Legate disappear, taking the Doctor and some of the Britons with them. They arrive in an alien dimension where the jellyfish-like Hajor declare themselves the new Lords of Time. The Hajor exist to 'smooth out' the paradoxes created by time travellers, and they were attracted by Giovanni's dreams of a regulated universe, seeing a way to impose order through active rather than passive means. Giovanni aims to create a mighty army to restart history along sterile lines, but the Doctor accesses images of the time stream to show him that the aliens will not give him the perfect world he craves: they will mechanise everything and destroy the human race. Meanwhile, with the aid of the psychic paper, Rose and the other women prisoners stage a breakout. The Doctor reminds Giovanni of his feelings for Altea, which caused him to spare her in Milan. Giovanni then breaks his link with the Hajor and teleports back to the prison to protect Altea from an attack by a soldier, but dies by the soldier's sword. The Doctor realises that Valente is linked to the Hajor in the same way Giovanni was, which gives him the power to destroy the creatures. This done, the Earth returns to normality.

## INTERSTELLAR OVERDRIVE

Story: Jonathan Morris
Pencils: Mike Collins; Inks: David A Roach; Colours: James Offredi; Letters: Roger Langridge; Editors: Clayton Hickman and Scott Gray
Publication: Issues 375-376; 8 November 2006, 6 December 2006

PLOT

The TARDIS brings the Doctor and Rose to a Magellan-class Star Cruiser inhabited by a famous rock group, Pakafroon Wabster. The group have been recording for 300 years and are now on their sixty-third line-up but are still led by the cadaverous form of their founder, Wabster, who was animatronically reanimated following his death in a rollerblading accident. The Doctor, mistaken for a representative from the group's record label, warns that the ship's engines are about to blow, but is disregarded. The explosion tears a hole in the side of the ship, and Rose discovers that the spacesuits all have burn holes in them. The Doctor, realising that there is a saboteur on board, tries to flush him out by jettisoning the ship's only escape pod. Suddenly the ship splits apart, sending Rose and the band members falling into space. The Doctor manages to cling on to a door handle and avoid this fate, but suddenly the whole ship explodes … However, the ship is in a time loop, and the Doctor and Rose find themselves back at the point where they first arrived. Armed with foreknowledge of what is to happen, the Doctor declares that one of those on the ship is a murderer – or is going to be, at any rate. Events start to occur as before, and the saboteur is revealed to be the band's manager, Jacey, who believes that their tragic deaths will give them legendary status. She is working with the record label, who are planning a major back-catalogue promotion for the band, and so realised all along that the Doctor was an imposter. Jacey is killed by Wabster, who is restored to full life after taking a blast from her gun. The band then get away in the escape pod before the ship explodes, while the Doctor and Rose depart in the TARDIS.

## THE GREEN-EYED MONSTER

Story: Nev Fountain
Art and Lettering: Roger Langridge; Colours: James Offredi; Editors: Clayton Hickman and Scott Gray
Publication: Issue 377; 3 January 2007

PLOT

Rose emerges from the TARDIS to find herself in a TV studio, appearing as a star guest on the Vanexxa Skank talk show. Other guests on the show are Mickey Smith and Jackie Tyler, who tell stories about the Doctor seemingly designed to make Rose jealous. When Jackie and the Doctor actually kiss, a green, slug-like monster squirts out of Rose's ear, to be blasted by Mickey with a gun that traps it in a forcefield. The Doctor explains that the creature is the Iagnon, whose acolytes placed it in Rose's ear while she was asleep so that it could devour her essence. It loves to eat jealous emotions, so the Doctor caused Rose to feel so much jealousy that it eventually over-fed and expelled itself. The TV show was set up by the Doctor at Jackie's suggestion, using actors.

## THE WARKEEPER'S CROWN

Story: Alan Barnes
Pencils: Martin Geraghty; Inks: David A Roach; Colours: James Offredi; Lettering: Roger Langridge; Editors: Hickman and Gray
Publication: Issues 378-380; 31 January 2007, 28 February 2007,

PLOT

The retired Brigadier Lethbridge-Stewart is attending a military parade when a whirlwind whips up and deposits him on an alien planet. There he is greeted by the Doctor, newly-arrived himself, and proclaimed by some hawk-like living statues to be their Warkeeper-Elect. As they come under attack by a red harpy-like creature, the Hawk Leader whisks the Doctor and the Brigadier into the sky, from which vantage point they see that a war is raging across the planet. They are taken to meet the current Warkeeper, a blue-skinned alien, who is close to death. The Warkeeper tells them that they are in the Slough of the Disunited Planets. A tactical genius is needed to take over the Warkeeper's Crown when he dies, in order to prevent the troll-like creatures outside from overrunning the place, and he has chosen the Brigadier for this role, having learned about his leadership skills from scanning the Doctor's mind. He has also brought to the planet a man named Mike Yates ... but, as the Doctor and the Brigadier quickly realise, this is not their old friend who formerly served in UNIT, but a prospective MEP for Upper

Wardleswick. The Doctor, the Brigadier and Yates escape after a thwarted attack by the trolls. They meet an elf-like nurse called Tilly who takes them to her field station. However, Tilly's two fellow nurses then transform into harpies. The Doctor and the Bridgadier are rescued by the hawks, but Tilly escapes, taking Yates with her. The Warkeeper dies, and Tilly gives the Crown to Yates. The Doctor realises that this whole planet is a laboratory and the creatures its experimental subjects, put here to devise new weapons and battle techniques. Yates gains control of the hawks and takes them and the three harpies to Upper Wardleswick. He declares war on France in revenge for the Battle of Hastings, but the harpies are growing restless for carrion and want to begin eating the assembled onlookers. The Doctor and the Brigadier have followed them to Earth. The Brigadier dislodges the Crown from Yates's head and the Doctor puts it on his own, but his mind is too sophisticated to access it. The harpies want the Brigadier to accept the Crown, but he refuses, and one of them shoots him with his own revolver. However, a whole army of duplicate Brigadiers then appears. The Doctor explains that he created the duplicates in the Warkeeper's clone factories and brought them all to Earth in the TARDIS. The harpies replace the Crown on Yates's head and instruct him to use it to dissipate the clones, which he does … but the hawks are clones too, and are thus destroyed. As army tanks arrive, the three harpies take refuge in a nearby pub, which is where the Doctor has left the real Brigadier. The Brigadier finally dons the Warkeeper's Crown and tells the harpies to 'Go to blazes', sending them flying off into space. Mike Yates is arrested, and the Doctor bids farewell to the Brigadier.

## THE WOMAN WHO SOLD THE WORLD

Story: Rob Davis
Pencils: Mike Collins; Inks: David A Roach; Colours: James Offredi; Lettering: Roger Langridge; Editors: Hickman and Gray
Publication: Issues 381-384; 2 May 2007, 30 May 2007,

PLOT

Responding to a distress beacon, the Doctor and Martha arrive on the planet Loam, which is under attack by High Goliax – huge, ornate robots that are actually inhabited demolition machines controlled by children. The planet's former Prime Minister, Baroness Hellyer, known as Sugarpea, and her partner, Sweetleaf, rescue Martha in a flying chair when she is ejected from the mouth of one of the High Goliax. The Doctor meanwhile is taken through a portal to a pyramidal spaceship called the Krib, which is the biggest bank in the universe. The manager, Mr Kingfish, explains that Loam is a property being cleared for resale, having fallen into the bank's hands after being used as collateral for a loan that was not repaid. Martha learns that Sugarpea took out the loan when she was Prime Minister, so this is all her fault, but now she is trying to make amends by saving the world. Sugarpea reactivates a giant, coal-fired statue of herself called the Diplomat, but known as Brassneck to the people, which was designed as an armoured peace negotiator for battle zones. The Doctor finds his way to the bank's computer, known as the Speculator, and discovers that its organic processors are effectively enslaved within it. He frees the processors, which then develop spider-like 'legs' and start to overrun the bank. On Loam, Sugarpea uses Brassneck to stage a coup, forcing the current Prime Minister to resign. As a dictator, she takes on personal responsibility for the loan to the Krib, which cannot then be enforced against the planet, but the sentence for this is death. Brassneck carries Sugarpea and Martha into one of the High Goliax and through a portal to the Krib, where Sugarpea tells Kingfish what she has done. On her prior instruction, Sugarpea is then executed by Brassneck. Brassneck returns to Loam with the Doctor and Martha via a High Goliax, and the processors follow. The processors are actually the minds of the High Goliax, and their 'legs' the nerves that were severed when they were ripped from the creatures' skulls centuries earlier. The processors return to their rightful places, and the High Goliax become benign creatures – but not before Kingfish has been killed by one operated by his son.

## DOCTOR WHO ADVENTURES

### FRIED DEATH

Script: Alan Barnes
Script Editor: Gareth Roberts
Artwork: John Ross; Colouring: Adrian Salmon; Lettering: Paul Vyse
Publication: Issue 8; 13 July 2006

PLOT

The Doctor and Rose visit Terry's Café on present day Earth and encounter the alien Gastronauts, led by the fearsome Rammzi, and their Chopbot drones.[133] The Doctor starts a rumour that there is good food to be found at a restaurant called the Fat Buck[134] in the Horse Head Nebula, and the Gastronauts move on to check it out.

### BIZARRE ZERO

Script: Stewart Sheargold
Script Editor: Gareth Roberts
Art: John Ross; Colours: Adrian Salmon; Letters: Paul Lang
Publication: Issue 9; 27 July 2006

PLOT

Winter seems to have come three months early when the Doctor and Rose arrive at the Powell Estate to visit Jackie, but the 'ice' is really an alien entity that freezes people on contact. The Doctor finds the aliens' weather control machine and switches it off, causing a temperature rise that the aliens are unable to survive.

---

[133] The character Rammzi is based on the celebrity chef Gordon Ramsey. A fellow Gastronaut mentioned in dialogue, Pukka Olifa, is named after another celebrity chef, Jamie Oliver.

[134] A name inspired by that of the Fat Duck, Heston Blumenthal's award-winning restaurant in London.

**SAVE THE HUMANS!**

Script: Alan Barnes
Script Editor: Gareth Roberts
Art: John Ross; Colours: Adrian Salmon; Letters: Paul Lang
Publication: Issue 10; 10 August 2006

PLOT

On arriving in an alien safari park called Wumba's World of Wild, the Doctor and Rose are captured by the keepers and put on display with a colony of humans. Genetically-altered dinosaurs are let loose on them, but the Doctor draws the creatures off with a promise of pizza, liberating the colony and causing the keepers to flee. The Doctor offers the humans Adam and Steve a lift off the planet, but they decline, saying that they want to make a go of it here, despite the hostile wildlife.

**BAT ATTACK!/THE BATTLE OF READING GAOL**

Script: Alan Barnes
Script Editor: Gary Russell
Art: John Ross; Colours: Adrian Salmon; Letters: Paul Lang
Publication: Issues 11-12; 24 August 2006, 7 September 2006

PLOT

The Doctor and Rose visit London in 1897, where Bram Stoker is giving a reading of his shortly-to-be-published novel *Dracula*, prior to its first presentation as a stage play ... only to be accosted by the newly-arrived Frederick von Dracula, Count of Wallachia, who wants to protect his family name. Bram is rescued by his wife Florence, who turns out to be a real vampire. She was infected by vampirism – an alien virus – 20 years earlier by Oscar Wilde. The Doctor visits Oscar in Reading Gaol, while Rose and Florence use the psychic paper to pose as prison inspectors, only to find that the governor and warders are all vampires. The Doctor drinks some of the vampire virus, against which Time Lords were routinely immunised, and makes it safe, then cures all the infected staff and prisoners by burping out the anti-virus.

**TRISKAIDEKAPHOBIA**

Script: Alan Barnes
Script Editor: Gary Russell
Art: John Ross; Colours: Lee Sullivan; Letters: Paul Vyse
Publication: Issue 13; 21 September 2006

PLOT

Arriving at galactic coordinates 13:13:13:13:13:13 – the thirteenth moon of the thirteenth planet of the thirteenth galaxy on the thirteenth day of the thirteenth year of the 13th Century – the Doctor and Rose encounter a group of aliens who consider themselves the unluckiest in the galaxy. The Doctor finds a four leaf clover, but then a lightning monster attacks. The moster is really a matter transporter. It takes the Doctor and Rose up to a spaceship hovering in a cloud overhead, where they meet the alien Bob Kreesus. Kreesus ensures that those below encounter only bad luck, which his computer then absorbs and converts into good luck for himself. The Doctor destroys the computer with his sonic screwdriver and takes Bob down to the planet, where the sun has started shining and things are looking brighter. Bob pulls a gun on Rose but unluckily falls off a cliff.

## SMART BOMBS

Script: Alan Barnes
Script Editor: Gary Russell
Art: John Ross; Colours: Adrian Salmon; Letters: Paul Lang
Publication: Issue 14; 3 October 2006

## PLOT

After he and Rose arrive on a planet with orange trees and purple skies, the Doctor falls down a hole in the ground, but is saved from harm by a group of living missiles called Fat Boy, Little Man, Whizz Bang and Sharkey. Rose meanwhile meets a businessman, apparently from Arcadian Independent Traders, who reunites her with the Doctor.[135] The man states that the living missiles are the evolved survivors of a war that wiped out the planet's original inhabitants thousands of years earlier. They cannot venture above ground as sunlight will cause them to explode, but the man offers to transport them through a teleportal to the planet Zlaow, which he claims is in perpetual darkness. The Doctor sees through this deception, realising that the man is actually an arms dealer who wants to blow up the planet beyond the portal. He causes the man to fall through the portal, then closes it. This angers the missiles, who send their 'big brother' – a long-range nuclear missile – to try to kill the Doctor and Rose. The two travellers escape in the TARDIS, but the missile detonation causes a 'nuclear winter' on the planet that finally allows the other missiles to emerge onto the surface.

## PINBALL WIZARD

Script: Davey Moore
Script Editor: Gary Russell
Art: John Ross; Colours: Adrian Salmon; Letters: Paul Lang
Publication: Issue 15; 17 October 2006

---

[135] It appears from hints in the story that the arms dealer character is intended to be the villainous Mephistopheles Arkadian from Big Finish's audio CD drama series *Gallifrey*.

## PLOT

The TARDIS malfunctions and materialises in what appears to be a giant pinball game ... which is exactly what it is. But the game has a sinister purpose, as it serves as a form of punishment for offending members of a blue-skinned alien race who are sentenced to play on it for set periods of time, their fate being decided by public vote. Rose is sent into the game, but the Doctor takes control of it from inside the workings and gets her out by catching her inside a giant silver ball, which also slams into the TARDIS and thereby cures its fault.

## GANGSTER'S PARADISE/HEADS YOU LOSE

Script: Alan Barnes
Script Editor: Gary Russell
Art: John Ross; Colours: Adrian Salmon; Letters: Paul Vyse and Kerrie Lockyer for Part One, Paul Lang for Part Two
Publication: Issues 16-17; 1 November 2006, 15 November 2006

## PLOT

The Doctor and Rose arrive on a planet known as Sunset Strip, which is populated by a strange assortment of gangster types. There is a price on the Doctor's head, and he gets taken prisoner by mob boss Mr Lippizzaner. Rose meanwhile meets Doll, a blonde who is on the run from her father, the rival boss Don Corpulone. Lippizzaner and Corpulone are vying to obtain a treasure referred to as 'the bird'. But all is not what it seems: Doll is really a robot with a detachable head. A mad scientist once made a number of such 'talking heads' to act as company for the old and lonely, but they got out of control. The treasure everyone is seeking turns out to be the egg of a glitter bird, a rare and endangered robot species, the droppings of which are studded with diamonds. It is currently in the possession of a Cyber Detective, correctly deduced by the Doctor to be an Acme Industries android. As Don comes to accept that Doll is really the 'head' of their family, the Doctor and Rose seize a spaceship and turn its backburners on the egg. The intense heat causes the egg to hatch, and the glitter bird flies away into space. Don and Doll are arrested by the android authorities, and the Detective vows to clean up Sunset Strip.

## A DATE TO REMEMBER/SNOW FAKES

Script: Davey Moore
Script Editor: Gary Russell
Art: John Ross; Colours: Adrian Salmon; Letters: Paul Lang
Publication: Issues 18-19; 29 November 2006, 13 December 2006

## PLOT

The Doctor takes Rose to Paris to enjoy the sights, but the peace of the beautiful city is shattered as beret-wearing gunmen appear as if from nowhere and do battle with robotic security guards. Rose is seized by an interloper and disappears through a rift in space ... to find herself in the *real* Paris, now a semi-ruined city. The sights that she and the Doctor saw before were all an enhanced illusion created by a computer program called the Façade. The gunmen are trying to bring down the Façade with a computer virus. They discover that the computer is being operated by a haggard young man who built it years ago with the aim of creating the perfect city but then became taken over by it. They free him and the illusion is broken.

## THE HUNTERS/CLIFFHANGER

Script: Trevor Baxendale
Script Editor: Gary Russell
Art: John Ross; Colours: Adrian Salmon; Letters: Paul Vyse
Publication: Issues 20-21; 3 January 2007, 17 January 2007

PLOT

The Doctor, travelling alone now, arrives on a planet and promptly becomes separated from the TARDIS when it falls down a cliff. He meets a woman called Kara McGravy who has been charting the planet's flora and fauna for Outworld University, and who has discovered that all life there is carnivorous. The Doctor and Kara are attacked by huge purple creatures, identified by the Time Lord as human-hunters from Untralo IV. They try to throw the hunters off the scent by wading through quicksand-like mud, but the Doctor suddenly finds himself caught in the jaws of a huge green plant-creature – a meat-eating Marorda Plant. The Plant is intelligent, and the Doctor befriends it, but it is shot by the Untra, who have finally caught up with their intended prey. Kara rescues the Doctor by assailing the Untra with mushrooms that emit a foul stench. They narrowly escape via some carnivorous vines, which then eat the Untra.

## 13 O'CLOCK

Script: Trevor Baxendale
Art: John Ross; Colours: Adrian Salmon; Letters: Paul Vyse
Publication: Issues 22-23; 31 January 2007, 14 February 2007

PLOT

The TARDIS arrives at Croxton Hall, home of Lord Percival Tubbs, where the Doctor plans to attend a party. The house is strangely deserted save for a caterer named Daisy White, who warns the Doctor that the place is haunted – and that if the ghosts touch you, you die and come back as a ghost yourself. The Doctor and Daisy take refuge in a room full of clocks, where the Doctor comes face to face with the ghost of Lord Tubbs. Daisy pushes the Doctor to safety, but at the cost of being turned into a ghost herself. After discovering the remains of a broken clock, the Doctor deduces what has happened. The clock was an ancient horologe built by master chronosmiths from the older worlds to measure the passage of time across different dimensions. It was broken in a struggle when someone tried to steal it, and the damage has extended into time itself, causing those nearest to it to slip into a different kind of time. The Doctor manages to repair the clock with his sonic screwdriver, and everything returns to normality. Daisy learns that the clock was originally given to Lord Tubbs as a wedding present by the Doctor.

## GREEN FINGERS

Script: Mike Tucker
Art: John Ross; Colours: Alan Craddock; Letters: Paul Vyse
Publication: Issues 24-25; 28 February 2007, 14 March 2007

PLOT

The TARDIS brings the Doctor to a darkened biodome on a spaceship. The scientist Professor Flynt explains that the crops in the biodome have been adapted so as to grow with the faintest hint of light, the aim being to revolutionise the lives of planetary colonists. There is only one problem: strong light causes the plants to react violently. Flynt is currently trying to rectify this. Her colleague Professor Brask, on the other hand, wishes to increase the effect and sell the plants as military weapons. Brask steals some genetically modified seed samples and blasts off in an escape pod, to be met by a Weapontek Battlecruiser. He has also sabotaged the biodome ship's systems so that the plants are exposed to direct light from a nearby sun, causing them to run wild. The Doctor manages to gain access to the secondary systems and instructs the ship's robot guards to treat the plants as weeds. He also activates a tractor beam, dragging the Weapontek Battlescruiser back to a point where it blocks out the sunlight, causing the plants to wither and die. Brask and his Weapontek paymaster Jerrix are arrested by the robots.

## THE SNAG FINDERS

Script: Trevor Baxendale
Art: John Ross; Colours: Alan Craddock; Letters: Paul Vyse
Publication: Issues 26-27; 29 March 2007, 12 April 2007

PLOT

In the year 3769, Space Station Alpha is under construction. Snag-hunter Jimmy and his welding-robot mate Bert are carrying out maintenance work when Bert develops a fault. The Doctor, visiting the ship, realises that Bert's systems have been scrambled by a signal being broadcast on an unauthorised wavelength. He disables Bert's receptors so that the robot can function again. Two android intruders push the Doctor, Jimmy and Bert into a septic tank, where they encounter a fearsome creature called the Klytode. The Klytode plans to transform the Earth into a world suitable for its own kind – but uninhabitable by humans – and also to blow up the Station with a cobalt bomb. On the Doctor's instructions, Bert sends out a signal that causes the Klytode's androids to go haywire and allows the Doctor to take possession of the cobalt bomb, which Jimmy then fires out into space. The Klytode is arrested.

## THE SKRAWN INHERITANCE

Script: Trevor Baxendale
Art: John Ross; Colours: Adrian Salmon; Letters: Paul Vyse
Publication: Issues 28-29; 26 April 2007, 10 May 2007

PLOT

The Doctor and Martha arrive on the luxury astroliner *Tritanic* in the 59th Century. The TARDIS is lost somewhere out in space, having been ravaged by the unpredictable time winds of the Kolox Nebula. The *Tritanic* is forcibly boarded by the Skrawn – described by the Doctor as one of this galaxy's nastier creatures, whose sting can be lethal to humans. The Kolox Nebula, otherwise known as the Skrawn Inheritance, is comprised of the remains of their home planet, Kolox, which was destroyed in the Time War. The Skrawn have come to steal the *Tritanic*'s experimental time-nav system, which the Doctor had hoped to use to find the TARDIS. They hope that with this they will be able to control the whole Nebula. They leave in their ship, taking the time-nav with them, but the Doctor and Martha follow by teleport. The Skrawn have the TARDIS on board their ship, and plan to use it in conjuction with the time-nav to regenerate their entire planet. Martha manages to disorientate the Skrawn using the sonic screwdriver, and she and the Doctor return to the *Tritanic* in the TARDIS, taking the time-nav with them. The Skrawn are left to fly their ship blind through the Nebula, victims of the Time War twice over.

## THE GREEN, THE BAD AND THE UGLY

Script: Martin Day
Art: John Ross; Colours: Alan Craddock; Letters: Paul Vyse
Publication: Issues 30-31; 24 May 2007, 7 June 2007

PLOT

The TARDIS arrives on the planet Maught, where water is so rare that it is literally worth its weight in gold. The Doctor and Martha get caught up in the machinations of a trio of unscrupulous creatures each bidding to be the first to learn the location of a legendary underground river that holds the key to untold wealth and power. One of the three, the lizard-like Blontt, is killed, but not before telling the Doctor the depth co-ordinate for the river. The Doctor is forced to give this information to the other two, the insectoid Angelo and the horse-like Tu, when they join forces and threaten to kill Martha, but he deliberately gets it wrong, causing them to bore down too far. A torrent of water is unleashed, thwarting the creatures' plans, and the Doctor and Martha return to the TARDIS.

## MINUS SEVEN WONDERS

Script: Trevor Baxendale
Art: John Ross; Colours: Alan Craddock; Letters: Paul Vyse
Publication: Issues 32-33; 21 June 2007, 5 July 2007

PLOT

The Doctor and Martha are visiting the Great Pyramid of Cheops in Egypt when it suddenly disappears. Following its time track in the TARDIS, they discover that all seven wonders of the ancient world are being stolen in turn. The culprit is Pholonius Ginn, a Talithan dealer in antiquities and relics – or, as the Doctor calls him, a swindler – who is about to auction the stolen wonders as a job lot on G-Bay. An unforeseen development occurs when a creature called Sylven, representing the Fatkat Corporation, gazumps Polonius and purchases the whole planet Earth. The Doctor and Martha manage to gain access to the office of Trongus Squum, Managing Director of Fatkat … only to discover that it has been taken over by Pholonius. On checking the sale contract for the Earth, however, the Doctor discovers that it is null and void: the sale was to have included every man, woman and child born in the Humanian Era, but there was one who was absent from the planet when it was concluded: Martha, who was here at the Fatkat Corporation offices instead. Pholonius is arrested by Sylven as the Fatkats arrive and Squum resumes control.

## BATTLES IN TIME[136]

## THE POWER OF THE CYBERMEN/DRONES OF DOOM/ENEMY MINE/TIME OF THE CYBERMEN

Written by: Steve Cole
Inks: Lee Sullivan; Colours: Alan Craddock
Publication: Issues 8-11; 27 December 2006, 10 January 2007, 24 January 2007, 7 February 2007

PLOT

The Doctor is sunbathing on the planet Centuria when he is seized by a Cyberman and, along with a group of other holidaymakers, taken off in a truck to be upgraded. He meets Jayne Kadett, an undercover investigator who was tracking down an interplanetary info-thief when she was captured. The thief stole secret files from the Torchwood Archive and used their designs to build his own Cybermen, intending to sell them as hi-tech soldiers – but the Cybermen had other ideas, and made him their slave. The Doctor and Jayne manage to escape when the

---

[136] The first seven issues of *Battles in Time* reprinted comic strips that had already appeared in a regional 'trial run' for the magazine earlier in 2006. For details of these, see *Second Flight: The Unofficial and Unauthorised Guide to Doctor Who 2006* by Shaun Lyon (Telos Publishing, 2006).

truck stops at the Cybermen's base. Using his sonic screwdriver, the Doctor causes a power surge through the base's systems, destroying all the Cybermen there ... but it seems there are still others at large elsewhere on Centuria. Tracking the Cybermen's transmissions to the planet's most deserted continent, Azlon, the Doctor and Jayne discover that the local population have succumbed to a hypnotic signal and are offering no resistance. The Doctor manages to switch off the signal, and the part-converted humans start to think for themselves and fight with each other. The fuel banks are ruptured and the Cybermen's base destroyed in the resultant explosion. The Doctor and Jayne still need to discover what the Cybermen were really after on Centuria. Following a map they found, they make their way to the planet's arctic zone, where the Cybermen are forcing part-converted slaves to mine precious gems called hargstones. A spaceship stands by to transport the gems away. The Cybermen at the mine are destroyed by indigenous creatures called ice-snakes, and the Doctor and Jayne learn from a slave whose mental implants have failed that the gems are headed for Centuria Central. They are too late to stop the Cybermen's ship taking off, but they follow it in the TARDIS. On arrival in Centuria Central, the Doctor discovers that the population – including Jayne – are frozen into immobility by a temporal stasis field, created by the Cybermen using a machine powered by the hargstones. The Doctor manages to infiltrate the Cybermen's base in the city's bank, where he finds the stasis machine in the vault and destroys it. The Cybermen die with their machine, and the population are freed. The Doctor then bids farewell to Jayne and leaves in the TARDIS ... but are the Cybermen really gone for good?

## BENEATH THE SKIN/THE SKY BELOW/BEYOND THE SEA/LONELY PLANET

Written by: Steve Cole
Inks: Lee Sullivan; Colours: Alan Craddock
Publication: Issues 12-15; 21 February 2007, 7 March 2007, 21 March 2007, 4 April 2007

PLOT

The TARDIS is forced down to the surface of a planet where many other spaceships are also trapped. The Tragellan occupants of one of these ships mistake the Doctor for an indigenous life form and take him prisoner with a paralysis ray. When the Tragellans plant a flag in the planet's surface, however, they are attacked by rock-like creatures that emerge from the ground, and the Doctor's paralysis is broken. The Doctor realises that the planet is actually a living being, and that the creatures are antibodies come to fight off what they believe are attacking organisms. He manages to repair the planet's 'skin', causing the antibodies to retreat, but then discovers that the TARDIS has disappeared down a hole in the ground. Descending with the aid of an anti-grav pack from one of the crashed ships, the Doctor gets past a different, serpent-like type of antibody and encounters a group of aliens who have been living in the planet's 'bloodstream' on floating islands made out of bits of stone and spaceship debris. There he finds the TARDIS. He helps the aliens to safety on the surface by showing them how to use the bodies of the serpent-like antibodies as 'living ladders'. While he has been doing this, however, the TARDIS has been drawn still further down toward the planet's centre. Accompanied by one of the aliens, Kul, the Doctor explores the plasma sea of the planet's 'bloodstream' on an aquabike. Fleeing from some new, giant-eyeball-like antibodies, they find themselves inside the Life Ark in which Kul's ancestors first came to the planet. The ship's cleaning robots hold off the antibodies until the Doctor is able to expel them with a burst of gas. The Time Lord then discovers that the ship's info-banks have been drained by nerve endings leading down toward the planet's brain. The Doctor and Kul make their way down to the core, where they fight off yet another variety of antibodies. The living planet extrudes 'roots' that enable the Doctor to link with its mind. He discovers that its actions are motivated by loneliness. It is never able to commune with the organic occupants of the spaceships it attracts to itself, because its antibodies always mistake them for infections and drive them off. Computers, however, present no such problems, so the planet communes with them instead. The Doctor neutralises the antibodies, enabling the planet at last to live in harmony with Kul and his kind, whose home it has now become. The Doctor leaves in the TARDIS.

## PLAGUE PANIC

Written by: Claire Lister
Inks: Lee Sullivan; Colours: Alan Craddock
Publication: Issue 16; 18 April 2007

PLOT

The Doctor arrives in 1348 in Melcombe Regis, the time and place where the Black Death first appeared in England. Local villagers are turning green and acting like zombies, and two frightened children lead the Doctor to what they believe is a 'fairy nest', a pink-and-purple ovoid on the ground nearby. The Doctor identifies this as a trans-galactic tour bus carrying a group of aliens called Zeerover. The Zeerover are taking over the bodies of the villagers – hence their condition – because their ship has run out of fuel and the air on Earth is poisonous to them in their natural forms. The Doctor makes a bargain with the Zeerover: they heal the villagers, and he gives their ship a new fuel cell, which is good enough to enable them to get back into space.

## EXHAUSTING EVIL

Written by: Claire Lister
Inks: Lee Sullivan; Colours: Alan Craddock
Publication: Issue 17; 2 May 2007

PLOT

The Doctor and Martha go sightseeing in Harankast, a supposedly tranquil human colony on an alien planet. There they are accosted by some giant-frog-like creatures called the Ranfo, who show them that outside the confines of the city the planet has been reduced to a wasteland – a devastation they attribute to pollution from a new kind of car that the humans are driving. The Doctor can hear a buzzing noise that is inaudible to everyone else, and he realises that this is a brainwashing wave inducing the human population into buying the cars. The wave is being transmitted by robotic flies created by a car dealer called Joseph Manvers, but the Doctor defeats him by disabling one of the flies with his sonic screwdriver and thereby disorientating the others via their shared network, allowing the Ranfo to devour them. Manvers is arrested by the police.

## WRATH OF THE WARRIOR/THE SCREAMING PRISON/FORCE AND FURY

Written by: Steve Cole
Inks: Lee Sullivan; Colours: Alan Craddock
Publication: Issues 18-21; 16 May 2007, 30 May 2007, 6 June 2007, 20 June 2007

PLOT

The Doctor and Martha encounter a giant alien warrior called Thaur, who is rampaging around a supermarket. They learn that he is one of three great warrior kings banished from their home world, Norsum, to live on primitive planets. This is the work of an enemy called Angboda, who is building war-craft with which she can crush a hundred worlds. The Doctor agrees to help Thaur rescue his warrior brothers and return to Norsum to defeat Angboda. He directs the TARDIS to an unnamed planetoid where one of the other warriors, Vulstarg the Vast, is held in chains, guarded by strange flying creatures that emit a deafening screeching noise. The Doctor rigs up specially-adjusted hearing aids for himself, Martha and Thaur that cancel out the noise and allow them to release Vulstarg. Alerted by the screeching noise, a giant green creature attacks, but the Doctor defeats it by restoring the hearing aids to their normal function and placing them on its ears, so that the noise renders it unconscious. The Doctor next takes the TARDIS to the planet Haklok, where the third warrior, Jotastar, is located. Dodging robotic assassins and laser-beam defences, the Doctor, Martha, Thaur and Vulstarg find Jotastar within a maxi-secure centre – but he is not trying to break out, but to break in, to gain access to a battlecruiser. The Doctor and Martha have been tricked: the 'warships' being constructed in the Norsum system are actually hospital ships, and Angboda is really seeking to aid populations that the three warriors previously conquered and crushed. The warriors blast off in the battlecruiser, leaving the Doctor and Martha behind. Resolving to warn Angboda, the Doctor materialises the TARDIS on the bridge of her ship. The warriors teleport aboard, but the Doctor reverses the teleport feed, sending them back to their battlecruiser. Thaur then launches a thermal laser strike on Angboda's ship, but the Doctor has ejected a pile of foil blankets from the cargo bay, and these form a reflective barrier. The laser beam bounces back and causes the battlecruiser to crash on a barren asteroid, where the three warriors are stranded.

# APPENDIX G
# OTHER ORIGINAL FICTION

In addition to the novels and comic strip stories covered in the preceding Appendices, there were three other places where original, officially-sanctioned new series *Doctor Who* fiction could be found during the period covered by this book. Details are given below.

## DOCTOR WHO FILES BOOKS

The *Doctor Who Files* are a range of children's books, each of which covers one character or race of monsters from *Doctor Who*, presenting various factual items, 'Test Your Knowledge' quizzes and the like, and also one short piece of original fiction.

### TAKING MICKEY

Written by: Justin Richards
Publication: *Doctor Who Files: Mickey*, BBC Children's Books; 5 October 2006.

PLOT

Mickey is contacted by a woman called Jill Ongar who wants to discuss the Doctor, but she turns out to be the wife of a Trimestrian Warlord who was killed by a booby trap he had set for the Doctor. Jill – whose real name is Jillonga – blames the Doctor for her husband's death and wants revenge. Her house is really a spaceship, and she plans to take Mickey with her on the 60 year journey back to her home planet, so that she can question him as to the Doctor's whereabouts. Mickey tricks her two children into letting him out of the airlock, and he escapes just as the spaceship takes off.

### A DOG'S LIFE

Written by: Justin Richards
Publication: *Doctor Who Files: K-9*, BBC Children's Books; 5 October 2006.

PLOT

K-9 Mark III is old and his systems are failing. He uses the last of his energy to repel two burglars who break into Sarah Jane Smith's house, then becomes inactive. He is revived when the Doctor fixes his self repair systems.[137]

---

[137] This story effectively serves as a prequel to 'School Reunion'.

**MISSION TO GALACTON**

Written by: Justin Richards
Publication: *Doctor Who Files: The Daleks*, BBC Children's Books; 5 October 2006.

PLOT

At some point prior to the Time War, a Dalek saucer ship visits the planet Galacton to mine it for fuel. The saucer lands on the planet's surface and the Daleks begin drilling, only to find themselves attacked by indigenous rock creatures against which their fire power is ineffective. The saucer returns to orbit, but the Dalek Attack Squad Leader is left behind, having been knocked down a drill shaft by one of the creatures. Determined to complete the mission, it blasts its way down to the planet's core and energises it. The planet is destroyed, providing the Daleks with the power source they sought. Victorious, they chant 'Daleks conquer and destroy'.

**GOING OFF THE RAILS**

Written by: Justin Richards
Publication: *Doctor Who Files: The Cybermen*, BBC Children's Books; 5 October 2006.

PLOT

Sam visits her schoolfriend Harry at his house, where his dad has been assembling a model train set in the garage. There, Sam finds what seem to be a collection of metal body parts amongst a pile of junk. The children try to reassemble these into a complete body. Suddenly the metal man stands up: it is a Cyberman, and the children have inadvertently initiated its self-repair systems. The Cyberman forces Sam to help it put together a piece of electronic apparatus, which it describes as 'upgrade equipment'. It plans to electrify the children's brains and burn out their emotions; bodily conversion will follow when the necessary components are available. Harry saves the day by causing one of the model trains to come flying off its track and strike the Cyberman in its chest, pushing the creature into the hastily-assembled upgrade equipment and electrocuting it. The Cyberman's head falls from its now-lifeless body and crashes to the floor.

**THE DOCTOR WHO STORYBOOK 2007**

This book was effectively a successor to Panini's *Doctor Who Annual 2006* (Penguin having now taken over publication of the *Annual* under its BBC Children's Books imprint and reformatted it to appeal to a much younger age group). It contained seven short pieces of text fiction with illustrations, plus a comic strip story entitled *Opera of Doom!*, all featuring the tenth Doctor and Rose Tyler. Most of the writers had previously contributed scripts to the TV series itself. Credits were as follows.

**CUCKOO-SPIT**
Written by Mark Gatiss. Illustrations by Daryl Joyce.

**THE CAT CAME BACK**
Written by Gareth Roberts. Illustrations by Martin Geraghty.

**ONCE UPON A TIME**
Written by Tom McRae. Illustrations by Adrian Salmon.

**GRAVESTONE HOUSE**
Written by Justin Richards. Illustrations by Andy Walker.

**UNTITLED**
Written by Robert Shearman. Illustrations by Brian Williamson.

**NO ONE DIED**
Written by Nicholas Briggs. Illustrations by Ben Willsher.

**CORNER OF THE EYE**
Written by Steven Moffat. Illustrations by Daryl Joyce.

**OPERA OF DOOM!**
Written by Jonathan Morris. Pencil art by Martin Geraghty.

## THE SUNDAY TIMES CHRISTMAS STORY

On Christmas Eve 2006, *The Sunday Times* published a *Doctor Who* short story for Christmas entitled *Deep and Dreamless Sleep*, written by Paul Cornell.

PLOT

The TARDIS apparently materialises in the bedroom of a young boy called Daniel, who goes inside and operates the controls, causing the ship to dematerialise. Glumly insisting that he wants to see Christmas, the boy takes the Doctor to the First World War trenches, where hostilities stop for a Christmas game of football. Then the Doctor organises a Christmas party for Daniel, inviting Laurel and Hardy and others to entertain him (and ensuring that none of them has any memory of it afterwards). But still the boy is sad. The Doctor takes him to see the Nativity, but to no avail. Finally, the truth is revealed: having been run down by a car on Christmas Eve, Daniel is really lying in a coma in hospital, and has come to the Doctor in his dreams. Travelling back in time, the Doctor makes numerous visits to the hospital over a period of several months to ensure that all is in readiness for Daniel to receive the best possible care from the staff when he is brought in. Daniel consequently survives, and is able to see Christmas.

# ABOUT THE AUTHOR

Stephen James Walker became hooked on *Doctor Who* as a young boy, right from its debut season in 1963/64, and has been a fan ever since. He first got involved in the series' fandom in the early 1970s, when he became a member of the original Doctor Who Fan Club (DWFC). He joined the Doctor Who Appreciation Society (DWAS) immediately on its formation in May 1976, and was an attendee and steward at the first ever *Doctor Who* convention in August 1977. He soon began to contribute articles to fanzines, and in the 1980s was editor of the seminal reference work *Doctor Who – An Adventure in Space and Time* and its sister publication *The Data-File Project*. He also became a frequent writer for the official *Doctor Who Magazine*. Between 1987 and 1993 he was co-editor and publisher, with David J Howe and Mark Stammers, of the leading *Doctor Who* fanzine *The Frame*. Since that time, he has gone on to write and co-write numerous *Doctor Who* books and articles, and is now widely acknowledged as one of the foremost chroniclers of the series' history. He was the initiator and, for the first two volumes, co-editor of Virgin Publishing's *Decalog* books – the first ever *Doctor Who* short story anthology range. More recently, he has written *Inside the Hub*, the definitive factual guide book on the *Doctor Who* spin-off *Torchwood*. He has a degree in Applied Physics from University College London, and his many other interests include cult TV, film noir, vintage crime fiction, Laurel and Hardy and an eclectic mix of soul, jazz, R&B and other popular music. Between July 1983 and March 2005 he acted as an adviser to successive Governments, latterly at senior assistant director level, responsible for policy on a range of issues relating mainly to individual employment rights. Most of his working time is now taken up with his role as co-owner and director of Telos Publishing Ltd. He lives in Kent with his wife and family.

# Other Cult TV Titles
# From Telos Publishing

**Back to the Vortex:** *Doctor Who* **2005**
**Second Flight:** *Doctor Who* **2006**
J Shaun Lyon

**Third Dimension:** *Doctor Who* **2007**
**Monsters Within:** *Doctor Who* **2008**
**End of Ten:** *Doctor Who* **2009**
**Cracks in Time:** *Doctor Who* **2010**
**River's Run:** *Doctor Who* **2011**
**Time of the Doctor:** *Doctor Who* **2012 and 2013**
Stephen James Walker

**The Television Companion (***Doctor Who***) Vols 1 and 2**
David J Howe, Stephen James Walker

**The Handbook (***Doctor Who***) Vols 1 and 2**
David J Howe, Stephen James Walker, Mark Stammers

**Talkback (***Doctor Who* **Interview Books) Vols 1, 2 and 3**
Ed. Stephen James Walker

**The Target Book (***Doctor Who* **Novelisations)**
David J Howe

**Doctor Who Exhibitions**
Bedwyr Gullidge

**Inside the Hub (Guide to** *Torchwood* **Season 1)**
**Something in the Darkness (Guide to** *Torchwood* **Season 2)**
Stephen James Walker

**A Day in the Life (Guide to Season 1 of 24)**
**Triquetra (Guide to** *Charmed***)**
**A Vault of Horror (Guide to 80 Great British Horror Films)**
**The Complete Slayer (Guide to** *Buffy the Vampire Slayer***)**
Keith Topping

**Liberation (Guide to** *Blake's 7***)**
**Fall Out (Guide to** *The Prisoner***)**
**By Your Command (Guide to** *Battlestar Galactica***, 2 Vols)**
Alan Stevens and Fiona Moore

**A Family at War (Guide to *Till Death Us Do Part*)**
Mark Ward

**Destination Moonbase Alpha (Guide to *Space 1999*)**
Robert E Wood

**Assigned (Guide to *Sapphire and Steel*)**
Richard Callaghan

**Hear the Roar (Guide to *Thundercats*)**
David Crichton

**Hunted (Guide to *Supernatural* Seasons 1-3)**
Sam Ford and Antony Fogg

**Bowler Hats and Kinky Boots (Guide to *The Avengers*)**
Michael Richardson

**Transform and Roll Out (Guide to The Transformers Franchise)**
Ryan Frost

**Songs for Europe (Guide to the UK in the
Eurovision Song Contest: 4 Volumes)**
Gordon Roxburgh

**Prophets of Doom (Guide to *Doomwatch*)**
Michael Seely and Phil Ware

**All available online from
www.telos.co.uk**

Printed in Great Britain
by Amazon